InfoPath 2010 Cookbook 5

Integrating InfoPath with Excel and Excel Services

S.Y.M. Wong-A-Ton

InfoPath 2010 Cookbook 5 – Integrating InfoPath with Excel and Excel Services

Copyright © 2013 by S.Y.M. Wong-A-Ton

Cover photo © by S.Y.M. Wong-A-Ton: Purakaunui River, South Island, New Zealand

Now is the time

Table of Contents

Introduction

The strength of Excel lies in performing calculations, while the strength of InfoPath lies in data-entry combined with making forms easily shareable through the use of XML. While Excel and InfoPath are both desktop applications, they were extended with features that allowed documents to be stored in SharePoint. Excel Services provides access to Excel workbooks that are stored in SharePoint and because it offers several extension points through Excel Web Access, web services, and User-Defined Functions (UDFs), you can now create powerful solutions – many of which do not require you to write a single line of code – that combine Excel workbooks with InfoPath forms.

The goal of this book is to help you understand and see how you can combine InfoPath forms with Excel workbooks, whether they are stored inside or outside of SharePoint. Because this book does not cover the basics of InfoPath, Excel, or SharePoint, the solutions presented herein may seem quite advanced at times, but are always aimed at getting the job done primarily without writing code, and secondarily, if code is written, it is kept simple enough so that InfoPath form templates do not require an administrator to publish them.

Who should read this book?

This book is neither an Excel book nor a SharePoint book. This book is an InfoPath-centric book that is not suitable for absolute beginners in any of the three aforementioned technologies. This book requires you to already be familiar with the basics of designing and publishing InfoPath forms as is taught in *InfoPath 2010 Cookbook: 101 Codeless Recipes for Beginners*, the basics of using InfoPath forms in SharePoint as is taught in *InfoPath 2010 Cookbook 2: 101 Codeless Recipes for SharePoint 2010*, and if you intend to follow the recipes in Chapter 3, the basics of writing code for InfoPath forms as is taught in either *InfoPath 2010 Cookbook 3: 101 Code Recipes for C# Developers* or *InfoPath 2010 Cookbook 4: 101 Code Recipes for VB Developers*. In addition, you must have a basic knowledge of Excel 2010, constructing Excel formulas, and writing Visual Basic for Applications (VBA) code if you intend to follow the recipes in Chapter 3.

This book was primarily written for InfoPath and Excel users who do not or cannot write code, and secondarily for developers who want to combine InfoPath with Excel. Since this book does not teach InfoPath, Excel, SharePoint, or writing VBA or .NET code (C# or Visual Basic) from the ground up, it assumes that you already have a basic proficiency in all of these Microsoft technologies.

This book follows a practical approach. Almost each chapter presents you first with a short amount of theory explaining a few key concepts and then slowly builds your skills with step-by-step recipes (tutorials) that follow a logical sequence.

Each recipe has a discussion section that expands on the solution presented in the recipe, and offers additional information on what you learned. The recipes in this book have one of two purposes: 1. To explain and demonstrate fundamental concepts for using InfoPath with Excel, or 2. To provide you with examples of techniques you can repeatedly use to create a large range of solutions that combine InfoPath and Excel.

While you will not find everything you can do with InfoPath and Excel explained in this book, it should provide you with enough examples and ideas for creating or extending your own solutions that combine InfoPath, Excel, and SharePoint.

How to use this book

This book has been set up in a cookbook style with 57 recipes. Each recipe consists of 3 parts: A description of the problem, a step-by-step outline of the solution, and further discussion highlighting important parts of the solution or expanding on what you have learned.

Chapters 1 and 2 are meant for users who do not want to write code. They explain how to get data in and out of Excel and InfoPath, manually or going through other applications such as Access and SharePoint. While it is recommended that you sequentially go through all of the recipes in this book, if you want to go straight to implementing a particular recipe, it is recommended that at the very least you go through recipes 7, 10, 11, 13, 18, 19, and 21 before doing any other recipe in Chapter 2. Where necessary, recipes reference each other so that you do not miss vital pieces of information. In addition, tips, notes, and warnings are repeated where necessary for those who choose not to sequentially go through the book.

Chapter 3 is meant for developers who can already write VBA, C#, or VB.NET code. They explain how to get data in and out of Excel and InfoPath by writing code in either Excel or InfoPath. In addition, the last section on User-Defined Functions requires you to have Visual Studio 2010 installed on your computer and to know how to use it.

Throughout this book you will find references to code snippets indicated by numbers (for example *code #: 3C144335-0D54-4F82-96CB-EFC6E0D03072*). These numbers correspond to text files, which you can download from www.bizsupportonline.com.

About the author

My name is S.Y.M. Wong-A-Ton and I have been a software developer since the start of my IT career back in 1997. The first Microsoft products I used as a developer were Visual Basic 4 and SQL Server 6.5. During my IT career I have developed as well as maintained and supported all types of applications ranging from desktop applications to web sites and web services. I have been a Microsoft Certified Professional since 1998 and have held the title of Microsoft Certified Solution Developer for almost as long as I have been in IT.

I was originally trained as a Geophysicist and co-wrote (as the main author) a scientific article while I was still a scientist. This article was published in 1997 in the Geophysical Research Letters of the American Geophysical Union.

I started exploring the first version of InfoPath in 2005 in my spare time and was hooked on it from day one. What I liked most about InfoPath was the simplicity with which I was able to quickly create electronic forms that were in reality small applications on their own; all this without writing a single line of code!

While exploring InfoPath, I started actively helping other InfoPath users, who were asking questions on the Internet, to come up with innovative solutions. And because the same questions were being asked frequently, I decided to start writing tutorials and articles about InfoPath on my web site "Enterprise Solutions", which evolved into what is known today as "Biz Support Online" and can be visited at http://www.bizsupportonline.net.

Shortly after starting to share my knowledge about InfoPath with others, I received recognition from Microsoft in the form of the Microsoft Most Valuable Professional (MVP) award, and have received this award every year after then, which as of writing has been 7 years in a row.

While the greatest joy I get from working with InfoPath is being able to stretch its boundaries without writing code, I also enjoy exploring other technologies that open pathways for finding new solutions. Needless to say, I had an immense pleasure putting the recipes in this book together for you, so I hope you enjoy reading it, that you learn a lot from it, and that it inspires you to find more InfoPath solutions that make use of Excel and Excel Services.

Support

Every effort has been made to ensure the accuracy of this book. Corrections for this book are provided at http://www.bizsupportonline.com.

If you have comments, suggestions, improvements, or ideas about this book, please send them to bizsupportonline@gmail.com with "InfoPath 2010 Cookbook 5" in the subject line.

Chapter 1: Import Excel Data in InfoPath

You can use InfoPath 2010 to retrieve data from specific data sources through data connections. You can retrieve data from Excel in InfoPath by using one of the following types of data connections:

1. Web Service (SOAP or REST)
2. SharePoint List
3. Database
4. XML File

From the aforementioned data connections, only Web Service data connections offer dynamic retrieval of data from Excel, while the rest of data connections require you to first statically export data to an external data source (XML file, database, or SharePoint list) before you can retrieve the data from within InfoPath. Once you have created a data connection to retrieve data, you can use it to populate controls on an InfoPath form.

You can also use InfoPath to submit data to a particular destination. If you want to submit data to an Excel workbook without having to write code, using a Web Service data connection is your only option.

In this chapter you will learn how you can statically export Excel data to several types of external data sources so that you can connect to and use that data in InfoPath.

1 Create an InfoPath form template from an Excel workbook

Problem

You have an Excel workbook that contains form-like cells which you want to convert into fields in an InfoPath form template.

Solution

You can use the **Convert Existing Form** functionality in InfoPath to convert an Excel workbook into an InfoPath form template.

To create an InfoPath form template from an Excel workbook:

1. Ensure that the workbook you want to import into InfoPath is not currently open in Excel. You can download a file named **ConvertXLToIP.xlsx** from www.bizsupportonline.com for use with this recipe.

2. In InfoPath, select **File ➤ New ➤ Convert Existing Form**, and then click **Design Form**.

Figure 1. The Convert Existing Form command in InfoPath 2010.

3. On the **Import Wizard**, select **InfoPath importer for Excel workbooks**, and click **Next**.

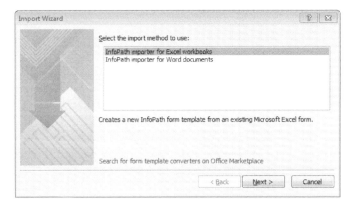

Figure 2. Importing an Excel workbook into InfoPath 2010.

4. On the **Import Wizard**, click **Browse**.

5. On the **Import Form** dialog box, browse to and select the Excel workbook you want to import, and click **Open**.

6. On the **Import Wizard**, click **Finish**.

7. On the **Import Wizard**, click **OK**.

The converted workbook should open in InfoPath with formatted cells having been converted into form fields and worksheets into views.

Discussion

In the solution described above, you saw how to use the **InfoPath importer for Excel workbooks** option on the **Import Wizard** in InfoPath to convert an existing Excel workbook into an InfoPath form template.

While you can select custom conversion settings, the solution described above used the default conversion settings. If you want to use custom conversion settings you must:

1. On the screen of the **Import Wizard** where you can click to browse to select an Excel workbook, click **Options**.

2. On the **Import Options** dialog box, select the **Layout and form fields (custom conversion)** option, and then select the settings of your choice.

Figure 3. Selecting custom conversion settings in InfoPath 2010.

3. On the **Import Options** dialog box, click **OK**.

When using the default conversion settings, an Excel workbook is converted as follows:

- The Excel workbook is converted into an InfoPath Filler Form template by default. If you want to make it a browser-compatible form template afterwards, you must change its **Compatibility** setting on the **Form Options** dialog box.

- Each worksheet that has cells that can be converted into InfoPath form fields or labels is converted into a separate **View** in the InfoPath form template. For example, if you have two worksheets named **PersonalInfo** and **Addresses** with convertible cells in an Excel workbook, these worksheets will be converted into views in InfoPath with the first view named **PersonalInfo** and the second view named **Addresses**.

- Only cells that have a border around them in an Excel workbook are converted into text fields in InfoPath. Cells that contain text but have no borders around them are converted into labels in InfoPath.

  To format a cell to have a border:

  1. In Excel, select the cell or range of cells you want to format.

  2. Select **Home ➤ Cells ➤ Format ➤ Format Cells**.

  3. On the **Format Cells** dialog box, click the **Border** tab, and then under **Presets**, click **Outline**.

  4. Click **OK** to close the **Format Cells** dialog box.

  Any text you prepend to such cells will not only be used as the labels for the corresponding fields in InfoPath, but also for naming the InfoPath form fields.

For example, if you enter the text "First Name" in cell **B2** and format cell **C2** to have borders in Excel, **FirstName** will become the name of the field in InfoPath and the text "First Name" will appear as the label for the field in InfoPath. Note that cells must be adjacent to each other for labels to be assigned to fields as names. For example, if you place the text "First Name" in cell **A2** and format cell **C2** to have borders, "First Name" will become a label in InfoPath, but will not be used to name the field. Instead, the field will be assigned a default name such as for example **field1**.

- To convert cells into a repeating table in InfoPath you must format adjacent cells on at least two rows on an Excel worksheet to have borders. Note that each row will be added as a default row to the repeating table (open the **Edit Default Values** dialog box via **Data ➤ Form Data ➤ Default Values** to access these default rows).

	A	B	C
1		Column 1	Column 2
2			
3			
4			

In the figure shown above, cells **B2**, **C2**, **B3**, and **C3** have been formatted to have borders, and because they are adjacent to each other, they will be converted into a repeating table that has two default rows in InfoPath. To add column labels, you can type column names in cells above the formatted cells. For example, in the figure above, you could enter "Column 1" in cell **B1** and "Column 2" in cell **C1** so that these labels are converted to column labels in the repeating table in InfoPath. While these column labels will not be automatically used as the names of the fields in the repeating table, they will appear as labels in the repeating table.

- The background colors of cells are preserved during the conversion. For example if you format cells to have a blue background color, the cells will be converted into InfoPath form fields with a blue background color.

To format a cell to have a background color:

1. In Excel, select the cell or range of cells you want to format.

2. Select **Home ➤ Cells ➤ Format ➤ Format Cells**.

3. On the **Format Cells** dialog box, click the **Fill** tab, and then under **Background Color**, select the color of your choice.

4. Click **OK** to close the **Format Cells** dialog box.

Note that cell background images, patterns, and gradients are not supported in InfoPath, so will not be preserved during the conversion.

- Excel formulas are not converted into InfoPath formulas. If you want to use formulas in InfoPath, you must manually construct them in InfoPath.

The conversion of an Excel workbook into an InfoPath form template provides basic functionality and has several limitations, but is good to use if you have a large amount of Excel cells to convert into InfoPath form fields. For a full list of Excel features and settings that are not fully supported during the conversion of an Excel workbook into an InfoPath form template, refer to the article entitled *"Convert an Excel workbook to an InfoPath form template"* on the Microsoft Office Online web site.

2   Import Excel data as XML in InfoPath – method 1

Problem

You want to import tabular data from an Excel worksheet into InfoPath so that you can use it as an XML data source in InfoPath forms.

Solution

Before you can use an Excel workbook as an XML data source in InfoPath, you must first save the Excel workbook as an XML file. And before you can save an Excel workbook as an XML file, you must first map the data you want to save as XML to an XML data source in Excel.

Suppose you have an Excel workbook named **Fruits.xlsx** (which you can download from www.bizsupportonline.com) that has the following contents:

	A	B	C
1	**Name**	**Color**	
2	Apple	Red	
3	Banana	Yellow	
4	Kiwi	Brown	
5	Melon	Green	
6	Orange	Orange	

To import Excel data as XML in InfoPath:

1. In Notepad, create a new file with the following contents:

```
<TabularData>
  <Fruit><Name/><Color/></Fruit>
  <Fruit><Name/><Color/></Fruit>
</TabularData>
```

and name the file **TabularData.xml**. You can also download a file named **TabularData.xml** from www.bizsupportonline.com for use with this recipe. You will use this XML file to perform the XML mapping in Excel. Note that at least two **Fruit** elements have been added to the XML file so that when Excel creates a schema for the XML data, it recognizes the **Fruit** element as a repeating element, and so that you can map a **Fruit** element to a row in an Excel table. Also note that you can name the elements in the **TabularData.xml** file whatever you like as long as you ensure that the amount of elements in each repeating element is the same as the amount of columns in the Excel table you want to map. In this case, the Excel table contains two columns named **Name** and **Color**, so the **Fruit** element in the **TabularData.xml** file also contains two child elements named **Name** and **Color**, respectively.

2. In Excel, open the **Fruits.xlsx** Excel workbook.

3. Click **Developer ➤ XML ➤ Source** to open the **XML Source** task pane.

Figure 4. The Source command on the Developer tab in Excel 2010.

Note: If the **Developer** tab is not present on the Ribbon, click **File ➤ Options**. On the **Excel Options** dialog box, click **Customize Ribbon**, and then on the right-hand side of the dialog box, select **Main Tabs** from the **Customize the Ribbon** drop-down list box, ensure that the **Developer** check box is selected, and then click **OK**.

4. On the **XML Source** task pane, click **XML Maps**.

5. On the **XML Maps** dialog box, click **Add**.

6. On the **Select XML Source** dialog box, browse to and select the **TabularData.xml** file, and then click **Open**. If Excel displays an informational message saying that it will create a schema based on the XML source data, click **OK** on that message box.

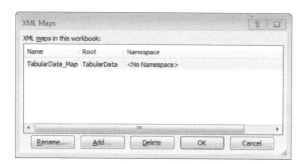

Figure 5. The XML Maps dialog box in Excel 2010.

7. On the **XML Maps** dialog box, click **OK**.

8. On the **XML Source** task pane, right-click the **Fruit** repeating group node, and then select **Map element** from the context menu that appears.

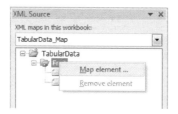

Figure 6. Mapping an element via the XML Source task pane in Excel 2010.

9. On the **Map XML Elements** dialog box, enter **A1:B6** in the text box or select the range of cells that contains the names and colors of fruits including headers on the Excel worksheet, and click **OK**.

Figure 7. The Map XML Elements dialog box in Excel 2010.

10. Click **File ➤ Save As**.

11. On the **Save As** dialog box, select **XML Data (*.xml)** from the **Save as type** drop-down list box, enter a name in the **File name** text box (for example **Fruits.xml**), and click **Save**. If Excel displays a warning message saying that you will lose worksheet features, click **Continue**.

12. In InfoPath, create a new form template or use an existing one.

13. Select **Data ➤ Get External Data ➤ From Other Sources ➤ From XML File** and follow the instructions to add an XML data connection for the **Fruits.xml** file you created via Excel. Name the data connection **Fruits** and leave the **Automatically retrieve data when form is opened** check box selected.

14. On the **Fields** task pane, select **Fruits (Secondary)** from the **Fields** drop-down list box, and then drag-and-drop the **Fruit** repeating group node onto the view of the form template. Select **Repeating Table** from the context menu when you drop the repeating group node.

15. Preview the form.

When the form opens, the data you exported from the Excel file and imported as an XML file in InfoPath should appear in the repeating table.

Discussion

In the solution described above, you saw how to save data from an Excel table as an XML file and then use this XML file as a secondary data source in an InfoPath form.

This is a static solution, meaning that if you change the data in the Excel workbook, you would have to export the data again to an XML file, refresh the XML file for the data connection in InfoPath, and republish the form template so that the updated data becomes available in InfoPath forms.

If you are looking for a dynamic solution where changes made to data in an Excel workbook are automatically propagated to InfoPath forms without having to modify and republish the InfoPath form template linked to the InfoPath forms, you must access the Excel workbook through one of the Excel Services web services (see Chapter 2) or write code that provides such functionality.

3   Import Excel data as XML in InfoPath – method 2

Problem

You have an Excel workbook that contains data that you want to use in lists on an InfoPath form, so you want to export the Excel data to an XML file so that you can use it as an XML data source in InfoPath forms.

Solution

You can use Access to import the data from Excel and then export the data as an XML file that can be used in InfoPath.

To import Excel data as XML in InfoPath:

1. In Excel, create a new workbook or use an existing one, and fill it with data. You can enter the data on worksheets or use one or more named ranges (also see *How to create a named range in Excel* in the Appendix) to define groups of data that can be imported into InfoPath. If you want to use a sample Excel workbook, you can download a file named **Fruits.xlsx** from www.bizsupportonline.com.

2. In Access, create a new **Blank database**.

3. Click **External Data ➤ Import & Link ➤ Excel**.

Figure 8. The Excel command in the Import & Link group on the External Data tab in Access.

4. On the **Get External Data – Excel Spreadsheet** dialog box, click **Browse**, and browse to, select, and open the Excel workbook that contains the data you want to use in InfoPath.

5. On the **Get External Data – Excel Spreadsheet** dialog box, leave the **Import the source data into a new table in the current database** option selected, and click **OK**.

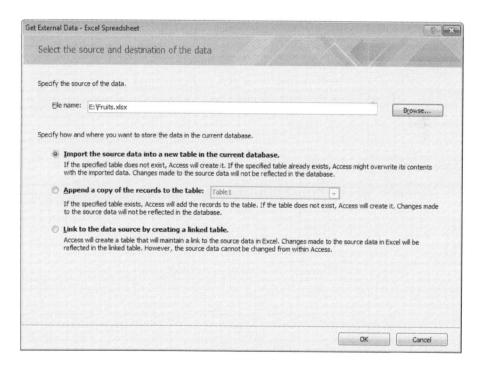

Figure 9. The Get External Data - Excel Spreadsheet dialog box in Access 2010.

6. On the **Import Spreadsheet Wizard**, leave the **Show Worksheets** option selected if the data you want to import is located on a spreadsheet; otherwise select the **Show**

Named Ranges option if you defined one or more named ranges for the data you want to import.

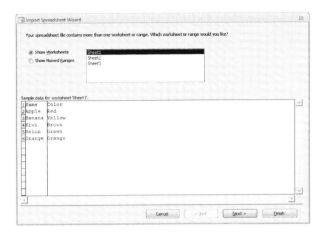

Figure 10. The Import Spreadsheet Wizard in Access 2010.

7. On the **Import Spreadsheet Wizard**, select the worksheet or named range from the list box depending on the selection you made in the previous step, and then click **Next**. Note that the sample **Fruits.xlsx** file contains a named range named **Fruits**, which you can use; or you can select **Sheet1** as the worksheet that contains the data and select the **First Row Contains Column Headings** check box in the next step.

8. On the **Import Spreadsheet Wizard**, select the **First Row Contains Column Headings** check box if the first row of the data you are importing contains header text; otherwise, leave this check box deselected. Click **Next**.

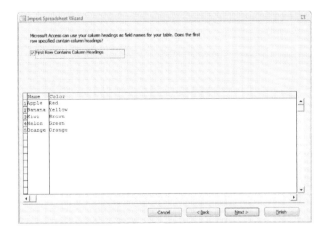

Figure 11. Selecting the column headings option on the Import Spreadsheet Wizard in Access.

9. On the **Import Spreadsheet Wizard**, click on the first column, enter a suitable name for the column in the **Field Name** text box, and leave all of the other field

options as is. Note that if you are using the sample **Fruits.xlsx** file and selected the **First Row Contains Column Headings** check box, the column names should already be correct.

10. Repeat the previous step for each column displayed on the **Import Spreadsheet Wizard**. Click **Next** when you are done.

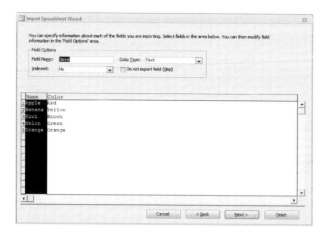

Figure 12. Specifying field (column) names on the Import Spreadsheet Wizard in Access 2010.

11. On the **Import Spreadsheet Wizard**, leave everything as is, and click **Next**.

12. On the **Import Spreadsheet Wizard**, enter a name for the table in the **Import to Table** text box (for example **Fruits**), and then click **Finish**.

13. On the **Get External Data – Excel Spreadsheet** dialog box, click **Close**.

14. Double-click the table that contains the data you imported from Excel (**Fruits** in this case) to open the table.

15. Click **External Data ➤ Export ➤ XML File**.

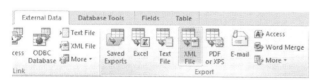

Figure 13. The XML File command in the Export group on the External Data tab in Access.

16. On the **Export – XML File** dialog box, enter a location on disk where you want to save the newly generated InfoPath form, specify a file name (for example **Fruits.xml**), and click **OK**.

17. On the **Export XML** dialog box, leave the **Data (XML)** check box selected, deselect the **Schema of the data (XSD)** check box, and click **OK**.

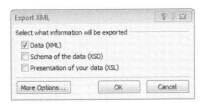

Figure 14. The Export XML dialog box in Access 2010.

18. On the **Export – XML File** dialog box, click **Close**. The resulting XML of the **Fruits.xml** file should be similar to the following XML fragment:

```
<dataroot xmlns:od="urn:schemas-microsoft-com:officedata">
  <Fruits>
    <ID>1</ID>
    <Name>Apple</Name>
    <Color>Red</Color>
  </Fruits>
  <Fruits>
    <ID>2</ID>
    <Name>Banana</Name>
    <Color>Yellow</Color>
  </Fruits>
  <Fruits>
    <ID>3</ID>
    <Name>Kiwi</Name>
    <Color>Brown</Color>
  </Fruits>
</dataroot>
```

As you can see from the XML fragment above, **Fruits** is a repeating group node that contains 3 elements (**ID**, **Name**, and **Color**), making such an XML data structure suitable for use in InfoPath as a secondary data source.

19. In InfoPath, create a new form template or use an existing one.

20. Select **Data ➤ Get External Data ➤ From Other Sources ➤ From XML File** and follow the instructions to add an XML data connection for the **Fruits.xml** file you created via Access. Name the data connection **Fruits** and leave the **Automatically retrieve data when form is opened** check box selected.

21. Add a **Drop-Down List Box** control to the view of the form template and name it **field1**.

22. Open the **Drop-Down List Box Properties** dialog box, and then on the **Data** tab, select the **Get choices from an external data source** option, select **Fruits** from the **Data Source** drop-down list box, and then click the button behind the **Entries** text box.

23. On the **Select a Field or Group** dialog box, select the **Fruits** repeating group node, and click **OK**.

24. On the **Drop-Down List Box Properties** dialog box, ensure **ID** is selected for the **Value** property and **Name** is selected for the **Display name** property, and then click **OK**.

25. Preview the form.

When the form opens, the drop-down list box should contain the values from the XML file that was exported from Access using data from Excel.

Discussion

In the solution described above, you saw how to save data from an Excel workbook as an XML file through Access and then use this XML file as a secondary data source in an InfoPath form.

This is a static solution, meaning that if you change the data in the Excel workbook, you would have to export the data again to an XML file, refresh the XML file for the data connection in InfoPath, and republish the form template so that the updated data becomes available in InfoPath forms.

If you are looking for a dynamic solution where changes made to data in the Excel workbook are automatically propagated to InfoPath forms without having to modify and republish the InfoPath form template linked to the InfoPath forms, you must access the Excel workbook through one of the Excel Services web services (see Chapter 2) or write code that provides such functionality.

While the solution described above displayed the data from Excel in a drop-down list box control on an InfoPath form, you could do anything with the imported data such as for example display it in a repeating table (see recipe *2 Import Excel data as XML in InfoPath – method 1*) or use it in rules to perform data validation.

Note that you do not have to export the Excel data as an XML file from within Access to be able to use it in InfoPath, but that you could have also added a database connection for the Access database table to the InfoPath form template to be able to access the Excel data that is stored in the database table. Importing the data as an XML file in InfoPath allows you to include the data in the form template without having the need to maintain an extra connection to a database. However, if you wanted to make the solution more dynamic and maintain the Excel data in Access, then adding a database connection would probably be a better option.

4 Import Excel data in InfoPath via a SharePoint list – method 1

Problem

You have tabular data in an Excel workbook which you want to display in a repeating table on an InfoPath form.

Solution

You can export data from a table in an Excel workbook to a SharePoint list and then add a data connection for that SharePoint list in InfoPath so that the data can be displayed in a repeating table control on an InfoPath form.

To import Excel data in InfoPath via a SharePoint list:

1. In Excel, create an Excel workbook with tabular data or use an existing one. You can also download a file named **Fruits.xlsx** from www.bizsupportonline.com for use with this recipe.

2. Select all of the tabular data including any headers by clicking in the top-left cell, holding the mouse button pressed down, dragging the cursor to the bottom-right cell, and then releasing the mouse button.

3. Click **Home ➤ Styles ➤ Format as Table** and select a table format from the drop-down list of table formats.

4. On the **Format As Table** dialog box, the **Where is the data for your table?** text box should already contain a correct reference to the cells on the worksheet. Select the **My table has headers** check box and click **OK**.

5. Click on any cell in the table, and then select **Table Tools ➤ Design ➤ External Table Data ➤ Export ➤ Export Table to SharePoint List**.

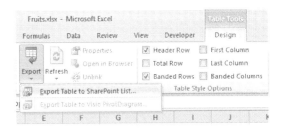

Figure 15. The Export Table to SharePoint List command in Excel 2010.

6. On the **Export Table to SharePoint List** dialog box, enter the URL of the SharePoint site (where you want to publish the table) in the **Address** combo box, enter a **Name** and **Description** for the SharePoint list, and click **Next**.

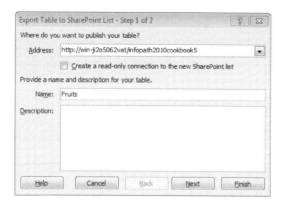

Figure 16. Selecting the SharePoint site to which to export the Excel data.

7. On the **Export Table to SharePoint List** dialog box, read the information displayed, and then click **Finish**.

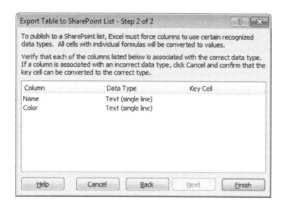

Figure 17. The last screen of the Export Table to SharePoint List dialog box in Excel 2010.

A confirmation message box should appear once the tabular data has been exported to SharePoint.

Figure 18. The confirmation message box that the table was successfully published.

You can verify whether the data was successfully exported to SharePoint by clicking on the link that Excel provides on the confirmation message box or by going to the SharePoint site, clicking on **Site Actions ➤ View All Site Content**, and searching for the SharePoint list on the **All Site Content** page.

8. In InfoPath, create a new form template or use an existing one.

9. Click **Data ➤ Get External Data ➤ From SharePoint List** and follow the instructions to add a **Receive** data connection to the SharePoint list you just created for the tabular data in Excel to the form template. Leave the **Automatically retrieve data when form is opened** check box selected and name the data connection **ExcelData**.

10. On the **Fields** task pane, select **ExcelData (Secondary)** from the **Fields** drop-down list box, expand the **dataFields** group node, and then drag-and-drop the **SharePointListItem_RW** repeating group node onto the view of the form template. Select **Repeating Table** from the context menu that appears when you drop the repeating group node onto the view.

11. Preview the form.

When the form opens, the data from the table in the Excel workbook that you exported to a SharePoint list should appear in the repeating table.

Discussion

In the solution described above, you exported data from a table in an Excel workbook to a SharePoint list. Such a solution is a static solution, since there is no live connection between the Excel workbook and the SharePoint list. This also means that you cannot make changes to the data in the table in the Excel workbook after you have already exported it to SharePoint and then synchronize the data in the Excel workbook with the data in the existing SharePoint list.

In step 6 of the solution described above, you could have selected the **Create a read-only connection to the new SharePoint list** check box on the **Export Table to SharePoint List** dialog box to create a live one-way connection between the Excel workbook and the SharePoint list. In this case, you would be able to update data in the SharePoint list and then when you click **Data ➤ Connections ➤ Refresh All** or **Table Tools ➤ Design ➤ External Table Data ➤ Refresh** in Excel, the data you added or updated in SharePoint should appear in the table in the Excel workbook.

You could also make use of for example SharePoint Workspace together with the **Sync to SharePoint Workspace** command of the SharePoint list to maintain the data in the SharePoint list, and then if you wanted to recreate the data in Excel using the data from the SharePoint list, you could use the **List Tools ➤ List ➤ Connect & Export ➤ Export to Excel** command of the SharePoint list to export the data in the SharePoint list to an **.iqy** file, which you could then open in Excel. The discussion of SharePoint Workspace is beyond the scope of this book, but you are encouraged to explore its features and capabilities.

To be able to dynamically display data from an Excel workbook in an InfoPath form, you must either write code to achieve such functionality or publish the Excel workbook to SharePoint and then make use of one of the Excel Services web services as discussed in Chapter 2. Another option would be to go through an application such as Access, which offers live two-way connections with SharePoint (see recipe *5 Import Excel data in InfoPath via a SharePoint list – method 2*).

5　Import Excel data in InfoPath via a SharePoint list – method 2

Problem

You have tabular data in an Excel workbook which you want to display in a repeating table on an InfoPath form.

Solution

You can import data from a table in an Excel workbook into Access, use Access to create a live connection with a SharePoint list, and then add a data connection for that SharePoint list in InfoPath so that the data can be displayed in a repeating table control on an InfoPath form.

To import Excel data in InfoPath via a SharePoint list:

1.　Follow steps 1 through 13 of recipe *3 Import Excel data as XML in InfoPath – method 2* to import Excel data into an Access database.

2.　In Access, click the table that contains the Excel data you just imported to select it, and then select **External Data ➤ Export ➤ More ➤ SharePoint List**.

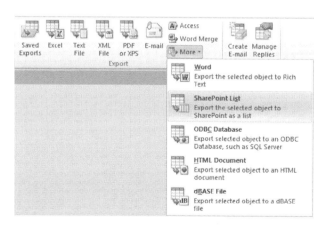

Figure 19. The SharePoint List command in the Export group on the External Data tab.

3.　On the **Export – SharePoint Site** dialog box, select an existing SharePoint site or enter the URL of the SharePoint site to where you want to export the data, enter a name for the new SharePoint list that should be created (for example **Fruits**), deselect the **Open the list when finished** check box, and then click **OK**.

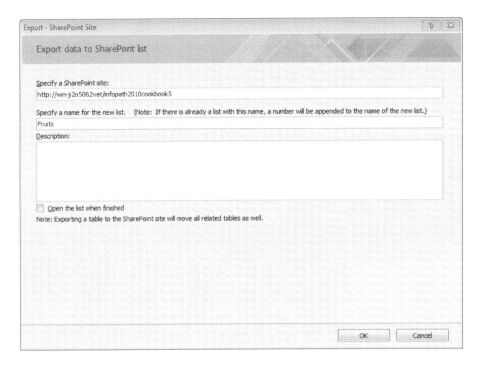

Figure 20. Exporting data from a table to a SharePoint list in Access 2010.

4. On the **Export – SharePoint Site** dialog box, click **Close**.

5. Once the SharePoint list with the Excel data has been created, you can create a live connection in Access by linking to the existing SharePoint list. So select **External Data ➤ Import & Link ➤ More ➤ SharePoint List**.

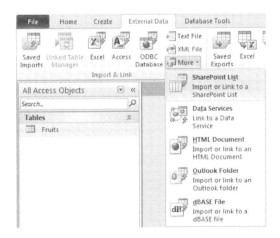

Figure 21. The SharePoint List command in the Import & Link group on the External Data tab.

6. On the **Get External Data – SharePoint Site** dialog box, select the same SharePoint site you selected in step 3, select the **Link to the data source by creating a linked table** option, and click **Next**.

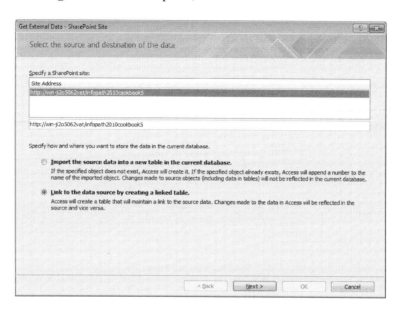

Figure 22. Selecting to create a linked table for data stored in a SharePoint list in Access 2010.

7. On the **Get External Data – SharePoint Site** dialog box, select the SharePoint list you created in step 3, and click **OK**.

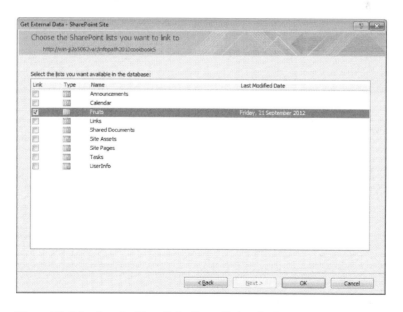

Figure 23. Selecting the SharePoint list to link to in Access 2010.

A linked table for the SharePoint list should now be present in the database. You can maintain data in this table and the data should automatically get updated in the SharePoint list.

Figure 24. Fruits1 is an Access table linked to a SharePoint list.

8. In InfoPath, create a new form template or use an existing one.

9. Click **Data ➤ Get External Data ➤ From SharePoint List** and follow the instructions to add a **Receive** data connection to the SharePoint list you created in step 3 for the tabular data in Excel to the form template. Leave the **Automatically retrieve data when form is opened** check box selected and name the data connection **ExcelData**.

10. On the **Fields** task pane, select **ExcelData (Secondary)** from the **Fields** drop-down list box, expand the **dataFields** group node, and then drag-and-drop the **SharePointListItem_RW** repeating group node onto the view of the form template. Select **Repeating Table** from the context menu that appears when you drop the repeating group node onto the view.

11. Add a **Button** control to the view of the form template and set its **Action** property to **Refresh**.

12. Preview the form.

When the form opens, the data from the Excel spreadsheet should appear in the repeating table. In SharePoint, navigate to the SharePoint list and add a new item. In InfoPath, click the **Refresh** button. The newly added item should appear in the repeating table. In Access, open the linked table. The item you added to the SharePoint list should be present in the table. Add a new record to the table in Access. In InfoPath, click the **Refresh** button. The newly added record should appear in the repeating table. And if you go to the SharePoint list again and refresh the data, the record you added in Access should also be present in the SharePoint list.

Once you have a database table that is linked to a SharePoint list, you can import data from Excel into the linked table and thereby immediately synchronize the data in the SharePoint list with the data in the linked table.

To import data into the linked table you created in step 7:

1. In Access, ensure that the linked table is closed. If it is not closed, right-click its tab, and select **Close** from the context menu that appears.

2. Click **External Data ➤ Import & Link ➤ Excel**.

3. On the **Get External Data – Excel Spreadsheet** dialog box, click **Browse**, and browse to, select, and open the Excel workbook from which you want to import data.

4. On the **Get External Data – Excel Spreadsheet** dialog box, select the **Append a copy of the records to the table** option, select the linked table from the drop-down list box, and click **OK**.

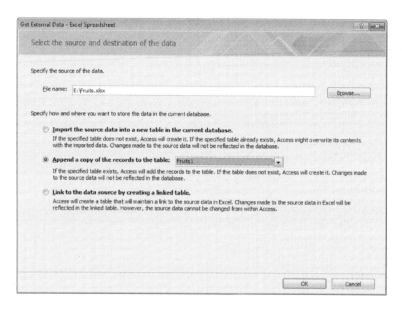

Figure 25. Importing data from Excel into a linked table in Access 2010.

5. On the **Import Spreadsheet Wizard**, leave the **Show Worksheets** option selected if the data you want to import is located on a spreadsheet; otherwise select the **Show Named Ranges** option if you defined one or more named ranges for the data you want to import. Note: Ensure that the data you are importing has one or more columns (except for an ID column) that are also present in the existing linked table, that the Excel data has column headings, and that the column headings have the same name as the columns that are present in the existing linked table, otherwise the import might fail.

6. On the **Import Spreadsheet Wizard**, select the worksheet or named range from the list box depending on the selection you made in the previous step, and then click **Next**.

7. On the **Import Spreadsheet Wizard**, the **First Row Contains Column Headings** check box should automatically be selected, but if it is not, select it, and then click **Next**.

8. On the **Import Spreadsheet Wizard**, click **Finish**.

9. On the **Get External Data – Excel Spreadsheet** dialog box, click **Close**.

The linked table should now contain the data imported from Excel and this data should also be present in the SharePoint list that is linked to the linked table in Access.

To export data from the linked table to an Excel workbook:

1. In Access, click the linked table to select it, and then click **External Data ➤ Export ➤ Excel**.

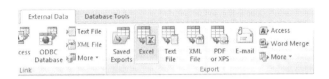

Figure 26. The Excel command in the Export group on the External Data tab in Access 2010.

2. On the **Export – Excel Spreadsheet** dialog box, click **Browse** and browse to and select an existing Excel workbook to which you want to export the data in the linked table; or enter the file path to create a new Excel workbook to which the data should be exported.

3. On the **Export – Excel Spreadsheet** dialog box, leave **Excel Workbook (*.xlsx)** selected in the **File format** drop-down list box, leave all check boxes deselected, and click **OK**.

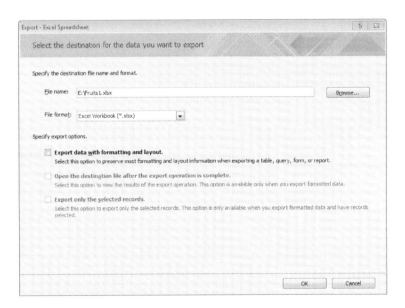

Figure 27. Exporting the contents of the linked table in Access 2010 to an Excel workbook.

4. On the **Export – Excel Spreadsheet** dialog box, click **Close**.

The data from the linked table should appear on a new worksheet that has the same name as the linked table in the Excel workbook to which you exported the data.

Discussion

In the solution described above, you saw how to use Access to export Excel data to a SharePoint list and then use a linked table in Access to manage this data. Note that instead of first exporting a database table to a SharePoint list and then creating a linked table as you have done in the solution above, you could have also used the **Database Tools ➤ Move Data ➤ SharePoint** command. However, the aforementioned command would have published all of the tables in the database to SharePoint instead of just one.

If you want to avoid having to go through an application such as Access to be able to dynamically display data from an Excel workbook in an InfoPath form, you must either write code to achieve such functionality or publish the Excel workbook to SharePoint and then make use of one of the Excel Services web services as discussed in Chapter 2.

6   Generate an InfoPath form from Excel data using XSLT

Problem

You have data in an Excel workbook from which you would like to create a new InfoPath form without having to write VBA or .NET code to be able to do so.

Solution

You can use the **Excel** import functionality in Access to import data from an Excel workbook and then use the **XML File** export functionality in Access along with an XSL stylesheet to export the data to an XML format that represents an InfoPath form.

To generate an InfoPath form from Excel data using XSLT:

1. In InfoPath, create a new form template or use an existing one. If you are creating your own form template, continue with step 2. If you want to use a sample form template, you can download a file named **GenerateFromExcel.xsn** from www.bizsupportonline.com and then continue with step 5.

2. Add a **Text Box** control to the view of the form template and name it **field1**.

3. Add a **Repeating Table** control with 3 columns to the view of the form template, and ensure that the fields within the repeating table have the names **field2**, **field3**, and **field4**, respectively.

4. Save the form template locally on disk.

5. In Windows Explorer, navigate to the location where you saved the form template, double-click it, and then when it opens in InfoPath Filler, save the InfoPath form as a file named **BlankForm.xml**.

    If you are using the downloaded form template, do the following before trying to create a blank form:

a. In Windows Explorer, navigate to the location where you saved the form template (.xsn).

b. Right-click the form template (.xsn), and select **Design** from the context menu that appears. This should open the form template in InfoPath Designer 2010.

c. In InfoPath, click **Save** and save the form template to a location on disk.

6. In Excel, create a new workbook or use an existing one, and fill it with data. You can enter the data on worksheets or use one or more named ranges (also see *How to create a named range in Excel* in the Appendix) to define groups of data that should be used to create the InfoPath form. If you want to use a sample Excel workbook, you can download a file named **Fruits.xlsx** from www.bizsupportonline.com.

7. In Access, create a new **Blank database**.

8. Click **External Data** ➤ **Import & Link** ➤ **Excel**.

9. On the **Get External Data – Excel Spreadsheet** dialog box, click **Browse**, and browse to, select, and open the Excel workbook that contains the data you want to use to create a new InfoPath form.

10. On the **Get External Data – Excel Spreadsheet** dialog box, leave the **Import the source data into a new table in the current database** option selected, and click **OK**.

11. On the **Import Spreadsheet Wizard**, leave the **Show Worksheets** option selected if the data you want to import is located on a spreadsheet; otherwise select the **Show Named Ranges** option if you defined one or more named ranges for the data you want to import. If you are using the **Fruits.xlsx** Excel workbook, select the **Show Named Ranges** option and then in the next step, select the **Fruits** named range.

12. On the **Import Spreadsheet Wizard**, select the worksheet or named range from the list box depending on the selection you made in the previous step, and then click **Next**. Note that the sample **Fruits.xlsx** file contains a named range named **Fruits**, which you can use; or you can select **Sheet1** as the worksheet that contains the data and select the **First Row Contains Column Headings** check box in the next step.

13. On the **Import Spreadsheet Wizard**, select the **First Row Contains Column Headings** check box if the first row of the data you are importing contains header text; otherwise, leave this check box deselected. If you are using the **Fruits** named range in the **Fruits.xlsx** Excel workbook, leave this check box deselected. Click **Next**.

14. On the **Import Spreadsheet Wizard**, click on the first column, enter a suitable name for the column in the **Field Name** text box, and leave all of the other field options as is. If you are using the **Fruits** named range in the **Fruits.xlsx** Excel workbook, name the first column **Name**.

15. Repeat the previous step for each column displayed on the **Import Spreadsheet Wizard**. If you are using the **Fruits** named range in the **Fruits.xlsx** Excel workbook, name the second column **Color**. Click **Next** when you are done.

16. On the **Import Spreadsheet Wizard**, leave everything as is, and click **Next**.

17. On the **Import Spreadsheet Wizard**, enter a name for the table in the **Import to Table** text box (for example **Fruits**), and then click **Finish**.

18. On the **Get External Data – Excel Spreadsheet** dialog box, click **Close**.

19. In Notepad, open the **BlankForm.xml** InfoPath form you saved in step 5 and copy all of its contents to the Windows clipboard by pressing **Ctrl+A** and then **Ctrl+C**.

20. In Windows Explorer, create a new text file named **CreateIPForm.xsl**, and then open this file in Notepad.

21. In Notepad, press **Ctrl+V** to paste the contents from the Windows clipboard. The contents should resemble the following:

```
<?xml version="1.0" encoding="UTF-8"?><?mso-infoPathSolution
solutionVersion="1.0.0.2" productVersion="14.0.0" PIVersion="1.0.0.0"
href="file:///E:\GenerateFromExcel.xsn" name="urn:schemas-microsoft-
com:office:infopath:GenerateFromExcel:-myXSD-2012-07-27T03-59-09" ?><?mso-
application progid="InfoPath.Document"
versionProgid="InfoPath.Document.3"?><my:myFields
xmlns:my="http://schemas.microsoft.com/office/infopath/2003/myXSD/2012-07-
27T03:59:09" xml:lang="en-us">
<my:field1></my:field1>
   <my:group1>
     <my:group2>
       <my:field2></my:field2>
       <my:field3></my:field3>
       <my:field4></my:field4>
     </my:group2>
   </my:group1>
</my:myFields>
```

This is the XML of the blank InfoPath form that contains no data.

22. Add the following XSL code just before the `<?mso-infoPathSolution ...?>` processing instruction:

```
<xsl:stylesheet version="1.0"
xmlns:xsl="http://www.w3.org/1999/XSL/Transform"
xmlns:my="http://schemas.microsoft.com/office/infopath/2003/myXSD/2012-07-
27T03:59:09">
   <xsl:output method="xml" encoding="UTF-8" indent="yes"/>
   <xsl:template match="//dataroot">
```

where you should replace the namespace URI (`http://schemas.microsoft.com/office/infopath/2003/myXSD/2012-07-27T03:59:09`) for the **my** namespace prefix with the namespace URI for the **my** namespace prefix used in your own form. And if your form contains any other namespace declarations, you can declare them in the **xsl:stylesheet** element as is done for the **my** namespace declaration.

The **CreateIPForm.xsl** file should now resemble the following:

```
<?xml version="1.0" encoding="UTF-8"?>
<xsl:stylesheet version="1.0"
xmlns:xsl="http://www.w3.org/1999/XSL/Transform"
xmlns:my="http://schemas.microsoft.com/office/infopath/2003/myXSD/2012-07-
27T03:59:09">
  <xsl:output method="xml" encoding="UTF-8" indent="yes"/>
  <xsl:template match="//dataroot"><?mso-infoPathSolution
solutionVersion="1.0.0.2" productVersion="14.0.0" PIVersion="1.0.0.0"
href="file:///E:\GenerateFromExcel.xsn" name="urn:schemas-microsoft-
com:office:infopath:GenerateFromExcel:-myXSD-2012-07-27T03-59-09" ?><?mso-
application progid="InfoPath.Document"
versionProgid="InfoPath.Document.3"?><my:myFields
xmlns:my="http://schemas.microsoft.com/office/infopath/2003/myXSD/2012-07-
27T03:59:09" xml:lang="en-us">
<my:field1></my:field1>
  <my:group1>
    <my:group2>
      <my:field2></my:field2>
      <my:field3></my:field3>
      <my:field4></my:field4>
    </my:group2>
  </my:group1>
</my:myFields>
```

23. Add the following XSL code at the end of the file:

```
    </xsl:template>
</xsl:stylesheet>
```

The **CreateIPForm.xsl** file should now resemble the following:

```
<?xml version="1.0" encoding="UTF-8"?>
<xsl:stylesheet version="1.0"
xmlns:xsl="http://www.w3.org/1999/XSL/Transform"
xmlns:my="http://schemas.microsoft.com/office/infopath/2003/myXSD/2012-07-
27T03:59:09">
  <xsl:output method="xml" encoding="UTF-8" indent="yes"/>
  <xsl:template match="//dataroot"><?mso-infoPathSolution
solutionVersion="1.0.0.2" productVersion="14.0.0" PIVersion="1.0.0.0"
href="file:///E:\GenerateFromExcel.xsn" name="urn:schemas-microsoft-
com:office:infopath:GenerateFromExcel:-myXSD-2012-07-27T03-59-09" ?><?mso-
application progid="InfoPath.Document"
versionProgid="InfoPath.Document.3"?>
  <my:myFields
xmlns:my="http://schemas.microsoft.com/office/infopath/2003/myXSD/2012-07-
27T03:59:09" xml:lang="en-us">
  <my:field1></my:field1>
    <my:group1>
      <my:group2>
        <my:field2></my:field2>
        <my:field3></my:field3>
        <my:field4></my:field4>
      </my:group2>
    </my:group1>
  </my:myFields>
```

```
    </xsl:template>
</xsl:stylesheet>
```

24. Replace the entire **mso-infoPathSolution** processing instruction

```
<?mso-infoPathSolution solutionVersion="1.0.0.2" productVersion="14.0.0"
PIVersion="1.0.0.0" href="file:///E:\GenerateFromExcel.xsn"
name="urn:schemas-microsoft-com:office:infopath:GenerateFromExcel:-myXSD-
2012-07-27T03-59-09" ?>
```

with the following XSL code:

```
<xsl:processing-instruction name="mso-infoPathSolution">
  <xsl:text>solutionVersion="1.0.0.2" productVersion="14.0.0"
PIVersion="1.0.0.0" href="file:///E:\GenerateFromExcel.xsn"
name="urn:schemas-microsoft-com:office:infopath:GenerateFromExcel:-myXSD-
2012-07-27T03-59-09"</xsl:text>
</xsl:processing-instruction>
```

where you must set the value of the **xsl:text** element to be the same as the attributes that were present in the **mso-infoPathSolution** processing instruction you replaced.

The **CreateIPForm.xsl** file should now resemble the following:

```
<?xml version="1.0" encoding="UTF-8"?>
<xsl:stylesheet version="1.0"
xmlns:xsl="http://www.w3.org/1999/XSL/Transform"
xmlns:my="http://schemas.microsoft.com/office/infopath/2003/myXSD/2012-07-
27T03:59:09">
  <xsl:output method="xml" encoding="UTF-8" indent="yes"/>
  <xsl:template match="//dataroot">
  <xsl:processing-instruction name="mso-infoPathSolution">
    <xsl:text>solutionVersion="1.0.0.2" productVersion="14.0.0"
PIVersion="1.0.0.0" href="file:///E:\GenerateFromExcel.xsn"
name="urn:schemas-microsoft-com:office:infopath:GenerateFromExcel:-myXSD-
2012-07-27T03-59-09"</xsl:text>
  </xsl:processing-instruction>
<?mso-application progid="InfoPath.Document"
versionProgid="InfoPath.Document.3"?>
  <my:myFields
xmlns:my="http://schemas.microsoft.com/office/infopath/2003/myXSD/2012-07-
27T03:59:09" xml:lang="en-us">
  <my:field1></my:field1>
    <my:group1>
      <my:group2>
        <my:field2></my:field2>
        <my:field3></my:field3>
        <my:field4></my:field4>
      </my:group2>
    </my:group1>
  </my:myFields>
  </xsl:template>
</xsl:stylesheet>
```

25. Replace the entire **mso-application** processing instruction

```
<?mso-application progid="InfoPath.Document"
versionProgid="InfoPath.Document.3"?>
```

with the following XSL code:

```
<xsl:processing-instruction name="mso-application">
  <xsl:text>progid="InfoPath.Document"
versionProgid="InfoPath.Document.3"</xsl:text>
</xsl:processing-instruction>
```

where you must set the value of the **xsl:text** element to be the same as the attributes that were present in the **mso-application** processing instruction you replaced.

The **CreateIPForm.xsl** file should now resemble the following:

```
<?xml version="1.0" encoding="UTF-8"?>
<xsl:stylesheet version="1.0"
xmlns:xsl="http://www.w3.org/1999/XSL/Transform"
xmlns:my="http://schemas.microsoft.com/office/infopath/2003/myXSD/2012-07-
27T03:59:09">
  <xsl:output method="xml" encoding="UTF-8" indent="yes"/>
  <xsl:template match="//dataroot">
  <xsl:processing-instruction name="mso-infoPathSolution">
    <xsl:text>solutionVersion="1.0.0.2" productVersion="14.0.0"
PIVersion="1.0.0.0" href="file:///E:\GenerateFromExcel.xsn"
name="urn:schemas-microsoft-com:office:infopath:GenerateFromExcel:-myXSD-
2012-07-27T03-59-09"</xsl:text>
  </xsl:processing-instruction>
  <xsl:processing-instruction name="mso-application">
    <xsl:text>progid="InfoPath.Document"
versionProgid="InfoPath.Document.3"</xsl:text>
  </xsl:processing-instruction>
  <my:myFields
xmlns:my="http://schemas.microsoft.com/office/infopath/2003/myXSD/2012-07-
27T03:59:09" xml:lang="en-us">
  <my:field1></my:field1>
    <my:group1>
      <my:group2>
        <my:field2></my:field2>
        <my:field3></my:field3>
        <my:field4></my:field4>
      </my:group2>
    </my:group1>
  </my:myFields>
  </xsl:template>
</xsl:stylesheet>
```

26. Once you have the base XSL file in place, you can start adding XSL code to it that will loop through the rows of the database table (**Fruits** in this case)

```
<xsl:for-each select="Fruits">
...
</xsl:for-each>
```

and retrieve the values of fields. For example, the following XSL code retrieves the value of the **Name** field in a row:

```
<xsl:value-of select="Name"/>
```

So replace all of the XML elements that are located within the **my:group1** element with the following XSL code:

```
<xsl:for-each select="Fruits">
  <my:group2>
    <my:field2><xsl:value-of select="Name"/></my:field2>
    <my:field3><xsl:value-of select="Color"/></my:field3>
    <my:field4></my:field4>
  </my:group2>
</xsl:for-each>
```

As you can see from the XSL code displayed above, the **my:field4** element remains empty and only the **my:field2** and **my:field3** elements are filled with the names and colors of fruits stored in the **Fruits** database table.

The final **CreateIPForm.xsl** file should resemble the following:

```
<?xml version="1.0" encoding="UTF-8"?>
<xsl:stylesheet version="1.0"
xmlns:xsl="http://www.w3.org/1999/XSL/Transform"
xmlns:my="http://schemas.microsoft.com/office/infopath/2003/myXSD/2012-07-
27T03:59:09">
  <xsl:output method="xml" encoding="UTF-8" indent="yes"/>
  <xsl:template match="//dataroot">
  <xsl:processing-instruction name="mso-infoPathSolution">
    <xsl:text>solutionVersion="1.0.0.2" productVersion="14.0.0"
PIVersion="1.0.0.0" href="file:///E:\GenerateFromExcel.xsn"
name="urn:schemas-microsoft-com:office:infopath:GenerateFromExcel:-myXSD-
2012-07-27T03-59-09"</xsl:text>
  </xsl:processing-instruction>
  <xsl:processing-instruction name="mso-application">
    <xsl:text>progid="InfoPath.Document"
versionProgid="InfoPath.Document.3"</xsl:text>
  </xsl:processing-instruction>
  <my:myFields
xmlns:my="http://schemas.microsoft.com/office/infopath/2003/myXSD/2012-07-
27T03:59:09" xml:lang="en-us">
  <my:field1></my:field1>
    <my:group1>
    <xsl:for-each select="Fruits">
      <my:group2>
        <my:field2><xsl:value-of select="Name"/></my:field2>
        <my:field3><xsl:value-of select="Color"/></my:field3>
        <my:field4></my:field4>
      </my:group2>
    </xsl:for-each>
    </my:group1>
  </my:myFields>
  </xsl:template>
</xsl:stylesheet>
```

27. Save the **CreateIPForm.xsl** file and close Notepad.

28. In Access, double-click the table that contains the data you imported from Excel (**Fruits** in this case) to open the table.

29. Click **External Data** ➤ **Export** ➤ **XML File**.

30. On the **Export – XML File** dialog box, enter a location on disk where you want to save the newly generated InfoPath form, and click **OK**.

31. On the **Export XML** dialog box, leave the **Data (XML)** check box selected, deselect the **Schema of the data (XSD)** check box, and then click **More Options**.

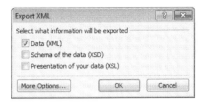

Figure 28. The Export XML dialog box in Access 2010.

32. On the **Export XML** dialog box, click **Transforms**.

33. On the **Export Transforms** dialog box, click **Add**.

34. On the **Add New Transform** dialog box, browse to and select the **CreateIPForm.xsl** file you created earlier, and click **Add**.

35. On the **Export Transforms** dialog box, click **OK**.

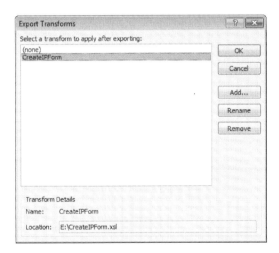

Figure 29. The Export Transforms dialog box in Access 2010.

36. On the **Export XML** dialog box, click **OK**.

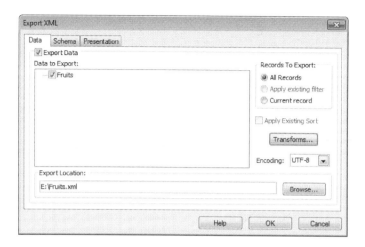

Figure 30. The Export XML dialog box in Access 2010.

37. On the **Export – XML File** dialog box, click **Close**.

In Windows Explorer, navigate to the location where you exported the Access database table and verify that an XML file with an InfoPath form icon was created. Double-click the file. It should open in InfoPath Filler 2010. Verify that it contains the data from the Access database table and thus also from the Excel workbook.

Discussion

In the solution described above, you saw how to use Access to create an InfoPath form based on data from an Excel workbook. You thereby used the **XML File** export functionality in Access together with an XSL transformation to be able to get the Excel data in the format for a specific InfoPath form.

When you export a table from Access as an XML file without performing any data transformations, the XML file will have the following structure:

```
<dataroot>
  <TableName>
    <Field1Name>Value</Field1Name>
    <Field2Name>Value</Field2Name>
  </TableName>
  <TableName>
    <Field1Name>Value</Field1Name>
    <Field2Name>Value</Field2Name>
  </TableName>
  ...
</dataroot>
```

where a **TableName** element is added for each row in the table you exported and each **TableName** element contains elements for the fields (columns) in a row. In the case of the **Fruits.xlsx** Excel workbook, the **Fruits** table, when exported without performing a data transformation, generates the following XML:

```
<dataroot>
  <Fruits>
    <Name>Apple</Name>
    <Color>Red</Color>
  </Fruits>
  <Fruits>
    <Name>Banana</Name>
    <Color>Yellow</Color>
  </Fruits>
  ...
</dataroot>
```

Because this XML does not have the structure of the XML of the InfoPath form you want to create, you must use an XSL transformation to get it into the correct structure. The **CreateIPForm.xsl** you constructed in steps 20 through 27 of the solution described above does just that. In addition, you added InfoPath-specific processing instructions to the generated XML file (see steps 24 and 25), so that the resulting XML file would be linked to the correct form template and recognized as an InfoPath form on your system.

The solution described above does not make use of compiled code to generate an InfoPath form. If you want to create an InfoPath form directly from within Excel and know how to write VBA code, you can use the solution described in recipe *39 Generate an InfoPath form from Excel data*.

Chapter 2: Excel Services in SharePoint

You can use Excel Services in SharePoint to display and access data from Excel workbooks in SharePoint. Excel Services consists of the following three components:

1.   Excel Calculation Services

2.   Excel Web Access

3.   Excel Web Services

Excel Calculation Services provides the core functionality for Excel Services (loading spreadsheets and workbooks, refreshing external data, maintaining session state, etc.). Excel Web Access is a web part and browser interface that you can use to display data and charts from an Excel workbook. Excel Web Services are web services hosted in SharePoint that you can use to get or set data in workbooks, create workbooks, perform calculations, etc.

Excel Services provides two web services: A SOAP web service and a REST web service. While the REST web service is easier to use, it is limited to getting data from Excel workbooks. And while you can use the REST web service to set values in an Excel workbook, those changes only affect the request you make (and no other REST requests or Excel Web Access browser sessions) and are not persisted in the workbook. To permanently store data in an Excel workbook, you must make use of the Excel Services SOAP web service or write code.

In this chapter you will not only see examples of using the Excel Web Access web part, but you will also learn how to work with the two web services of Excel Services without having to write code.

7   Publish an Excel workbook to SharePoint

Configure show options for an Excel workbook

Problem

You have an Excel workbook, which you want to access through Excel Services in SharePoint.

Solution

You can publish an entire workbook or parts of a workbook to a trusted file location in SharePoint so that it can be used with Excel Services.

To publish an Excel workbook to SharePoint:

1. In Excel, create a new workbook or use an existing one.

2. Click **File ➤ Save & Send ➤ Save to SharePoint** and then click **Publish Options**.

Figure 31. Saving a workbook to SharePoint in Excel 2010.

3. On the **Publish Options** dialog box on the **Show** tab, select **Sheets** from the drop-down list box, select the check box for the sheet(s) that have data you want to publish to SharePoint, and then click **OK**.

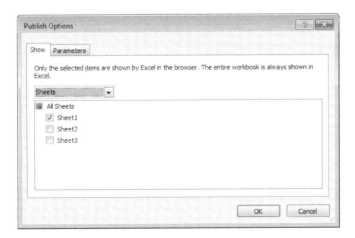

Figure 32. The Publish Options dialog box in Excel 2010.

Alternatively, if you want to publish the entire workbook to SharePoint, select **Entire Workbook** from the drop-down list box. And if you only want to publish certain items, for example a chart, select **Items in the Workbook** from the drop-down list box, and then select the check boxes for the individual items you want to publish.

Note that the publish options only apply to Excel Web Access and not to the Excel Services web services, which means that if for example you only publish **Sheet1** in a workbook to SharePoint, you will only be able to view the data from **Sheet1** if you use Excel Web Access (that is, view the Excel workbook in the browser or in an Excel Web Access web part), but you will still be able to access data from other worksheets through either the Excel Services REST or SOAP web service. So if you are going to use the Excel Services web services, it does not really matter which publish options you choose.

Refer to *Configure parameters for an Excel workbook* later in this recipe for the meaning and use of the **Parameters** tab on the **Publish Options** dialog box.

4.   Click **File ➤ Save & Send ➤ Save to SharePoint** and then click **Save As**.

5.   On the **Save As** dialog box, enter the URL of the SharePoint site where you want to publish the Excel workbook in the address bar at the top of the dialog box, and press **Enter**.

6.   On the **Save As** dialog box, select a document library in which to store the Excel workbook (for example the **Shared Documents** library), enter a name for the workbook in the **File name** combo box, deselect the **Open with Excel in the browser** check box, and click **Save**.

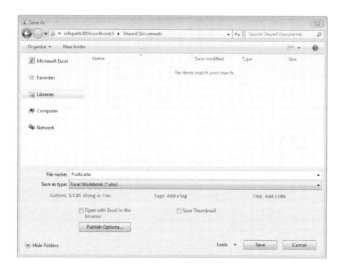

Figure 33. The Save As dialog box to save the Excel workbook to SharePoint 2010.

Note that you can also access the **Publish Options** dialog box by clicking the **Publish Options** button on the **Save As** dialog box instead of clicking the **Publish Options** button on the **Save & Send** tab in Excel.

Instead of saving the file to a document library via Excel, you could have also uploaded the Excel workbook to a document library from within SharePoint via the **Library Tools** ➤ **Documents** ➤ **Upload Document** functionality of the document library in SharePoint. However, performing such an action would not allow you to specify parameters or specific items to access in the workbook unless you have configured them (as described in step 3) before uploading the document.

You should now be able to access the Excel workbook through Excel Services (Excel Web Access or web services) in SharePoint.

Discussion

In the solution described above, you saw how to publish an Excel workbook to SharePoint so that it could be viewed using Excel Web Access or accessed through the Excel Services web services. If you want to provide interactivity with the Excel workbook through Excel Web Access (the browser or the web part), you must expose workbook cells through parameters (as discussed in *Configure parameters for an Excel workbook* later in this recipe), so that data can be passed to and used by the Excel workbook when it is being viewed using Excel Web Access.

All SharePoint sites are configured by default as trusted file locations when SharePoint is first installed, so you need not explicitly define the document library to which you publish an Excel workbook as a trusted file location. But if a solution that makes use of Excel Services is not working for you, you may want to have your administrator check whether the document library in which you saved the Excel file is indeed a trusted file location.

Your administrator can verify the existence of trusted file locations as follows:

1. In SharePoint 2010 Central Administration under **Application Management**, click **Manage service applications**.

2. On the **Manage Service Applications** page ensure that the **Excel Services Application** has a status of **Started**, and then click **Excel Services Application**.

3. On the **Manage Excel Services Application** page, click **Trusted File Locations**.

4. On the **Trusted File Locations** page, ensure that **http://** has been added as a trusted file location or click **Add Trusted File Location** and follow the instructions to add a trusted file location.

Tip:

> If you already uploaded an Excel workbook once before and then republish it
> because you made changes to it, but then see that those latest changes did not
> come through, try deleting the Excel workbook from the SharePoint document
> library and then republish the Excel workbook again to SharePoint by following
> the steps outlined in the solution above.
>
> If you changed data in an Excel workbook and do not see the changes appear
> when viewing the workbook in the browser or an Excel Web Access web part, try
> refreshing the data by clicking **File ➤ Reload Workbook** in the browser or the
> Excel Web Access web part.

Configure parameters for an Excel workbook

Problem

You have an Excel workbook to which you want to pass data to certain cells in the
workbook via Excel Web Access (the browser or the web part).

Solution

You can define names for cells in an Excel workbook to which you want to pass values
and then add the named ranges as parameters to the workbook before publishing the
workbook to SharePoint.

To configure an Excel workbook cell to receive input data:

1.   In Excel, create a new workbook or use an existing one.

2.   Select a cell on a worksheet in the workbook to which data should be passed. For
     example, cell **B3** on **Sheet3**. Note: To expose a cell through a parameter, you must
     use a single cell (not multiple cells) and the cell must not be used to perform a
     calculation using a formula. Named ranges that span multiple cells or that contain
     formulas cannot be added as parameters to an Excel workbook.

3.   Click **Formulas ➤ Defined Names ➤ Define Name**.

4.   On the **New Name** dialog box, enter a **Name** for the cell (for example
     InputParam1), leave **Workbook** selected as the **Scope**, and click **OK**.

5.   Click **File ➤ Save & Send ➤ Save to SharePoint** and then click **Publish Options**.

6. On the **Publish Options** dialog box, select the **Parameters** tab, and then click **Add**.

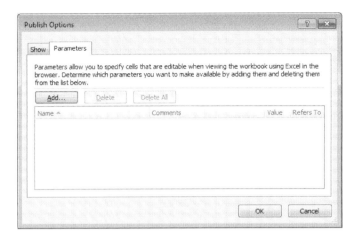

Figure 34. Adding a parameter to a workbook in Excel 2010.

7. On the **Add Parameters** dialog box, select the check box for the **InputParam1** named range you defined earlier, and click **OK**.

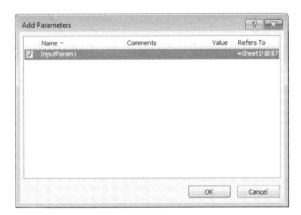

Figure 35. Selecting a named range to be used as a parameter in Excel 2010.

8. On the **Publish Options** dialog box, click **OK**.

9. Follow steps 4 through 6 of the first solution in this recipe to finish publishing the Excel workbook to SharePoint.

Now when you view the workbook in the browser or embed the workbook in an Excel Web Access web part (see recipe *8 Send an InfoPath form value to an Excel workbook*), you should be able to enter or pass a value for the **InputParam1** parameter.

Use Excel Web Access

8   Send an InfoPath form value to an Excel workbook

Problem

You have an InfoPath form and an Excel workbook, and you want to enter data in a field on the InfoPath form, click a button to send the data to the Excel workbook, and then use the data passed to the Excel workbook in a formula to perform a calculation and display the result on a worksheet in the Excel workbook.

Solution

You can embed both an InfoPath form and an Excel workbook in web parts on a SharePoint page and then set up web part connections to pass data from the InfoPath form to the Excel workbook.

To set up an Excel workbook to receive parameters:

1. In Excel, create a new workbook and name it **WeekNumber.xlsx** or download the **WeekNumber.xlsx** file from www.bizsupportonline.com and continue with step 6.

2. Place the cursor in cell **A1** on **Sheet1**, enter a date such as for example **2012-12-20**, and then click in another cell. The data type for the cell should automatically change to **Date**.

3. Place the cursor again in cell **A1** on **Sheet1**, and then click **Formulas ➤ Defined Names ➤ Define name**.

4. On the **New Name** dialog box, type **startDate** in the **Name** text box, leave **Workbook** selected in the **Scope** drop-down list box, and click **OK**. You will use this named range later as a parameter.

5. Place the cursor in cell **A2** on **Sheet1**, and enter the following formula:

```
=WEEKNUM(A1,2)
```

   This formula returns the week number for a specific date with the 2 indicating that the week begins on a Monday.

6. Click **File ➤ Save & Send ➤ Save to SharePoint** and publish the Excel workbook to SharePoint as described in recipe *7 Publish an Excel workbook to SharePoint*, thereby making the **startDate** named range a parameter.

Once you have published an Excel workbook with parameters, you can design an InfoPath form template that sends data to that Excel workbook. To create an InfoPath form template that can send data to an Excel workbook:

1. In InfoPath, create a new browser-compatible form template or use an existing one.

2. Add a **Date Picker** control and a **Button** control to the view of the form template. Name the date picker control **startDate** and label the button control **Send Data to Excel**.

3. Add an **Action** rule to the **Send Data to Excel** button that has the following action:

    ```
    Send data to Web Part
    ```

    and then on the **Rule Details** dialog box, click **Property Promotion**.

4. On the **Form Options** dialog box, click **Add** in the section for managing SharePoint Web Part connection parameters (the bottom section).

5. On the **Select a field** dialog box, select **startDate** in the tree view, leave **Start Date** as the **Parameter name**, select the **Output** option, and click **OK**. With this you have created an output web part connection parameter for the **startDate** field.

6. On the **Form Options** dialog box, click **OK**.

7. On the **Rule Details** dialog box, click **OK**.

8. Publish the form template to a SharePoint form library on the same site where you published the Excel workbook.

Once you have created and published both the Excel workbook and the InfoPath form template to SharePoint, you can embed them in web parts on a SharePoint page and set up web part connections between them to send or receive data. To send a value from the InfoPath form to the Excel workbook:

1. In SharePoint, navigate to a wiki page or a web part page on which you want to place the InfoPath form and Excel workbook, and edit the page.

2. Add an **InfoPath Form Web Part** (located under the **Forms** category of web parts) to the page.

3. Add an **Excel Web Access** web part (located under the **Business Data** category of web parts) to the page.

4. On the **InfoPath Form Web Part**, click the **Click here to open the tool pane** link.

5. On the web part tool pane, select the SharePoint form library where you published the InfoPath form template from the **List or Library** drop-down list box, and click **OK**.

6. On the **Excel Web Access** web part, click the **Click here to open the tool pane** link.

7. On the web part tool pane, click the ellipsis (...) button behind the **Workbook** text box.

8. On the **Select an Asset** webpage dialog, navigate to the location where you published the Excel workbook, select the **WeekNumber** Excel workbook, and click **OK**.

9. On the web part tool pane under the **Navigation and Interactivity** section, deselect the **Display Parameters Task Pane** check box, and then click **OK**.

10. Click the drop-down arrow in the upper right-hand corner of the **InfoPath Form Web Part**, and then select **Edit Web Part** from the drop-down menu that appears.

11. Click the drop-down arrow in the upper right-hand corner of the **InfoPath Form Web Part**, and then select **Connections ➤ Send Data To ➤ Excel Web Access – WeekNumber** from the drop-down menu that appears.

12. On the **Configure Connection** webpage dialog, select **Start Date** from the **Provider Field Name** drop-down list box, select **startDate** from the **Consumer Field Name** drop-down list box, and click **Finish**. With this you have configured the **InfoPath Form Web Part** to send data to the **Excel Web Access** web part.

13. Click **OK** on the InfoPath Form Web Part tool pane.

14. Save or stop editing the page.

In SharePoint, navigate to the page on which you placed the two web parts. Select a date from the date picker control on the InfoPath form and then click the button. The date you selected should appear in cell **A1** and its corresponding week number should appear in cell **A2** on **Sheet1** in the Excel workbook.

Discussion

In the solution described above, you saw how to use the Excel Web Access web part to embed an Excel workbook on a SharePoint page and send data from an InfoPath form embedded in an InfoPath Form Web Part to that Excel workbook through web part connection parameters.

You thereby used the **Send data to Web Part** action in InfoPath to send the value of one InfoPath form field to the Excel workbook. If your scenario calls for passing multiple parameters to an Excel workbook, you could set up multiple web part connection parameters in InfoPath, define multiple parameters in the Excel workbook, and then use SharePoint Designer 2010 as described in recipe *9 Send repeating table data to an Excel workbook for display in an Excel chart* to set up the web part connections between the InfoPath Form Web Part and the Excel Web Access web part in SharePoint.

The power of Excel lies in its ability to perform complex calculations. The formula used in the solution described above was kept simple for demonstration purposes, but you could make it as complex as you like.

9 Send repeating table data to an Excel workbook for display in an Excel chart

Problem

You have a repeating table control on an InfoPath form and want to use it to pass data to an Excel workbook for use and display in a chart.

Solution

You can use an InfoPath Form Web Part and Excel Web Access web part to pass data from a repeating table on an InfoPath form to an Excel workbook for display in a chart.

This solution consists of the following three parts:

1. Create an InfoPath form template that formats data in a special way so that it can be parsed in Excel.

2. Create an Excel workbook that contains formulas that can parse data from the repeating table on the InfoPath form and use this data to display a chart.

3. Embed the InfoPath form and the Excel workbook in web parts in SharePoint and set up web part connections.

To create an InfoPath form template that formats data for use in Excel:

1. In InfoPath, create a new browser-compatible form template or use an existing one.

2. Add a **Repeating Table** control with 2 columns to the view of the form template and name the fields in the repeating table **field1** and **field2**, respectively.

3. Add a **Validation** rule to **field2** with a **Condition** that says:

```
field2 does not match pattern Custom Pattern: 000.00
```

and a **ScreenTip** that says:

```
Please enter a number with the following format: 999.99
```

You can use the following custom pattern for the condition:

```
\d?\d?\d\.\d{2}
```

The intention is for users to only be able to enter numbers that have 3 digits before and 2 digits after the decimal point.

4. On the **Fields** task pane, add two **Field (element)** fields that have the data type **Text (string)** and the names **productNames** and **productPrices** to the Main data source.

5. Set the **Default Value** of the **productNames** field to be equal to the following formula (*code #: FEFE4EDE-07E5-4A79-8171-8A91066D259F*):

```
concat(xdMath:Eval(xdMath:Eval(../my:group1/my:group2, "my:field1"), ".."),
xdMath:Eval(xdMath:Eval(../my:group1/my:group2,
'concat(substring(concat("000", sum(xdMath:Eval(preceding::my:field1,
"string-length(.)")) + 1), string-length(concat("000",
sum(xdMath:Eval(preceding::my:field1, "string-length(.)")) + 1)) - 2, 3),
".", substring(concat("000", string-length(my:field1)), string-
length(concat("000", string-length(my:field1))) - 2, 3))'), ".."),
substring(concat("000", count(../my:group1/my:group2)), string-
length(concat("000", count(../my:group1/my:group2))) - 2, 3))
```

This formula should produce a text string such as for example "First sentenceSecond sentenceLast sentence001.014015.015030.013003" where the text string consists of values from **field1** in the repeating table where the first value is "First sentence" (the value of **field1** in the first row of the repeating table), the second value is "Second sentence" (the value of **field1** in the second row of the repeating table), and the third value is "Last sentence" (the value of **field1** in the third row of the repeating table). In addition, the starting position and length of each string is appended to the string. For example, "001.014" in the text string means that the first value starts at position number **1** in the string and has a length of **14** characters. Likewise, the second value starts at position number **15** in the string and has a length of **15** characters ("015.015"), and the third value starts at position number **30** in the string and has a length of **13** characters ("030.013"). The last 3 digits in the text string (**003**) indicate that there is a total of **3** values in the text string. This format has been chosen to make it easier to split the text string in the Excel workbook as you will see later.

6. Set the **Default Value** of the **productPrices** field to be equal to the following formula (*code #: 93488B80-D59E-4A9B-A7D2-2433D29A1BAD*):

```
xdMath:Eval(xdMath:Eval(../my:group1/my:group2, 'substring(concat("000",
my:field2), string-length(my:field2) - 2, 6)'), "..")
```

This formula should produce a text string such as for example "123.25088.55012.95" where each number from a **field2** in the repeating table consists of a total of 6 characters. The preceding text string consists of numbers (**123.25**, **88.55**, and **12.95**) from the **field2** fields in 3 rows of the repeating table concatenated to each other. In addition, **88.55** is displayed as "088.55" and **12.95** is displayed as "012.95" to make them consist of 6 characters each in the text string. This format has been chosen to make it easier to split the text string in the Excel workbook as you will see later.

7. Click **File ➤ Info ➤ Form Options**.

8. On the **Form Options** dialog box, select **Property Promotion** in the **Category** list, and then click **Add** in the section for managing SharePoint Web Part connection parameters (the bottom section).

9. On the **Select a field** dialog box, select **productNames**, leave the **Parameter name** as **Product Names**, select the **Output** option, and then click **OK**. You will use this parameter to pass the value of the **productNames** field to an Excel Web Access web part.

10. Repeat the previous step for the **productPrices** field, and name the parameter **Product Prices**.

11. On the **Form Options** dialog box, click **OK**.

12. Add a **Button** control to the view of the form template and label it **Display Excel Chart**.

13. Add an **Action** rule to the **Display Excel Chart** button with an action that says:

```
Send data to Web Part
```

This action will be used to send the values of the **productNames** and **productPrices** fields to an Excel Web Access web part.

14. Publish the form template to a SharePoint form library located on the same site where you will also be publishing the Excel workbook.

To create an Excel workbook that can parse data from an InfoPath repeating table:

1. In Excel, create a new workbook or use an existing one. Name the Excel workbook **Products.xlsx** or download the **Products.xlsx** file from www.bizsupportonline.com and continue with step 11.

2. Create a named range for cell **A1** on **Sheet1** as described in *Configure parameters for an Excel workbook* in recipe *7 Publish an Excel workbook to SharePoint* and name it **productNames**. The value of the **productNames** field in the InfoPath form will be passed to this cell.

3. Repeat the previous step for cell **A2** on **Sheet1** and name the named range **productPrices**. The value of the **productPrices** field in the InfoPath form will be passed to this cell.

4. Select cells **B5** through **B15** or as many rows as you think users may enter into the repeating table, enter the following formula in the formula box (*code #: E82DB2B2-24D3-4EF4-976F-986708C89FED*):

```
=MID(A1, LEFT(MID(MID(A1, LEN(A1) - 3 - VALUE(RIGHT(A1, 3))*7 + 1,
VALUE(RIGHT(A1, 3))*7), (ROW()-5)*7+1, 7), 3), RIGHT(MID(MID(A1, LEN(A1) -
3 - VALUE(RIGHT(A1, 3))*7 + 1, VALUE(RIGHT(A1, 3))*7), (ROW()-5)*7+1, 7),
3))
```

and then press **Shift+Ctrl+Enter** to create an array formula. This formula parses the value of cell **A1**, which contains the value of the **productNames** field in the InfoPath form, and places the parsed strings vertically in column **B** of the worksheet starting from cell **B5** downwards.

5. Select cells **C5** through **C15** or as many rows as you think users may enter into the repeating table, enter the following formula in the formula box (*code #: 4978444B-E1E2-4AD1-B78A-380687336651*):

```
=VALUE(MID(A2,((ROW()-5)*6+1),6))
```

    and then press **Shift+Ctrl+Enter** to create an array formula. This formula parses the value of cell **A2**, which contains the value of the **productPrices** field in the InfoPath form, and places the parsed numbers vertically in column **C** of the worksheet starting from cell **C5** downwards.

6. Select **Insert ➤ Charts ➤ Bar ➤ 2-D Bar** to add a bar chart to the worksheet.

7. Right-click the bar chart and select **Select Data** from the context menu that appears.

8. Select cells **C5** through **C15** on the worksheet to populate the **Chart data range** text box on the **Select Data Source** dialog box.

9. On the **Select Data Source** dialog box, click **Edit** in the **Horizontal (Category) Axis Labels** list box, select cells **B5** through **B15** on the worksheet, and then click **OK** on the **Axis Labels** dialog box.

10. On the **Select Data Source** dialog box, click **OK**.

11. Publish the Excel workbook to SharePoint as described in recipe *7 Publish an Excel workbook to SharePoint* thereby adding the **productNames** and **productPrices** named ranges as parameters via the **Publish Options** command.

To embed the InfoPath form and the Excel workbook in web parts in SharePoint and set up web part connections:

1. In SharePoint, navigate to a wiki page or a web part page on which you want to place the InfoPath form and Excel workbook, and edit the page.

2. Add an **InfoPath Form Web Part** (located under the **Forms** category of web parts) to the page.

3. Add an **Excel Web Access** web part (located under the **Business Data** category of web parts) to the page.

4. On the **InfoPath Form Web Part**, click the **Click here to open the tool pane** link.

5. On the web part tool pane, select the SharePoint form library where you published the InfoPath form template from the **List or Library** drop-down list box, and click **OK**.

6. On the **Excel Web Access** web part, click the **Click here to open the tool pane** link.

7. On the web part tool pane, click the ellipsis (...) button behind the **Workbook** text box.

8. On the **Select an Asset** webpage dialog, navigate to the location where you published the Excel workbook, select the **Products** Excel workbook, and click **OK**.

9. On the web part tool pane under the **Navigation and Interactivity** section, deselect the **Display Parameters Task Pane** check box, and then click **OK**.

10. Save or stop editing the page.

11. Because you must set up more than one web part connection, you must continue editing the page in SharePoint Designer. So in SharePoint, select **Site Actions ➤ Edit in SharePoint Designer**.

12. In SharePoint Designer, click **Site Pages** (or navigate to the location where you saved the SharePoint wiki or web part page) in the left navigation pane, and then click the page on which you placed the two web parts.

13. When the page editor opens, under **Customization**, click **Edit file**.

14. Click the InfoPath Form Web Part that is located on the page to select it, and then click **Web Part Tools ➤ Format ➤ Connections ➤ Add Connection**.

15. On the **Web Part Connections Wizard**, select **Send Data To** from the drop-down list box, and click **Next**.

16. On the **Web Part Connections Wizard**, leave the **Connect to a Web Part on this page** option selected, and click **Next**. If the **Connect to a Web Part on this page** option is disabled, double-check whether you added the **productNames** and **productPrices** named ranges as parameters when you published the Excel workbook to SharePoint.

17. On the **Web Part Connections Wizard**, select **Excel Web Access – Products** from the **Target Web Part** drop-down list box, select **Get Values for Multiple Parameters From** from the **Target action** drop-down list box, and click **Next**.

18. On the **Web Part Connections Wizard**, select **productNames** in both the **Columns in InfoPath Form Web Part** and the **Inputs to Excel Web Access – Products** columns in the same row of the grid. Do the same for **productPrices** on the second row in the grid, and then click **Next**.

19. On the **Web Part Connections Wizard**, click **Finish**.

20. Save the changes.

In SharePoint, navigate to the page on which you placed the two web parts. Add a couple of rows with data to the repeating table, and then click the **Display Excel Chart** button. The data should appear in the Excel workbook and the Excel chart should have been updated to display the data you entered in the InfoPath form.

Discussion

The solution described above is similar to the solution described in recipe *8 Send an InfoPath form value to an Excel workbook*, but instead of sending one value from the InfoPath form to the Excel workbook, you are sending two values that are concatenated strings of fields in two columns of a repeating table control on the InfoPath form.

In addition, instead of using a normal formula in the Excel workbook, you used vertical array formulas to parse and place text strings that are passed from the InfoPath form in columns (either column **B** or **C**) starting from the fifth row on a worksheet. The Excel formula for parsing the product prices resembles the following:

```
=VALUE(MID(A2,((ROW()-5)*6+1),6))
```

The format for the numbers in the text string passed from the InfoPath form resembles the following:

```
111.11222.22333.33
```

There are 3 numbers in this text string (**111.11**, **222.22**, and **333.33**) with each number consisting of 6 characters (including the decimal symbol). The Excel formula first uses the **ROW** function to determine the row number the formula is located in. In this case, row numbers start at **5**, since the first cell to contain the array formula is cell **C5**. Because the row numbers are used to calculate the starting position for the **MID** function, a **5** must be subtracted from the **ROW** function, so that row numbers start at **0**.

```
ROW()-5
```

Therefore, cell **C5** would return **0**, cell **C6** would return **1**, cell **C7** would return **2**, etc. for the formula shown above. The starting position for **111.11** in the text string is **1**, 7 for **222.22**, and **13** for **333.33**. So the following formula would return starting positions **1**, **7**, and **13** for cells **C5**, **C6**, and **C7**:

```
((ROW()-5)*6+1)
```

This formula would continue to return the correct starting positions for all cells in column **C** downwards if the text string consisted of more than 3 numbers. To complete the **MID** function, each number is **6** characters long (the last argument), and the **MID** function should be run on the text string (the first argument), which results in the following formula:

```
MID(A2,((ROW()-5)*6+1),6)
```

And finally, the **VALUE** function is used to convert the extracted string into a number.

```
VALUE(MID(A2,((ROW()-5)*6+1),6))
```

The formula for parsing the product names is slightly more complex, but follows the same principles.

```
=MID(A1, LEFT(MID(MID(A1, LEN(A1) - 3 - VALUE(RIGHT(A1, 3))*7 + 1,
VALUE(RIGHT(A1, 3))*7), (ROW()-5)*7+1, 7), 3), RIGHT(MID(MID(A1, LEN(A1) - 3 -
VALUE(RIGHT(A1, 3))*7 + 1, VALUE(RIGHT(A1, 3))*7), (ROW()-5)*7+1, 7), 3))
```

The format for the text string containing product names resembles the following:

```
Product Name 1Product Name 2Product Name 3001.014015.014029.014003
```

where the last 3 digits (**003**) refer to the amount of product names in the string (3 in this case). The numbers at the end of the text string describe the starting position and length of each product name in the string. For example, **001.014** stands for starting position 1 (**001**) and a length of 14 characters (**014**). And because each of these numbers consists of a total of 7 characters, you know that the last **21** characters (**3*7**) in the text string describe the starting positions and lengths of 3 product names in the text string. With this information, you can now start to construct a formula that can parse the string.

First you must retrieve the amount of product names in the string (so the last 3 digits).

```
VALUE(RIGHT(A1, 3))
```

The formula above should return **3** once **003** has been converted into a number using the **VALUE** function. Then you must retrieve the numbers at the end of the string (minus the last 3 digits) that represent the starting positions and lengths of the product names.

```
MID(A1, LEN(A1) - 3 - VALUE(RIGHT(A1, 3))*7 + 1, VALUE(RIGHT(A1, 3))*7)
```

The formula above should return **001.014015.014029.014**. The **ROW** function is used similarly to the formula that retrieves the product prices to find the individual number pairs (**001.014**, **015.014**, and **029.014**).

```
(ROW()-5)*7+1
```

Each number pair is then parsed using the **LEFT** or **RIGHT** function to retrieve 3 characters representing either the starting position or the length of a product name in the text string.

```
LEFT(MID(MID(A1, LEN(A1) - 3 - VALUE(RIGHT(A1, 3))*7 + 1, VALUE(RIGHT(A1,
3))*7), (ROW()-5)*7+1, 7), 3)
```

is used to retrieve the starting position of a product name in the text string (for example **001** for the first product name) and

```
RIGHT(MID(MID(A1, LEN(A1) - 3 - VALUE(RIGHT(A1, 3))*7 + 1, VALUE(RIGHT(A1,
3))*7), (ROW()-5)*7+1, 7), 3)
```

is used to retrieve the length of a product name in the text string (for example **014** for the first product name). And finally, the **MID** function is used to extract the individual product names from the text string, which results in the final formula:

```
MID(A1, LEFT(MID(MID(A1, LEN(A1) - 3 - VALUE(RIGHT(A1, 3))*7 + 1,
VALUE(RIGHT(A1, 3))*7), (ROW()-5)*7+1, 7), 3), RIGHT(MID(MID(A1, LEN(A1) - 3 -
VALUE(RIGHT(A1, 3))*7 + 1, VALUE(RIGHT(A1, 3))*7), (ROW()-5)*7+1, 7), 3))
```

Note that all cells for which no value can be calculated will be filled with the **#VALUE!** error value in Excel. You can replace this error value with a blank value by checking for errors using the **IF** and **ISERROR** functions as follows:

```
IF(ISERROR([original formula goes here]), "", [original formula goes here])
```

where you must replace **[original formula goes here]** with the Excel formula you constructed in step 4 or step 5.

On the InfoPath side of the solution, the text strings are constructed using the **eval()** function. The formula for constructing the text string for the product prices resembles the following:

```
xdMath:Eval(xdMath:Eval(../my:group1/my:group2, 'substring(concat("000",
my:field2), string-length(my:field2) - 2, 6)'), "..")
```

The way you would go about constructing such a formula is to start with the base formula that returns the contents of all **group2** group nodes concatenated to each other.

```
eval(my:group2, "..")
```

Then for each **group2** group node, you must retrieve the **field2** field which contains product prices in the repeating table.

```
eval(eval(my:group2, "my:field2"), "..")
```

But because you want to format each price as **000.00**, you must use the **substring()**, **concat()**, and **string-length()** functions to construct such a price format. So first you prepend **000** to **field2** using the **concat()** function.

```
concat("000", my:field2)
```

Because you know that the final price should consist of 6 characters, you must then use a combination of the **substring()** and **string-length()** functions to retrieve the right 6 characters of the concatenated string, since InfoPath does not have a **right()** function you can use.

```
substring(concat("000", my:field2), string-length(my:field2) - 2, 6)
```

You can use the formula above to replace the **my:field2** part in the following formula

```
eval(eval(my:group2, "my:field2"), "..")
```

which should then result in

```
eval(eval(my:group2, 'substring(concat("000", my:field2), string-
length(my:field2) - 2, 6)'), "..")
```

where the double quotes around **my:field2** have been replaced by single quotes to allow the use of double quotes in the formula that replaced **my:field2**.

The formula that constructs the text string for the product names is slightly more complex, but you can follow a similar technique to construct it. The base formula uses the **concat()** function to concatenate a string for the product names with a string for the numbers that represent the starting positions and lengths of the strings. And finally the amount of product names should be appended at the end of the text string as 3 digits. So something like:

```
concat([product names formula goes here], [starting positions and lengths
formula goes here], [amount of products formula goes here])
```

For the product names formula you must again use the **eval()** function.

```
eval(eval(my:group2, "my:field1"), "..")
```

For the starting positions and lengths formula you must also use the **eval()** function with a combinations of the **sum()** function and the **preceding** XPath axis to be able to calculate the starting position for each product name.

```
eval(eval(my:group2, 'concat(substring(concat("000",
sum(xdMath:Eval(preceding::my:field1, "string-length(.)")) + 1), string-
length(concat("000", sum(xdMath:Eval(preceding::my:field1, "string-length(.)"))
+ 1)) - 2, 3), ".", substring(concat("000", string-length(my:field1)), string-
length(concat("000", string-length(my:field1))) - 2, 3))'), "..")
```

For example, while the **eval()** function is looping through the **group2** group nodes and the third **group2** group node is the context node, **preceding** is used to retrieve the first and second **group2** group nodes. Then the **string-length()** function is used on the **field1** field below each one of those **group2** group nodes to find the lengths of the product names. And finally, the **sum()** function is then used to calculate the total length of the first and second product names, which can then be used as a starting position for the third product name.

```
sum(xdMath:Eval(preceding::my:field1, "string-length(.)")) + 1
```

As you can see from the formula above, the **eval()** function is used again within the
sum() function to be able to run the **string-length()** function on each **field1** field and
return a node-set that can then be used in the **sum()** function to perform a summation.
And then to make the starting positions have a format equal to **000**, you can again
combine the **substring()**, **concat()**, and **string-length()** functions.

```
substring(concat("000", sum(xdMath:Eval(preceding::my:field1, "string-
length(.)")) + 1), string-length(concat("000",
sum(xdMath:Eval(preceding::my:field1, "string-length(.)")) + 1)) - 2, 3)
```

The last part of the formula for the starting positions and string lengths retrieves the
string lengths for each product name by using the **string-length()** function on each **field1**
field.

```
substring(concat("000", string-length(my:field1)), string-length(concat("000",
string-length(my:field1))) - 2, 3)
```

The starting positions and string lengths are then concatenated to each other and
separated by a period by using the **concat()** function.

```
concat(substring(concat("000", sum(xdMath:Eval(preceding::my:field1, "string-
length(.)")) + 1), string-length(concat("000",
sum(xdMath:Eval(preceding::my:field1, "string-length(.)")) + 1)) - 2, 3), ".",
substring(concat("000", string-length(my:field1)), string-length(concat("000",
string-length(my:field1))) - 2, 3))
```

For the amount of products formula you can use the **count()** function and combine this
with the **substring()**, **concat()**, and **string-length()** functions to make the final string
have a format like **000**.

```
substring(concat("000", count(my:group2)), string-length(concat("000",
count(my:group2))) - 2, 3)
```

Note that the solution described in this recipe does not permanently store data in the
Excel workbook; it just passes data to the workbook for display. If you want to
permanently store InfoPath repeating table data in the Excel workbook, see recipe *27
Send a repeating table row to Excel – method 2*.

Use the Excel Services REST Web Service

The Excel Services REST web service allows you to access resources such as charts,
tables, and named ranges in an Excel workbook directly through an URL. Note that you
should always test a REST web service URL in the browser to verify that it is working
properly before you use it in InfoPath, because if it does not work in the browser, it is
likely not to work in InfoPath either.

The Excel Services REST web service is generally easier to use than the Excel Services SOAP web service and typically requires less actions or rules to run. In addition, you can use it to retrieve Excel data in situations where data retrieval through the Excel Services SOAP web service might fail.

The REST URL for Excel Services consists of four parts:

1. A REST ASPX page URI – This is the entry point to the **ExcelREST.aspx** page. For example:

    ```
    http://serverName/siteName/_vti_bin/ExcelRest.aspx
    ```

2. A workbook location – This is the path to the workbook. For example:

    ```
    /DocumentLibraryName/WorkbookName.xlsx
    ```

3. A resource location – This is the path to the requested resource inside the workbook. For example:

    ```
    /model/Tables('TableName')
    ```

    or

    ```
    /model/Ranges('Sheet1!A1|G5')
    ```

    or

    ```
    /model/Ranges('NameOfTheNamedRange')
    ```

    or

    ```
    /model/Charts('ChartName')
    ```

4. The format in which to return the data. For example:

    ```
    $format=atom
    ```

    or

    ```
    $format=html
    ```

For more information about Excel Services and its REST web service, consult the MSDN documentation.

10 Get the value of an Excel cell in InfoPath

Problem

You have an Excel workbook from which you want to retrieve the value of a particular cell so that you can display this value on an InfoPath form.

Solution

You can create an Excel workbook that contains data, publish this Excel workbook to a trusted file location for Excel Services in SharePoint, and then call the Excel Services REST web service from within an InfoPath form to retrieve data that is stored in the Excel workbook.

To get the value of a cell in an Excel workbook from within an InfoPath form:

1. In Excel, create an Excel workbook that has login names of employees in column **A** of **Sheet1** and their corresponding leave balances in column **B** of **Sheet1**.

    Sample data in the Excel workbook:

	A	B	C
1	jane.doe	25	
2	john.doe	15	
3	clovis.carvalho	33	
4			

    Name the Excel workbook **LeaveBalances.xlsx**. You can also download a file named **LeaveBalances.xlsx** from www.bizsupportonline.com for use with this recipe.

2. Click **File ➤ Save & Send ➤ Save to SharePoint ➤ Save As** and save the entire workbook (including all of its sheets) to a document library (for example the **Shared Documents** library) on the SharePoint site to which the InfoPath form will be connecting (also see recipe *7 Publish an Excel workbook to SharePoint*).

3. In InfoPath, create a new browser-compatible form template or use an existing one.

4. Select **Data ➤ Get External Data ➤From Web Service ➤ From REST Web Service**.

Figure 36. Adding a REST web service data connection in InfoPath 2010.

5. On the **Data Connection Wizard**, enter the URL of the Excel Services REST web service and the Excel workbook, for example:

```
http://servername/sitename/_vti_bin/ExcelREST.aspx/Shared%20Documents/Leave
Balances.xlsx/model/Ranges('B1')?$format=atom
```

and click **Next**. Here, **servername** is the name of the SharePoint server and **sitename** is the name of the site where the **LeaveBalances.xlsx** workbook has been stored in the **Shared Documents** document library. **B1** is the name of the cell in the Excel workbook from which a value should be retrieved.

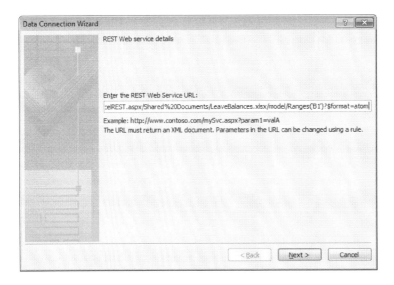

Figure 37. Entering the REST URL on the Data Connection Wizard in InfoPath 2010.

If you enter this same URL in the browser, you should get back a page displaying the XML that will be returned to the InfoPath form. The **content** element should contain the following XML fragment:

```
<x:range name="B1">
  <x:row>
    <x:c>
      <x:v>25</x:v>
      <x:fv>25</x:fv>
    </x:c>
  </x:row>
</x:range>
```

So now you also know that you must use either the **v** or the **fv** field in InfoPath to display the leave balance retrieved from cell **B1**. Note that **v** stands for "value" and **fv** stands for "formatted value". For example if you format a number such as **2.2** in a cell as a currency, the **v** field would contain **2.2** and the **fv** field would contain **$2.20**.

6. On the **Data Connection Wizard**, name the data connection **GetLeaveBalance**, leave the **Automatically retrieve data when form is opened** check box selected,

and click **Finish**.

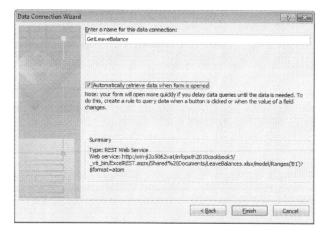

Figure 38. The last screen of the Data Connection Wizard in InfoPath 2010.

7. On the **Fields** task pane, select **GetLeaveBalance (Secondary)** from the Fields drop-down list box, expand all of the group nodes under the **content** group node, and then drag-and-drop the **fv** field under the **c** group node under the **row** group node under the **range** group node onto the view of the form template. It should automatically get bound to a text box control.

Figure 39. The Fields task pane in InfoPath 2010 displaying the secondary data source.

8. Preview the form.

When the form opens, **25** should appear in the text box.

Discussion

In the solution described above, you used the following REST URL:

```
http://servername/sitename/_vti_bin/ExcelREST.aspx/Shared%20Documents/LeaveBalan
ces.xlsx/model/Ranges('B1')?$format=atom
```

to retrieve the value of a cell (cell **B1** on **Sheet1** in this case) from an Excel workbook. Note that you could have also retrieved the value of cell **B1** by using the following URL, which explicitly specifies the name of the worksheet:

```
http://servername/sitename/_vti_bin/ExcelREST.aspx/Shared%20Documents/LeaveBalan
ces.xlsx/model/Ranges('Sheet1!B1')?$format=atom
```

Such an URL is handy to use when a cell is located on a worksheet other than the first worksheet in the Excel workbook. For example, to retrieve the value of cell **C1** on a worksheet named **DateDiffCalculation**, you would have to use the following REST URL:

```
http://servername/sitename/_vti_bin/ExcelREST.aspx/Shared%20Documents/LeaveBalan
ces.xlsx/model/Ranges('DateDiffCalculation!C1')?$format=atom
```

The solution described above used a static URL to retrieve data from one particular cell in an Excel workbook. However, if you wanted to allow users to specify the cell to use when retrieving a value, you could take the solution a step further as follows:

1. Add a **Text Box** control to the view of the form template and name it **cellReference**.

2. Add a **Button** control to the view of the form template and label it **Get Cell Value**.

3. Add an **Action** rule to the button with an action that says:

   ```
   Change REST URL: GetLeaveBalance
   ```

   where you must change the formula that sets the value of the **REST Web Service URL** to be the following:

   ```
   concat("http://servername/sitename/_vti_bin/ExcelREST.aspx/Shared%20Docu
   ments/LeaveBalances.xlsx/model/Ranges('", cellReference,
   "')?$format=atom")
   ```

   where **cellReference** is the field in the Main data source that is bound to the text box control. With this you have made the REST URL dynamic by using the **concat()** function to construct the REST URL based on a static base URL and the value of a field on the InfoPath form.

4. Add a second action to the **Action** rule on the button that says:

```
Query using a data connection: GetLeaveBalance
```

This action refreshes the data in the **GetLeaveBalance** secondary data source by retrieving data using the modified REST URL.

5. Preview the form.

When the form opens, enter a value (for example **B3**) in the **cellReference** text box, and then click the **Get Cell Value** button. **33** should appear in the text box for the **fv** field. And if you enter for example **A2** in the **cellReference** text box and then click the button, **john.doe** should appear in the text box for the **fv** field.

11 Set the value of an Excel cell in InfoPath

Problem

You have an Excel workbook in which you want to set the value of a cell so that you can perform a calculation and retrieve the result for display on an InfoPath form.

Solution

You can create an Excel workbook that contains data and a formula, publish this Excel workbook to a trusted file location for Excel Services in SharePoint, and then call the Excel Services REST web service from within an InfoPath form to perform data submission and retrieval.

To set the value of a cell in an Excel workbook from within an InfoPath form:

1. Use the same Excel workbook from step 1 of recipe *10 Get the value of an Excel cell in InfoPath*, but rename **Sheet2** to **Calculations**, and add the following formula to cell **A2** on the **Calculations** worksheet:

```
=VLOOKUP(A1, Sheet1!A1:B3, 2, FALSE)
```

Save the Excel workbook back to SharePoint once you have modified it. Note that if you downloaded the **LeaveBalance.xlsx** file from www.bizsupportonline.com, the Excel workbook should already contain the **Calculations** worksheet and the formula.

2. In InfoPath, create a new browser-compatible form template or use an existing one.

3. Select **Data ➤ Get External Data ➤From Web Service ➤ From REST Web Service**.

4. On the **Data Connection Wizard**, enter the URL of the Excel Services REST web service and the Excel workbook, for example:

```
http://servername/sitename/_vti_bin/ExcelREST.aspx/Shared%20Documents/Leave
Balances.xlsx/model/Ranges('Calculations!A2')?Ranges('Calculations!A1')=joh
n.doe&$format=atom
```

and click **Next**. Here, **servername** is the name of the SharePoint server and **sitename** is the name of the site where the **LeaveBalances.xlsx** workbook has been stored in the **Shared Documents** document library. **Calculations!A1** is the name of the cell on the **Calculations** worksheet in the Excel workbook that should receive the input for the formula. **Calculations!A2** is the name of the cell on the **Calculations** worksheet in the Excel workbook that contains the result of the calculation.

The first query string parameter in the REST URL that comes after the question mark

```
Ranges('Calculations!A1')=john.doe
```

sets the value of cell **A1** on the **Calculations** worksheet in the Excel workbook to be equal to **john.doe**, while the part of the REST URL that comes before the question mark

```
Ranges('Calculations!A2')
```

retrieves the value of cell **A2** on the **Calculations** worksheet in the Excel workbook.

5. On the **Data Connection Wizard**, name the data connection **GetLeaveBalance**, deselect the **Automatically retrieve data when form is opened** check box, and click **Finish**.

6. Add a **Text Box** control to the view of the form template and name it **userName**.

7. Add a **Button** control to the view of the form template and label it **Get Leave Balance**.

8. Add an **Action** rule to the button with an action that says:

```
Change REST URL: GetLeaveBalance
```

where you must change the formula that sets the value of the **REST Web Service URL** to be the following:

```
concat("http://servername/sitename/_vti_bin/ExcelREST.aspx/Shared%20Documen
ts/LeaveBalances.xlsx/model/Ranges('Calculations!A2')?Ranges('Calculations!
A1')=", userName ,"&$format=atom")
```

where **userName** is the field in the Main data source that is bound to the text box control. With this you have made the REST URL dynamic by using the **concat()** function to construct the REST URL based on a static base URL and the value of a field on the InfoPath form.

9. Add a second action to the **Action** rule on the button that says:

```
Query using a data connection: GetLeaveBalance
```

This action refreshes the data in the **GetLeaveBalance** secondary data source by retrieving data using the modified REST URL.

10. On the **Fields** task pane, select **GetLeaveBalance (Secondary)** from the **Fields** drop-down list box, expand all of the group nodes under the **content** group node, and then drag-and-drop the **fv** field under the **c** group node under the **row** group node under the **range** group node onto the view of the form template. It should automatically get bound to a text box control.

11. Preview the form.

When the form opens, enter one of the user names from the Excel workbook (for example **jane.doe**) into the text box and click the button. The leave balance for the user name you entered should appear in the text box for the **fv** field.

Discussion

In the solution described above, you used a **Change REST URL** action in a rule in InfoPath to be able to dynamically change the REST URL used to perform a calculation and then retrieve the result of the calculation from an Excel workbook that is stored in SharePoint and that is accessible through Excel Services.

Note that the value you passed as a query string parameter of the REST URL (refer to the beginning of the *Use the Excel Services REST Web Service* section in this chapter for general information about using the Excel Services REST web service in InfoPath and for an explanation of the different parts of the REST URL)

```
?Ranges('Calculations!A1')=john.doe
```

to the Excel workbook was not permanently stored in the Excel workbook. You can open the workbook and verify that the value of cell **A1** on the **Calculations** worksheet still has the same value it had when you first published the Excel workbook to SharePoint.

Query string parameter values exist only for the duration of a request you send to Excel Services and do not affect other Excel Services sessions that may be active on the server. To make permanent changes to an Excel workbook that is stored in SharePoint, you can use Excel Services SOAP web service operations without having to write code.

Tip:

If you get any of the errors listed below when trying to retrieve data through the Excel Services REST web service, double-check whether the URL is correct. Chances are that you missed (for example an ampersand) or have an invalid character in the URL. You can also verify whether the URL you used in InfoPath is correct by copying it to a browser window and testing whether it returns XML data in the browser.

> *The query cannot be run for the following DataObject: GetLeaveBalance*
>
> *InfoPath cannot run the specified query.*
>
> *The file is not a valid XML file.*
>
> *The form contains XML that cannot be parsed:*
>
> *Reference to undefined entity 'nbsp'.*

12 Display an Excel chart on an InfoPath form

Problem

You have an Excel workbook that contains a chart and that is stored in a SharePoint document library and you want to be able to display this chart statically on an InfoPath browser form.

Solution

You can use the Excel Services REST web service to access a chart that is located in an Excel workbook and display this chart statically on an InfoPath form.

To display an Excel chart on an InfoPath form:

1. In Excel, create a new workbook or use an existing one and name it **Chart.xlsx**.

2. Add a chart to one of the worksheets in the workbook and configure the chart to display data. You can also download a file named **Chart.xlsx** from www.bizsupportonline.com for use with this recipe.

3. Click **File ➤ Save & Send ➤ Save to SharePoint ➤ Save As** and save the entire workbook (including all of its sheets) to a document library (for example the **Shared Documents** library) on the SharePoint site to which the InfoPath form will be connecting (also see recipe *7 Publish an Excel workbook to SharePoint*).

4. Once the Excel file has been published to SharePoint, you should test whether you can access the chart (**Chart1** if you downloaded the **Chart.xlsx** file from www.bizsupportonline.com) by entering an URL such as the following in the browser:

```
http://servername/sitename/_vti_bin/ExcelREST.aspx/Shared%20Documents/Chart
.xlsx/model/Charts('Chart1')
```

where `http://servername/sitename/_vti_bin/ExcelREST.aspx` is the URL to access the Excel Services REST web service, **Shared%20Documents** is the document library to which you published the Excel workbook, **Chart.xlsx** is the name of the Excel workbook you published to SharePoint and **Chart1** is the name of the chart you want to access in the Excel workbook. Note that you must replace **servername** and **sitename** with the appropriate names for your own SharePoint server and site where the **Shared%20Documents** document library is located.

5. In InfoPath, create a new browser-compatible form template or use an existing one.

6. Add a **Picture** control to the view of the form template, select the **As a link** option on the **Insert Picture Control** dialog box when you add the picture control, and name the picture control **field1**.

7. Set the **Default Value** of the picture control to be equal to the following formula:

```
concat(SharePointSiteUrl(),
"/_vti_bin/ExcelREST.aspx/Shared%20Documents/Chart.xlsx/model/Charts('Chart
1')")
```

where **SharePointSiteUrl()** retrieves the URL of the site where the Excel workbook is located and to which you will be publishing the form template, `/_vti_bin/ExcelREST.aspx` is the part of the URL that accesses the Excel Services REST web service, **Shared%20Documents** is the document library to which you published the Excel workbook, **Chart.xlsx** is the name of the Excel workbook you published to SharePoint, and **Chart1** is the name of the chart you want to access in the Excel workbook.

8. Publish the form template to a form library that is located on the same SharePoint site where the Excel workbook is located.

In SharePoint, navigate to the form library where you published the form template and add a new form. When the form opens, you should see the Excel chart appear in the picture control.

Discussion

In the solution described above, you saw how to use an Excel Services REST URL to access a chart that is stored in an Excel workbook that was published to SharePoint. In addition, you saw how to assign this URL to a picture control on an InfoPath form so that you could display the Excel chart on the InfoPath form.

Because the Excel Services REST web service does not return the image for the Excel chart as a base64-encoded string, you cannot include the chart in the form, but must select to link to it through a picture control instead.

And because you used the **SharePointSiteUrl()** function to construct the REST URL

```
concat(SharePointSiteUrl(),
"/_vti_bin/ExcelREST.aspx/Shared%20Documents/Chart.xlsx/model/Charts('Chart1')")
```

you must publish the form template to the same SharePoint site where the Excel workbook is located for the solution to work. If you want to display an Excel chart while filling out a form in InfoPath Filler or use an Excel workbook that is located on a different SharePoint site than where the InfoPath form is located, you must replace the **SharePointSiteUrl()** function with a static URL, for example

```
"http://servername/sitename/_vti_bin/ExcelREST.aspx/Shared%20Documents/Chart.xls
x/model/Charts('Chart1')"
```

where you must replace **servername** and **sitename** with the correct names for the SharePoint server and site where the Excel workbook is located. Refer to the beginning of the *Use the Excel Services REST Web Service* section in this chapter for general information about using the Excel Services REST web service in InfoPath and for an explanation of the different parts of the REST URL.

At this point, the Excel chart is displayed statically on an InfoPath form. If you want to dynamically update and display a chart, you must use the Excel Services SOAP web service to change values for the chart in the Excel workbook and then refresh the Excel chart by retrieving its image through the Excel Services REST web service as described in recipe *20 Update an Excel chart on an InfoPath form*.

13 Get the values of a range of Excel cells in InfoPath

Problem

You want to use an InfoPath form to retrieve data from a range of cells in an Excel workbook that is stored in a SharePoint document library.

Solution

You can create an Excel workbook that contains tabular data, publish this Excel workbook to a trusted file location for Excel Services, and then call the Excel Services REST web service from within an InfoPath form to retrieve data.

To get the values of a range of cells in an Excel workbook from within an InfoPath form:

1. In Excel, create an Excel workbook that contains a list of fruit names and their corresponding fruit colors as described in recipe *2 Import Excel data as XML in InfoPath – method 1* or download a file named **Fruits.xlsx** from www.bizsupportonline.com. Note that the Excel workbook contains a named range named **Fruits** that spans cells **A2** through **B6**.

2. Click **File ➤ Save & Send ➤ Save to SharePoint ➤ Save As** and save the entire workbook (including all of its sheets) to a document library (for example the **Shared Documents** library) on the SharePoint site to which the InfoPath form will be connecting (also see recipe *7 Publish an Excel workbook to SharePoint*).

3. In InfoPath, create a new browser-compatible form template or use an existing one.

4. Select **Data ➤ Get External Data ➤ From Web Service ➤ From REST Web Service**.

5. On the **Data Connection Wizard**, enter the URL of the Excel Services REST web service and the Excel workbook, for example:

```
http://servername/sitename/_vti_bin/ExcelREST.aspx/Shared%20Documents/Fruit
s.xlsx/model/Ranges('Fruits')?$format=atom
```

and click **Next**. Here, **servername** is the name of the SharePoint server and **sitename** is the name of the site where the **Fruits.xlsx** workbook has been stored in the **Shared Documents** document library. **Fruits** is a named range in the Excel workbook that spans the list of fruit names and fruit colors.

6. On the **Data Connection Wizard**, name the data connection **GetFruits**, leave the **Automatically retrieve data when form is opened** check box selected, and click **Finish**.

7. On the **Fields** task pane, select **GetFruits (Secondary)** from the **Fields** drop-down list box, expand the **content** group node under the **entry** group node, expand the **range** group node under the **content** group node, drag the **row** repeating group node to the view of the form template, drop it, and select **Repeating Section with Controls** from the context menu that appears.

8. Publish the form template to a SharePoint form library.

In SharePoint, navigate to the form library where you published the form template and add a new form. When the form opens, all of the values from the **Fruits** named range in the Excel workbook should appear in sections of the repeating section control.

Discussion

In the solution described above, you saw how to use a named range to retrieve the values of a range of cells in an Excel workbook. In this case, the REST URL resembled the following:

```
http://servername/sitename/_vti_bin/ExcelREST.aspx/Shared%20Documents/Fruits.xls
x/model/Ranges('Fruits')?$format=atom
```

where **Fruits** is a named range in the Excel workbook. However, you could have also specified the range of cells in the REST URL as follows:

```
http://servername/sitename/_vti_bin/ExcelREST.aspx/Shared%20Documents/Fruits.xls
x/model/Ranges('Sheet1!A2%7CB6')?$format=atom
```

because the **Fruits** named range is located on **Sheet1** and spans cells **A2** through **B6**. Refer to the beginning of the *Use the Excel Services REST Web Service* section in this chapter for general information about using the Excel Services REST web service in InfoPath and for an explanation of the different parts of the REST URL.

Part of the XML returned by the Excel Services REST web service resembles the following:

```
<x:range name="Fruits">
  <x:row>
    <x:c>
       <x:fv>Apple</x:fv>
    </x:c>
    <x:c>
       <x:fv>Red</x:fv>
    </x:c>
  </x:row>
  <x:row>
    <x:c>
       <x:fv>Banana</x:fv>
    </x:c>
    <x:c>
       <x:fv>Yellow</x:fv>
    </x:c>
  </x:row>
</x:range>
```

The **row** and the **c** group nodes are repeating group nodes. As you can see, each **row** group node contains two **c** group nodes with the first **c** group node always containing the fruit name in its **fv** child field and the second **c** group node containing the fruit color in its **fv** child field.

The **row** repeating group node represents a row on a worksheet, the **c** repeating group node represents a cell in a row on a worksheet, and **fv** stands for "formatted value".

A **c** group node may sometimes also contain both a **v** field and an **fv** field. The **v** field would then contain the actual unformatted value, while the **fv** field would contain the formatted value of a cell. For example when you format a number like **2.2** in a cell as a currency, the **v** field would contain **2.2** and the **fv** field would contain **$2.20**.

In the solution described above, you dragged-and-dropped fields from the secondary data source onto the view of the form template to visualize the data. In the next recipe you will learn one of several methods you can use to extract data from the secondary data source for the REST web service to populate fields on an InfoPath form.

Note that you can also use the Excel Services SOAP web service to retrieve the values of a range of cells (see recipe *21 Get the values of a range of Excel cells in InfoPath*).

14 Populate a drop-down list in InfoPath with data from an Excel workbook

Problem

You have data on an Excel spreadsheet, which you would like to use to populate a drop-down list box on an InfoPath form. In addition, whenever a user selects an item from the drop-down list box, you want a text box to display additional information for the selected item.

Solution

You can create an Excel workbook that contains tabular data, publish this Excel workbook to a trusted file location for Excel Services, and then call the Excel Services REST web service from within an InfoPath form to perform data retrieval so that you can populate controls on the InfoPath form.

To populate a drop-down list box in InfoPath with data from an Excel workbook through the Excel Services REST web service:

1. In Excel, create an Excel workbook that contains a list of fruit names and their corresponding fruit colors as described in recipe *2 Import Excel data as XML in InfoPath – method 1*.

2. Click **File** ➤ **Save & Send** ➤ **Save to SharePoint** ➤ **Save As** and save the entire workbook (including all of its sheets) to a document library (for example the **Shared Documents** library) on the SharePoint site to which the InfoPath form will be connecting (also see recipe *7 Publish an Excel workbook to SharePoint*).

3. In InfoPath, create a new browser-compatible form template or use an existing one.

4. Select **Data** ➤ **Get External Data** ➤**From Web Service** ➤ **From REST Web Service**.

5. On the **Data Connection Wizard**, enter the URL of the Excel Services REST web service and the Excel workbook, for example:

```
http://servername/sitename/_vti_bin/ExcelREST.aspx/Shared%20Documents/Fruit
s.xlsx/model/Ranges('Fruits')?$format=atom
```

and click **Next**. Here, **servername** is the name of the SharePoint server and **sitename** is the name of the site where the **Fruits.xlsx** workbook has been stored in the **Shared Documents** document library. **Fruits** is a named range in the Excel workbook that contains the list of fruit names and fruit colors.

6. On the **Data Connection Wizard**, name the data connection **GetFruits**, leave the **Automatically retrieve data when form is opened** check box selected, and click **Finish**.

7. Add a **Drop-Down List Box** control to the view of the form template and name it **field1**.

8. Open the **Drop-Down List Box Properties** dialog box, and then on the **Data** tab, select the **Get choices from an external data source** option, select **GetFruits** from the **Data source** drop-down list box, and then click the button behind the **Entries** text box.

9. On the **Select a Field or Group** dialog box, expand all of the group nodes under the **content** group node until you see a repeating group node named **c**, which should be located under a repeating group node named **row**. Select the **c** repeating group node and then click **Filter Data**.

10. On the **Filter Data** dialog box, click **Add**.

11. On the **Specify Filter Conditions** dialog box, select **The expression** from the first drop-down list box, and then enter the following expression into the text box:

    ```
    count(preceding-sibling::ns2:c) = 0
    ```

    Note that you may have to change the namespace prefix **ns2** to suit your own scenario. What this expression does is look for the one **c** repeating group node that has no sibling nodes preceding it. So basically it looks for the first **c** repeating group node under each **row** repeating group node.

    Part of the XML returned by the REST web service resembles the following:

    ```
    <x:range name="Fruits">
      <x:row>
        <x:c>
          <x:fv>Apple</x:fv>
        </x:c>
        <x:c>
          <x:fv>Red</x:fv>
        </x:c>
      </x:row>
      <x:row>
        <x:c>
          <x:fv>Banana</x:fv>
        </x:c>
        <x:c>
          <x:fv>Yellow</x:fv>
        </x:c>
      </x:row>
    </x:range>
    ```

    The **row** and the **c** group nodes are repeating group nodes. As you can see, each **row** group node contains two **c** group nodes with the first **c** group node containing the fruit name in its **fv** child field and the second **c** group node containing the fruit color in its **fv** child field. And because you want to display only the fruit names in the drop-down list box, you must only retrieve the first **c** group node under each **row** group node from the resulting XML, which is what the filter expression you defined in this step helps you achieve.

12. On the **Specify Filter Conditions** dialog box, click **OK**.

13. On the **Filter Data** dialog box, click **OK**.

14. On the **Select a Field or Group** dialog box, click **OK**. The final expression in the **Entries** text box on the **Drop-Down List Box Properties** dialog box should resemble the following:

```
/ns1:entry/ns1:content/ns2:range/ns2:row/ns2:c[count(preceding-
sibling::ns2:c) = 0]
```

15. On the **Drop-Down List Box Properties** dialog box, ensure that the **fv** field has been selected for both the **Value** and **Display name** properties, and then click **OK**.

16. Add a **Calculated Value** control to the view of the form template. This should open the **Insert Calculated Value** dialog box.

17. On the **Insert Calculated Value** dialog box, click the formula button behind the **XPath** text box.

18. On the **Insert Formula** dialog box, construct a formula that resembles the following (*code #: D0DD9698-8314-4390-8AF4-027E9B5D7884*):

```
xdXDocument:GetDOM("GetFruits")/ns1:entry/ns1:content/ns2:range/ns2:row/ns2
:c/ns2:fv[../preceding-sibling::ns2:c/ns2:fv = xdXDocument:get-
DOM()/my:myFields/my:field1]
```

This formula retrieves the values of all of the **fv** fields in the **GetFruits** secondary data source

```
xdXDocument:GetDOM("GetFruits")/ns1:entry/ns1:content/ns2:range/ns2:row/ns2
:c/ns2:fv
```

and then filters them on the value of a preceding sibling **fv** field of the context node

```
[../preceding-sibling::ns2:c/ns2:fv
```

being equal to the value of **field1**, which is located in the Main data source (xdXDocument:get-DOM()) and which is bound to the drop-down list box (the selected item).

```
= xdXDocument:get-DOM()/my:myFields/my:field1]
```

In step 11 you saw that the first **c** group nodes under the **row** group nodes contain fruit names. The XPath filter expression in the formula above uses this information to find only those **fv** fields that are located in the second **c** group nodes under the **row** group nodes in the **GetFruits** secondary data source, since those **fv** fields contain the fruit colors, which is what you want to display in the calculated value control. Note that whenever the context node is an **fv** field located under one of the first **c** group nodes under a **row** group node, the left-hand side of the XPath filter expression will return nothing (because the first **c** group node under each **row** group node does not have any sibling nodes preceding it), so the **fv** fields under the first **c** group nodes will never be returned by the formula.

Another way of writing the formula for this step would be as follows (*code #: EF90B4C2-5374-4085-B7EB-F9EC34458233*):

67

```
xdXDocument:GetDOM("GetFruits")/ns1:entry/ns1:content/ns2:range/ns2:row/ns2
:c[2]/ns2:fv[../../ns2:c[1]/ns2:fv = xdXDocument:get-
DOM()/my:myFields/my:field1]
```

This formula should render the same result as the first formula and is perhaps easier to understand if you do not want to or cannot work with the **preceding-sibling** XPath axis.

Note that you can also use the formula in this step when setting the value of another field on the form by adding an **Action** rule on the drop-down list box.

19. On the **Insert Formula** dialog box, click **OK**.

20. On the **Insert Calculated Value** dialog box, click **OK**.

21. Publish the form template to a SharePoint form library.

In SharePoint, navigate to the form library where you published the form template and add a new form. When the form opens, verify that the drop-down list box was populated with the names of fruits from the Excel workbook. Select a fruit from the drop-down list box. The color of the selected fruit should appear in the calculated value control.

Discussion

In the solution described above, you saw how to populate a drop-down list box control with data from an Excel spreadsheet. However, the solution is not limited to drop-down list boxes, but can be used with any type of list box (normal list box, combo box, and multiple-selection list box) which you can bind to an external data source.

Refer to the discussion section of recipe *13 Get the values of a range of Excel cells in InfoPath* for an explanation of working with an Excel Services REST URL and the data returned by it.

If you want to achieve similar functionality as described in this recipe by using the Excel Services SOAP web service, see recipe *22 Populate a drop-down list in InfoPath with data from an Excel workbook*.

15 Submit Excel data to a SharePoint list via a SharePoint List form – method 1

Problem

You have data on an Excel spreadsheet, which you would like to use to populate fields on a SharePoint List form, so that the data can be submitted as an item to a SharePoint list.

Solution

You can create an Excel workbook that contains tabular data, publish this Excel workbook to a trusted file location for Excel Services, and then use the Excel Services

REST web service from within a SharePoint List form to perform data retrieval and then submit the data as a SharePoint list item to SharePoint.

To submit Excel data to a SharePoint list via a SharePoint List form:

1. In Excel, create an Excel workbook that contains a list of fruit names and their corresponding fruit colors as described in recipe *2 Import Excel data as XML in InfoPath – method 1*.

2. Click **File ➤ Save & Send ➤ Save to SharePoint ➤ Save As** and save the entire workbook (including all of its sheets) to a document library (for example the **Shared Documents** library) on the SharePoint site to which the InfoPath form will be connecting (also see recipe *7 Publish an Excel workbook to SharePoint*).

3. In SharePoint, create a new custom SharePoint list named **Fruits** that has 3 columns with the data type **Single line of text** and the names **Title**, **Field1**, and **Field2**, respectively.

4. Click **List Tools ➤ List ➤ Customize List ➤ Customize Form** to create a SharePoint List form and open it in InfoPath Designer 2010. Note that you will be able to create or edit only one item at a time with such an InfoPath form. If you want to create or edit multiple list items at a time, you may want to consider using the solution in recipe *16 Submit Excel data to a SharePoint list via a SharePoint List form – method 2* or the solution in recipe *17 Submit Excel data to a SharePoint list via a SharePoint List form – method 3*.

5. In InfoPath, select **Data ➤ Get External Data ➤From Web Service ➤ From REST Web Service**.

6. On the **Data Connection Wizard**, enter the URL of the Excel Services REST web service and the Excel workbook, for example:

   ```
   http://servername/sitename/_vti_bin/ExcelREST.aspx/Shared%20Documents/Fruit
   s.xlsx/model/Ranges('Fruits')?$format=atom
   ```

   and click **Next**. Here, **servername** is the name of the SharePoint server and **sitename** is the name of the site where the **Fruits.xlsx** workbook has been stored in the **Shared Documents** document library. **Fruits** is a named range in the Excel workbook that contains the list of fruit names and fruit colors.

7. On the **Data Connection Wizard**, name the data connection **GetFruits**, leave the **Automatically retrieve data when form is opened** check box selected, and click **Finish**.

8. Right-click the text box that was added to the form template for **Field1**, and select **Change Control ➤ Drop-Down List Box** from the context menu that appears.

9. Open the **Drop-Down List Box Properties** dialog box, and then on the **Data** tab, select the **Get choices from an external data source** option, select **GetFruits** from the **Data source** drop-down list box, and then click the button behind the **Entries** text box.

10. On the **Select a Field or Group** dialog box, expand all of the group nodes under the **content** group node until you see a repeating group node named **c**, which should be located under a repeating group node named **row**. Select the **c** repeating group node and then click **Filter Data**.

11. On the **Filter Data** dialog box, click **Add**.

12. On the **Specify Filter Conditions** dialog box, select **The expression** from the first drop-down list box, and then enter the following expression into the text box:

```
count(preceding-sibling::ns2:c) = 0
```

Note that you may have to change the namespace prefix **ns2** to suit your own scenario. What this expression does is look for the one **c** repeating group node that has no sibling nodes preceding it. So basically it looks for the first **c** repeating group node under each **row** repeating group node. Refer to the discussion section of recipe *13 Get the values of a range of Excel cells in InfoPath* for an explanation of the structure of the XML that is returned by the Excel Services REST web service.

13. On the **Specify Filter Conditions** dialog box, click **OK**.

14. On the **Filter Data** dialog box, click **OK**.

15. On the **Select a Field or Group** dialog box, click **OK**. The final expression in the **Entries** text box on the **Drop-Down List Box Properties** dialog box should resemble the following:

```
/ns3:entry/ns3:content/ns2:range/ns2:row/ns2:c[count(preceding-
sibling::ns2:c) = 0]
```

16. On the **Drop-Down List Box Properties** dialog box, ensure that the **fv** field has been selected for both the **Value** and **Display name** properties, and then click **OK**.

17. Add an **Action** rule to **Field1** (the drop-down list box) with an action that says:

```
Set a field's value: Field2 = c[2]/fv[c[1]/fv = Field1]
```

where **Field1** and **Field2** are located in the Main data source and the rest of the fields are all located in the secondary data source for the REST web service. You can construct this formula by entering the following in the **Formula** text box on the **Insert Formula** dialog box (*code #: 13ADF64A-8621-455A-9F46-F6430AA3CAAC*):

```
xdXDocument:GetDOM("GetFruits")/ns3:entry/ns3:content/ns2:range/ns2:row/ns2
:c[2]/ns2:fv[../../ns2:c[1]/ns2:fv = xdXDocument:get-
DOM()/dfs:myFields/dfs:dataFields/my:SharePointListItem_RW/my:Field1]
```

This formula retrieves the values of all of the **fv** fields under the second **c** group node under each **row** group node in the **GetFruits** secondary data source and then filters them on the value of the **fv** field under the first **c** group node under a **row** group node being equal to the value of **Field1** (which is equivalent to the selected value in the drop-down list box) in the Main data source.

18. Click **File ➤ Info ➤ Quick Publish** to publish the form template to the SharePoint list.

In SharePoint, navigate to the SharePoint list for which you published the form template and add a new item. When the form opens, verify that the drop-down list box was populated with the names of fruits from the Excel workbook. Select a fruit from the drop-down list box. The color of the selected fruit should appear in **Field2** on the form. Fill out all of the other required fields on the form and then click **Save**. The item should appear in the SharePoint list with the data from Excel.

Discussion

In the solution described above, you saw how to access and store data from an Excel workbook in a SharePoint list item by making use of the Excel Services REST web service and a SharePoint List form.

While the Excel Services REST web service allows you to retrieve data and also submit data to perform Excel calculations, it does not allow you to permanently store data in Excel workbooks. For the latter, you must make use of the Excel Services SOAP web service. You can use the Excel Services SOAP web service to retrieve data from (see recipe *18 Get the value of an Excel cell in InfoPath*) or submit data to (see recipe *19 Set the value of an Excel cell in InfoPath*) an Excel workbook from within a SharePoint List form (see recipe *25 Submit SharePoint List form values to a new Excel workbook* for an example).

16 Submit Excel data to a SharePoint list via a SharePoint List form – method 2

Problem

You have data on an Excel spreadsheet, which you would like to use to populate fields on a SharePoint List form, so that you can submit multiple items at once to a SharePoint list.

Solution

You can create an Excel workbook that contains tabular data, publish this Excel workbook to a trusted file location for Excel Services, and then call the Excel Services REST web service from within a SharePoint List form to perform data retrieval and then submit the data as SharePoint list items to SharePoint.

To submit Excel data to a SharePoint list via a SharePoint List form:

1. In Excel, create an Excel workbook that contains a list of fruit names and their corresponding fruit colors as described in recipe *2 Import Excel data as XML in InfoPath – method 1*.

2. Click **File ➤ Save & Send ➤ Save to SharePoint ➤ Save As** and save the entire workbook (including all of its sheets) to a document library (for example the **Shared**

Documents library) on the SharePoint site to which the InfoPath form will be connecting (also see recipe *7 Publish an Excel workbook to SharePoint*).

3. In SharePoint, create a new custom SharePoint list named **Fruits** that has 3 columns with the data type **Single line of text** and the names **Title**, **Field1**, and **Field2**, respectively.

4. In InfoPath, click **File ➤ New ➤ SharePoint List**, and then click **Design Form**.

5. On the **Data Connection Wizard**, enter the URL of the SharePoint site where the **Fruits** SharePoint list is located, and then click **Next**.

6. On the **Data Connection Wizard**, select the **Customize an existing SharePoint list** option, select the **Fruits** SharePoint list from the list of SharePoint lists, and then click **Next**.

7. On the **Data Connection Wizard**, select the **Manage multiple list items with this form** check box, and then click **Finish**.

8. Select and then delete the repeating section control that has been automatically added to the view of the form template.

9. On the **Fields** task pane, click **Show advanced view** if the basic view is currently being displayed.

10. On the **Fields** task pane, expand the **dataFields** group node, right-click the **my:SharePointListItem_RW** repeating group node, drag it to the view of the form template, drop it, and select **Repeating Table** from the context menu when you drop it.

11. Delete all of the columns from the repeating table except for the **Title**, **Field1**, and **Field2** columns.

12. Select **Data ➤ Get External Data ➤From Web Service ➤ From REST Web Service**.

13. On the **Data Connection Wizard**, enter the URL of the Excel Services REST web service and the Excel workbook, for example:

```
http://servername/sitename/_vti_bin/ExcelREST.aspx/Shared%20Documents/Fruit
s.xlsx/model/Ranges('Fruits')?$format=atom
```

and click **Next**. Here, **servername** is the name of the SharePoint server and **sitename** is the name of the site where the **Fruits.xlsx** workbook has been stored in the **Shared Documents** document library. **Fruits** is a named range in the Excel workbook that contains the list of fruit names and fruit colors.

14. On the **Data Connection Wizard**, name the data connection **GetFruits**, leave the **Automatically retrieve data when form is opened** check box selected, and click **Finish**.

15. In this solution, the fields in the repeating table are going to automatically pull in data from the secondary data source for the REST web service based on position. For example, the first row of the repeating table should automatically contain the data from the first row in the secondary data source and the second row of the repeating table should automatically contain the data from the second row in the secondary data source, etc. whenever a user clicks **Insert item** to add a row to the repeating table. For this you need to configure the default values of the fields in the repeating table. So select **Field1**, and then click **Control Tools ➤ Properties ➤ Properties ➤ Default Value**.

16. On the **Field or Group Properties** dialog box, click the formula button behind the **Value** field under the **Default Value** section.

17. On the **Insert Formula** dialog box, enter a formula similar to the following:

```
xdXDocument:GetDOM("GetFruits")/ns3:entry/ns3:content/ns2:range/ns2:row[cou
nt(current()/../preceding-sibling::*) + 1]/ns2:c[1]/ns2:fv
```

This formula retrieves the value of the **fv** field (`ns2:fv`) that is located under the first **c** group node (`ns2:c[1]`) under the **row** group node that is located on the same position as the current row in the repeating table. The **current()** function is used to retrieve the current context node, which in this case is **Field1**. Then the double-dot notation (**..**) is used to navigate to the **my:SharePointListItem_RW** group node pertaining to the context node. Then all of the **my:SharePointListItem_RW** group nodes preceding the current group node are retrieved using the **preceding-sibling** XPath axis (`preceding-sibling::*`). And finally, the **count()** function is used to count how many group nodes precede the current group node and a **1** is added to the final amount to get the correct index number (`count(current()/../preceding-sibling::*) + 1`). The final index number is then used in a filter on the **row** group node in the secondary data source to find the correct row. Refer to the discussion section of recipe *13 Get the values of a range of Excel cells in InfoPath* for an explanation of the structure of the XML that is returned from making the call to the Excel Services REST web service.

18. On the **Insert Formula** dialog box, click **OK**.

19. On the **Field or Group Properties** dialog box, ensure that the **Refresh value when formula is recalculated** check box is selected, and then click **OK**.

20. Repeat steps 15 through 19 for **Field2**, but then use a formula similar to the following to set the **Default Value** of the field:

```
xdXDocument:GetDOM("GetFruits")/ns3:entry/ns3:content/ns2:range/ns2:row[cou
nt(current()/../preceding-sibling::*) + 1]/ns2:c[2]/ns2:fv
```

This formula is similar to the formula for **Field1** with the difference that the value of **fv** is retrieved from under the second **c** group node (`ns2:c[2]`) instead of the first **c** group node.

21. Click **File ➤ Info ➤ Quick Publish** to publish the form template to the SharePoint list.

In SharePoint, navigate to the SharePoint list for which you published the form template and add a new item. When the form opens, the values from the first row in the data source for the Excel workbook should appear in **Field1** and **Field2** in the first row of the repeating table. Click **Insert item** to add a new row to the repeating table. The values from the second row in the data source for the Excel workbook should appear in **Field1** and **Field2** in the second row of the repeating table. Continue inserting items, fill out the **Title** fields in all of the rows, and then click **Save**. The items you added to the repeating table should appear in the SharePoint list and should contain the data from the Excel workbook.

Discussion

In the solution described above, you saw how to access and store data from an Excel workbook in multiple SharePoint list items by making use of the Excel Services REST web service and a SharePoint List form.

Note that you can also prepopulate the repeating table with a couple of empty rows via the **Edit Default Values** dialog box, which you can open by clicking **Data ➤ SharePoint Form Data ➤ Default Values**. This way, when the form opens, it should open with a certain amount of repeating table rows already populated with data from the secondary data source for the Excel Services REST web service.

The solution described above does not offer much flexibility in that rows are copied automatically from the data source for the Excel Services REST web service and rows are mapped one-on-one with the data source. If you want to offer users the flexibility to select rows from the data source, refer to recipe *17 Submit Excel data to a SharePoint list via a SharePoint List form – method 3*.

17   Submit Excel data to a SharePoint list via a SharePoint List form – method 3

Problem

You have data on an Excel spreadsheet, which you would like to use to populate fields on a SharePoint List form, so that you can submit multiple items at once to a SharePoint list.

Solution

You can create an Excel workbook that contains tabular data, publish this Excel workbook to a trusted file location for Excel Services, and then call the Excel Services REST web service from within the SharePoint List form to perform data retrieval and then submit the data as SharePoint list items to SharePoint.

To submit Excel data to a SharePoint list via a SharePoint List form:

1. Follow steps 1 through 14 of recipe *16 Submit Excel data to a SharePoint list via a SharePoint List form – method 2.*

2. In Notepad, create an XML file that has the following contents:

    ```
    <FruitsExcelData>
      <Name/>
      <Color/>
    </FruitsExcelData>
    ```

    and name the XML file **FruitsExcelData.xml** or download the **FruitsExcelData.xml** file from www.bizsupportonline.com. You will use the fields in this XML file as helper fields to be able to place a drop-down list box control on the form without having to add fields to the Main data source (and thus also the SharePoint list) just to be able to select items from the data source for the Excel workbook.

3. In InfoPath, select **Data ➤ Get External Data ➤ From Other Sources ➤ From XML File** and follow the instructions to add an XML data connection for the **FruitsExcelData.xml** file. Accept the data connection name of **FruitsExcelData** and leave the **Automatically retrieve data when form is opened** check box selected.

4. On the **Fields** task pane, select **FruitsExcelData (Secondary)** from the **Fields** drop-down list box, right-click the **Name** field, drag it to the view of the form template, drop it, and select **Drop-Down List Box** from the context menu when you drop it.

5. Open the **Drop-Down List Box Properties** dialog box, and then on the **Data** tab, select the **Get choices from an external data source** option, select **GetFruits** from the **Data source** drop-down list box, and then click the button behind the **Entries** text box.

6. On the **Select a Field or Group** dialog box, expand all of the group nodes under the **content** group node until you see a repeating group node named **c**, which should be located under a repeating group node named **row**. Select the **c** repeating group node and then click **Filter Data**.

7. On the **Filter Data** dialog box, click **Add**.

8. On the **Specify Filter Conditions** dialog box, select **The expression** from the first drop-down list box, and then enter the following expression into the text box:

    ```
    count(preceding-sibling::ns2:c) = 0
    ```

    Note that you may have to change the namespace prefix **ns2** to suit your own scenario. This expression looks for the one **c** repeating group node that has no sibling nodes preceding it. So basically it looks for the first **c** repeating group node under each **row** repeating group node. Refer to the discussion section of recipe *13*

Get the values of a range of Excel cells in InfoPath for an explanation of the structure of the XML that is returned by the Excel Services REST web service.

9. On the **Specify Filter Conditions** dialog box, click **OK**.

10. On the **Filter Data** dialog box, click **OK**.

11. On the **Select a Field or Group** dialog box, click **OK**. The final expression in the **Entries** text box on the **Drop-Down List Box Properties** dialog box should resemble the following:

```
/ns3:entry/ns3:content/ns2:range/ns2:row/ns2:c[count(preceding-
sibling::ns2:c) = 0]
```

12. On the **Drop-Down List Box Properties** dialog box, ensure that the **fv** field has been selected for both the **Value** and **Display name** properties, and then click **OK**.

13. In this solution, the user is going to select an item from the drop-down list box, the second field in the **FruitsExcelData** secondary data source is then going to be populated behind the scenes with the color of the selected fruit in the drop-down list box, and then when the user clicks **Insert item** to add a row to the repeating table the values for **Field1** and **Field2** in the row of the repeating table will be copied from the **Name** and **Color** fields in the **FruitsExcelData** secondary data source (which is equivalent to the selected item in the drop-down list box). But first you need to set the value of the **Color** field in the **FruitsExcelData** secondary data source, so add an **Action** rule to the drop-down list box with an action that says:

```
Set a field's value: Color = c[2]/fv[c[1]/fv = Name]
```

where **Color** and **Name** are fields that are located in the **FruitsExcelData** secondary data source and the rest of fields are all located in the secondary data source for the Excel Services REST web service. You can construct this formula by entering the following formula in the text box on the **Insert Formula** dialog box (*code #: 14BE0052-B0F9-4B43-9818-6653161E0508*):

```
xdXDocument:GetDOM("GetFruits")/ns3:entry/ns3:content/ns2:range/ns2:row/ns2
:c[2]/ns2:fv[../../ns2:c[1]/ns2:fv =
xdXDocument:GetDOM("FruitsExcelData")/FruitsExcelData/Name]
```

This formula retrieves the values of all of the **fv** fields under the second **c** group node (`ns2:c[2]`) under each **row** group node in the **GetFruits** secondary data source and then filters them on the value of the **fv** field under the first **c** group node under a **row** group node (`../../ns2:c[1]/ns2:fv`) being equal to the value of the **Name** field, which is located in the **FruitsExcelData** secondary data source and is equivalent to the selected value in the drop-down list box.

14. Select **Field1** in the repeating table, click **Control Tools ➤ Properties ➤ Properties ➤ Default Value**, and then set the **Default Value** of **Field1** to be equal to the value of the **Name** field in the **FruitsExcelData** secondary data source. Ensure that the **Refresh value when formula is recalculated** check box is

deselected on the **Field or Group Properties** dialog box, and then click **OK**. Deselecting the check box ensures that the Excel data of the selected item in the drop-down list box is only added to the row that is currently being added and that the values in all other rows of the repeating table are not overwritten.

15. Repeat the previous step for **Field2** in the repeating table, but then set its **Default Value** to be equal to the value of the **Color** field in the **FruitsExcelData** secondary data source.

16. Click **Data ➤ SharePoint Form Data ➤ Default Values**.

17. On the **Edit Default Values** dialog box, expand the **dataFields** node, clear the check box in front of the **my:SharePointListItem_RW** node, and then click **OK**. This will ensure that the repeating table does not start up with a row containing empty fields.

18. Click **File ➤ Info ➤ Quick Publish** to publish the form template to the SharePoint list.

In SharePoint, navigate to the SharePoint list for which you published the form template and add a new item. When the form opens, verify that the drop-down list box contains values from the Excel workbook. Select an item from the drop-down list box and then click **Insert item** to add a row to the repeating table. The values from the selected item in the drop-down list box (so from a row in the data source for the Excel workbook) should appear in **Field1** and **Field2** of the row of the repeating table. Continue adding rows to the repeating table this way, fill out the **Title** fields in all of the rows, and then click **Save**. The items you added to the repeating table should appear in the SharePoint list and should contain the data from the Excel workbook.

Discussion

In the solution described above, you saw how to access and store data from an Excel workbook in multiple SharePoint list items by making use of the Excel Services REST web service and a SharePoint List form.

In addition, you saw how to use a secondary data source for an XML file to be able to bind a drop-down list box to a field without having to add extra fields to the Main data source of the form and thus also to the SharePoint list.

Use the Excel Services SOAP Web Service

Excel Services not only allows InfoPath forms to interact with Excel workbooks through an Excel Web Access web part, but also through web services (SOAP and REST) and User-Defined Functions (UDFs).

You can access the Excel Services SOAP web service and get a list of its operations by typing in an URL similar to the following into the browser:

```
http://servername/sitename/_vti_bin/ExcelService.asmx
```

where **servername** is the name of the SharePoint server where a site named **sitename** is located where an Excel workbook you want to access is located. You can also access the web service from the top-level site in a site collection as follows:

```
http://servername/_vti_bin/ExcelService.asmx
```

You can use either **Receive** or **Submit** web service data connections in InfoPath to call operations of the Excel Services SOAP web service to retrieve or submit data to Excel Services. If you click on any of the operations on the Excel Services ASMX page, you will see that the SOAP response contains a status element that has the following structure:

```
<status>
  <Status>
    <Name></Name>
    <Severity></Severity>
    <Message></Message>
  </Status>
  <Status>
    <Name></Name>
    <Severity></Severity>
    <Message></Message>
  </Status>
</status>
```

As a general rule-of-thumb you can assume that if the SOAP response contains nothing but a **status** element, you should create a **Submit** data connection in InfoPath to call the web service operation. And if the SOAP response contains an extra element that returns a result, you should create a **Receive** data connection in InfoPath to call the web service operation.

For example, the SOAP response of the **SetCellA1** operation resembles the following:

```
<soap:Envelope>
  <soap:Body>
    <SetCellA1Response>
      <status>
      ...
      </status>
    </SetCellA1Response>
  </soap:Body>
</soap:Envelope>
```

Because it only contains a **status** element, you should create a **Submit** data connection in InfoPath to call it. However, as mentioned previously, you can also use a **Receive** data connection in InfoPath to call such an operation to submit data to Excel Services (refer to the three solutions in recipe *19 Set the value of an Excel cell in InfoPath*).

While you can assume that all web service operations that start with the word **Set** can be called for data submission, not all data submission web service operations start with the word **Set**. For example, **CloseWorkbook**, **SaveWorkbook**, and **SaveWorkbookCopy** do not start with the word **Set**, but are still used for sending instructions to Excel Services and not for retrieving data. Likewise, not all web service operations with which you can retrieve data start with the word **Get**. For example, **OpenWorkbook** does not start with the word **Get**, but because it returns a result in its SOAP response, you can see it as a web service operation with which you can retrieve data.

```
<soap:Envelope>
  <soap:Body>
    <OpenWorkbookResponse>
      <OpenWorkbookResult></OpenWorkbookResult>
      <status>
      ...
      </status>
    </OpenWorkbookResponse>
  </soap:Body>
</soap:Envelope>
```

Almost all of the Excel Services SOAP web service operations require you to pass a session ID to them when calling them. You can retrieve a session ID by calling either the **OpenWorkbook** or **OpenWorkbookForEditing** web service operation. **OpenWorkbook** returns a session ID you can use to read data from an Excel workbook, while **OpenWorkbookForEditing** returns a session ID you can use to edit an Excel workbook. Once you have performed the web service operations you want to perform, you can close an Excel workbook by passing the same session ID you used to open the workbook to the **CloseWorkbook** web service operation.

Receive data connections add secondary data sources to an InfoPath form, while **Submit** data connections do not. These secondary data sources consist of query fields and data fields. You can use query fields to set the values of parameters of a web service operation before querying the data source. Data fields contain the data that is returned by the web service operation after you have executed a query on the data connection.

Figure 40. Query fields and data fields in the secondary data source for a web service operation.

While you could programmatically access the Excel Services web services, in this book you will primarily use rules and formulas (so no compiled code) to get or set data in Excel workbooks through Excel Services.

18 Get the value of an Excel cell in InfoPath

Problem

You have an Excel workbook from which you want to retrieve the value of a particular cell so that you can display this value on an InfoPath form.

Solution

You can create an Excel workbook that contains data, publish this Excel workbook to a trusted file location for Excel Services in SharePoint, and then call Excel Services SOAP web service operations from within an InfoPath form to perform data retrieval.

To get the value of an Excel cell in InfoPath:

1. Follow steps 1 and 2 of recipe *10 Get the value of an Excel cell in InfoPath*.

2. In InfoPath, create a new browser-compatible form template or use an existing one.

3. Select **Data ➤ Get External Data ➤ From Web Service ➤ From SOAP Web Service**.

Figure 41. The From SOAP Web Service command on the Data tab in InfoPath 2010.

4. On the **Data Connection Wizard**, enter the URL of the Excel Services SOAP web service on the site where the Excel workbook is located, for example:

```
http://servername/sitename/_vti_bin/ExcelService.asmx
```

where **servername** is the name of the SharePoint server, **sitename** is the name of the site where the Excel workbook is located, and **ExcelService.asmx** is the Excel Services SOAP web service ASMX page. Click **Next**.

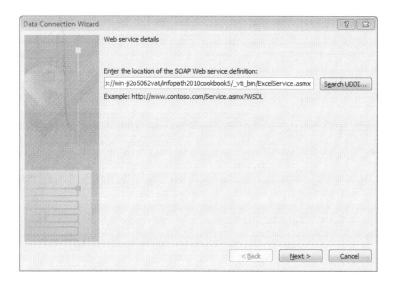

Figure 42. Entering the URL of the web service on the Data Connection Wizard in InfoPath.

5. On the **Data Connection Wizard**, select **OpenWorkbook** from the list of operations, and click **Next**.

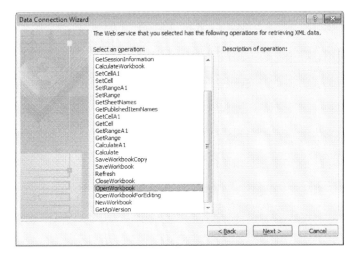

Figure 43. Selecting a web service operation in InfoPath 2010.

6.   On the **Data Connection Wizard**, leave **workbookPath** selected, and click **Set Value**.

7.   On the **Parameter Details** dialog box, enter the full URL of the Excel workbook location, for example:

```
http://servername/sitename/libraryname/LeaveBalances.xlsx
```

where **servername** is the name of the SharePoint server, **sitename** is the name of the site, and **libraryname** is the name of the document library and Excel Services trusted file location where the **LeaveBalances.xlsx** Excel workbook is located. Click **OK** when you are done.

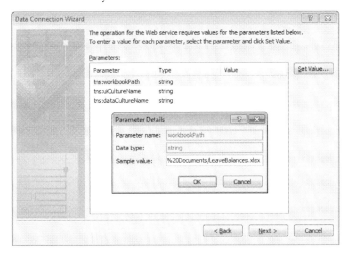

Figure 44. Entering the path of the Excel workbook to open.

8. On the **Data Connection Wizard**, leave the other two parameters as is, and click **Next**.

9. On the **Data Connection Wizard**, leave the **Store a copy of the data in the form template** check box deselected, and click **Next**.

10. On the **Data Connection Wizard**, accept the default name for the data connection (**OpenWorkbook**), deselect the **Automatically retrieve data when form is opened** check box, and click **Finish**. You will use this data connection to open the Excel workbook and get a session ID that you can use for all subsequent calls you make to Excel Services.

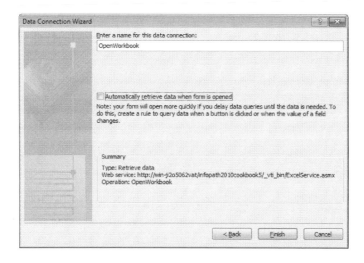

Figure 45. The final screen of the Data Connection Wizard in InfoPath 2010.

11. Select **Data ➤ Get External Data ➤ From Web Service ➤ From SOAP Web Service**.

12. On the **Data Connection Wizard**, enter the URL of the Excel Services SOAP web service on the site where the Excel workbook is located, for example:

```
http://servername/sitename/_vti_bin/ExcelService.asmx
```

where **servername** is the name of the SharePoint server, **sitename** is the name of the site where the Excel workbook is located, and **ExcelService.asmx** is the Excel Services SOAP web service ASMX page. Click **Next**.

13. On the **Data Connection Wizard**, select **GetCellA1** from the list of operations, and click **Next**.

14. On the **Data Connection Wizard**, do not set any values for the parameters (you will be using a rule later to set their values), and click **Next**.

15. On the **Data Connection Wizard**, leave the **Store a copy of the data in the form template** check box deselected, and click **Next**.

16. On the **Data Connection Wizard**, accept the default name for the data connection (**GetCellA1**), deselect the **Automatically retrieve data when form is opened** check box, and click **Finish**. You will use this data connection to retrieve the amount of leave for a particular employee from the Excel workbook.

17. Select **Data ➤ Get External Data ➤ From Web Service ➤ From SOAP Web Service**.

18. On the **Data Connection Wizard**, enter the URL of the Excel Services SOAP web service on the site where the Excel workbook is located, for example:

```
http://servername/sitename/_vti_bin/ExcelService.asmx
```

where **servername** is the name of the SharePoint server, **sitename** is the name of the site where the Excel workbook is located, and **ExcelService.asmx** is the Excel Services SOAP web service ASMX page. Click **Next**.

19. On the **Data Connection Wizard**, select **CloseWorkbook** from the list of operations, and click **Next**.

20. On the **Data Connection Wizard**, do not set the value of the **sessionId** parameter (you will be using a rule later to set its value), and click **Next**.

21. On the **Data Connection Wizard**, leave the **Store a copy of the data in the form template** check box deselected, and click **Next**.

22. On the **Data Connection Wizard**, accept the default name for the data connection (**CloseWorkbook**), deselect the **Automatically retrieve data when form is opened** check box, and click **Finish**. You will use this data connection to close the Excel workbook and the Excel Services session.

23. On the **Fields** task pane, select **GetCellA1 (Secondary)** from the **Fields** drop-down list box, expand the **dataFields** group node, expand the **GetCellA1Response** group node, and then drag-and-drop the **GetCellA1Result** field onto the view of the form template. The field should automatically get bound to a text box control.

Figure 46. The secondary data source for the GetCellA1 web service operation in InfoPath 2010.

24. Add a **Button** control to the view of the form template and label it **Get Leave Balance**.

25. Add an **Action** rule to the **Get Leave Balance** button control with the following 8 actions:

```
Query using a data connection: OpenWorkbook
```

This action calls the **OpenWorkbook** web service operation to retrieve a session ID.

```
Set a field's value: sessionId = OpenWorkbookResult
```

where **sessionId** is located under the **GetCellA1** group node under the **queryFields** group node in the **GetCellA1** secondary data source and **OpenWorkbookResult** is located under the **OpenWorkbookResponse** group node under the **dataFields** group node in the **OpenWorkbook** secondary data source.

```
Set a field's value: sheetName = "Sheet1"
```

where **sheetName** is located under the **GetCellA1** group node under the **queryFields** group node in the **GetCellA1** secondary data source and **Sheet1** is a static piece of text representing the name of the worksheet in the Excel workbook where the leave balances are located.

```
Set a field's value: rangeName = "B1"
```

where **rangeName** is located under the **GetCellA1** group node under the **queryFields** group node in the **GetCellA1** secondary data source and **B1** is a static piece of text representing cell **B1** on **Sheet1** in the Excel workbook that contains the leave balances.

```
Set a field's value: formatted = "false"
```

where **formatted** is located under the **GetCellA1** group node under the **queryFields** group node in the **GetCellA1** secondary data source and **false** is a static piece of text.

```
Query using a data connection: GetCellA1
```

This action calls the **GetCellA1** web service operation to retrieve the value of cell **B1**.

```
Set a field's value: sessionId = OpenWorkbookResult
```

where **sessionId** is located under the **CloseWorkbook** group node under the **queryFields** group node in the **CloseWorkbook** secondary data source and **OpenWorkbookResult** is located under the **OpenWorkbookResponse** group node under the **dataFields** group node in the **OpenWorkbook** secondary data source.

```
Query using a data connection: CloseWorkbook
```

This action closes the workbook and the Excel Services session.

26. Preview the form.

When the form opens, click the **Get Leave Balance** button. **25** should appear in the text box.

Discussion

In the solution described above, you saw how to use Excel Services SOAP web service operations to retrieve the value of a cell in an Excel workbook that is stored in a SharePoint document library. The sequence of Excel Services SOAP web service calls to retrieve the value of a cell in an Excel workbook was as follows:

1. Call **OpenWorkbook** to get an Excel Services session ID, which allowed you to read data from the Excel workbook and change but not permanently store data in the Excel workbook.

2. Call **GetCellA1** to retrieve the value of a cell in the Excel workbook.

3. Call **CloseWorkbook** to close the workbook and end the Excel Services session.

Before calling either the **GetCellA1** or **CloseWorkbook** operation, you had to set values of parameters to query them. In the case of **GetCellA1**, you had to set the value of the following four parameters:

1. sessionId

2. sheetName

3. rangeName

4. formatted

While you could have set the values of **sheetName**, **rangeName**, and **formatted** through the **Data Connection Wizard** when you added the data connection for the web service operation, you used actions in a rule in step 25 of the solution described above to set their values. Actions in a rule allow you to dynamically (when the form is being filled out) set the values of query parameters of a web service operation, while the **Data Connection Wizard** only allows you to set parameter values statically (when designing the form template). And because the session ID becomes available after you call the **OpenWorkbook** operation, you cannot use the **Data Connection Wizard** to set the **sessionId** parameter of the **GetCellA1** operation, but instead must use an action in a rule. Note that all query parameters are located under the **queryFields** group node of the secondary data source for the web service operation.

In the case of **CloseWorkbook**, you only had to set the value of a **sessionId** parameter, which you can retrieve from the **dataFields** group node in the secondary data source for the **OpenWorkbook** web service operation. Note that because **CloseWorkbook** returns only a status, it can be seen as a submit operation for sending data to Excel Services, so you could have also created a **Submit** data connection to call it instead of a **Receive** data connection (also see the second solution of recipe *19 Set the value of an Excel cell in InfoPath*).

The Excel Services SOAP web service provides two web service operations you can use to retrieve the value of a cell:

1. GetCellA1
2. GetCell

The difference between **GetCellA1** and **GetCell** is that you must specify the name of a cell when using the **GetCellA1** operation, while you must specify a row number and a column number of a particular cell when using the **GetCell** operation.

GetCellA1 works similar to the Excel Services REST web service (see recipe *10 Get the value of an Excel cell in InfoPath*) in that you can set its **rangeName** parameter to have a particular value, for example **B1** as in the solution described above. In terms of a row number and a column number, cell **B1** would correspond to row number **0** and column number **1** when you use the **GetCell** operation. Note that row and column numbers always start at **0** for Excel Service SOAP web service operations with cell **A1** having row number **0** and column number **0**.

The **GetCell** operation is good to use if you do not want to use a specific name of a cell, but rather want to dynamically change the row and column numbers of a cell at runtime (when a form is being filled out) from within InfoPath (see for example recipe *19 Set the value of an Excel cell in InfoPath* or recipe *35 Sequentially navigate through rows of an Excel table – method 1*).

Instead of the solution described in this recipe, you could have also used the Excel Services REST web service, which is easier and simpler to use and reference from within InfoPath, to retrieve the value of a cell (see recipe *10 Get the value of an Excel cell in InfoPath*). You generally require only one action rule to call it, while the SOAP web service almost always requires more than two actions to call it via a rule.

19   Set the value of an Excel cell in InfoPath

You can use browser-compatible and non-browser-compatible form templates to call Excel Services SOAP web service operations. If you are not going to publish a form template to SharePoint for filling out in the browser, the method you use for calling Excel Services SOAP web service operations does not really matter. However, if you are going to publish a form template to SharePoint for filling out in the browser, you must choose an appropriate method for calling Excel Services web service operations to prevent errors from taking place.

In this recipe, you will learn three methods you can use to call web service operations with which you can submit data to Excel Services. The following table shows which methods can be used with which types of form templates in InfoPath.

Form Template Type	Method 1	Method 2	Method 3
SharePoint List	✓		
SharePoint Form Library	✓	✓	
Blank Form	✓	✓	
InfoPath Filler	✓	✓	
Blank Form (InfoPath Filler)	✓	✓	
Web Service	✓	✓	✓

Table 1. InfoPath form template types and three ways to call the Excel Services web service.

Method 1: Use a form template with Receive data connections

Problem

You have an Excel workbook in which you want to set the value of a cell so that a calculation can be performed and the result returned to an InfoPath form for display.

Solution

You can create an Excel workbook that contains data and a formula, publish this Excel workbook to a trusted file location for Excel Services in SharePoint, and then call Excel Services SOAP web service operations from within the InfoPath form to perform data submission and retrieval.

To set the value of a cell in an Excel workbook from within an InfoPath form:

1. Use the same Excel workbook as described in step 1 of recipe *11 Set the value of an Excel cell in InfoPath*.

2. In InfoPath, create a new browser-compatible (**Blank**, **SharePoint Form Library**, or **SharePoint List**) form template or use an existing one.

3. Select **Data ➤ Get External Data ➤ From Web Service ➤ From SOAP Web Service** to add a **Receive** data connection for the **OpenWorkbook** operation of the Excel Services web service (also see recipe *18 Get the value of an Excel cell in InfoPath* for detailed instructions on how to connect to the Excel Services SOAP web service)

and configure its parameters as follows:

Parameter	Value
tns:workbookPath	`http://servername/sitename/libraryname/LeaveBalances.xlsx` where **servername** is the name of the SharePoint server, **sitename** is the name of the site, and **libraryname** is the name of the document library and Excel Services trusted file location where the **LeaveBalances.xlsx** Excel workbook is located.
tns:uiCultureName	
tns:dataCultureName	

Leave the **Store a copy of the data in the form template** check box deselected, name the data connection **OpenWorkbook**, and deselect the **Automatically retrieve data when form is opened** check box. You will use this data connection to open the Excel workbook and get a session ID that you can use for all subsequent calls you make to Excel Services.

4. Select **Data ➤ Get External Data ➤ From Web Service ➤ From SOAP Web Service** to add a **Receive** data connection for the **SetCellA1** operation of the Excel Services web service and configure its parameters as follows:

Parameter	Value
tns:sessionId	
tns:sheetName	Calculations where **Calculations** is the name of the worksheet in the **LeaveBalances.xlsx** Excel workbook that has a **VLOOKUP** formula defined on it.
tns:rangeName	A1 where **A1** is the name of the cell that contains the **VLOOKUP** formula on the **Calculations** worksheet in the **LeaveBalances.xlsx** Excel workbook.
tns:cellValue	

Leave the **Store a copy of the data in the form template** check box deselected, name the data connection **SetCellA1**, and deselect the **Automatically retrieve data when form is opened** check box. You will use this data connection to set the value of cell **A1** on the **Calculations** worksheet in the Excel workbook. At this point, the **sessionId** and **cellValue** parameters are still blank; you will use a rule later to set their values before making the web service call.

5. Select **Data ➤ Get External Data ➤ From Web Service ➤ From SOAP Web Service** to add a **Receive** data connection for the **GetCell** operation of the Excel Services web service and configure its parameters as follows:

Parameter	Value
tns:sessionId	
tns:sheetName	Calculations
	where **Calculations** is the name of the worksheet in the **LeaveBalances.xlsx** Excel workbook that has a **VLOOKUP** formula defined on it.
tns:row	1
	Because the result of the calculation is stored in cell **A2** of the **Calculations** worksheet in the Excel workbook, you must use number **1** to access the row for cell **A2**.
tns:column	0
	Because the result of the calculation is stored in cell **A2** of the **Calculations** worksheet in the Excel workbook, you must use number **0** to access the column for cell **A2**.
tns:formatted	false

Leave the **Store a copy of the data in the form template** check box deselected, name the data connection **GetCell**, and deselect the **Automatically retrieve data when form is opened** check box. You will use this data connection to get the result of the **VLOOKUP** calculation in the Excel workbook. Note that at this stage the **sessionId** parameter is still blank, since you will set its value later through a rule.

6. Select **Data ➤ Get External Data ➤ From Web Service ➤ From SOAP Web Service** to add a **Receive** data connection for the **CloseWorkbook** operation of the

Excel Services web service. Leave the **sessionId** parameter as is, leave the **Store a copy of the data in the form template** check box deselected, name the data connection **CloseWorkbook**, and deselect the **Automatically retrieve data when form is opened** check box. You will use this data connection to close the workbook and the Excel Services session. Note that at this stage the **sessionId** parameter is still blank, since you will set its value later through a rule.

7. On the **Fields** task pane, select **SetCellA1 (Secondary)** from the **Fields** drop-down list box, expand the **queryFields** group node, expand the **SetCellA1** group node, and then drag-and-drop the **cellValue** field onto the view of the form template. It should automatically get bound to a text box control.

8. Add a **Button** control to the view of the form template and label it **Get Leave Balance**.

9. Add an **Action** rule to the **Get Leave Balance** button control with the following 7 actions:

```
Query using a data connection: OpenWorkbook
```

This action calls the **OpenWorkbook** web service operation to retrieve a session ID.

```
Set a field's value: sessionId = OpenWorkbookResult
```

where **sessionId** is located under the **SetCellA1** group node under the **queryFields** group node in the **SetCellA1** secondary data source and **OpenWorkbookResult** is located under the **OpenWorkbookResponse** group node under the **dataFields** group node in the **OpenWorkbook** secondary data source.

```
Query using a data connection: SetCellA1
```

This action calls the **SetCellA1** web service operation to set the value of cell **A1** on the **Calculations** worksheet to be able to perform a **VLOOKUP** in the Excel workbook.

```
Set a field's value: sessionId = OpenWorkbookResult
```

where **sessionId** is located under the **GetCell** group node under the **queryFields** group node in the **GetCell** secondary data source and **OpenWorkbookResult** is located under the **OpenWorkbookResponse** group node under the **dataFields** group node in the **OpenWorkbook** secondary data source.

```
Query using a data connection: GetCell
```

This action calls the **GetCell** web service operation to retrieve the result of the **VLOOKUP** calculation.

```
Set a field's value: sessionId = OpenWorkbookResult
```

where **sessionId** is located under the **CloseWorkbook** group node under the **queryFields** group node in the **CloseWorkbook** secondary data source and

OpenWorkbookResult is located under the **OpenWorkbookResponse** group node under the **dataFields** group node in the **OpenWorkbook** secondary data source.

```
Query using a data connection: CloseWorkbook
```

This action closes the workbook and the Excel Services session.

10. On the **Fields** task pane, select **GetCell (Secondary)** from the **Fields** drop-down list box, expand the **dataFields** group node, expand the **GetCellResponse** group node, and then drag-and-drop the **GetCellResult** field onto the view of the form template. It should automatically get bound to a text box control.

11. Preview the form.

When the form opens, enter an employee name (for example **john.doe**) into the **cellValue** text box, and then click the **Get Leave Balance** button. **15** should appear in the **GetCellResult** text box.

Discussion

There are two ways you can call a web service using an InfoPath form: 1. By creating a **Web Service** form template that is based on a web service operation, or 2. By creating a normal InfoPath form template (browser-compatible or Filler) and adding a receive or submit data connection for a web service operation to the form template. In the solution described above, you created a browser-compatible (**Blank**, **SharePoint Form Library**, or **SharePoint List**) form template and used only **Receive** data connections to call Excel Services SOAP web service operations.

In the solution described above, you used Excel Services SOAP web service operations to perform a **VLOOKUP** calculation in an Excel workbook and return the result to an InfoPath form. You could have also used the Excel Services REST web service to perform the Excel calculation (see recipe *33 Calculate remaining leave in InfoPath using Excel* for how to perform a **VLOOKUP** calculation using the Excel Services REST web service instead of its SOAP web service).

Note that you could have also used the **GetCellA1** web service operation instead of the **GetCell** web service operation to get the value of the calculation. Refer to the discussion section of recipe *18 Get the value of an Excel cell in InfoPath* to learn about the difference between the **GetCell** and **GetCellA1** web service operations. Likewise, you could have also used the **SetCell** web service operation instead of the **SetCellA1** web service operation to set the value of a cell in the Excel workbook. It all depends on what you want to pass to the web service operation, that is, a cell name or row and column numbers representing a cell on a worksheet.

The sequence of Excel Services SOAP web service calls to update the value of a cell in an Excel workbook and then retrieve the result of a calculation is as follows:

1. Call **OpenWorkbook** to get an Excel Services session ID, which allows you to read data from the Excel workbook and change but not permanently store data in the Excel workbook.

2. Call **SetCell** or **SetCellA1** to update the value of a cell in the Excel workbook that is used to perform a calculation. Note that such a change is not permanent unless you open the Excel workbook for editing using the **OpenWorkbookForEditing** web service operation (also see recipe *20 Update an Excel chart on an InfoPath form*) instead of the **OpenWorkbook** web service operation.

3. Call **GetCell** or **GetCellA1** to retrieve the result of the calculation from a cell in the Excel workbook.

4. Call **CloseWorkbook** to close the workbook and end the Excel Services session.

Unlike the technique discussed in the next solution, the technique used in this solution can also be used with **SharePoint List** form templates. Refer to the discussion section of the next solution for more information.

Method 2: Use a form template with Receive and Submit data connections

Problem

You have an Excel workbook in which you want to set the value of a cell so that a calculation can be performed and the result returned to an InfoPath form for display.

Solution

You can create an Excel workbook that contains data and a formula, publish this Excel workbook to a trusted file location for Excel Services in SharePoint, and then call Excel Services SOAP web service operations from within the InfoPath form to perform data submission and retrieval.

To set the value of a cell in an Excel workbook from within an InfoPath form:

1. Use the same Excel workbook as described in step 1 of recipe *11 Set the value of an Excel cell in InfoPath*.

2. In Notepad, create an XML file that has the following contents:

```
<SetCellA1>
  <sheetName></sheetName>
  <rangeName></rangeName>
  <cellValue></cellValue>
</SetCellA1>
```

and name the XML file **SetCellA1.xml** or download the **SetCellA1.xml** file from www.bizsupportonline.com. You will use the fields in this XML file as helper fields to set the values of parameters for making one of the Excel Services SOAP web service calls. By using a separate secondary data source and not including these fields in the Main data source of the form, you will keep the InfoPath form free from irrelevant data.

3. In InfoPath, create a new browser-compatible (**Blank** or **SharePoint Form Library**) form template or use an existing one.

4. Select **Data ➤ Get External Data ➤ From Other Sources ➤ From XML File** and follow the instructions to add an XML data connection for the **SetCellA1.xml** file. Accept the data connection name of **SetCellA1** and leave the **Automatically retrieve data when form is opened** check box selected.

5. Select **Data ➤ Get External Data ➤ From Web Service ➤ From SOAP Web Service** to add a **Receive** data connection for the **OpenWorkbook** operation of the Excel Services web service (also see recipe *18 Get the value of an Excel cell in InfoPath* for detailed instructions on how to connect to the Excel Services SOAP web service) and configure its parameters as follows:

Parameter	Value
tns:workbookPath	`http://servername/sitename/libraryname/LeaveBalan ces.xlsx` where **servername** is the name of the SharePoint server, **sitename** is the name of the site, and **libraryname** is the name of the document library and Excel Services trusted file location where the **LeaveBalances.xlsx** Excel workbook is located.
tns:uiCultureName	
tns:dataCultureName	

Leave the **Store a copy of the data in the form template** check box deselected, name the data connection **OpenWorkbook**, and deselect the **Automatically retrieve data when form is opened** check box. You will use this data connection to open the Excel workbook and get a session ID that you can use for all subsequent calls you make to Excel Services.

6. Select **Data ➤ Submit Form ➤ To Other Locations ➤ To Web Service** to add a **Submit** data connection for the **SetCellA1** operation of the Excel Services web service.

7. On the **Data Connection Wizard** screen where you can configure parameters for the web service operation, select **sessionId** in the list of **Parameters**, and then click the button behind the **Field or group** text box.

8. On the **Select a Field or Group** dialog box, select **OpenWorkbook (Secondary)** from the **Fields** drop-down list box, expand the **dataFields** group node, expand the **OpenWorkbookResponse** group node, select the **OpenWorkbookResult** field, and then click **OK**. Repeat this step for the other parameters, but then configure them as follows:

Parameter	Element
tns:sheetName	/SetCellA1/sheetName where **sheetName** is located in the **SetCellA1** secondary data source.
tns:rangeName	/SetCellA1/rangeName where **rangeName** is located in the **SetCellA1** secondary data source.
tns:cellValue	/SetCellA1/ cellValue where **cellValue** is located in the **SetCellA1** secondary data source.

Select **Text and child elements only** from the **Include** drop-down list box and leave the **Submit data as a string** check box deselected for all of the parameters. Name the data connection **SetCellA1WS** and deselect the **Set as the default submit connection** check box. You will use this data connection to set the value of cell **A1** on the **Calculations** worksheet in the Excel workbook. At this point, the fields in the **SetCellA1** secondary data source are still blank; you will use a rule later to set their values before making the web service call.

9. Select **Data ➤ Get External Data ➤ From Web Service ➤ From SOAP Web Service** to add a **Receive** data connection for the **GetCellA1** operation of the Excel Services web service and configure its parameters as follows:

Parameter	Value
tns:sessionId	
tns:sheetName	Calculations where **Calculations** is the name of the worksheet in the **LeaveBalances.xlsx** Excel workbook that has a **VLOOKUP** formula defined on it.

tns:rangeName	A2
	where **A2** is the name of the cell on the **Calculations** worksheet in the **LeaveBalances.xlsx** Excel workbook that has a **VLOOKUP** formula defined on it.
tns:formatted	false

Leave the **Store a copy of the data in the form template** check box deselected, name the data connection **GetCellA1**, and deselect the **Automatically retrieve data when form is opened** check box. You will use this data connection to get the result of the **VLOOKUP** calculation in the Excel workbook. Note that at this stage the **sessionId** parameter is still blank, since you will set its value later through a rule.

10. Select **Data** ➤ **Submit Form** ➤ **To Other Locations** ➤ **To Web Service** to add a **Submit** data connection for the **CloseWorkbook** operation of the Excel Services web service and configure its parameter as follows:

Parameter	Element
tns:sessionId	`/dfs:myFields/dfs:dataFields/tns:OpenWorkbookResp onse/tns:OpenWorkbookResult`
	where **OpenWorkbookResult** is located under the **OpenWorkbookResponse** group node under the **dataFields** group node in the **OpenWorkbook** secondary data source.

Select **Text and child elements only** from the **Include** drop-down list box and leave the **Submit data as a string** check box deselected. Name the data connection **CloseWorkbook** and deselect the **Set as the default submit connection** check box. You will use this data connection to close the workbook and the Excel Services session.

11. On the **Fields** task pane, select **SetCellA1 (Secondary)** from the **Fields** drop-down list box, and then drag-and-drop the **cellValue** field onto the view of the form template. It should automatically get bound to a text box control.

12. Add a **Button** control to the view of the form template and label it **Get Leave Balance**.

13. Add an **Action** rule to the **Get Leave Balance** button control with the following 7 actions:

```
Query using a data connection: OpenWorkbook
```

This action calls the **OpenWorkbook** web service operation to retrieve a session ID.

```
Set a field's value: sheetName = "Calculations"
```

where **sheetName** is located in the **SetCellA1** secondary data source and **Calculations** is a static piece of text representing the name of the worksheet in the Excel workbook where the **VLOOKUP** calculation is performed.

```
Set a field's value: rangeName = "A1"
```

where **rangeName** is located in the **SetCellA1** secondary data source and **A1** is a static piece of text representing the name of the cell that is used as input for the **VLOOKUP** formula.

```
Submit using a data connection: SetCellA1WS
```

This action calls the **SetCellA1** web service operation to set the value of cell **A1** on the **Calculations** worksheet to be able to perform a **VLOOKUP** in the Excel workbook.

```
Set a field's value: sessionId = OpenWorkbookResult
```

where **sessionId** is located under the **GetCellA1** group node under the **queryFields** group node in the **GetCellA1** secondary data source and **OpenWorkbookResult** is located under the **OpenWorkbookResponse** group node under the **dataFields** group node in the **OpenWorkbook** secondary data source.

```
Query using a data connection: GetCellA1
```

This action calls the **GetCellA1** web service operation to retrieve the result of the **VLOOKUP** calculation.

```
Submit using a data connection: CloseWorkbook
```

This action closes the workbook and the Excel Services session.

14. On the **Fields** task pane, select **GetCellA1 (Secondary)** from the **Fields** drop-down list box, expand the **dataFields** group node, expand the **GetCellA1Response** group node, and then drag-and-drop the **GetCellA1Result** field onto the view of the form template. It should automatically get bound to a text box control.

15. If you are going to publish the form template to SharePoint and fill it out through the browser, add an **ArrayOfAnyType** node to the Main data source of the form as described in *How to add an ArrayOfAnyType to the Main data source* in the Appendix.

16. Preview the form.

When the form opens, enter an employee name (for example **john.doe**) into the **cellValue** text box, and then click the **Get Leave Balance** button. **15** should appear in the **GetCellA1Result** text box.

Discussion

There are two ways you can call a web service using an InfoPath form: 1. By creating a **Web Service** form template that is based on a web service operation, or 2. By creating a normal InfoPath form template (browser-compatible or Filler) and adding a receive or submit data connection for a web service operation to the form template. In the solution described above, you created a browser-compatible (**Blank** or **SharePoint Form Library**) form template and used a combination of **Receive** and **Submit** data connections to call Excel Services SOAP web service operations.

In the solution described above, you used Excel Services SOAP web service operations to perform a **VLOOKUP** calculation in an Excel workbook and return the result to an InfoPath form. You could have also used the Excel Services REST web service to perform the Excel calculation (see recipe *33 Calculate remaining leave in InfoPath using Excel* for how to perform a **VLOOKUP** calculation using the Excel Services REST web service instead of its SOAP web service).

Note that you could have also used the **GetCell** web service operation instead of the **GetCellA1** web service operation to get the value of the calculation. Refer to the discussion section of recipe *18 Get the value of an Excel cell in InfoPath* to learn about the difference between the **GetCell** and **GetCellA1** web service operations. Likewise, you could have also used the **SetCell** web service operation instead of the **SetCellA1** web service operation to set the value of a cell in the Excel workbook. It all depends on what you want to pass to the web service operation, that is, a cell name or row and column numbers representing a cell on a worksheet.

The sequence of Excel Services SOAP web service calls to update the value of a cell in an Excel workbook and then retrieve the result of a calculation is as follows:

1. Call **OpenWorkbook** to get an Excel Services session ID, which allows you to read data from the Excel workbook and change but not permanently store data in the Excel workbook.

2. Call **SetCell** or **SetCellA1** to update the value of a cell in the Excel workbook that is used to perform a calculation. Note that such a change is not permanent unless you open the Excel workbook for editing using the **OpenWorkbookForEditing** web service operation (also see recipe *20 Update an Excel chart on an InfoPath form*) instead of the **OpenWorkbook** web service operation.

3. Call **GetCell** or **GetCellA1** to retrieve the result of the calculation from a cell in the Excel workbook.

4. Call **CloseWorkbook** to close the workbook and end the Excel Services session.

Typically when you publish a form template, which makes use of **Submit** data connections to call Excel Services SOAP web service operations, to SharePoint and fill out forms that are based on that form template in the browser, you may receive a warning message that says:

There has been an error while processing the form.

Adding an **ArrayOfAnyType** node to the Main data source of the form as described in *How to add an ArrayOfAnyType to the Main data source* in the Appendix tends to solve this error. Because **SharePoint List** forms are bound to a SharePoint list and must abide by the data types that are available for SharePoint list columns and because the Main data source of such a form is typically locked, you cannot add an **ArrayOfAnyType** node to the Main data source of a **SharePoint List** form as you did in step 15 of the solution described above, so calling Excel Services SOAP web service operations through **Submit** data connections in a **SharePoint List** form might fail. However, you can still make use of the technique described in method 1 of this recipe or of the Excel Services REST web service to get and set values within an Excel workbook through a **SharePoint List** form.

Method 3: Use a Web Service template

Problem

You have an Excel workbook in which you want to set the value of a cell so that a calculation can be performed and the result returned to an InfoPath form for display.

Solution

You can create an Excel workbook that contains data and a formula, publish this Excel workbook to a trusted file location for Excel Services in SharePoint, and then call operations of the Excel Services SOAP web service from within the InfoPath form to perform data submission and retrieval.

To set the value of a cell in an Excel workbook from within an InfoPath form:

1. Use the same Excel workbook as described in step 1 of recipe *11 Set the value of an Excel cell in InfoPath*.

2. In InfoPath, click **File ➤ New ➤ Web Service** under **Advanced Form Templates**, and then click **Design Form**.

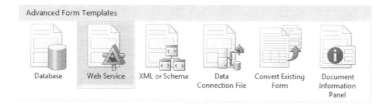

Figure 47. The Web Service command under Advanced Form Templates in InfoPath 2010.

3. On the **Data Connection Wizard**, leave the **Submit data** option selected, and click **Next**.

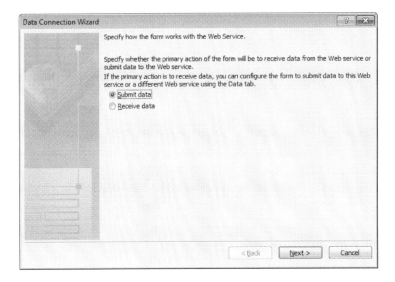

Figure 48. Selecting to submit data to a web service in InfoPath 2010.

4. On the **Data Connection Wizard**, enter the URL of the Excel Services SOAP web service on the site where the Excel workbook is located, for example:

```
http://servername/sitename/_vti_bin/ExcelService.asmx
```

where **servername** is the name of the SharePoint server, **sitename** is the name of the site where the Excel workbook is located, and **ExcelService.asmx** is the Excel Services SOAP web service ASMX page. Click **Next**.

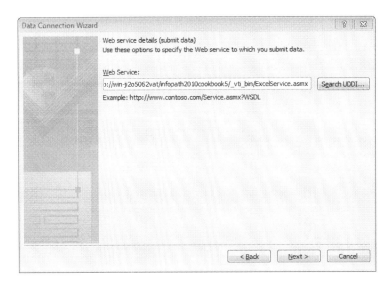

Figure 49. Specifying the Excel Services SOAP web service URL in InfoPath 2010.

5. On the **Data Connection Wizard**, select **SetCellA1** from the list of operations, and click **Next**.

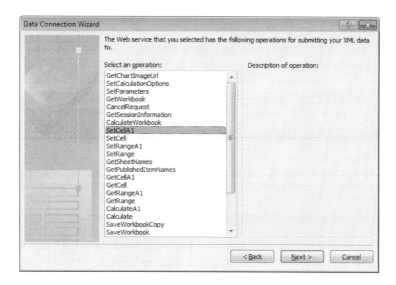

Figure 50. Selecting the SetCellA1 web service operation in InfoPath 2010.

6. On the **Data Connection Wizard**, accept the default name for the data connection (**Main submit**), and click **Finish**.

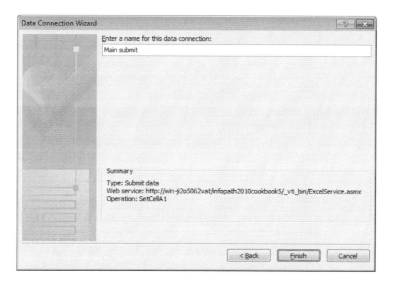

Figure 51. The last screen of the Data Connection Wizard in InfoPath 2010.

7. On the **Fields** task pane, expand all of the group nodes, double-click the **sheetName** field to open its **Field or Group Properties** dialog box, set its **Default Value** to be equal to the static piece of text **Calculations**, and then click **OK**.

Because the **VLOOKUP** formula is located on the **Calculations** worksheet in the Excel workbook, you must pass this sheet name to the web service operation.

Figure 52. The Main data source of the form bound to the SetCellA1 web service operation.

8. On the **Fields** task pane, double-click the **rangeName** field to open its **Field or Group Properties** dialog box, set its **Default Value** to be equal to the static piece of text **A1**, and then click **OK**. Because the **VLOOKUP** formula uses the value of cell **A1** on the **Calculations** worksheet as its input, you must pass this cell name to the web service operation.

9. On the **Fields** task pane, select the **cellValue** field, and drag-and-drop it onto the view of the form template. It should automatically get bound to a text box control. You are going to use this field to enter an employee name.

10. Select **Data ➤ Get External Data ➤ From Web Service ➤ From SOAP Web Service** to add a **Receive** data connection for the **OpenWorkbook** operation of the Excel Services web service (also see recipe *18 Get the value of an Excel cell in InfoPath* for detailed instructions on how to connect to the Excel Services SOAP web service) and configure its parameters as follows:

Parameter	Value
tns:workbookPath	`http://servername/sitename/libraryname/LeaveBalances.xlsx`
	where **servername** is the name of the SharePoint server, **sitename** is the name of the site, and **libraryname** is the name of the document library and Excel Services trusted file location where the **LeaveBalances.xlsx** Excel workbook is located.
tns:uiCultureName	

tns:dataCultureName	

Leave the **Store a copy of the data in the form template** check box deselected, name the data connection **OpenWorkbook**, and deselect the **Automatically retrieve data when form is opened** check box. You will use this data connection to open the Excel workbook and get a session ID that you can use for all subsequent calls you make to Excel Services.

11. Select **Data ➤ Get External Data ➤ From Web Service ➤ From SOAP Web Service** to add a **Receive** data connection for the **GetCell** operation of the Excel Services web service and configure its parameters as follows:

Parameter	Value
tns:sessionId	
tns:sheetName	Calculations
	where **Calculations** is the name of the worksheet in the **LeaveBalances.xlsx** Excel workbook that has a **VLOOKUP** formula defined on it.
tns:row	1
	Because the result of the calculation is stored in cell **A2** of the **Calculations** worksheet in the Excel workbook, you must use number **1** to access the row for cell **A2**.
tns:column	0
	Because the result of the calculation is stored in cell **A2** of the **Calculations** worksheet in the Excel workbook, you must use number **0** to access the column for cell **A2**.
tns:formatted	false

Leave the **Store a copy of the data in the form template** check box deselected, name the data connection **GetCell**, and deselect the **Automatically retrieve data when form is opened** check box. You will use this data connection to get the result of the **VLOOKUP** calculation in the Excel workbook. Note that at this stage the **sessionId** parameter is still blank, since you will set its value later through a rule.

12. Select **Data ➤ Submit Form ➤ To Other Locations ➤ To Web Service** to add a **Submit** data connection for the **CloseWorkbook** operation of the Excel Services web service and configure its parameter as follows:

Parameter	Element
tns:sessionId	/dfs:myFields/dfs:dataFields/tns:OpenWorkbookResp onse/tns:OpenWorkbookResult
	where **OpenWorkbookResult** is located under the **OpenWorkbookResponse** group node under the **dataFields** group node in the **OpenWorkbook** secondary data source.

Select **Text and child elements only** from the **Include** drop-down list box and leave the **Submit data as a string** check box deselected. Name the data connection **CloseWorkbook** and leave the **Set as the default submit connection** check box deselected. You will use this data connection to close the workbook and the Excel Services session.

13. While the submit button is automatically enabled for this form template, because you selected the **Submit data** option when you first created the form template, in this solution, you will add a separate button to call the web service operations. So add a **Button** control to the view of the form template and label it **Get Leave Balance**. For an example of how to call web service operations using the standard **Submit** button of a form, see recipe *24 Update an Excel workbook when submitting an InfoPath form to SharePoint*.

14. Add an **Action** rule to the **Get Leave Balance** button control with the following 6 actions:

```
Query using a data connection: OpenWorkbook
```

This action calls the **OpenWorkbook** web service operation to retrieve a session ID.

```
Set a field's value: sessionId = OpenWorkbookResult
```

where **sessionId** is located under the **SetCellA1** group node under the **dataFields** group node in the Main data source and **OpenWorkbookResult** is located under the **OpenWorkbookResponse** group node under the **dataFields** group node in the **OpenWorkbook** secondary data source.

```
Submit using a data connection: Main submit
```

This action calls the **SetCellA1** web service operation to perform the **VLOOKUP** calculation.

```
Set a field's value: sessionId = OpenWorkbookResult
```

where **sessionId** is located under the **GetCell** group node under the **queryFields** group node in the **GetCell** secondary data source and **OpenWorkbookResult** is located under the **OpenWorkbookResponse** group node under the **dataFields** group node in the **OpenWorkbook** secondary data source. Remember that this was the only parameter you did not already set when configuring the data connection itself, so you are setting it here using an action.

```
Query using a data connection: GetCell
```

This action calls the **GetCell** web service operation to retrieve the result of the **VLOOKUP** calculation.

```
Submit using a data connection: CloseWorkbook
```

This action closes the workbook and the Excel Services session.

15. On the **Fields** task pane, select **GetCell (Secondary)** from the **Fields** drop-down list box, expand the **dataFields** group node, expand the **GetCellResponse** group node, and then drag-and-drop the **GetCellResult** field onto the view of the form template. It should automatically get bound to a text box control.

16. Preview the form.

When the form opens, enter an employee name (for example **john.doe**) into the **cellValue** text box, and then click the **Get Leave Balance** button. **15** should appear in the **GetCellResult** text box.

Discussion

There are two ways you can call a web service using an InfoPath form: 1. By creating a **Web Service** form template that is based on a web service operation, or 2. By creating a normal InfoPath form template (browser-compatible or Filler) and adding a receive or submit data connection for a web service operation to the form template. In the solution described above, you created a **Web Service** form template to call Excel Services SOAP web service operations. And because you can bind the Main data source of a **Web Service** form template to only one web service operation, you added a combination of **Receive** and **Submit** data connections for other web service operations to the form template to be able to retrieve an Excel Services session ID, retrieve the result of a calculation, and close the Excel workbook when done.

A **Web Service** form template is browser-compatible by default, so you can publish it to SharePoint to be filled out as a browser form. The only difference with other browser-compatible form templates is that a **Web Service** form template is based on a web service operation and that part of its Main data source is locked from changes. Also note that you did not have to add an **ArrayOfAnyType** node to the Main data source of the form as you did in step 15 of method 2 in this recipe, because an **ArrayOfAnyType** node is automatically defined in the XML schema definition of a form template when you base that form template on an Excel Services SOAP web service operation.

When you create a **Web Service** form template that is based on a web service submit operation such as the **SetCellA1** operation of the Excel Services SOAP web service, fields for the input parameters of the web service operation are placed under a **dataFields** group node in the Main data source of the form. This **dataFields** group node and all of its child nodes are locked by default, which means that you cannot change anything about them. However, you can still add fields to the Main data source via the **Fields** task pane, since the root **myFields** group node is not locked. Also note that you cannot directly add a control (except for buttons) to the view of the form template, since InfoPath will then open a dialog box for you to select a field in the Main data source or a secondary data source you want to bind the control to. So you must first add a field to the Main data source via the **Fields** task pane and then afterwards bind it to a control on the view of the form template to be able to add a control.

Note that just like you did in method 1 of this recipe, you can also bind the **SetCellA1** operation to the Main data source of a **Web Service** form template that receives (instead of submits) data. In that case, the Main data source would consist of both **queryFields** and **dataFields** group nodes and the input parameters would then be located under the **queryFields** group node.

While you used the **GetCell** web service operation in the solution described above, you could have also used the **GetCellA1** web service operation to get the value of the calculation. Refer to the discussion section of recipe *18 Get the value of an Excel cell in InfoPath* to learn about the difference between the **GetCell** and **GetCellA1** web service operations. Likewise, you could have also bound the form template to the **SetCell** web service operation instead of the **SetCellA1** web service operation. It all depends on what you want to pass to the web service operation, that is, a range name or row and column numbers representing a cell on a worksheet.

20   Update an Excel chart on an InfoPath form

Problem

You want to display a chart on an InfoPath form, but because InfoPath does not come with a chart control, you want to use Excel to display the chart on the InfoPath form.

Solution

You can use the Excel Services SOAP web service to send data to an Excel workbook, use that data as the input for a chart in the workbook, and then use the Excel Services REST web service to access the chart and display it statically on an InfoPath form.

To update an Excel chart on an InfoPath form:

1.   In Excel, create an Excel workbook that contains a chart. If you want to use a sample Excel workbook, you can download a file named **Chart.xlsx** from www.bizsupportonline.com. The **Chart.xlsx** file contains a simple pie chart that displays data entered into cells **A1** and **A2** on **Sheet1**.

2. Click **File ➤ Save & Send ➤ Save to SharePoint ➤ Save As** and save the entire workbook (including all of its sheets) to a document library (for example the **Shared Documents** library) on the SharePoint site to which the InfoPath form will be connecting (also see recipe *7 Publish an Excel workbook to SharePoint*).

3. In InfoPath, create a new browser-compatible form template or use an existing one.

4. Add two **Text Box** controls to the view of the form template and name them **cellA1Value** and **cellA2Value**, respectively.

5. Add a **Button** control to the view of the form template and label it **Update Chart**.

6. Add a **Picture** control to the view of the form template, select the **As a link** option on the **Insert Picture Control** dialog box when you add the picture control, and name the picture control **chart**.

7. Open the **Picture Properties** dialog box, click the **Browser forms** tab, select the **Always** option, and click **OK**.

8. Select **Data ➤ Get External Data ➤ From Web Service ➤ From SOAP Web Service** to add a **Receive** data connection for the **OpenWorkbookForEditing** operation of the Excel Services web service (also see recipe *18 Get the value of an Excel cell in InfoPath* for detailed instructions on how to connect to the Excel Services SOAP web service) and configure its parameters as follows:

Parameter	Value
tns:workbookPath	`http://servername/sitename/libraryname/Chart.xlsx` where **servername** is the name of the SharePoint server, **sitename** is the name of the site, and **libraryname** is the name of the document library and Excel Services trusted file location where the **Chart.xlsx** Excel workbook is located.
tns:uiCultureName	
tns:dataCultureName	

Leave the **Store a copy of the data in the form template** check box deselected, name the data connection **OpenWorkbookForEditing**, and deselect the **Automatically retrieve data when form is opened** check box. You will use this data connection to open the Excel workbook and get a session ID that you can use for all subsequent calls you make to Excel Services.

9. Select **Data ➤ Get External Data ➤ From Web Service ➤ From SOAP Web Service** to add a **Receive** data connection for the **SetCellA1** operation of the Excel

Services web service (also see recipe *19 Set the value of an Excel cell in InfoPath*) and configure its parameters as follows:

Parameter	Value
tns:sessionId	
tns:sheetName	Sheet1 where **Sheet1** is a static piece of text representing the name of the worksheet in the **Chart.xlsx** Excel workbook on which the cells that are used to set the data for the chart are located.
tns:rangeName	
tns:cellValue	

Leave the **Store a copy of the data in the form template** check box deselected, name the data connection **SetCellA1**, and deselect the **Automatically retrieve data when form is opened** check box. You will use this data connection to set the values of cells **A1** and **A2** on **Sheet1** in the Excel workbook. At this point, the **sessionId**, **rangeName**, and **cellValue** parameters are still blank; you will use a rule later to set their values before making the web service call.

10. Select **Data ➤ Get External Data ➤ From Web Service ➤ From SOAP Web Service** to add a **Receive** data connection for the **SaveWorkbook** operation of the Excel Services web service. Leave the **sessionId** parameter as is, leave the **Store a copy of the data in the form template** check box deselected, name the data connection **SaveWorkbook**, and deselect the **Automatically retrieve data when form is opened** check box. You will use this data connection to save the Excel workbook. Note that at this stage the **sessionId** parameter is still blank, since you will set its value later through a rule.

11. Select **Data ➤ Get External Data ➤ From Web Service ➤ From SOAP Web Service** to add a **Receive** data connection for the **CloseWorkbook** operation of the Excel Services web service. Leave the **sessionId** parameter as is, leave the **Store a copy of the data in the form template** check box deselected, name the data connection **CloseWorkbook**, and deselect the **Automatically retrieve data when form is opened** check box. You will use this data connection to close the workbook and the Excel Services session. Note that at this stage the **sessionId** parameter is still blank, since you will set its value later through a rule.

12. Add an **Action** rule to the **Update Chart** button control with the following 13 actions:

```
Query using a data connection: OpenWorkbookForEditing
```

This action calls the **OpenWorkbookForEditing** web service operation to retrieve a session ID.

```
Set a field's value: sessionId = OpenWorkbookForEditingResult
```

where **sessionId** is located under the **SetCellA1** group node under the **queryFields** group node in the **SetCellA1** secondary data source and **OpenWorkbookForEditingResult** is located under the **OpenWorkbookForEditingResponse** group node under the **dataFields** group node in the **OpenWorkbookForEditing** secondary data source.

```
Set a field's value: rangeName = "A1"
```

where **rangeName** is located under the **SetCellA1** group node under the **queryFields** group node in the **SetCellA1** secondary data source and **A1** is a static piece of text representing cell **A1** on the worksheet in the Excel workbook that contains data for the chart.

```
Set a field's value: cellValue = cellA1Value
```

where **cellValue** is located under the **SetCellA1** group node under the **queryFields** group node in the **SetCellA1** secondary data source and **cellA1Value** is located in the Main data source of the form.

```
Query using a data connection: SetCellA1
```

This action calls the **SetCellA1** web service operation to update the value of cell **A1** in the Excel workbook.

```
Set a field's value: rangeName = "A2"
```

where **rangeName** is located under the **SetCellA1** group node under the **queryFields** group node in the **SetCellA1** secondary data source and **A2** is a static piece of text representing cell **A2** on the worksheet in the Excel workbook that contains data for the chart.

```
Set a field's value: cellValue = cellA2Value
```

where **cellValue** is located under the **SetCellA1** group node under the **queryFields** group node in the **SetCellA1** secondary data source and **cellA2Value** is located in the Main data source of the form.

```
Query using a data connection: SetCellA1
```

This action calls the **SetCellA1** web service operation to update the value of cell **A2** in the Excel workbook.

```
Set a field's value: sessionId = OpenWorkbookForEditingResult
```

109

where **sessionId** is located under the **SaveWorkbook** group node under the **queryFields** group node in the **SaveWorkbook** secondary data source and **OpenWorkbookForEditingResult** is located under the **OpenWorkbookForEditingResponse** group node under the **dataFields** group node in the **OpenWorkbookForEditing** secondary data source.

```
Query using a data connection: SaveWorkbook
```

This action saves the changes made to the Excel workbook.

```
Set a field's value: sessionId = OpenWorkbookForEditingResult
```

where **sessionId** is located under the **CloseWorkbook** group node under the **queryFields** group node in the **CloseWorkbook** secondary data source and **OpenWorkbookForEditingResult** is located under the **OpenWorkbookForEditingResponse** group node under the **dataFields** group node in the **OpenWorkbookForEditing** secondary data source.

```
Query using a data connection: CloseWorkbook
```

This action closes the workbook and the Excel Services session.

```
Set a field's value: chart =
"http://servername/sitename/_vti_bin/ExcelREST.aspx/libraryname/Chart.xlsx/
model/Charts('Chart1')"
```

where **chart** is the field that is bound to the picture control on the form and

```
"http://servername/sitename/_vti_bin/ExcelREST.aspx/libraryname/Chart.xlsx/
model/Charts('Chart1')"
```

is the a REST URL that retrieves the image for a chart named **Chart1** in the **Chart.xlsx** Excel workbook. Note that you must replace **servername**, **sitename**, and **libraryname** in the REST URL with appropriate values for your own scenario. Also see recipe *12 Display an Excel chart on an InfoPath form*.

13. Publish the form template to a SharePoint form library.

In SharePoint, navigate to the form library where you published the form template and add a new form. When the form opens, enter values into the **cellA1Value** and **cellA2Value** text boxes, and then click the **Update Chart** button. The chart should appear using the values you entered.

Discussion

In the solution described above, you saw how to use the **OpenWorkbookForEditing** and **SaveWorkbook** Excel Services SOAP web service operations to permanently update data in an Excel workbook that is stored in a SharePoint document library and use this data to display a chart on an InfoPath form by making use of the Excel Services REST web service as was first discussed in recipe *12 Display an Excel chart on an InfoPath form*.

The sequence of Excel Services SOAP web service calls to update data in an Excel workbook is as follows:

1. Call **OpenWorkbookForEditing** to get an Excel Services session ID, which allows you to edit the Excel workbook.

2. Call **SetCell** or **SetCellA1** to edit data in the Excel workbook.

3. Call **SaveWorkbook** to permanently save the changes to the Excel workbook. Note that if you intend to immediately close the Excel workbook after calling **SetCell** or **SetCellA1** to update values in the workbook, you do not have to call **SaveWorkbook** to save the changes, since any changes you made to data in the workbook should automatically be saved when you close the workbook. **SaveWorkbook** is used in this recipe to properly update the data in the Excel workbook and thus also the chart while the InfoPath form is still open.

4. Call **CloseWorkbook** to close the workbook and end the Excel Services session.

While you used **Receive** data connections for calling all of the web service operations in the solution described above, you could have also used **Submit** data connections as described in method 2 of recipe *19 Set the value of an Excel cell in InfoPath* to call the **SetCellA1**, **SaveWorkbook**, and **CloseWorkbook** web service operations.

Note that the **Always** option on the **Browser forms** tab of the **Picture Properties** dialog box only works for browser forms and ensures that after each update of data in the Excel workbook, the image for the chart displayed in the picture control is refreshed. This repeatedly refreshing of the chart image does not work when you are filling out a form in InfoPath Filler. Once the chart has been displayed for the first time in InfoPath Filler, it will not be refreshed on subsequent updates of the data in the Excel workbook.

21 Get the values of a range of Excel cells in InfoPath

Problem

You have an Excel workbook from which you want to retrieve the values of a range of cells so that you can display these values on an InfoPath form.

Solution

You can create an Excel workbook that contains data, publish this Excel workbook to a trusted file location for Excel Services in SharePoint, and then call Excel Services SOAP web service operations from within an InfoPath form to perform data retrieval.

Suppose you have an Excel workbook named **Fruits2.xlsx** (which you can also download from www.bizsupportonline.com for use with this recipe) that has the following contents:

	A	B	C
1	**Name**		**Color**
2	Apple	|	Red
3	Banana	|	Yellow
4	Kiwi	|	Brown
5	Melon	|	Green
6	Orange	|	Orange

To get the values of a range of Excel cells from within an InfoPath form:

1. Click **File ➤ Save & Send ➤ Save to SharePoint ➤ Save As** and save the entire **Fruits2.xlsx** workbook (including all of its sheets) to a document library (for example the **Shared Documents** library) on the SharePoint site to which the InfoPath form will be connecting (also see recipe *7 Publish an Excel workbook to SharePoint*).

2. In InfoPath, create a new browser-compatible form template or use an existing one.

3. Select **Data ➤ Get External Data ➤ From Web Service ➤ From SOAP Web Service** to add a **Receive** data connection for the **OpenWorkbook** operation of the Excel Services web service (also see recipe *18 Get the value of an Excel cell in InfoPath* for detailed instructions on how to connect to the Excel Services SOAP web service) and configure its parameters as follows:

Parameter	Value
tns:workbookPath	`http://servername/sitename/libraryname/Fruits2.xlsx` where **servername** is the name of the SharePoint server, **sitename** is the name of the site, and **libraryname** is the name of the document library and Excel Services trusted file location where the **Fruits2.xlsx** Excel workbook is located.
tns:uiCultureName	
tns:dataCultureName	

Leave the **Store a copy of the data in the form template** check box deselected, name the data connection **OpenWorkbook**, and deselect the **Automatically retrieve data when form is opened** check box. You will use this data connection to open the Excel workbook and get a session ID that you can use for all subsequent calls you make to Excel Services.

4. Select **Data ➤ Get External Data ➤ From Web Service ➤ From SOAP Web Service** to add a **Receive** data connection for the **GetRangeA1** operation of the Excel Services web service, leave all parameters as is, leave the **Store a copy of the data in the form template** check box deselected, name the data connection **GetRangeA1**, and deselect the **Automatically retrieve data when form is opened** check box. You will use this data connection to retrieve the values of a range of cells from the Excel workbook.

5. Select **Data ➤ Get External Data ➤ From Web Service ➤ From SOAP Web Service** to add a **Receive** data connection for the **CloseWorkbook** operation of the Excel Services web service. Leave the **sessionId** parameter as is, leave the **Store a copy of the data in the form template** check box deselected, name the data connection **CloseWorkbook**, and deselect the **Automatically retrieve data when form is opened** check box. You will use this data connection to close the workbook and the Excel Services session. Note that at this stage the **sessionId** parameter is still blank, since you will set its value later through a rule.

6. On the **Fields** task pane, select **GetRangeA1 (Secondary)** from the **Fields** drop-down list box, expand the **dataFields** group node, expand the **GetRangeA1Response** group node, expand the **GetRangeA1Result** group node, and then drag-and-drop the **anyType** repeating field onto the view of the form template. Select **Repeating Table** from the context menu when you drop the field onto the view.

7. Add a **Button** control to the view of the form template and label it **Get Fruits**.

8. Add an **Action** rule to the **Get Fruits** button with the following 8 actions:

    ```
    Query using a data connection: OpenWorkbook
    ```

    This action calls the **OpenWorkbook** web service operation to retrieve a session ID.

    ```
    Set a field's value: sessionId = OpenWorkbookResult
    ```

    where **sessionId** is located under the **GetRangeA1** group node under the **queryFields** group node in the **GetRangeA1** secondary data source and **OpenWorkbookResult** is located under the **OpenWorkbookResponse** group node under the **dataFields** group node in the **OpenWorkbook** secondary data source.

    ```
    Set a field's value: sheetName = "Sheet1"
    ```

    where **sheetName** is located under the **GetRangeA1** group node under the queryFields group node in the **GetRangeA1** secondary data source and **Sheet1** is a static piece of text representing the name of the worksheet in the Excel workbook where the fruits are located.

```
Set a field's value: rangeName = "A2:C6"
```

where **rangeName** is located under the **GetRangeA1** group node under the queryFields group node in the **GetRangeA1** secondary data source and **A2:C6** is a static piece of text representing a range of cells on **Sheet1** in the Excel workbook that contains the fruit names and colors.

```
Set a field's value: formatted = "false"
```

where **formatted** is located under the **GetRangeA1** group node under the queryFields group node in the **GetRangeA1** secondary data source and **false** is a static piece of text.

```
Query using a data connection: GetRangeA1
```

This action calls the **GetRangeA1** web service operation to retrieve the values of cells **A2** through **C6** on **Sheet1** in the Excel workbook.

```
Set a field's value: sessionId = OpenWorkbookResult
```

where **sessionId** is located under the **CloseWorkbook** group node under the queryFields group node in the **CloseWorkbook** secondary data source and **OpenWorkbookResult** is located under the **OpenWorkbookResponse** group node under the **dataFields** group node in the **OpenWorkbook** secondary data source.

```
Query using a data connection: CloseWorkbook
```

This action closes the workbook and the Excel Services session.

9. Preview the form.

When the form opens, click the **Get Fruits** button. The fruit names and colors should appear in the repeating table with a pipe (|) symbol separating them. For example, the value "Apple|Red" should appear in the first row of the repeating table.

Discussion

A range in an Excel workbook spans specific rows and columns, which means that a range can span one cell (for example cell **C5**) or a range can span multiple cells (for example **A1** through **C3**). You can select a group of cells on a worksheet and then give the group of selected cells a name, thereby making the group a named range. For example, you could select cells **B2**, **B3**, **C2**, and **C3** while holding the left mouse button pressed down and then click **Formulas ➤ Defined Names ➤ Define Name** to give the group of four cells a name, thereby making that group a named range.

	A	B	C	D
1	A1	B1	C1	D1
2	A2	B2	C2	D2
3	A3	B3	C3	D3
4	A4	B4	C4	D4
5	A5	B5	C5	D5

Figure 53. A range in an Excel workbook spanning cells B2, B3, C2, and C3.

When an Excel workbook is stored in a SharePoint document library and you want to access data from a range of cells in the workbook without writing code, you can make use of either the Excel Services SOAP web service or the Excel Services REST web service (see recipe *13 Get the values of a range of Excel cells in InfoPath*). Note that while you can use non-adjacent cells (for example **A1**, **B2**, and **C3**) in an Excel workbook to define a named range, you cannot use such a range when retrieving data through the Excel Services web services. If you try to do this, Excel Services will return an error that says:

Unable to parse the range request.

Suppose you defined a named range called **MyNamedRange** for the selected cells shown in Figure 53. To retrieve the values of the cells contained in the range through Excel Services, you could use one of the following references for the range of cells:

- MyNamedRange

- B2:C3

The Excel Services SOAP web service provides two operations you can call to retrieve the values of a range of cells:

1. GetRangeA1

2. GetRange

You can set the **rangeName** parameter of **GetRangeA1** to have a particular value (**MyNamedRange** or **B2:C3** for the example given above) to be able to retrieve values from a range of cells in an Excel workbook. **GetRange** on the other hand works slightly different in that you must specify the row and column numbers of the top-left cell in the range and then the amount of cells in terms of the height and width of the range (moving downwards and to the right). For the example given above this would be row number **1** and column number **1** with a height of **2** and a width of **2**.

Note that row and column numbers start at **0** when you are using the **GetRange** web service operation. So to retrieve the value of cell **A1** you would have to specify the following values for parameters of the **GetRange** web service operation:

- Row = 0

- Column = 0

- Height = 1

- Width = 1

And to retrieve the values of cells **B3** and **B4**, you would have to specify the following values for parameters of the **GetRange** web service operation:

- Row = 2

- Column = 1

- Height = 2

- Width = 1

GetRange is good to use if you want to dynamically change the range of cells at runtime (when the user is filling out the form) from within InfoPath and is also handy if you want to dynamically reduce or increase the amount of cells retrieved. The advantage of using this web service operation is that you would not have to modify and republish the InfoPath form template if users need to retrieve a different range of cells from an Excel workbook. **GetRangeA1** is good to use if you always have a fixed range of cells to retrieve. While it offers less flexibility in InfoPath at runtime, you can however modify the range itself in an Excel workbook to span more or less cells without having to modify and republish the InfoPath form template.

You can also use the Excel Services REST web service to retrieve the values of a range of cells (see recipe *13 Get the values of a range of Excel cells in InfoPath*). The Excel Services REST web service is easier and simpler to use and reference from within InfoPath. You generally require only one action rule to call it, while the SOAP web service almost always requires more than two actions in a rule. In addition, when you retrieve values from more than one column using the Excel Services SOAP web service, the values will generally be concatenated in one field. For example, if you retrieved the values of the **MyNamedRange** range defined in the example given above, the values would be returned as

```
<GetRangeA1Result>
  <anyType>B2C2</anyType>
  <anyType>B3C3<anyType>
</GetRangeA1Result>
```

This means that if you want to distinguish between the values from columns **B** and **C**, you would have to add a separator between them. For example, you could add an extra column in between columns **B** and **C** (so column **C** would become column **D**), add only pipe symbols to the cells in column **C**, make column **C** hidden in Excel, and expand the range in InfoPath to retrieve cells **B2** through **D3** where cells **C2** and **C3** contain only pipe symbols. The result returned to InfoPath would then be the following:

```
<GetRangeA1Result>
  <anyType>B2|C2</anyType>
  <anyType>B3|C3<anyType>
</GetRangeA1Result>
```

This technique was used in the solution described above. You can then use the **substring-before()** or **substring-after()** functions in InfoPath to recognize the pipe symbol and parse the string to extract the values from the individual cells.

With the Excel Services REST web service you do not have this issue of having to use a separator to distinguish between the individual cells, since the value of each cell is returned separately in its own field. The XML structure returned by the Excel Services REST web service would resemble the following for the **MyNamedRange** example:

```
<x:range name="MyNamedRange">
  <x:row>
    <x:c>
      <x:fv>B2</x:fv>
    </x:c>
    <x:c>
      <x:fv>C2</x:fv>
    </x:c>
  </x:row>
  <x:row>
    <x:c>
      <x:fv>B3</x:fv>
    </x:c>
    <x:c>
      <x:fv>C3</x:fv>
    </x:c>
  </x:row>
</x:range>
```

where a **row** group node represents a row and a **c** group node represents a cell in a row in the Excel workbook.

22 Populate a drop-down list in InfoPath with data from an Excel workbook

Problem

You have data on an Excel spreadsheet, which you would like to use to populate a drop-down list box on an InfoPath form. In addition, whenever a user selects an item from the drop-down list box, you want a text box to display additional information for the selected item.

Solution

You can create an Excel workbook that contains tabular data and a calculation for performing a **VLOOKUP** in the data, publish this Excel workbook to a trusted file location for Excel Services, and then call Excel Services SOAP web service operations

117

from within an InfoPath form to perform data retrieval and lookups so that you can populate controls on the InfoPath form.

To populate a drop-down list box in InfoPath with data from an Excel workbook through the Excel Services SOAP web service:

1. In Excel, create an Excel workbook named **Fruits.xlsx** that contains a list of fruit names and their corresponding fruit colors as described in recipe *2 Import Excel data as XML in InfoPath – method 1*. Add the following formula to cell **C2** on **Sheet1**:

   ```
   =VLOOKUP(C1,Fruits,2)
   ```

   where cell **C1** on **Sheet1** contains a static piece of text from column **A** and **Fruits** is a named range that spans cells **A2** through **B6**. The value of cell **C1** will be set from within InfoPath, so that whenever a fruit name is selected from the drop-down list box, its corresponding color can be retrieved using the **VLOOKUP** function in Excel. Note that if you are not using a named range, you could also use a formula that contains the cell range of data such as for example the following:

   ```
   =VLOOKUP(C1,A2:B6,2)
   ```

   The Excel workbook should also contain a second named range named **FruitNames** that spans cells **A2** through **A6**. This named range will be used by one of the web service operations to be able to retrieve the fruit names for the drop-down list box. The advantage of using named ranges instead of static cell names is that after you have designed your InfoPath form template and published it to SharePoint and later want to update the data in the Excel workbook, you can do so without having to make any changes in InfoPath. Just remember to also edit the named ranges to contain the updated data or cells. After you republish the Excel workbook to SharePoint, all InfoPath forms should then automatically display the newly updated Excel data in the drop-down list box.

2. Click **File ➤ Save & Send ➤ Save to SharePoint ➤ Save As** and save the entire workbook (including all of its sheets) to a document library (for example the **Shared Documents** library) on the SharePoint site to which the InfoPath form will be connecting (also see recipe *7 Publish an Excel workbook to SharePoint*).

3. In InfoPath, create a new browser-compatible form template or use an existing one.

4. Add a **Drop-Down List Box** control to the view of the form template and name it **field1**.

5. Add a **Text Box** control to the view of the form template and name it **field2**.

6. Add a **Button** control to the view of the form template and label it **Retrieve Fruits**.

7. Select **Data ➤ Get External Data ➤ From Web Service ➤ From SOAP Web Service** to add a **Receive** data connection for the **OpenWorkbook** operation of the Excel Services web service (also see recipe *18 Get the value of an Excel cell in InfoPath* for detailed instructions on how to connect to the Excel Services SOAP web service)

and configure its parameters as follows:

Parameter	Value
tns:workbookPath	`http://servername/sitename/libraryname/Fruits.xlsx` where **servername** is the name of the SharePoint server, **sitename** is the name of the site, and **libraryname** is the name of the document library and Excel Services trusted file location where the **Fruits.xlsx** Excel workbook is located.
tns:uiCultureName	
tns:dataCultureName	

Leave the **Store a copy of the data in the form template** check box deselected, name the data connection **OpenWorkbook**, and deselect the **Automatically retrieve data when form is opened** check box. You will use this data connection to open the Excel workbook and get a session ID that you can use for all subsequent calls you make to Excel Services.

8. Select **Data ➤ Get External Data ➤ From Web Service ➤ From SOAP Web Service** to add a **Receive** data connection for the **GetRangeA1** operation of the Excel Services web service and configure its parameters as follows:

Parameter	Value
tns:sessionId	
tns:sheetName	Sheet1 where **Sheet1** is a static piece of text representing the name of the worksheet in the Excel workbook where the list of fruit names and colors is located.
tns:rangeName	FruitNames where **FruitNames** is a static piece of text representing the name of the named range on **Sheet1** in the Excel workbook that contains the list of fruit names.
tns:formatted*	false

Leave the **Store a copy of the data in the form template** check box deselected, name the data connection **GetRangeA1**, and deselect the **Automatically retrieve data when form is opened** check box. You will use this data connection to retrieve the list of fruit names. Note that at this stage the **sessionId** parameter is still blank, since you will set its value later through a rule.

9. Select **Data ➤ Get External Data ➤ From Web Service ➤ From SOAP Web Service** to add a **Receive** data connection for the **SetCellA1** operation of the Excel Services web service (also see recipe *19 Set the value of an Excel cell in InfoPath*) and configure its parameters as follows:

Parameter	Value
tns:sessionId	
tns:sheetName	Sheet1 where **Sheet1** is a static piece of text representing the name of the worksheet in the Excel workbook where the list of fruit names and colors is located.
tns:rangeName	C1 where **C1** is a static piece of text representing the name of the cell that accepts the input for the **VLOOKUP** calculation that looks up the color of a fruit based on its name.
tns:cellValue	

Leave the **Store a copy of the data in the form template** check box deselected, name the data connection **SetCellA1**, and deselect the **Automatically retrieve data when form is opened** check box. You will use this data connection to set the value of cell **C1** which should receive the name of a fruit and that is subsequently used to perform a **VLOOKUP** to find a fruit color. At this point, the **sessionId** and **cellValue** parameters are still blank; you will use a rule later to set their values before making the web service call.

10. Select **Data ➤ Get External Data ➤ From Web Service ➤ From SOAP Web Service** to add a **Receive** data connection for the **GetCellA1** operation of the Excel Services web service and configure its parameters as follows:

Parameter	Value
tns:sessionId	
tns:sheetName	Sheet1 where **Sheet1** is a static piece of text representing the name of the worksheet in the Excel workbook where the list of fruit names and colors is located.
tns:rangeName	C2 where **C2** is a static piece of text representing the name of the cell that contains the result of the **VLOOKUP** calculation that looks up the color of a fruit based on its name.
tns:formatted*	false

Leave the **Store a copy of the data in the form template** check box deselected, name the data connection **GetCellA1**, and deselect the **Automatically retrieve data when form is opened** check box. You will use this data connection to retrieve the result of the **VLOOKUP** calculation from the Excel workbook. Note that at this stage the **sessionId** parameter is still blank, since you will set its value later through a rule.

11. Select **Data ➤ Get External Data ➤ From Web Service ➤ From SOAP Web Service** to add a **Receive** data connection for the **CloseWorkbook** operation of the Excel Services web service. Leave the **sessionId** parameter as is, leave the **Store a copy of the data in the form template** check box deselected, name the data connection **CloseWorkbook**, and deselect the **Automatically retrieve data when form is opened** check box. You will use this data connection to close the workbook and the Excel Services session. Note that at this stage the **sessionId** parameter is still blank, since you will set its value later through a rule.

12. Add an **Action** rule to the **Retrieve Fruits** button with the following 5 actions:

```
Query using a data connection: OpenWorkbook
```

This action calls the **OpenWorkbook** web service operation to retrieve a session ID.

```
Set a field's value: sessionId = OpenWorkbookResult
```

where **sessionId** is located under the **GetRangeA1** group node under the **queryFields** group node in the **GetRangeA1** secondary data source and **OpenWorkbookResult** is located under the **OpenWorkbookResponse** group node under the **dataFields** group node in the **OpenWorkbook** secondary data source.

```
Query using a data connection: GetRangeA1
```

This action calls the **GetRangeA1** web service operation to retrieve the list of fruit names.

```
Set a field's value: sessionId = OpenWorkbookResult
```

where **sessionId** is located under the **CloseWorkbook** group node under the **queryFields** group node in the **CloseWorkbook** secondary data source and **OpenWorkbookResult** is located under the **OpenWorkbookResponse** group node under the **dataFields** group node in the **OpenWorkbook** secondary data source.

```
Query using a data connection: CloseWorkbook
```

This action closes the workbook and the Excel Services session.

13. Add an **Action** rule to the drop-down list box with the following 9 actions:

```
Query using a data connection: OpenWorkbook
```

This action calls the **OpenWorkbook** web service operation to retrieve a session ID.

```
Set a field's value: sessionId = OpenWorkbookResult
```

where **sessionId** is located under the **SetCellA1** group node under the **queryFields** group node in the **SetCellA1** secondary data source and **OpenWorkbookResult** is located under the **OpenWorkbookResponse** group node under the **dataFields** group node in the **OpenWorkbook** secondary data source.

```
Set a field's value: cellValue = .
```

where **cellValue** is located under the **SetCellA1** group node under the **queryFields** group node in the **SetCellA1** secondary data source and **.** represents the value of the selected item in the drop-down list box.

```
Query using a data connection: SetCellA1
```

This action calls the **SetCellA1** web service operation to set the value of the cell in the Excel workbook that contains the name of the fruit for which a color should be retrieved.

```
Set a field's value: sessionId = OpenWorkbookResult
```

where **sessionId** is located under the **GetCellA1** group node under the **queryFields** group node in the **GetCellA1** secondary data source and **OpenWorkbookResult** is located under the **OpenWorkbookResponse** group node under the **dataFields** group node in the **OpenWorkbook** secondary data source.

```
Query using a data connection: GetCellA1
```

This action calls the **GetCellA1** web service operation to retrieve the color of the fruit that was selected in the drop-down list box.

```
Set a field's value: field2 = GetCellA1Result
```

where **field2** is a field that is located in the Main data source and that is bound to the text box control on the form and **GetCellA1Result** is located under the **GetCellA1Response** group node under the **dataFields** group node in the **GetCellA1** secondary data source.

```
Set a field's value: sessionId = OpenWorkbookResult
```

where **sessionId** is located under the **CloseWorkbook** group node under the **queryFields** group node in the **CloseWorkbook** secondary data source and **OpenWorkbookResult** is located under the **OpenWorkbookResponse** group node under the **dataFields** group node in the **OpenWorkbook** secondary data source.

```
Query using a data connection: CloseWorkbook
```

This action closes the workbook and the Excel Services session.

14. Open the **Drop-Down List Box Properties** dialog box, and then on the **Data** tab, select the **Get choices from an external data source** option, select **GetRangeA1** from the **Data Source** drop-down list box, and click the button behind the **Entries** text box.

15. On the **Select a Field or Group** dialog box, expand the **GetRangeA1Response** group node, expand the **GetRangeA1Result** group node, select the **anyType** repeating field, and click **OK**.

16. On the **Drop-Down List Box Properties** dialog box, ensure **.** is selected for both the **Value** property and the **Display name** property, and then click **OK**.

17. Publish the form template to a SharePoint form library.

In SharePoint, navigate to the form library where you published the form template and add a new form. When the form opens, verify that the drop-down list box does not contain any items. Click the **Retrieve Fruits** button and then verify that the drop-down list box was populated with the names of fruits from the Excel workbook. Select a fruit from the drop-down list box. The color of the selected fruit should appear in the text box.

Discussion

In the solution described above, you saw how to call Excel Services SOAP web service operations to populate a drop-down list box on an InfoPath form with data from an Excel workbook and also perform a lookup for data in the workbook to populate a text box control on the InfoPath form.

You thereby used a sequence of Excel Services web service calls on a button control to:

1. Call **OpenWorkbook** to get an Excel Services session ID, which allowed you to open an Excel workbook to be able to read data from it.

2. Call **GetRangeA1** to retrieve a list of fruit names from the Excel workbook thereby making use of a named range in the Excel workbook.

3. Call **CloseWorkbook** to close the workbook and end the Excel Services session.

You then used the data that was retrieved by this sequence of Excel Services web service calls to populate a drop-down list box on an InfoPath form. Note that you could have used the data that was returned by Excel Services to populate any type of list box (normal list box, combo box, and multiple-selection list box) that you can bind to an external data source.

You then used a second sequence of Excel Services web service calls on the drop-down list box control to:

1. Call **OpenWorkbook** to get an Excel Services session ID, which allowed you to open the Excel workbook again to be able to run a calculation and return its results.

2. Call **SetCellA1** to set the value of cell **C1** on **Sheet1** in the Excel workbook, so that it could be used to perform a **VLOOKUP** calculation using the fruit name passed to the Excel workbook.

3. Call **GetCellA1** to retrieve the value of cell **C2** on **Sheet1** in the Excel workbook that contained the result of the **VLOOKUP** calculation. You then used this value to set the value of the text box control on the InfoPath form.

4. Call **CloseWorkbook** to close the workbook and end the Excel Services session.

Designing a form template that makes use of Excel Services SOAP web service calls can require quite a few steps to complete and/or action rules that could cause time-outs. Using the Excel Services REST web service is much easier and requires less rules. If you want to implement similar functionality as in the solution described above but use the Excel Services REST web service instead, see recipe *14 Populate a drop-down list in InfoPath with data from an Excel workbook.*

23 Create a new Excel workbook in SharePoint from within an InfoPath form

Problem

You want to use an InfoPath form to create a new Excel workbook in a SharePoint document library.

Solution

You can call Excel Services SOAP web service operations from within an InfoPath form to copy an existing blank Excel workbook and store a copy of it with a new name in a SharePoint document library.

To create a new Excel workbook in SharePoint from within an InfoPath form:

1. In Excel, create a new Excel workbook that does not contain any data and then click **File ➤ Save & Send ➤ Save to SharePoint ➤ Save As** and save the entire workbook (including all of its sheets) with the name **BlankWorkbook.xlsx** to a document library (for example the **Shared Documents** library) on the SharePoint site to which the InfoPath form will be connecting (also see recipe *7 Publish an Excel workbook to SharePoint*).

2. In InfoPath, create a new browser-compatible form template or use an existing one.

3. Add a **Text Box** control to the view of the form template and name it **filename**.

4. Add a **Button** control to the view of the form template and label it **Create New Workbook**.

5. Select **Data ➤ Get External Data ➤ From Web Service ➤ From SOAP Web Service** to add a **Receive** data connection for the **OpenWorkbook** operation of the Excel Services web service and configure its parameters as follows:

Parameter	Value
tns:workbookPath	http://servername/sitename/libraryname/ BlankWorkbook.xlsx where **servername** is the name of the SharePoint server, **sitename** is the name of the site, and **libraryname** is the name of the document library and Excel Services trusted file location where the **BlankWorkbook.xlsx** Excel workbook is located.
tns:uiCultureName	
tns:dataCultureName	

Leave the **Store a copy of the data in the form template** check box deselected, name the data connection **OpenWorkbook**, and deselect the **Automatically retrieve data when form is opened** check box. You will use this data connection to open the Excel workbook and get a session ID that you can use for all subsequent calls you make to Excel Services.

6. Select **Data ▶ Get External Data ▶ From Web Service ▶ From SOAP Web Service** to add a **Receive** data connection for the **SaveWorkbookCopy** operation of the Excel Services web service and configure its parameters as follows:

Parameter	Value
tns:sessionId	
tns:workbookPath	
tns:workbookType	FullWorkbook where **FullWorkbook** is one of three values you can select for the type of Excel workbook to create. Other possible values are **FullSnapshot** and **PublishedItemsSnapshot**.
tns:saveOptions	None where **None** is a static piece of text representing a save option. You could also use **AllowOverwrite** as a save option.

Leave the **Store a copy of the data in the form template** check box deselected, name the data connection **SaveWorkbookCopy**, and deselect the **Automatically retrieve data when form is opened** check box. You will use this data connection to make a copy of the existing Excel workbook in SharePoint and save it with a new name.

7. Select **Data ▶ Get External Data ▶ From Web Service ▶ From SOAP Web Service** to add a **Receive** data connection for the **CloseWorkbook** operation of the Excel Services web service. Leave the **sessionId** parameter as is, leave the **Store a copy of the data in the form template** check box deselected, name the data connection **CloseWorkbook**, and deselect the **Automatically retrieve data when form is opened** check box. You will use this data connection to close the workbook and the Excel Services session. Note that at this stage the **sessionId** parameter is still blank, since you will set its value later through a rule.

8. Add an **Action** rule to the **Create New Workbook** button control with the following 6 actions:

```
Query using a data connection: OpenWorkbook
```

This action calls the **OpenWorkbook** web service operation to retrieve a session ID.

```
Set a field's value: sessionId = OpenWorkbookResult
```

where **sessionId** is located under the **SaveWorkbookCopy** group node under the **queryFields** group node in the **SaveWorkbookCopy** secondary data source and **OpenWorkbookResult** is located under the **OpenWorkbookResponse** group node under the **dataFields** group node in the **OpenWorkbook** secondary data source.

```
Set a field's value: workbookPath =
concat("http://servername/sitename/libraryname/", filename)
```

where **workbookPath** is located under the **SaveWorkbookCopy** group node under the **queryFields** group node in the **SaveWorkbookCopy** secondary data source, `http://servername/sitename/libraryname/` is the URL of the SharePoint document library where you want to save the new Excel workbook (this URL can point to a different SharePoint library on a different site than where the **BlankWorkbook.xlsx** Excel workbook is located), and **filename** is the field that is bound to the text box control on the form. The **concat()** function is used here to generate the full URL for the new Excel workbook.

```
Query using a data connection: SaveWorkbookCopy
```

This action calls the **SaveWorkbookCopy** web service operation to save a copy of the **BlankWorkbook.xlsx** Excel workbook in SharePoint.

```
Set a field's value: sessionId = OpenWorkbookResult
```

where **sessionId** is located under the **CloseWorkbook** group node under the **queryFields** group node in the **CloseWorkbook** secondary data source and **OpenWorkbookResult** is located under the **OpenWorkbookResponse** group node under the **dataFields** group node in the **OpenWorkbook** secondary data source.

```
Query using a data connection: CloseWorkbook
```

This action closes the workbook and the Excel Services session.

9. Publish the form template to a SharePoint form library.

In SharePoint, navigate to the form library where you published the form template and add a new form. When the form opens, enter a name (including the **.xlsx** file extension) for the new Excel workbook in the **filename** text box, and then click the **Create New Workbook** button. Navigate to the SharePoint document library where the new Excel workbook should have been created and verify that it is indeed present in the document library.

Discussion

In the solution described above, you saw how to use a browser-compatible form template to call Excel Services SOAP web service operations with which you can create a new Excel workbook in a SharePoint document library. You thereby copied an existing blank

Excel workbook and saved it with a different name in either the same or a different SharePoint document library than where the original Excel workbook was located.

The sequence of Excel Services SOAP web service calls to create a new Excel workbook based on an existing Excel workbook was as follows:

1. Call **OpenWorkbook** to get an Excel Services session ID, which allowed you to open an existing Excel workbook.

2. Call **SaveWorkbookCopy** to copy the Excel workbook that was opened using **OpenWorkbook** and save it with a new name.

3. Call **CloseWorkbook** to close the workbook and end the Excel Services session.

While you added a normal button control to the view of the form template with an action rule to create the new Excel workbook in SharePoint, you could have also added a rule to the **Form Submit** event of the form to submit the form and create a new Excel workbook.

Note that you could have also created a **Web Service** form template as described in method 3 of recipe *19 Set the value of an Excel cell in InfoPath* or a **SharePoint List** form template as described in recipe *25 Submit SharePoint List form values to a new Excel workbook* to create and save a new Excel workbook to SharePoint.

In the solution described above, you did not have to write code to create a new Excel workbook. However, this solution is limited to creating a new Excel workbook and does not offer the ability to also add new worksheets to the new workbook. For the latter you would have to write code as described in recipe *44 Create a new Excel workbook from within InfoPath* or recipe *49 Create a new Excel workbook in SharePoint from within InfoPath*.

24 Update an Excel workbook when submitting an InfoPath form to SharePoint

Problem

You have an Excel workbook that is stored in a SharePoint document library and want to have the ability to update specific cells on worksheets within the workbook when an InfoPath form is submitted to a SharePoint form library.

Solution

You can call Excel Services SOAP web service operations from within an InfoPath form to perform data submission and updates in an Excel workbook that is stored in a SharePoint document library.

To update an Excel workbook when submitting an InfoPath form to SharePoint:

1. In Excel, create an Excel workbook that contains the following four named ranges: **firstName**, **lastName**, **addressLine1**, and **addressLine2**. Each named range should span only one cell, must have a scope of **Workbook**, and can be located on

any worksheet in the Excel workbook (also see *How to create a named range in Excel* in the Appendix). You can download a sample Excel file named **UpdateFromInfoPath.xlsx** from www.bizsupportonline.com for use with this recipe.

2. Click **File ➤ Save & Send ➤ Save to SharePoint ➤ Save As** and save the entire workbook (including all of its sheets) to a document library (for example the **Shared Documents** library) on the SharePoint site to which the InfoPath form will be connecting (also see recipe *7 Publish an Excel workbook to SharePoint*).

3. In InfoPath, create a new browser-compatible form template or use an existing one.

4. Add four **Text Box** controls to the view of the form template and name them **firstName**, **lastName**, **addressLine1**, and **addressLine2**, respectively.

5. Click **Data ➤ Submit Form ➤ To SharePoint Library** and follow the instructions to add a data connection to submit the InfoPath form to a SharePoint form library (if you do not have an existing form library, create one in SharePoint before adding the data connection to the InfoPath form template). Accept the default name for the data connection (**SharePoint Library Submit**) and leave the **Set as the default submit connection** check box selected.

6. Click **File ➤ Info ➤ Form Options** to open the **Form Options** dialog box, deselect the **Save** and **Save As** check boxes under the **Web Browser** category, and then click **OK**.

7. Select **Data ➤ Get External Data ➤ From Web Service ➤ From SOAP Web Service** to add a **Receive** data connection for the **OpenWorkbookForEditing** operation of the Excel Services web service (also see recipe *18 Get the value of an Excel cell in InfoPath* for detailed instructions on how to connect to the Excel Services SOAP web service) and configure its parameters as follows:

Parameter	Value

tns:workbookPath	`http://servername/sitename/libraryname/UpdateFrom`
	`InfoPath.xlsx`
	
	where **servername** is the name of the SharePoint server, **sitename** is the name of the site, and **libraryname** is the name of the document library and Excel Services trusted file location where the **UpdateFromInfoPath.xlsx** Excel workbook is located.

tns:uiCultureName	
tns:dataCultureName	

Leave the **Store a copy of the data in the form template** check box deselected, name the data connection **OpenWorkbookForEditing**, and deselect the **Automatically retrieve data when form is opened** check box. You will use this data connection to open the Excel workbook and get a session ID that you can use for all subsequent calls you make to Excel Services.

8. Select **Data ➤ Get External Data ➤ From Web Service ➤ From SOAP Web Service** to add a **Receive** data connection for the **SetCellA1** operation of the Excel Services web service (also see recipe *19 Set the value of an Excel cell in InfoPath*). Leave all parameters as is, leave the **Store a copy of the data in the form template** check box deselected, name the data connection **SetCellA1**, and deselect the **Automatically retrieve data when form is opened** check box. You will use this data connection to set the values of the named ranges in the Excel workbook.

9. Select **Data ➤ Get External Data ➤ From Web Service ➤ From SOAP Web Service** to add a **Receive** data connection for the **CloseWorkbook** operation of the Excel Services web service. Leave the **sessionId** parameter as is, leave the **Store a copy of the data in the form template** check box deselected, name the data connection **CloseWorkbook**, and deselect the **Automatically retrieve data when form is opened** check box. You will use this data connection to close the workbook and the Excel Services session. Note that at this stage the **sessionId** parameter is still blank, since you will set its value later through a rule.

10. Click **Data ➤ Submit Form ➤ Submit Options**.

11. On the **Submit Options** dialog box, select the **Perform custom action using Rules** option, and then click **OK**.

12. On the **Rules** task pane, there should already be one rule present for submitting the form to the SharePoint form library. Add a new **Action** rule and then move it up so that it is executed before the rule that was already present for submitting the form.

13. Add the following 17 actions to the new **Action** rule you just added:

```
Query using a data connection: OpenWorkbookForEditing
```

This action calls the **OpenWorkbookForEditing** web service operation to retrieve a session ID.

```
Set a field's value: sessionId = OpenWorkbookResult
```

where **sessionId** is located under the **SetCellA1** group node under the **queryFields** group node in the **SetCellA1** secondary data source and **OpenWorkbookForEditingResult** is located under the **OpenWorkbookForEditingResponse** group node under the **dataFields** group node in the **OpenWorkbookForEditing** secondary data source.

```
Set a field's value: sheetName = ""
```

where **sheetName** is located under the **SetCellA1** group node under the **queryFields** group node in the **SetCellA1** secondary data source. The worksheet name is set to be equal to an empty string, because you will be using named ranges, which can be located anywhere in the workbook (not on a specific worksheet) to submit data to the Excel workbook.

```
Set a field's value: rangeName = "firstName"
```

where **rangeName** is located under the **SetCellA1** group node under the **queryFields** group node in the **SetCellA1** secondary data source and **firstName** is a static piece of text representing the name of a named range in the Excel workbook.

```
Set a field's value: cellValue = firstName
```

where **cellValue** is located under the **SetCellA1** group node under the **queryFields** group node in the **SetCellA1** secondary data source and **firstName** is located in the Main data source.

```
Query using a data connection: SetCellA1
```

This action calls the **SetCellA1** web service operation to update the value of the **firstName** named range in the Excel workbook.

```
Set a field's value: rangeName = "lastName"
```

where **rangeName** is located under the **SetCellA1** group node under the **queryFields** group node in the **SetCellA1** secondary data source and **lastName** is a static piece of text representing the name of a named range in the Excel workbook.

```
Set a field's value: cellValue = lastName
```

where **cellValue** is located under the **SetCellA1** group node under the **queryFields** group node in the **SetCellA1** secondary data source and **lastName** is located in the Main data source.

```
Query using a data connection: SetCellA1
```

This action calls the **SetCellA1** web service operation to update the value of the **lastName** named range in the Excel workbook.

```
Set a field's value: rangeName = "addressLine1"
```

where **rangeName** is located under the **SetCellA1** group node under the **queryFields** group node in the **SetCellA1** secondary data source and **addressLine1** is a static piece of text representing the name of a named range in the Excel workbook.

```
Set a field's value: cellValue = addressLine1
```

where **cellValue** is located under the **SetCellA1** group node under the **queryFields** group node in the **SetCellA1** secondary data source and **addressLine1** is located in the Main data source.

```
Query using a data connection: SetCellA1
```

This action calls the **SetCellA1** web service operation to update the value of the **addressLine1** named range in the Excel workbook.

```
Set a field's value: rangeName = "addressLine2"
```

where **rangeName** is located under the **SetCellA1** group node under the **queryFields** group node in the **SetCellA1** secondary data source and **addressLine2** is a static piece of text representing the name of a named range in the Excel workbook.

```
Set a field's value: cellValue = addressLine2
```

where **cellValue** is located under the **SetCellA1** group node under the **queryFields** group node in the **SetCellA1** secondary data source and **addressLine2** is located in the Main data source.

```
Query using a data connection: SetCellA1
```

This action calls the **SetCellA1** web service operation to update the value of the **addressLine2** named range in the Excel workbook.

```
Set a field's value: sessionId = OpenWorkbookResult
```

where **sessionId** is located under the **CloseWorkbook** group node under the **queryFields** group node in the **CloseWorkbook** secondary data source and **OpenWorkbookForEditingResult** is located under the **OpenWorkbookForEditingResponse** group node under the **dataFields** group node in the **OpenWorkbookForEditing** secondary data source.

```
Query using a data connection: CloseWorkbook
```

This action closes the workbook and the Excel Services session.

14. Publish the form template to the form library you specified in the data connection in step 5.

In SharePoint, navigate to the form library where you published the form template and add a new form. When the form opens, enter values in all of the text boxes, and then click the **Submit** button on the toolbar. Once you have submitted the form, navigate to the document library that contains the Excel workbook, open the workbook, and verify that the data you submitted from within the InfoPath form was written to the named ranges in the Excel workbook.

Discussion

In the solution described above, you saw how to update cells that have been defined with names in an Excel workbook with data from an InfoPath form when submitting the form to a SharePoint form library.

The sequence of Excel Services SOAP web service calls to update the values of cells in an Excel workbook with data from an InfoPath form when the form is submitted to a SharePoint form library is as follows:

1. Call **OpenWorkbookForEditing** to get an Excel Services session ID, which allows you to edit the Excel workbook.

2. Call **SetCell** or **SetCellA1** to edit the value of a cell in the Excel workbook. You can call these operations repeatedly for each cell you need to update in the workbook. Note that in the solution described above, the **sheetName** parameter of the **SetCellA1** web service operation was set to be equal to an empty string, because the named ranges in the Excel workbook were defined with a scope of **Workbook**, so they should automatically be found through their names and not a particular worksheet in the Excel workbook.

3. Call **CloseWorkbook** to save the changes made to the workbook, close the workbook, and end the Excel Services session.

While the Excel workbook and the SharePoint form library need not be on the same SharePoint site for the solution to work, if you place them on different SharePoint sites, you must ensure that users can access the InfoPath form and Excel workbook on both SharePoint sites.

You could extend the solution described above by combining it with the solution in recipe *23 Create a new Excel workbook in SharePoint from within an InfoPath form*, so that users can create a new Excel workbook and then update it with data when the form is submitted to the SharePoint form library. For an example that makes use of a **SharePoint List** form instead of a **SharePoint Form Library** form, see recipe *25 Submit SharePoint List form values to a new Excel workbook*.

Note:

When you use the **OpenWorkbookForEditing** web service operation to open an Excel workbook for editing, you generally do not need to explicitly call the **SaveWorkbook** operation to save the changes made to the workbook before calling the **CloseWorkbook** operation to close the workbook, since any changes made to the workbook should automatically and permanently be stored in the workbook when you close it. But if the changes you made are not being persisted in your workbook, you may want to try adding the **SaveWorkbook** operation (see for example recipe *20 Update an Excel chart on an InfoPath form*) just before calling the **CloseWorkbook** operation to see whether the additional operation solves the issue.

25   Submit SharePoint List form values to a new Excel workbook

Problem

You have a SharePoint List form which you want to use to create a new Excel workbook and then submit values from the form to the newly created Excel workbook.

Solution

You can call Excel Services SOAP web service operations from within a SharePoint List form to copy an existing blank Excel workbook, store a copy of it with a new name in a SharePoint document library, and then edit the newly created Excel workbook to contain values from the SharePoint List form.

To submit SharePoint List form values to a new Excel workbook:

1.   In Excel, create a new Excel workbook that does not contain any data and then click **File ➤ Save & Send ➤ Save to SharePoint ➤ Save As** and save the entire workbook (including all of its sheets) with the name **BlankWorkbook.xlsx** to a document library (for example the **Shared Documents** library) on the SharePoint site to which the InfoPath form will be connecting (also see recipe *7 Publish an Excel workbook to SharePoint*).

2.   In SharePoint, create a new custom SharePoint list named **Employees** that has 4 columns with the data type **Single line of text** and the names **Title**, **FirstName**, **LastName**, and **ExcelFileName**, respectively.

3.   Click **List Tools ➤ List ➤ Customize List ➤ Customize Form** to create a SharePoint List form and open it in InfoPath Designer 2010.

4.   In InfoPath, select **Data ➤ Get External Data ➤ From Web Service ➤ From SOAP Web Service** to add a **Receive** data connection for the **OpenWorkbook** operation of the Excel Services web service (also see recipe *18 Get the value of an Excel cell in InfoPath* for detailed instructions on how to connect to the Excel Services SOAP web service) and configure its parameters as follows:

Parameter	Value

tns:workbookPath	`http://servername/sitename/libraryname/`
	`BlankWorkbook.xlsx`
	
	where **servername** is the name of the SharePoint server, **sitename** is the name of the site, and **libraryname** is the name of the document library and Excel Services trusted file location where the **BlankWorkbook.xlsx** Excel workbook is located.

tns:uiCultureName	
tns:dataCultureName	

Leave the **Store a copy of the data in the form template** check box deselected, name the data connection **OpenWorkbook**, and deselect the **Automatically retrieve data when form is opened** check box. You will use this data connection to open the Excel workbook and get a session ID that you can use in subsequent calls you make to Excel Services.

5. Select **Data ➤ Get External Data ➤ From Web Service ➤ From SOAP Web Service** to add a **Receive** data connection for the **SaveWorkbookCopy** operation of the Excel Services web service and configure its parameters as follows:

Parameter	Value
tns:sessionId	
tns:workbookPath	
tns:workbookType	FullWorkbook where **FullWorkbook** is an item you must select from a list of items (**FullWorkbook**, **FullSnapshot**, or **PublishedItemsSnapshot**).
tns:saveOptions	None where **None** is a static piece of text representing a save option. **AllowOverwrite** is another save option you could use.

Leave the **Store a copy of the data in the form template** check box deselected, name the data connection **SaveWorkbookCopy**, and deselect the **Automatically retrieve data when form is opened** check box. Note that you left the **sessionId** and **workbookPath** parameters blank, since you will be using a rule to set them later. You will use this data connection to save a copy of the **BlankWorkbook.xlsx** Excel workbook.

6. Select **Data ➤ Get External Data ➤ From Web Service ➤ From SOAP Web Service** to add a **Receive** data connection for the **CloseWorkbook** operation of the Excel Services web service. Leave the **sessionId** parameter as is, leave the **Store a copy of the data in the form template** check box deselected, name the data connection **CloseWorkbook**, and deselect the **Automatically retrieve data when**

form is opened check box. You will use this data connection to close the Excel workbook and Excel Services session.

7. Select **Data ➤ Get External Data ➤ From Web Service ➤ From SOAP Web Service** to add a **Receive** data connection for the **OpenWorkbookForEditing** operation of the Excel Services web service. Leave all parameters as is, leave the **Store a copy of the data in the form template** check box deselected, name the data connection **OpenWorkbookForEditing**, and deselect the **Automatically retrieve data when form is opened** check box. You will use this data connection to open the Excel workbook for editing and get a session ID that you can use in subsequent calls you make to Excel Services.

8. Select **Data ➤ Get External Data ➤ From Web Service ➤ From SOAP Web Service** to add a **Receive** data connection for the **SetCellA1** operation of the Excel Services web service (also see recipe *19 Set the value of an Excel cell in InfoPath*). Leave all parameters as is, leave the **Store a copy of the data in the form template** check box deselected, name the data connection **SetCellA1**, and deselect the **Automatically retrieve data when form is opened** check box. You will use this data connection to set the value of a cell in the Excel workbook.

9. Click **Data ➤ Submit Form ➤ Submit Options**.

10. On the **Submit Options** dialog box, select the **Perform custom action using Rules** option, and click **OK**.

11. On the **Rules** task pane, one **Action** rule should already be present. This **Action** rule is used to save the item back to the SharePoint list, so leave the rule as is. Add a new **Action** rule with the following 18 actions:

```
Query using a data connection: OpenWorkbook
```

This action calls the **OpenWorkbook** web service operation to retrieve a session ID.

```
Set a field's value: sessionId = OpenWorkbookResult
```

where **sessionId** is located under the **SaveWorkbookCopy** group node under the **queryFields** group node in the **SaveWorkbookCopy** secondary data source and **OpenWorkbookResult** is located under the **OpenWorkbookResponse** group node under the **dataFields** group node in the **OpenWorkbook** secondary data source.

```
Set a field's value: workbookPath =
concat("http://servername/sitename/libraryname/", ExcelFileName)
```

where **workbookPath** is located under the **SaveWorkbookCopy** group node under the **queryFields** group node in the **SaveWorkbookCopy** secondary data source and **ExcelFileName** is located under the **SharePointListItem_RW** group node under the **dataFields** group node in the Main data source. Note that you must replace **servername**, **sitename**, and **libraryname** in the formula with the correct values for your own scenario. The URL in the **concat()** function represents the location where the newly created Excel workbook should be stored. This location can be a different document library than where the original Excel workbook is located.

```
Query using a data connection: SaveWorkbookCopy
```

This action calls the **SaveWorkbookCopy** web service operation to save the workbook.

```
Set a field's value: sessionId = OpenWorkbookResult
```

where **sessionId** is located under the **CloseWorkbook** group node under the **queryFields** group node in the **CloseWorkbook** secondary data source and **OpenWorkbookResult** is located under the **OpenWorkbookResponse** group node under the **dataFields** group node in the **OpenWorkbook** secondary data source.

```
Query using a data connection: CloseWorkbook
```

This action closes the workbook and the Excel Services session.

```
Set a field's value: workbookPath =
concat("http://servername/sitename/libraryname/", ExcelFileName)
```

where **workbookPath** is located under the **OpenWorkbookForEditing** group node under the **queryFields** group node in the **OpenWorkbookForEditing** secondary data source and **ExcelFileName** is located under the **SharePointListItem_RW** group node under the **dataFields** group node in the Main data source. Note that you must replace **servername**, **sitename**, and **libraryname** in the formula with the correct values for your own scenario. The URL in the **concat()** function represents the location where the newly created Excel workbook was stored.

```
Query using a data connection: OpenWorkbookForEditing
```

This action calls the **OpenWorkbookForEditing** web service operation to retrieve a session ID.

```
Set a field's value: sessionId = OpenWorkbookForEditingResult
```

where **sessionId** is located under the **SetCellA1** group node under the **queryFields** group node in the **SetCellA1** secondary data source and **OpenWorkbookForEditingResult** is located under the **OpenWorkbookForEditingResponse** group node under the **dataFields** group node in the **OpenWorkbookForEditing** secondary data source.

```
Set a field's value: sheetName = "Sheet1"
```

where **sheetName** is located under the **SetCellA1** group node under the **queryFields** group node in the **SetCellA1** secondary data source and **Sheet1** is a static piece of text representing the worksheet in the Excel workbook where the cell that should be written to is located.

```
Set a field's value: rangeName = "A1"
```

where **rangeName** is located under the **SetCellA1** group node under the **queryFields** group node in the **SetCellA1** secondary data source and **A1** is a static piece of text representing the name of the cell that should receive data.

```
Set a field's value: cellValue = FirstName
```

where **cellValue** is located under the **SetCellA1** group node under the **queryFields** group node in the **SetCellA1** secondary data source and **FirstName** is located under the **SharePointListItem_RW** group node under the **dataFields** group node in the Main data source.

```
Query using a data connection: SetCellA1
```

This action sets the value of cell **A1** in the Excel workbook to be equal to the value of the **FirstName** text box on the InfoPath form.

```
Set a field's value: rangeName = "B1"
```

where **rangeName** is located under the **SetCellA1** group node under the **queryFields** group node in the **SetCellA1** secondary data source and **B1** is a static piece of text representing the name of the cell that should receive data.

```
Set a field's value: cellValue = LastName
```

where **cellValue** is located under the **SetCellA1** group node under the **queryFields** group node in the **SetCellA1** secondary data source and **LastName** is located under the **SharePointListItem_RW** group node under the **dataFields** group node in the Main data source.

```
Query using a data connection: SetCellA1
```

This action sets the value of cell **B1** in the Excel workbook to be equal to the value of the **LastName** text box on the InfoPath form.

```
Set a field's value: sessionId = OpenWorkbookForEditingResult
```

where **sessionId** is located under the **CloseWorkbook** group node under the **queryFields** group node in the **CloseWorkbook** secondary data source and **OpenWorkbookForEditingResult** is located under the **OpenWorkbookForEditingResponse** group node under the **dataFields** group node in the **OpenWorkbookForEditing** secondary data source.

```
Query using a data connection: CloseWorkbook
```

This action closes the workbook and the Excel Services session.

12. Click **File ➤ Info ➤ Quick Publish** to publish the form template to the SharePoint list.

In SharePoint, navigate to the SharePoint list for which you customized the form template and add a new item. When the form opens, enter values into the **Title**, **FirstName**, and **LastName** text boxes, enter a file name (for example **JaneDoe.xlsx**) in the **ExcelFileName** text box, and then click **Save**. The item should appear in the SharePoint list and a new Excel workbook should have been created. Navigate to the document library where the new Excel workbook should have been created, open the Excel workbook, and verify that the values from the SharePoint List form were written to and saved in the new Excel workbook.

Discussion

In the solution described above, you saw how to combine the techniques from recipe *23 Create a new Excel workbook in SharePoint from within an InfoPath form* and recipe *24 Update an Excel workbook when submitting an InfoPath form to SharePoint* to call Excel Services SOAP web service operations to submit values that are entered into a SharePoint List form to an Excel workbook stored in a SharePoint document library. You thereby copied an existing blank Excel workbook, saved it with a different name in either the same or a different SharePoint document library than where the original Excel workbook was located, and then edited it afterwards to contain the values from the SharePoint List form.

While you used rules in the **Form Submit** event of the form to submit the form and create a new Excel workbook containing values from the form, you could have also added a normal button control to the view of the form template with an action rule to perform the same actions as the rule does in the **Form Submit** event.

Note that because a SharePoint List form is tightly bound to the SharePoint list it belongs to, the InfoPath form must abide by the data types of fields in the SharePoint list and the data types that are available in SharePoint. Because an **ArrayOfAnyType** data type is not available in SharePoint, you cannot add it to the Main data source (also see *How to add an ArrayOfAnyType to the Main data source* in the Appendix) of a SharePoint List form with the purpose of preventing errors from taking place when calling Excel Services SOAP web service operations that are called through **Submit** data connections. And therefore, all of the web service operations were called through **Receive** data connections as described in method 1 of recipe *19 Set the value of an Excel cell in InfoPath* instead of a mixture of **Receive** and **Submit** data connections. Had you created a **SharePoint Form Library** form template instead of a **SharePoint List** form template, then you could have used a mixture of **Receive** and **Submit** data connections as described in method 2 of recipe *19 Set the value of an Excel cell in InfoPath* and added the **ArrayOfAnyType** node to the Main data source of the form to prevent errors from occurring.

26 Send a repeating table row to Excel – method 1

Problem

You have a repeating table on an InfoPath form and want to send data that is contained in the fields of a specific row of the repeating table to an Excel workbook for storage.

Solution

You can use Excel Services SOAP web service operations to send data to an Excel workbook and then in the Excel workbook, use Excel formulas to retrieve and parse the data that was sent from a repeating table on an InfoPath form.

To send a repeating table row to Excel:

1. In Excel, create an Excel workbook that has the following 3 formulas defined in cells in columns **B**, **C**, and **D** (*code #: E00CAAD6-F5DB-4C8C-95A8-67F2A20301DB*).

    Formula for the first row in column **B**:

    ```
    =MID(A1, 1, FIND("|", A1)-1)
    ```

    Formula for the first row in column **C**:

    ```
    =MID(MID(A1, FIND("|", A1) + 1, LEN(A1) - FIND("|", A1) ), 1, FIND("|",
    MID(A1, FIND("|", A1) + 1, LEN(A1) - FIND("|", A1) )  ) - 1)
    ```

    Formula for the first row in column **D**:

    ```
    =MID(MID(A1, FIND("|", A1) + 1, LEN(A1) - FIND("|", A1) ), FIND("|",
    MID(A1, FIND("|", A1) + 1, LEN(A1) - FIND("|", A1) )) + 1, LEN(MID(A1,
    FIND("|", A1) + 1, LEN(A1) - FIND("|", A1) )))
    ```

    Note that these formulas can be copied downwards to more cells in a column by dragging the lower-right corner of the first cell that contains a formula downwards to cover more cells.

    The way the formulas work is as follows:

    a. The data that is contained in the repeating table is expected to be stored in cells **A1**, **A2**, **A3**, etc. and passed in a format where the values of the fields in a row of the repeating are separated by a pipe (|) symbol. For example:

        ```
        Value of field 1|Value of field 2|Value of field 3
        ```

    b. The **FIND** function is then used in Excel to locate the position of the pipe (|) symbol and then used in combination with the **MID** and **LEN** functions to parse the value of one of the cells in column **A**. Note that the complexity of the formula will increase with the amount of columns you want to fill in Excel, that is, the formula will become more and more complex with each extra column of data you add to the worksheet.

Name the Excel workbook **SendRepeatingTableToExcel.xlsx**. You can also download a file named **SendRepeatingTableToExcel-method1.xlsx** from www.bizsupportonline.com for use with this recipe.

2. Click **File ➤ Save & Send ➤ Save to SharePoint ➤ Save As** and save the entire workbook (including all of its sheets) to a document library (for example the **Shared Documents** library) on the SharePoint site to which the InfoPath form will be connecting (also see recipe *7 Publish an Excel workbook to SharePoint*).

3. In InfoPath, create a new browser-compatible form template or use an existing one.

4. Add a **Repeating Table** control with 4 columns to the view of the form template and name the fields within the repeating table **field1**, **field2**, **field3**, and **field4**, respectively.

5. Replace the field in the fourth column (**field4**) in the repeating table with a **Button** control and label the button **Send To Excel**. You can delete **field4** from the Main data source since you will not be using it.

6. Add a **Text Box** control to the view of the form template and name it **cellReference**. This text box will serve to enter a cell reference, for example **A1**, **A2**, **A3**, etc.

7. Add a hidden **Field (element)** with the data type **Text (string)** and the name **cellValue** to the Main data source of the form.

8. Select **Data ➤ Get External Data ➤ From Web Service ➤ From SOAP Web Service** to add a **Receive** data connection for the **OpenWorkbookForEditing** operation of the Excel Services web service (also see recipe *18 Get the value of an Excel cell in InfoPath* for detailed instructions on how to connect to the Excel Services SOAP web service) and configure its parameters as follows:

Parameter	Value

tns:workbookPath	`http://servername/sitename/libraryname/`
	`SendRepeatingTableToExcel.xlsx`
	
	where **servername** is the name of the SharePoint server, **sitename** is the name of the site, and **libraryname** is the name of the document library and Excel Services trusted file location where the **SendRepeatingTableToExcel.xlsx** Excel workbook is located.

tns:uiCultureName	

---

tns:dataCultureName

Leave the **Store a copy of the data in the form template** check box deselected, name the data connection **OpenWorkbookForEditing**, and deselect the **Automatically retrieve data when form is opened** check box. You will use this data connection to open the Excel workbook and get a session ID that you can use for all subsequent calls you make to Excel Services.

9. Select **Data ➤ Get External Data ➤ From Web Service ➤ From SOAP Web Service** to add a **Receive** data connection for the **SetCellA1** operation of the Excel Services web service (also see recipe *19 Set the value of an Excel cell in InfoPath*). Leave all parameters as is, leave the **Store a copy of the data in the form template** check box deselected, name the data connection **SetCellA1**, and deselect the **Automatically retrieve data when form is opened** check box. You will use this data connection to set the value of a cell in the Excel workbook to be equal to the value specified in the **cellValue** text box on the form. You will use a rule later to set the values of the parameters of the **SetCellA1** operation before making the web service call.

10. Select **Data ➤ Get External Data ➤ From Web Service ➤ From SOAP Web Service** to add a **Receive** data connection for the **CloseWorkbook** operation of the Excel Services web service. Leave the **sessionId** parameter as is, leave the **Store a copy of the data in the form template** check box deselected, name the data connection **CloseWorkbook**, and deselect the **Automatically retrieve data when form is opened** check box. You will use this data connection to close the Excel workbook and Excel Services session.

11. Add an **Action** rule to the **Send To Excel** button in the repeating table with the following 9 actions:

```
Set a field's value: cellValue = eval(eval(., 'concat(my:field1, "|",
my:field2, "|", my:field3)'), "..")
```

where **cellValue** is the hidden field in the Main data source. Note that the **eval()** and **concat()** functions are used to concatenate the values of **field1**, **field2**, and **field3** that are located in the repeating table and separate them with pipe (|) symbols, since the Excel workbook expects the data from a repeating table row to be sent in this format.

```
Query using a data connection: OpenWorkbookForEditing
```

This action calls the **OpenWorkbookForEditing** web service operation to retrieve a session ID.

```
Set a field's value: sessionId = OpenWorkbookForEditingResult
```

where **sessionId** is located under the **SetCellA1** group node under the **queryFields** group node in the **SetCellA1** secondary data source and

OpenWorkbookForEditingResult is located under the
OpenWorkbookForEditingResponse group node under the **dataFields** group
node in the **OpenWorkbookForEditing** secondary data source.

```
Set a field's value: sheetName = "Sheet1"
```

where **sheetName** is located under the **SetCellA1** group node under the
queryFields group node in the **SetCellA1** secondary data source and **Sheet1** is a
static piece of text representing the name of the worksheet in the Excel workbook
where the data is stored. Note that you could also provide an extra field on the form
so that the name of the worksheet can be dynamically changed by users at runtime.

```
Set a field's value: rangeName = cellReference
```

where **rangeName** is located under the **SetCellA1** group node under the
queryFields group node in the **SetCellA1** secondary data source and **cellReference**
is located in the Main data source of the form.

```
Set a field's value: cellValue = cellValue
```

where the first **cellValue** is located under the **SetCellA1** group node under the
queryFields group node in the **SetCellA1** secondary data source and the second
cellValue is located in the Main data source of the form.

```
Query using a data connection: SetCellA1
```

This action calls the **SetCellA1** web service operation to update the value of a cell in
the Excel workbook.

```
Set a field's value: sessionId = OpenWorkbookForEditingResult
```

where **sessionId** is located under the **CloseWorkbook** group node under the
queryFields group node in the **CloseWorkbook** secondary data source and
OpenWorkbookForEditingResult is located under the
OpenWorkbookForEditingResponse group node under the **dataFields** group
node in the **OpenWorkbookForEditing** secondary data source.

```
Query using a data connection: CloseWorkbook
```

This action closes the workbook and the Excel Services session.

12. Publish the form template to a SharePoint form library.

In SharePoint, navigate to the form library where you published the form template and
add a new form. When the form opens, enter the name of a cell in the Excel workbook to
which you want to send data (for example **A1**) in the **cellReference** field. Add a row to
the repeating table, fill its fields with data, and then click the **Send To Excel** button in
the same row. Enter the name of another cell (for example **A2**) in the **cellReference** field.
Add another row to the repeating table, fill its fields with data, and then click the **Send
To Excel** button in the same row. Navigate to the document library that contains the

SendRepeatingTableToExcel.xlsx Excel workbook, open the workbook, and verify that the workbook contains the data sent from the repeating table rows and that the formulas correctly parsed and stored the data in the different columns.

Discussion

In the solution described above, you saw how to use Excel formulas to parse data that was sent from a repeating table row on an InfoPath form and split the data into columns in Excel. The Excel formulas combined the **FIND**, **MID**, and **LEN** functions to parse and split values. Such Excel formulas can become quite complex.

If you do not want to use complex formulas in Excel to parse data and split it into cells, and you do not mind parsing the data manually, you can combine the technique of passing individual rows of a repeating table to Excel along with the **Text to Columns** command in Excel to parse and split the data into separate rows and columns.

How this would work is that you can follow all of the steps outlined in the solution above, but skip the first step. Then after you have transferred data from repeating table rows to the Excel workbook, you must open the workbook in Excel and do the following:

1. Select all of the cells (for example **A1**, **A2**, and **A3**) that contain data from repeating table rows. This data should contain the values for the fields in the repeating table separated by pipe (|) symbols.

2. Click **Data ➤ Data Tools ➤ Text To Columns**.

3. On the **Convert Text to Columns Wizard**, leave the **Delimited** option selected, and click **Next**.

4. On the **Convert Text to Columns Wizard**, select the **Other** check box (deselect all other check boxes if there are any selected), enter a pipe (|) symbol into the text box behind the **Other** check box, and click **Next**.

5. On the **Convert Text to Columns Wizard**, accept the **Destination** cell or select a different **Destination** cell if you wish. This cell represents the cell in the top-left corner in a range of destination cells on the Excel worksheet where the converted data should be placed.

6. On the **Convert Text to Columns Wizard**, click **Finish**.

The previously concatenated repeating table data should now be located in separate rows and columns on the Excel worksheet.

The sequence of Excel Services SOAP web service calls to update the value of a cell in an Excel workbook with data from a repeating table row on an InfoPath form is as follows:

1. Call **OpenWorkbookForEditing** to get an Excel Services session ID, which allows you to edit the Excel workbook.

2. Call **SetCell** or **SetCellA1** to update the value of a cell in the Excel workbook.

3. Call **CloseWorkbook** to save the changes made to the workbook, close the workbook, and end the Excel Services session.

Note:

> When you use the **OpenWorkbookForEditing** web service operation to open an Excel workbook for editing, you generally do not need to explicitly call the **SaveWorkbook** operation to save the changes made to the workbook before calling the **CloseWorkbook** operation to close the workbook, since any changes made to the workbook should automatically and permanently be stored in the workbook when you close it. But if the changes you made are not being persisted in your workbook, you may want to try adding the **SaveWorkbook** operation (see for example recipe *20 Update an Excel chart on an InfoPath form*) just before calling the **CloseWorkbook** operation to see whether the additional operation solves the issue.

In the next recipe you will learn a second way of parsing data from a repeating table row in InfoPath by using an array formula in Excel.

27   Send a repeating table row to Excel – method 2

Problem

You have a repeating table on an InfoPath form and want to send data that is contained in the fields of a specific row of the repeating table to an Excel workbook for storage.

Solution

You can use Excel Services SOAP web service operations to send data to an Excel workbook and then in the Excel workbook, use Excel formulas to retrieve and parse the data that was sent from a repeating table on an InfoPath form.

To send a repeating table row to Excel:

1. In Excel, create an Excel workbook that has the following horizontal array formula defined in cells **A1**, **B1**, and **C1** (*code #: 948C7BDA-0CA2-4914-BBD9-144B381AAC47*):

```
=MID(Sheet2!A1, VALUE(LEFT(MID(RIGHT(Sheet2!A1, 21), (COLUMN() - 1) * 7 +
1, 7),3)), VALUE(RIGHT(MID(RIGHT(Sheet2!A1, 21), (COLUMN() - 1) * 7 + 1,
7),3)))
```

Note that you must press **Shift+Ctrl+Enter** after entering the formula to create an array formula. Once you have defined the array formula, select cells **A1**, **B1**, and **C1**, hover over the lower right-hand corner of cell **C1** until the cursor becomes a cross, and then click and pull the cursor downwards to cover more rows. For example, the horizontal array formula should say:

```
=MID(Sheet2!A2, VALUE(LEFT(MID(RIGHT(Sheet2!A2, 21), (COLUMN() - 1) * 7 +
1, 7),3)), VALUE(RIGHT(MID(RIGHT(Sheet2!A2, 21), (COLUMN() - 1) * 7 + 1,
```

```
7),3)))
```

for cells **A2**, **B2**, and **C2**, and it should say:

```
=MID(Sheet2!A3, VALUE(LEFT(MID(RIGHT(Sheet2!A3, 21), (COLUMN() - 1) * 7 +
1, 7),3)), VALUE(RIGHT(MID(RIGHT(Sheet2!A3, 21), (COLUMN() - 1) * 7 + 1,
7),3)))
```

for cells **A3**, **B3**, and **C3**, etc. As you can see, the value for the first argument of the **MID** function now depends on the row in which the horizontal array formula is located. For example, the horizontal array formula in the first row gets its value from cell **A1** on **Sheet2**, the horizontal array formula in the second row gets its value from cell **A2** on **Sheet2**, etc. You will be passing strings to cells **A1**, **A2**, **A3**, etc. on **Sheet2** from a repeating table on an InfoPath form and then the horizontal array formulas should parse the data and place them in columns **A**, **B**, and **C** of **Sheet1**. Save the Excel workbook as **SendRepeatingTableToExcel.xlsx**. You can also download a file named **SendRepeatingTableToExcel-method2.xlsx** from www.bizsupportonline.com for use with this recipe.

2. Click **File ➤ Save & Send ➤ Save to SharePoint ➤ Save As** and save the entire workbook (including all of its sheets) to a document library (for example the **Shared Documents** library) on the SharePoint site to which the InfoPath form will be connecting (also see recipe *7 Publish an Excel workbook to SharePoint*).

3. In InfoPath, create a new browser-compatible form template or use an existing one.

4. Add a **Repeating Table** control with 4 columns to the view of the form template and name the fields within the repeating table **field1**, **field2**, **field3**, and **field4**, respectively.

5. Replace **field4** in the repeating table with a **Button** control and label the button **Send To Excel**. You can delete **field4** from the Main data source since you will not be using it.

6. Add a **Text Box** control to the view of the form template and name it **cellReference**. This text box will serve to enter a cell reference, for example **A1**, **A2**, **A3**, etc.

7. Select **Data ➤ Get External Data ➤ From Web Service ➤ From SOAP Web Service** to add a **Receive** data connection for the **OpenWorkbookForEditing** operation of the Excel Services web service (also see recipe *18 Get the value of an Excel cell in InfoPath* for detailed instructions on how to connect to the Excel Services SOAP web service) and configure its parameters as follows:

Parameter	Value
tns:workbookPath	http://servername/sitename/libraryname/ SendRepeatingTableToExcel.xlsx

where **servername** is the name of the SharePoint server, **sitename** is the name of the site, and **libraryname** is the name of the document library and Excel Services trusted file location where the **SendRepeatingTableToExcel.xlsx** Excel workbook is located.

---

tns:uiCultureName

---

tns:dataCultureName

Leave the **Store a copy of the data in the form template** check box deselected, name the data connection **OpenWorkbookForEditing**, and deselect the **Automatically retrieve data when form is opened** check box. You will use this data connection to open the Excel workbook and get a session ID that you can use for all subsequent calls you make to Excel Services.

8. Select **Data ➤ Get External Data ➤ From Web Service ➤ From SOAP Web Service** to add a **Receive** data connection for the **SetCellA1** operation of the Excel Services web service (also see recipe *19 Set the value of an Excel cell in InfoPath*). Leave all parameters as is, leave the **Store a copy of the data in the form template** check box deselected, name the data connection **SetCellA1**, and deselect the **Automatically retrieve data when form is opened** check box. You will use this data connection to send the values from a row of the repeating table to a cell in the Excel workbook. You will use a rule later to set the values of the parameters of the **SetCellA1** operation before making the web service call.

9. Select **Data ➤ Get External Data ➤ From Web Service ➤ From SOAP Web Service** to add a **Receive** data connection for the **CloseWorkbook** operation of the Excel Services web service. Leave the **sessionId** parameter as is, leave the **Store a copy of the data in the form template** check box deselected, name the data connection **CloseWorkbook**, and deselect the **Automatically retrieve data when form is opened** check box. You will use this data connection to close the Excel workbook and Excel Services session.

10. Add an **Action** rule to the **Send To Excel** button in the repeating table with the following 8 actions:

```
Query using a data connection: OpenWorkbookForEditing
```

This action calls the **OpenWorkbookForEditing** web service operation to retrieve a session ID.

```
Set a field's value: sessionId = OpenWorkbookForEditingResult
```

where **sessionId** is located under the **SetCellA1** group node under the **queryFields** group node in the **SetCellA1** secondary data source and

OpenWorkbookForEditingResult is located under the
OpenWorkbookForEditingResponse group node under the **dataFields** group
node in the **OpenWorkbookForEditing** secondary data source.

```
Set a field's value: sheetName = "Sheet2"
```

where **sheetName** is located under the **SetCellA1** group node under the
queryFields group node in the **SetCellA1** secondary data source and **Sheet2** is a
static piece of text representing the worksheet in the Excel workbook where the data
is stored. In this case, the data from a repeating table row should be sent to a cell in
column **A** of **Sheet2** in the Excel workbook.

```
Set a field's value: rangeName = cellReference
```

where **rangeName** is located under the **SetCellA1** group node under the
queryFields group node in the **SetCellA1** secondary data source and **cellReference**
is located in the Main data source of the form.

```
Set a field's value: cellValue = concat(my:field1, my:field2, my:field3,
concat("001.", substring(concat("000", string-length(my:field1)), string-
length(concat("000", string-length(my:field1))) - 2, 3)),
concat(substring(concat("000", string-length(my:field1) + 1), string-
length(concat("000", string-length(my:field1) + 1)) - 2, 3), ".",
substring(concat("000", string-length(my:field2)), string-
length(concat("000", string-length(my:field2))) - 2, 3)),
concat(substring(concat("000", string-length(my:field1) + string-
length(my:field2) + 1), string-length(concat("000", string-
length(my:field1) + string-length(my:field2) + 1)) - 2, 3), ".",
substring(concat("000", string-length(my:field3)), string-
length(concat("000", string-length(my:field3))) - 2, 3)))
```

(*code #: 0FAF2460-DBD9-4C20-A81D-EA52E267D943*) where **cellValue** is located under
the **SetCellA1** group node under the **queryFields** group node in the **SetCellA1**
secondary data source and the formula is used to concatenate the values of **field1**,
field2, and **field3** that are located in the repeating table row with their starting
positions and lengths appended at the end of the string. For example, if the repeating
table contains the values "1" in **field1**, "test 1" in **field2**, and "test 2" in **field3**, the
string resulting from the formula should be "1test 1test 2001.001002.006008.006"
where the last 21 characters of the string represent the starting position and length of
each one of the 3 strings in the concatenated string. Such a string is fairly easy to
parse in Excel (also see the discussion section of recipe *9 Send repeating table data to
an Excel workbook for display in an Excel chart*).

```
Query using a data connection: SetCellA1
```

This action calls the **SetCellA1** web service operation to send the concatenated
string for the repeating table row to a cell in the Excel workbook.

```
Set a field's value: sessionId = OpenWorkbookForEditingResult
```

where **sessionId** is located under the **CloseWorkbook** group node under the

queryFields group node in the **CloseWorkbook** secondary data source and **OpenWorkbookForEditingResult** is located under the **OpenWorkbookForEditingResponse** group node under the **dataFields** group node in the **OpenWorkbookForEditing** secondary data source.

```
Query using a data connection: CloseWorkbook
```

This action closes the workbook and the Excel Services session.

11. Publish the form template to a SharePoint form library.

In SharePoint, navigate to the form library where you published the form template and add a new form. When the form opens, enter the name of a cell in the Excel workbook to which you want to send data (for example **A1**) in the **cellReference** text box. Add a row to the repeating table, fill its fields with data, and then click the **Send To Excel** button in the same row. Enter the name of another cell (for example **A2**) in the **cellReference** text box. Add another row to the repeating table, fill its fields with data, and then click the **Send To Excel** button in the same row. Navigate to the document library that contains the **SendRepeatingTableToExcel.xlsx** Excel workbook, open the workbook, and verify that the workbook contains the data sent from the repeating table rows and that the formulas correctly parsed and stored the data in the different columns.

Discussion

In the solution described above, you used a combination of string concatenation in InfoPath with string parsing in Excel similar to the technique discussed in recipe *9 Send repeating table data to an Excel workbook for display in an Excel chart* to send values from a particular row in a repeating table on an InfoPath form to a particular cell in an Excel workbook. While you used the **ROW** function in recipe *9 Send repeating table data to an Excel workbook for display in an Excel chart* to be able to parse a string passed from an InfoPath form and place the extracted values in a column of the Excel workbook through a vertical array formula, you used the **COLUMN** function in this recipe to parse a string passed from InfoPath and place the extracted values in a row of the Excel workbook through a horizontal array formula. And just like in recipe *9 Send repeating table data to an Excel workbook for display in an Excel chart*, you added the starting position and length of the value of each field in the repeating table row at the end of the concatenated string to make it easier to parse the data in Excel.

The main difference between this recipe and recipe *9 Send repeating table data to an Excel workbook for display in an Excel chart* is the InfoPath formula used to construct the concatenated string that is passed to Excel. Because you do not have to loop through rows of a repeating table but rather only concatenate values from one particular row in the repeating table, you do not have to use the **eval()** function, but can suffice with using a combination of the **concat()**, **substring()**, and **string-length()** functions in InfoPath to generate the concatenated string.

Note that instead of opening an Excel Services session, saving the workbook, and closing the workbook and Excel Services session every time a button in the repeating table is clicked, you could also for example:

1. Call **OpenWorkbookForEditing** to open the Excel Services session when the form loads.

2. Call **SetCellA1** when the button in a repeating table row is clicked.

3. Provide a separate button that calls **CloseWorkbook** to save the changes made to the workbook, close the workbook, and close the Excel Services session. Another option is to call **CloseWorkbook** when you submit the form.

Note:

> When you use the **OpenWorkbookForEditing** web service operation to open an Excel workbook for editing, you generally do not need to explicitly call the **SaveWorkbook** operation to save the changes made to the workbook before calling the **CloseWorkbook** operation to close the workbook, since any changes made to the workbook should automatically and permanently be stored in the workbook when you close it. But if the changes you made are not being persisted in your workbook, you may want to try adding the **SaveWorkbook** operation (see for example recipe *20 Update an Excel chart on an InfoPath form*) just before calling the **CloseWorkbook** operation to see whether the additional operation solves the issue.

28 Send an entire repeating table to Excel – method 1

Problem

You have a repeating table on an InfoPath form and want to send the data that is contained in the fields of the repeating table to an Excel workbook that is stored in SharePoint.

Solution

You can use Excel Services SOAP web service operations to send data to an Excel workbook and then in the Excel workbook, use a macro to parse the data that was sent from a repeating table on an InfoPath form and place that data in cells in the Excel workbook.

To send an entire repeating table to Excel:

1. In Excel, create an Excel workbook or use an existing one. In this solution, the repeating table data is going to be sent to cell **A1** on **Sheet1** in the Excel workbook. Name the Excel workbook **ParseRepeatingTable.xlsx**. Because Excel Services

does not support macros in Excel workbooks and because a workbook that contains a VBA project cannot be edited through Excel Services, you must save the Excel workbook as a macro-free workbook. You will add and remove a macro to parse the data from the repeating table later.

2. Click **File ➤ Save & Send ➤ Save to SharePoint ➤ Save As** and save the entire workbook (including all of its sheets) to a document library (for example the **Shared Documents** library) on the SharePoint site to which the InfoPath form will be connecting (also see recipe *7 Publish an Excel workbook to SharePoint*).

3. In InfoPath, create a new browser-compatible form template or use an existing one.

4. Add a **Repeating Table** control with 3 columns to the view of the form template and name the fields within the repeating table **field1**, **field2**, and **field3**, respectively.

5. Add a **Button** control to the view of the form template and label it **Send To Excel**.

6. Select **Data ➤ Get External Data ➤ From Web Service ➤ From SOAP Web Service** to add a **Receive** data connection for the **OpenWorkbookForEditing** operation of the Excel Services web service (also see recipe *18 Get the value of an Excel cell in InfoPath* for detailed instructions on how to connect to the Excel Services SOAP web service) and configure its parameters as follows:

Parameter	Value

tns:workbookPath	`http://servername/sitename/libraryname/ParseRepea`
	`tingTable.xlsx`
	
	where **servername** is the name of the SharePoint server, **sitename** is the name of the site, and **libraryname** is the name of the document library and Excel Services trusted file location where the **ParseRepeatingTable.xlsx** Excel workbook is located.

tns:uiCultureName	
tns:dataCultureName	

Leave the **Store a copy of the data in the form template** check box deselected, name the data connection **OpenWorkbookForEditing**, and deselect the **Automatically retrieve data when form is opened** check box. You will use this data connection to open the Excel workbook and get a session ID that you can use for all subsequent calls you make to Excel Services.

7. Select **Data ➤ Get External Data ➤ From Web Service ➤ From SOAP Web Service** to add a **Receive** data connection for the **SetCellA1** operation of the Excel

Services web service (also see recipe *19 Set the value of an Excel cell in InfoPath*). Leave all parameters as is, leave the **Store a copy of the data in the form template** check box deselected, name the data connection **SetCellA1**, and deselect the **Automatically retrieve data when form is opened** check box. You will use this data connection to set the value of cell **A1** on **Sheet1** in the Excel workbook to be equal to the value specified in the **cellValue** field in the **SetCellA1** secondary data source. You will use a rule later to set the values of the parameters of the **SetCellA1** operation before making the web service call.

8. Select **Data ➤ Get External Data ➤ From Web Service ➤ From SOAP Web Service** to add a **Receive** data connection for the **CloseWorkbook** operation of the Excel Services web service. Leave the **sessionId** parameter as is, leave the **Store a copy of the data in the form template** check box deselected, name the data connection **CloseWorkbook**, and deselect the **Automatically retrieve data when form is opened** check box. You will use this data connection to close the Excel workbook and Excel Services session.

9. Add an **Action** rule to the **Send To Excel** button with the following 8 actions:

    ```
    Query using a data connection: OpenWorkbookForEditing
    ```

    This action calls the **OpenWorkbookForEditing** web service operation to retrieve a session ID.

    ```
    Set a field's value: sessionId = OpenWorkbookForEditingResult
    ```

    where **sessionId** is located under the **SetCellA1** group node under the **queryFields** group node in the **SetCellA1** secondary data source and **OpenWorkbookForEditingResult** is located under the **OpenWorkbookForEditingResponse** group node under the **dataFields** group node in the **OpenWorkbookForEditing** secondary data source.

    ```
    Set a field's value: sheetName = "Sheet1"
    ```

    where **sheetName** is located under the **SetCellA1** group node under the **queryFields** group node in the **SetCellA1** secondary data source and **Sheet1** is a static piece of text representing the name of the worksheet in the Excel workbook where the data is stored. Note that you could also provide an extra field on the form so that the value of the worksheet can be dynamically changed by users at runtime.

    ```
    Set a field's value: rangeName = "A1"
    ```

    where **rangeName** is located under the **SetCellA1** group node under the **queryFields** group node in the **SetCellA1** secondary data source and **A1** is a static piece of text representing the name of the cell on the worksheet in the Excel workbook that should receive the data. Note that you could also provide an extra field on the form so that the name of the cell can be dynamically changed by users at runtime.

    ```
    Set a field's value: cellValue = eval(eval(group2, 'concat(my:field1, "|",
    ```

```
my:field2, "|", my:field3, ";")'), "..")
```

where **cellValue** is located under the **SetCellA1** group node under the **queryFields** group node in the **SetCellA1** secondary data source. Note that the **eval()** and **concat()** functions are used to concatenate the values of **field1**, **field2**, and **field3** that are located in the repeating table and separate them with pipe (|) symbols. The rows of the repeating table are separated with semi-colons (;). The Excel workbook expects the data from the repeating table row to be sent in this format.

```
Query using a data connection: SetCellA1
```

This action calls the **SetCellA1** web service operation to update the value of cell **A1** on **Sheet1** in the Excel workbook.

```
Set a field's value: sessionId = OpenWorkbookForEditingResult
```

where **sessionId** is located under the **CloseWorkbook** group node under the **queryFields** group node in the **CloseWorkbook** secondary data source and **OpenWorkbookForEditingResult** is located under the **OpenWorkbookForEditingResponse** group node under the **dataFields** group node in the **OpenWorkbookForEditing** secondary data source.

```
Query using a data connection: CloseWorkbook
```

This action closes the workbook and the Excel Services session.

10. Publish the form template to a SharePoint form library.

In SharePoint, navigate to the form library where you published the form template and add a new form. Add a couple of rows to the repeating table, fill the fields with data, and then click the **Send To Excel** button. Close the form and then navigate to the SharePoint document library where the **ParseRepeatingTable.xlsx** Excel workbook is located. Open the Excel workbook in Excel and verify that cell **A1** on **Sheet1** contains the concatenated string from the repeating table.

To parse the repeating table data in Excel using VBA code in a macro:

1. In Excel, click **Developer ➤ Code ➤ Macros**. If the **Developer** tab is not present on the Ribbon, click **File ➤ Options**, on the **Excel Options** dialog box, click **Customize Ribbon**, and then on the right-hand side of the dialog box, select **Main Tabs** from the **Customize the Ribbon** drop-down list box, ensure that the **Developer** check box is selected, and then click **OK**.

2. On the **Macro** dialog box, enter **ParseRepeatingTable** in the **Macro name** text box, select **This Workbook** from the **Macros in** drop-down list box, and then click **Create**. This should open Microsoft Visual Basic for Applications.

3. In Microsoft Visual Basic for Applications, add the following code to the ParseRepeatingTable() procedure in **Module1** (*code #: 10B5E914-4BC7-4684-B906-CD5741DA1DAB*):

```
Dim rtRows() As String
Dim rtCells() As String
Dim startingRowIndex As Integer
Dim startingColIndex As Integer

startingRowIndex = 0
startingColIndex = 0

If Selection.Areas.Count > 0 Then
   startingRowIndex = Selection.Areas(1).Cells(1, 1).Row
   startingColIndex = Selection.Areas(1).Cells(1, 1).Column
End If

rtRows = Split(Sheet1.Range("A1").Value, ";")

For i = 0 To UBound(rtRows) - 1

  rtCells = Split(rtRows(i), "|")

  For j = 0 To UBound(rtCells)

    Sheet1.Range( _
      Cells(startingRowIndex + i, startingColIndex + j), _
      Cells(startingRowIndex + i, startingColIndex + j)) _
      .Value = rtCells(j)

  Next j

Next i
```

4. Switch back to Excel and select a cell, for example **B1**.

5. Click **Developer ➤ Code ➤ Macros**.

6. On the **Macro** dialog box, select **ParseRepeatingTable**, and then click **Run**.

7. Click **Developer ➤ Code ➤ Macros**.

8. On the **Macro** dialog box, select **ParseRepeatingTable**, and then click **Delete**.

9. On the **Microsoft Excel** dialog box, click **Yes** to confirm that you want to delete the macro.

10. Click **File ➤ Save** to save the Excel workbook back to SharePoint.

11. On the **Microsoft Excel** dialog box, click **Yes** to save the workbook as a macro-free workbook.

Discussion

In the solution described above, you saw how to use Excel Services SOAP web service operations to save the concatenated values from rows of a repeating table to a cell in an Excel workbook, and then use a macro afterwards to parse the data and place the repeating table values into separate cells in the Excel workbook.

The sequence of Excel Services SOAP web service calls to send the concatenated values from rows of the repeating table to a cell in the Excel workbook was as follows:

1. Call **OpenWorkbookForEditing** to get an Excel Services session ID, which allowed you to open the Excel workbook with the purpose of editing it.

2. Call **SetCellA1** to update the value of cell **A1** on **Sheet1** in the Excel workbook. You could have also used **SetCell** instead of **SetCellA1** to achieve the same result.

3. Call **CloseWorkbook** to save the changes made to the workbook, close the workbook, and end the Excel Services session.

Note:

> When you use the **OpenWorkbookForEditing** web service operation to open an Excel workbook for editing, you generally do not need to explicitly call the **SaveWorkbook** operation to save the changes made to the workbook before calling the **CloseWorkbook** operation to close the workbook, since any changes made to the workbook should automatically and permanently be stored in the workbook when you close it. But if the changes you made are not being persisted in your workbook, you may want to try adding the **SaveWorkbook** operation (see for example recipe *20 Update an Excel chart on an InfoPath form*) just before calling the **CloseWorkbook** operation to see whether the additional operation solves the issue.

The VBA code in the macro first gets the row number and column number of the cell in the upper-left corner of a selected range of cells in the workbook.

```
If Selection.Areas.Count > 0 Then
  startingRowIndex = Selection.Areas(1).Cells(1, 1).Row
  startingColIndex = Selection.Areas(1).Cells(1, 1).Column
End If
```

The code then parses the concatenated string of the repeating table by splitting the values using a semi-colon (;) as the data separator.

```
rtRows = Split(Sheet1.Range("A1").Value, ";")
```

This returns an array of strings that represent the concatenated values in each row of the repeating table. The code loops through the concatenated strings for the rows thereby parsing each row by splitting the values using a pipe (|) symbol as the data separator.

```
For i = 0 To UBound(rtRows) - 1

  rtCells = Split(rtRows(i), "|")

  ...

Next i
```

This returns an array of strings that represent the individual fields in a row of the repeating table. Finally, the code loops through the fields and uses the `Value` property of the `Range` property of the `Sheet1` object to set the value of each cell on the worksheet in a particular row to be equal to the value of one of the fields in the repeating table.

```
For j = 0 To UBound(rtCells)

  Sheet1.Range( _
    Cells(startingRowIndex + i, startingColIndex + j), _
    Cells(startingRowIndex + i, startingColIndex + j)) _
    .Value = rtCells(j)

Next j
```

If you do not want to or cannot write code, and you do not mind parsing the data manually, you can combine the technique of passing data from an entire repeating table as a concatenated string to the Excel workbook along with the **Text to Columns** and **Transpose** commands in Excel to parse and split the data into separate rows and columns.

How this would work is that you can follow all of the steps outlined in the solution above, but skip the last part where a macro must be created and run. Then after you have transferred the data from the repeating table to the Excel workbook, you must open the workbook in Excel and do the following assuming that sample repeating table data such as

```
1|2|3;A2|B2|C2;
```

was passed to cell **A1** in the Excel workbook:

1. Select cell **A1**.

2. Click **Data ➤ Data Tools ➤ Text To Columns**.

3. On the **Convert Text to Columns Wizard**, select the **Delimited** option, and click **Next**.

4. On the **Convert Text to Columns Wizard**, select the **Semicolon** check box (deselect all other check boxes if there are any selected), and click **Next**.

5. On the **Convert Text to Columns Wizard**, accept the **Destination** cell or select a different **Destination** cell if you wish. This cell represents the cell in the top-left corner in a range of destination cells on the Excel worksheet where the converted data should be placed.

6. On the **Convert Text to Columns Wizard**, click **Finish**. After this the text

    ```
    1|2|3
    ```

    should be located in the first column (**A1** if you accepted the default destination), and the text

A2 | B2 | C2

should be located in the second column (**B1** if you accepted the default destination).

7. Select the cells that contain the data (cells **A1** and **B1** if you accepted the default destination), and then click **Home ➤ Clipboard ➤ Copy**.

8. Select another cell (for example cell **A5**) and then select **Home ➤ Clipboard ➤ Paste ➤ Transpose (T)**.

Figure 54. The Transpose command under the Paste command in Excel 2010.

After this the text

1 | 2 | 3

should be located in the first row (cell **A5** if you followed the example), and the text

A2 | B2 | C2

should be located in the second row (cell **A6** if you followed the example).

9. Select cells **A5** and **A6**.

10. Click **Data ➤ Data Tools ➤ Text To Columns**.

11. On the **Convert Text to Columns Wizard**, leave the **Delimited** option selected, and click **Next**.

12. On the **Convert Text to Columns Wizard**, select the **Other** check box (deselect all other check boxes if there are any selected), enter a pipe (|) symbol into the text box behind the **Other** check box, and click **Next**.

13. On the **Convert Text to Columns Wizard**, accept the **Destination** cell or select a different **Destination** cell if you wish. This cell represents the cell in the top-left corner in a range of destination cells on the Excel worksheet where the converted data should be placed.

14. On the **Convert Text to Columns Wizard**, click **Finish**.

The previously concatenated repeating table data should now be located in separate rows and columns on the Excel worksheet.

In the next recipe, you will learn how you can automate sending repeating table data to an Excel workbook without having to perform any manual steps by making use of relatively complex formulas in InfoPath and array formulas in Excel.

29 Send an entire repeating table to Excel – method 2

Problem

You have a repeating table on an InfoPath form and want to send the data that is contained in rows and columns of the repeating table to an Excel workbook that is stored in SharePoint.

Solution

You can use Excel Services SOAP web service operations to send data to an Excel workbook and then in the Excel workbook, use an array formula to parse the data that was sent from a repeating table on an InfoPath form and place that data in cells in the Excel workbook.

To send an entire repeating table to Excel:

1. In Excel, create an Excel workbook or use an existing one. This solution makes use of the same technique described in recipe *9 Send repeating table data to an Excel workbook for display in an Excel chart* to parse repeating table data, so you can refer to the aforementioned recipe for background information about the technique used here. Repeating table data is going to be sent to cells **A1**, **B1**, and **C1** on **Sheet2** in the Excel workbook. These cells expect to receive data in the following format:

    ```
    Value 1Value 2Value 3001.007008.007015.007003
    ```

    Add the following vertical array formula to cells **A1** through **A10** on **Sheet1** (*code #: 980F3BBD-D11D-4C36-9F2E-12B4BB93B31E*):

    ```
    =MID(Sheet2!A1, LEFT(MID(MID(Sheet2!A1, LEN(Sheet2!A1) - 3 -
    VALUE(RIGHT(Sheet2!A1, 3))*7 + 1, VALUE(RIGHT(Sheet2!A1, 3))*7), (ROW()-
    1)*7+1, 7), 3), RIGHT(MID(MID(Sheet2!A1, LEN(Sheet2!A1) - 3 -
    VALUE(RIGHT(Sheet2!A1, 3))*7 + 1, VALUE(RIGHT(Sheet2!A1, 3))*7), (ROW()-
    1)*7+1, 7), 3))
    ```

    Note that you must press **Shift+Ctrl+Enter** after entering the formula to create an array formula. Cells **A1** through **A10** on **Sheet1** will contain all of the values from the rows in the first column of the repeating table on the InfoPath form.

    Add the following vertical array formula to cells **B1** through **B10** on **Sheet1** (*code #: 980F3BBD-D11D-4C36-9F2E-12B4BB93B31E*):

    ```
    =MID(Sheet2!B1, LEFT(MID(MID(Sheet2!B1, LEN(Sheet2!B1) - 3 -
    VALUE(RIGHT(Sheet2!B1, 3))*7 + 1, VALUE(RIGHT(Sheet2!B1, 3))*7), (ROW()-
    1)*7+1, 7), 3), RIGHT(MID(MID(Sheet2!B1, LEN(Sheet2!B1) - 3 -
    VALUE(RIGHT(Sheet2!B1, 3))*7 + 1, VALUE(RIGHT(Sheet2!B1, 3))*7), (ROW()-
    1)*7+1, 7), 3))
    ```

    Note that you must press **Shift+Ctrl+Enter** after entering the formula to create an array formula. Cells **B1** through **B10** on **Sheet1** will contain all of the values from the rows in the second column of the repeating table on the InfoPath form.

Add the following vertical array formula to cells **C1** through **C10** on **Sheet1** (*code #: 980F3BBD-D11D-4C36-9F2E-12B4BB93B31E*):

```
=MID(Sheet2!C1, LEFT(MID(MID(Sheet2!C1, LEN(Sheet2!C1) - 3 -
VALUE(RIGHT(Sheet2!C1, 3))*7 + 1, VALUE(RIGHT(Sheet2!C1, 3))*7), (ROW()-
1)*7+1, 7), 3), RIGHT(MID(MID(Sheet2!C1, LEN(Sheet2!C1) - 3 -
VALUE(RIGHT(Sheet2!C1, 3))*7 + 1, VALUE(RIGHT(Sheet2!C1, 3))*7), (ROW()-
1)*7+1, 7), 3))
```

Note that you must press **Shift+Ctrl+Enter** after entering the formula to create an array formula. Cells **C1** through **C10** on **Sheet1** will contain all of the values from the rows in the third column of the repeating table on the InfoPath form. Name the Excel workbook **ParseRepeatingTable.xlsx**. You can also download a file named **ParseRepeatingTable.xlsx** from www.bizsupportonline.com for use with this recipe.

2.   Click **File ➤ Save & Send ➤ Save to SharePoint ➤ Save As** and save the entire workbook (including all of its sheets) to a document library (for example the **Shared Documents** library) on the SharePoint site to which the InfoPath form will be connecting (also see recipe *7 Publish an Excel workbook to SharePoint*).

3.   In InfoPath, create a new browser-compatible form template or use an existing one.

4.   Add a **Repeating Table** control with 3 columns to the view of the form template and name the fields within the repeating table **field1**, **field2**, and **field3**, respectively.

5.   Add a **Button** control to the view of the form template and label it **Send To Excel**.

6.   Select **Data ➤ Get External Data ➤ From Web Service ➤ From SOAP Web Service** to add a **Receive** data connection for the **OpenWorkbookForEditing** operation of the Excel Services web service (also see recipe *18 Get the value of an Excel cell in InfoPath* for detailed instructions on how to connect to the Excel Services SOAP web service) and configure its parameters as follows:

Parameter	Value
tns:workbookPath	`http://servername/sitename/libraryname/ParseRepea` `tingTable.xlsx`
	where **servername** is the name of the SharePoint server, **sitename** is the name of the site, and **libraryname** is the name of the document library and Excel Services trusted file location where the **ParseRepeatingTable.xlsx** Excel workbook is located.

tns:uiCultureName
tns:dataCultureName

Leave the **Store a copy of the data in the form template** check box deselected, name the data connection **OpenWorkbookForEditing**, and deselect the **Automatically retrieve data when form is opened** check box. You will use this data connection to open the Excel workbook and get a session ID that you can use for all subsequent calls you make to Excel Services.

7. Select **Data ➤ Get External Data ➤ From Web Service ➤ From SOAP Web Service** to add a **Receive** data connection for the **SetCellA1** operation of the Excel Services web service (also see recipe *19 Set the value of an Excel cell in InfoPath*). Leave all parameters as is, leave the **Store a copy of the data in the form template** check box deselected, name the data connection **SetCellA1**, and deselect the **Automatically retrieve data when form is opened** check box. You will use this data connection to set the values of cells **A1**, **B1**, and **C1** on **Sheet2** in the Excel workbook to be equal to the concatenated values from the repeating table on the InfoPath form. You will use a rule later to set the values of the parameters of the **SetCellA1** operation before making the web service call.

8. Select **Data ➤ Get External Data ➤ From Web Service ➤ From SOAP Web Service** to add a **Receive** data connection for the **CloseWorkbook** operation of the Excel Services web service. Leave the **sessionId** parameter as is, leave the **Store a copy of the data in the form template** check box deselected, name the data connection **CloseWorkbook**, and deselect the **Automatically retrieve data when form is opened** check box. You will use this data connection to close the Excel workbook and Excel Services session.

9. Add an **Action** rule to the **Send To Excel** button with the following 14 actions:

    ```
    Query using a data connection: OpenWorkbookForEditing
    ```

    This action calls the **OpenWorkbookForEditing** web service operation to retrieve a session ID.

    ```
    Set a field's value: sessionId = OpenWorkbookForEditingResult
    ```

    where **sessionId** is located under the **SetCellA1** group node under the **queryFields** group node in the **SetCellA1** secondary data source and **OpenWorkbookForEditingResult** is located under the **OpenWorkbookForEditingResponse** group node under the **dataFields** group node in the **OpenWorkbookForEditing** secondary data source.

    ```
    Set a field's value: sheetName = "Sheet2"
    ```

    where **sheetName** is located under the **SetCellA1** group node under the **queryFields** group node in the **SetCellA1** secondary data source and **Sheet2** is a static piece of text representing the name of the worksheet in the Excel workbook where the original data from the repeating table is stored.

```
Set a field's value: rangeName = "A1"
```

where **rangeName** is located under the **SetCellA1** group node under the **queryFields** group node in the **SetCellA1** secondary data source and **A1** is a static piece of text representing the name of the cell on the worksheet in the Excel workbook that should receive the data.

```
Set a field's value: cellValue =
concat(xdMath:Eval(xdMath:Eval(my:group1/my:group2, "my:field1"), ".."),
xdMath:Eval(xdMath:Eval(my:group1/my:group2,
'concat(substring(concat("000", sum(xdMath:Eval(preceding::my:field1,
"string-length(.)")) + 1), string-length(concat("000",
sum(xdMath:Eval(preceding::my:field1, "string-length(.)")) + 1)) - 2, 3),
".", substring(concat("000", string-length(my:field1)), string-
length(concat("000", string-length(my:field1))) - 2, 3))'), ".."),
substring(concat("000", count(my:group1/my:group2)), string-
length(concat("000", count(my:group1/my:group2))) - 2, 3))
```

(*code #: D7400AB8-09DF-413B-A29B-C22EBC1F1CB5*) where **cellValue** is located under the **SetCellA1** group node under the **queryFields** group node in the **SetCellA1** secondary data source. Refer to recipe *9 Send repeating table data to an Excel workbook for display in an Excel chart* for an explanation of how the formula is constructed. The basic idea is that this formula loops through all of the **field1** fields in the rows of the repeating table and concatenates them to form a string such as for example "First sentenceSecond sentenceLast sentence001.014015.015030.013003", which can then be parsed in the Excel workbook.

```
Query using a data connection: SetCellA1
```

This action calls the **SetCellA1** web service operation to update the value of cell **A1** on **Sheet2** in the Excel workbook.

```
Set a field's value: rangeName = "B1"
```

where **rangeName** is located under the **SetCellA1** group node under the **queryFields** group node in the **SetCellA1** secondary data source and **B1** is a static piece of text representing the name of the cell on the worksheet in the Excel workbook that should receive the data.

```
Set a field's value: cellValue =
concat(xdMath:Eval(xdMath:Eval(my:group1/my:group2, "my:field2"), ".."),
xdMath:Eval(xdMath:Eval(my:group1/my:group2,
'concat(substring(concat("000", sum(xdMath:Eval(preceding::my:field2,
"string-length(.)")) + 1), string-length(concat("000",
sum(xdMath:Eval(preceding::my:field2, "string-length(.)")) + 1)) - 2, 3),
".", substring(concat("000", string-length(my:field2)), string-
length(concat("000", string-length(my:field2))) - 2, 3))'), ".."),
substring(concat("000", count(my:group1/my:group2)), string-
length(concat("000", count(my:group1/my:group2))) - 2, 3))
```

(*code #: 37BE4434-2EED-4A30-B7E9-89EFFE76A156*) where **cellValue** is located under the **SetCellA1** group node under the **queryFields** group node in the **SetCellA1** secondary data source and the formula concatenates values from all of the **field2** fields in the repeating table.

```
Query using a data connection: SetCellA1
```

This action calls the **SetCellA1** web service operation to update the value of cell **B1** on **Sheet2** in the Excel workbook.

```
Set a field's value: rangeName = "C1"
```

where **rangeName** is located under the **SetCellA1** group node under the **queryFields** group node in the **SetCellA1** secondary data source and **C1** is a static piece of text representing the name of the cell on the worksheet in the Excel workbook that should receive the data.

```
Set a field's value: cellValue =
concat(xdMath:Eval(xdMath:Eval(my:group1/my:group2, "my:field3"), ".."),
xdMath:Eval(xdMath:Eval(my:group1/my:group2,
'concat(substring(concat("000", sum(xdMath:Eval(preceding::my:field3,
"string-length(.)")) + 1), string-length(concat("000",
sum(xdMath:Eval(preceding::my:field3, "string-length(.)")) + 1)) - 2, 3),
".", substring(concat("000", string-length(my:field3)), string-
length(concat("000", string-length(my:field3))) - 2, 3))'), ".."),
substring(concat("000", count(my:group1/my:group2)), string-
length(concat("000", count(my:group1/my:group2))) - 2, 3))
```

(*code #: C0300AE4-5B0D-47E5-8445-8611DC828268*) where **cellValue** is located under the **SetCellA1** group node under the **queryFields** group node in the **SetCellA1** secondary data source and the formula concatenates values from all of the **field3** fields in the repeating table.

```
Query using a data connection: SetCellA1
```

This action calls the **SetCellA1** web service operation to update the value of cell **C1** on **Sheet2** in the Excel workbook.

```
Set a field's value: sessionId = OpenWorkbookForEditingResult
```

where **sessionId** is located under the **CloseWorkbook** group node under the **queryFields** group node in the **CloseWorkbook** secondary data source and **OpenWorkbookForEditingResult** is located under the **OpenWorkbookForEditingResponse** group node under the **dataFields** group node in the **OpenWorkbookForEditing** secondary data source.

```
Query using a data connection: CloseWorkbook
```

This action closes the workbook and the Excel Services session.

10. Publish the form template to a SharePoint form library.

In SharePoint, navigate to the form library where you published the form template and add a new form. Add a couple of rows to the repeating table, fill the fields with data, and then click the **Send To Excel** button. Close the form and then navigate to the SharePoint document library where the **ParseRepeatingTable.xlsx** Excel workbook is located. Open the Excel workbook and verify that cells contain the data from the repeating table.

Discussion

In the solution described above, you saw how to use Excel Services SOAP web service operations to send the data from columns in a repeating table to separate cells in an Excel workbook, which then used vertical array formulas to parse and extract the data from the repeating table. The solution used a technique that was already discussed in recipe *9 Send repeating table data to an Excel workbook for display in an Excel chart*.

The sequence of Excel Services SOAP web service calls to update the Excel workbook was as follows:

1. Call **OpenWorkbookForEditing** to get an Excel Services session ID, which allowed you to open the Excel workbook with the purpose of editing it.

2. Call **SetCellA1** three times to update the values of cells **A1**, **B1**, and **C1** on **Sheet2** in the Excel workbook. You could have also used **SetCell** instead of **SetCellA1** to achieve the same result.

3. Call **CloseWorkbook** to save the changes made to the workbook, close the workbook, and end the Excel Services session.

Note:

> When you use the **OpenWorkbookForEditing** web service operation to open an Excel workbook for editing, you generally do not need to explicitly call the **SaveWorkbook** operation to save the changes made to the workbook before calling the **CloseWorkbook** operation to close the workbook, since any changes made to the workbook should automatically and permanently be stored in the workbook when you close it. But if the changes you made are not being persisted in your workbook, you may want to try adding the **SaveWorkbook** operation (see for example recipe *20 Update an Excel chart on an InfoPath form*) just before calling the **CloseWorkbook** operation to see whether the additional operation solves the issue.

Note that all cells for which no value can be calculated will be filled with the **#VALUE!** error value. And just like in recipe *9 Send repeating table data to an Excel workbook for display in an Excel chart*, you can replace this error value with a blank value by checking for errors using the **IF** and **ISERROR** functions as follows:

```
IF(ISERROR([original formula goes here]), "", [original formula goes here])
```

where you must replace **[original formula goes here]** with the Excel formulas from step 1. For example, the formula for column **A** on **Sheet1** in the Excel workbook would then become:

```
=IF(ISERROR(MID(Sheet2!A1,LEFT(MID(MID(Sheet2!A1,LEN(Sheet2!A1)-3-
VALUE(RIGHT(Sheet2!A1,3))*7+1,VALUE(RIGHT(Sheet2!A1,3))*7),(ROW()-
1)*7+1,7),3),RIGHT(MID(MID(Sheet2!A1,LEN(Sheet2!A1)-3-
VALUE(RIGHT(Sheet2!A1,3))*7+1,VALUE(RIGHT(Sheet2!A1,3))*7),(ROW()-
1)*7+1,7),3))), "", MID(Sheet2!A1,LEFT(MID(MID(Sheet2!A1,LEN(Sheet2!A1)-3-
VALUE(RIGHT(Sheet2!A1,3))*7+1,VALUE(RIGHT(Sheet2!A1,3))*7),(ROW()-
1)*7+1,7),3),RIGHT(MID(MID(Sheet2!A1,LEN(Sheet2!A1)-3-
VALUE(RIGHT(Sheet2!A1,3))*7+1,VALUE(RIGHT(Sheet2!A1,3))*7),(ROW()-1)*7+1,7),3)))
```

Run Formulas through Excel Services

30 Add the URL of a form as a link to an Excel workbook from within InfoPath

Problem

You have a few Excel workbooks stored in a SharePoint document library and you want to add a link of an existing InfoPath browser form to any one of those Excel workbooks by clicking on a button in an InfoPath form.

Solution

You can use the Excel Services SOAP web service to send a formula that makes use of the **HYPERLINK** function with the URL of an existing InfoPath form to an Excel workbook and then save the Excel workbook from within the InfoPath form.

To add the URL of a browser form as a link to an Excel workbook from within InfoPath:

1. In Excel, create a couple of workbooks, add a named range of one cell with a scope of **Workbook** (also see *How to create a named range in Excel* in the Appendix) to each one of the workbooks, name the named range **InfoPathLink**, and publish the workbooks to a document library (for example the **Shared Documents** library) on the SharePoint site to which the InfoPath form will be connecting (also see recipe *7 Publish an Excel workbook to SharePoint*). In SharePoint, ensure that the **Title** properties of all of the workbooks contain the actual file name (including the file extension) of each workbook.

2. In InfoPath, create a new browser-compatible form template or use an existing one.

3. Select **Data ➤ Get External Data ➤ From SharePoint List** and follow the instructions to add a data connection to the SharePoint document library that contains the Excel workbooks. Ensure that you select the **ID** and **Title** fields to be

included in the data source, name the data connection **ExcelWorkbooks**, and leave the **Automatically retrieve data when form is opened** check box selected.

4. Add a **Drop-Down List Box** control to the view of the form template, name it **field1**, and configure it to get its items from the **ExcelWorkbooks** secondary data source with the **Title** field configured for both its **Value** and **Display name** properties.

5. Publish the form template to a SharePoint form library.

6. Select **Data ➤ Get External Data ➤ From SharePoint List** and follow the instructions to add a data connection to the SharePoint form library to which you published the form template. Ensure that you select the **ID** and **Title** fields to be included in the data source, select the **Include data for the active form only** check box, name the data connection **CurrentFormData**, and leave the **Automatically retrieve data when form is opened** check box selected. You will use this data connection to retrieve the name of the current form when a user opens an existing form in the browser. This name will be used to construct the link that should be added to the Excel workbook the user selects from the drop-down list box.

7. Select **Data ➤ Get External Data ➤ From Web Service ➤ From SOAP Web Service** to add a **Receive** data connection for the **OpenWorkbookForEditing** operation of the Excel Services web service (also see recipe *18 Get the value of an Excel cell in InfoPath* for detailed instructions on how to connect to the Excel Services SOAP web service), leave all of the parameters as is, leave the **Store a copy of the data in the form template** check box deselected, name the data connection **OpenWorkbookForEditing**, and deselect the **Automatically retrieve data when form is opened** check box. You will use this data connection to open the Excel workbook and get a session ID that you can use for all subsequent calls you make to Excel Services. Note that you will set the **workbookPath** parameter later through a rule, since the URL depends on the workbook that is selected from the drop-down list box.

8. Select **Data ➤ Get External Data ➤ From Web Service ➤ From SOAP Web Service** to add a **Receive** data connection for the **SetCellA1** operation of the Excel Services web service. Leave all parameters as is, leave the **Store a copy of the data in the form template** check box deselected, name the data connection **SetCellA1**, and deselect the **Automatically retrieve data when form is opened** check box. You will use this data connection to set the value of a named range named **InfoPathLink** that should exist in the Excel workbooks that a user can select from the drop-down list box to be equal to the URL of the form that the user currently has open. You will use a rule later to set the values of the parameters for the **SetCellA1** operation before making the web service call.

9. Select **Data ➤ Get External Data ➤ From Web Service ➤ From SOAP Web Service** to add a **Receive** data connection for the **CloseWorkbook** operation of the Excel Services web service. Leave the **sessionId** parameter as is, leave the **Store a copy of the data in the form template** check box deselected, name the data

connection **CloseWorkbook**, and deselect the **Automatically retrieve data when form is opened** check box. You will use this data connection to close the Excel workbook and Excel Services session.

10. Add a **Button** control to the view of the form template and label it **Add Form Link**.

11. Add an **Action** rule to the **Add Form Link** button with the following 9 actions:

```
Set a field's value: workbookPath =
concat("http://servername/sitename/libraryname/", field1)
```

where **workbookPath** is located under the **OpenWorkbookForEditing** group node under the **queryFields** group node in the **OpenWorkbookForEditing** secondary data source and **field1** is the field in the Main data source that is bound to the drop-down list box containing the titles of Excel workbooks. Note that the **concat()** function is used to construct the full URL of an Excel workbook that is selected from the drop-down list box. You must replace **servername**, **sitename**, and **libraryname** with the correct values for the SharePoint document library where the Excel workbooks are located and which you chose in step 1.

```
Query using a data connection: OpenWorkbookForEditing
```

This action calls the **OpenWorkbookForEditing** web service operation to retrieve a session ID.

```
Set a field's value: sessionId = OpenWorkbookForEditingResult
```

where **sessionId** is located under the **SetCellA1** group node under the **queryFields** group node in the **SetCellA1** secondary data source and **OpenWorkbookForEditingResult** is located under the **OpenWorkbookForEditingResponse** group node under the **dataFields** group node in the **OpenWorkbookForEditing** secondary data source.

```
Set a field's value: sheetName = ""
```

where **sheetName** is located under the **SetCellA1** group node under the **queryFields** group node in the **SetCellA1** secondary data source. This will clear the value of the **sheetName** field in the **SetCellA1** secondary data source. Because you defined a specific named range (**InfoPathLink**) with a scope of **Workbook** in each workbook and this named range could be located on any sheet in the workbook, you do not have to pass the sheet name to Excel; the named range that was defined should automatically be found.

```
Set a field's value: rangeName = "InfoPathLink"
```

where **rangeName** is located under the **SetCellA1** group node under the **queryFields** group node in the **SetCellA1** secondary data source and **InfoPathLink** is a static piece of text representing the name of the cell on the worksheet in the Excel workbook that should receive the data.

```
Set a field's value: cellValue = concat('=HYPERLINK("',
"http://servername/sitename/_layouts/FormServer.aspx?XmlLocation=/sitename/
libraryname/", Title, "&DefaultItemOpen=1", '", "InfoPathForm"')
```

where **cellValue** is located under the **SetCellA1** group node under the **queryFields** group node in the **SetCellA1** secondary data source. Note that the **concat()** function is used to construct an Excel formula that makes use of the **HYPERLINK** function. The first argument passed to the **HYPERLINK** function is the URL of the form that is currently open and which is constructed using a browser form URL where **libraryname** is the SharePoint form library to which you published the form template in step 5 (you must replace **servername**, **sitename**, and **libraryname** with the correct values for your own scenario), and **Title** is the **Title** field under the **SharePointListItem_RW** repeating group node under the **dataFields** group node in the **CurrentFormData** secondary data source. The second argument passed to the **HYPERLINK** function is a static piece of text (**InfoPathForm**) representing the friendly name that the hyperlink should get in the Excel workbook. Note that in this case an entire formula is sent to Excel instead of a value that should be used in a formula.

```
Query using a data connection: SetCellA1
```

This action calls the **SetCellA1** web service operation to update the value of the **InfoPathLink** named range in the Excel workbook.

```
Set a field's value: sessionId = OpenWorkbookForEditingResult
```

where **sessionId** is located under the **CloseWorkbook** group node under the **queryFields** group node in the **CloseWorkbook** secondary data source and **OpenWorkbookForEditingResult** is located under the **OpenWorkbookForEditingResponse** group node under the **dataFields** group node in the **OpenWorkbookForEditing** secondary data source.

```
Query using a data connection: CloseWorkbook
```

This action closes the workbook and the Excel Services session.

12. Add a **Formatting** rule to the **Add Form Link** button with a condition that says:

```
Number of occurrences of SharePointListItem_RW = 0
```

with a formatting of **Disable this control**. Here **SharePointListItem_RW** is the repeating group node located under the **dataFields** group node in the **CurrentFormData** secondary data source. You can construct the condition for the rule by using an expression such as the following:

```
count(xdXDocument:GetDOM("CurrentFormData")/dfs:myFields/dfs:dataFields/d:S
harePointListItem_RW) = 0
```

This formatting rule disables the button if the InfoPath form is a new form instead of an existing form.

13. Copy and paste the **Formatting** rule you just added onto the drop-down list box that contains the names of Excel workbooks.

14. Republish the form template to the same SharePoint form library you published the form template to in step 5.

In SharePoint, navigate to the form library where you published the form template and add a new form. When the form opens, the drop-down list box and button controls should be disabled. Save the form back to the form library, close it, and then reopen it. When the form opens, the drop-down list box and button controls should be enabled. Select an Excel workbook from the drop-down list box and click the **Add Form Link** button. Close the form. Navigate to the document library where the Excel workbook you added the form link to is located and open the workbook. Verify that it contains the link to the InfoPath form. Click on the link and verify that the form opens in the browser. Note that if you are using Excel Web Access to view the workbook, you may have to select **File ➤ Reload Workbook** to refresh the data in the workbook to see the latest changes that were made to the workbook.

Discussion

In the solution described above, you used the **HYPERLINK** function in Excel and Excel Services SOAP web service operations to add a link for an existing InfoPath browser form to an Excel workbook.

In this case, you selected an existing Excel workbook from a list of workbooks to add a link to. However, you could have also first created a new Excel workbook as described in recipe *23 Create a new Excel workbook in SharePoint from within an InfoPath form* and then updated the newly created workbook to contain a link to the existing InfoPath browser form with which the Excel workbook was created. This way you can easily use an InfoPath form to create a new Excel workbook that contains a link back to the original InfoPath form that created it.

The **HYPERLINK** function creates a shortcut or jump that opens a document stored on a network server, an intranet, or the Internet. When you click the cell that contains the **HYPERLINK** function, Excel opens the file that is stored at the location specified by the first argument of the function.

Note that while you used the **SetCell** or **SetCellA1** in other recipes in this book to set the value of a cell in an Excel workbook that could then be used to perform a calculation using an Excel formula in another cell in the Excel workbook (see for example recipe *19 Set the value of an Excel cell in InfoPath*), in this recipe you used the **SetCellA1** operation to directly set the value of a cell in an Excel workbook to be equal to an Excel formula.

```
Set a field's value: cellValue = concat('=HYPERLINK("',
"http://servername/sitename/_layouts/FormServer.aspx?XmlLocation=/sitename/libra
ryname/", Title, "&DefaultItemOpen=1", '"', "InfoPathForm"')
```

Note:

> When you use the **OpenWorkbookForEditing** web service operation to open an Excel workbook for editing, you generally do not need to explicitly call the **SaveWorkbook** operation to save the changes made to the workbook before calling the **CloseWorkbook** operation to close the workbook, since any changes made to the workbook should automatically and permanently be stored in the workbook when you close it. But if the changes you made are not being persisted in your workbook, you may want to try adding the **SaveWorkbook** operation (see for example recipe *20 Update an Excel chart on an InfoPath form*) just before calling the **CloseWorkbook** operation to see whether the additional operation solves the issue.

31 Validate that a date falls at least 7 business days before a due date

Problem

You have two date picker controls on an InfoPath form and you want the date that a user selects from the second date picker to always fall 7 business days or more before the date that the user selects from the first date picker.

Solution

You can use the Excel Services REST web service to send data to an Excel workbook and then in the Excel workbook use the **WORKDAY** function to perform a calculation and return the result to an InfoPath form through the REST web service call, so that you can use data validation to validate the data that was entered by a user.

To validate that a date falls at least 7 business days before a due date:

1. In Excel, create an Excel workbook named **Workdays.xlsx** that has the following formula defined in cell **A3** of **Sheet1**:

```
=CONCATENATE(YEAR(WORKDAY(A1,A2)),"-
",RIGHT(CONCATENATE("00",MONTH(WORKDAY(A1,A2))),2),"-",
RIGHT(CONCATENATE("00",DAY(WORKDAY(A1,A2))),2))
```

   This formula returns a date (in the **YYYY-MM-DD** format) that is the indicated number of workdays specified in cell **A2** before or after the date specified in cell **A1**. Note that you can also download a file named **Workdays.xlsx** from www.bizsupportonline.com for use with this recipe.

2. Click **File ➤ Save & Send ➤ Save to SharePoint ➤ Save As** and save the entire workbook (including all of its sheets) to a document library (for example the **Shared**

Documents library) on the SharePoint site to which the InfoPath form will be connecting (also see recipe *7 Publish an Excel workbook to SharePoint*).

3. In InfoPath, create a new browser-compatible form template or use an existing one.

4. Select **Data ➤ Get External Data ➤From Web Service ➤ From REST Web Service**.

5. On the **Data Connection Wizard**, enter the URL of the Excel Services REST web service and the Excel workbook, for example:

```
http://servername/sitename/_vti_bin/ExcelREST.aspx/Shared%20Workd
ays.xlsx/model/Ranges('A3')?Ranges('A1')=2012-12-20&Ranges('A2')=-
7&$format=atom
```

and click **Next**. Here, **servername** is the name of the SharePoint server and **sitename** is the name of the site where the **Workdays.xlsx** workbook has been stored in the **Shared Documents** document library. **A1** is the name of the cell on the first worksheet in the Excel workbook that should receive the start date to use in the formula. **A2** is the name of the cell on the first worksheet in the Excel workbook that should receive the amount of days to use in the formula. **A3** is the name of the cell on the first worksheet that contains the result of the calculation.

The query string parameters in the REST URL that come after the question mark

```
Ranges('A1')=2012-12-20&Ranges('A2')=-7
```

set the values of cells **A1** and **A2** in the Excel workbook, while the part of the REST URL that comes before the question mark

```
Ranges('A3')
```

returns the value of cell **A3** from the Excel workbook.

6. On the **Data Connection Wizard**, name the data connection **CalculateDate**, deselect the **Automatically retrieve data when form is opened** check box, and click **Finish**.

7. Add two **Date Picker** controls to the view of the form template and name them **dueDate** and **selectedDate**, respectively.

8. Add an **Action** rule to the **dueDate** date picker with an action that says:

```
Change REST URL: CalculateDate
```

where you must change the formula that sets the value of the **REST Web Service URL** to be the following:

```
concat("http://servername/sitename/_vti_bin/ExcelREST.aspx/Shared%20Documen
ts/Workdays.xlsx/model/Ranges('A3')?Ranges('A1')=", ., "&Ranges('A2')=-
7&$format=atom")
```

where **.** is the field in the Main data source that is bound to the **dueDate** date picker. With this you have made the REST URL dynamic by using the **concat()** function to construct the REST URL based on a static base URL and the value of a field on the InfoPath form.

9. Add a second action to the **Action** rule for the **dueDate** date picker that says:

```
Query using a data connection: CalculateDate
```

This action refreshes the data in the **CalculateDate** secondary data source by retrieving the result of the **WORKDAY** calculation from the Excel workbook using the new REST URL.

10. Add a **Validation** rule to the **selectedDate** date picker with a condition that says:

```
selectedDate ≥ fv
```

and

```
dueDate is not blank
```

where **selectedDate** and **dueDate** are located in the Main data source and **fv** is located under the **c** group node under the **row** group node under the **range** group node under the **content** group node under the **entry** group node in the **CalculateDate** secondary data source. Set the **ScreenTip** of the validation rule to say:

```
Please select a date that is more than 7 business days before the due date.
```

11. Publish the form template to a SharePoint form library.

In SharePoint, navigate to the form library where you published the form template and add a new form. When the form opens, select a due date and then select a date for the **selectedDate** date picker that falls within a date range of 7 business days before the due date. You should see a validation error appear. Select a date for the **selectedDate** date picker that falls outside a date range of 7 business days before the due date (for example a date that falls 10 business days before the due date). The validation error should disappear.

Discussion

The **WORKDAY** function in Excel returns a number that represents a date that is the indicated number of work days before or after a date (the start date). Work days exclude weekends and any dates identified as holidays. You can use the **WORKDAY** function to take holidays into account by specifying a range of cells that contains dates for holidays in the Excel workbook as the third argument of the **WORKDAY** function similar to the **NETWORKDAYS** function described in recipe *32 Calculate work days between two dates in InfoPath using Excel.*

In the solution described above, you used the **WORKDAY** function to ensure that the date a user selects falls a certain amount of days (7 days in this case) before a selected due date. To perform the Excel calculation, you passed the value of the **dueDate** date picker and a value of **-7** business days to Excel Services through a REST web service URL.

```
concat("http://servername/sitename/_vti_bin/ExcelREST.aspx/Shared%20Documents/Wo
rkdays.xlsx/model/Ranges('A3')?Ranges('A1')=", ., "&Ranges('A2')=-
7&$format=atom")
```

Note that while the **-7** business days was statically passed in the REST web service URL, you could have also made this amount dynamic by adding a field to the form and then replacing the **-7** in the URL with the value of the field when using the **concat()** function to dynamically construct the REST web service URL.

You then used the result of the Excel calculation (stored in the **fv** field under the **c** group node under the **row** group node under the **range** group node under the **content** group node under the **entry** group node in the **CalculateDate** secondary data source) in a validation rule on the **selectedDate** date picker to enforce the **7** business days condition.

Note that while it is theoretically possible to perform such a calculation in InfoPath without using Excel Services or writing code, it becomes a bit more difficult when you want to take holidays into account when performing the calculation. In the latter case, the Excel Services solution offers a codeless option that is fairly quick and easy to implement compared to an InfoPath-only solution.

32 Calculate work days between two dates in InfoPath using Excel

Problem

You have two date picker controls on an InfoPath form and want to calculate the difference in business days between two dates excluding holidays and weekends.

Solution

You can create an Excel workbook that contains the calculation for the amount of work days between two dates and a list of dates for holidays, publish this Excel workbook to a trusted file location for Excel Services, and then call the Excel Services REST web service from within an InfoPath form to perform the calculation.

To calculate work days between two dates in InfoPath using Excel:

1. In Excel, modify the **LeaveBalances.xlsx** Excel workbook of recipe *10 Get the value of an Excel cell in InfoPath* to contain a worksheet named **DateDiffCalculation** that contains a list of dates for holidays (or download the **LeaveBalances.xlsx** sample file from www.bizsupportonline.com) and add the following formula to cell **A3** on the **DateDiffCalculation** worksheet:

```
=NETWORKDAYS(A1,A2,C1:C11)
```

where cell **A1** on the **DateDiffCalculation** worksheet contains a start date, cell **A2** on the **DateDiffCalculation** worksheet contains an end date, and cells **C1** through **C11** on the **DateDiffCalculation** worksheet contain a range of dates that represent holidays. Ensure that all of the cells containing dates have the **Date** data type assigned to them. You will be changing the values of cells **A1** and **A2** later through InfoPath. The Excel formula uses the **NETWORKDAYS** function to calculate the amount of work days between two given dates minus holidays.

2. Click **File ➤ Save & Send ➤ Save to SharePoint ➤ Save As** and save the entire workbook (including all of its sheets) to a document library (for example the **Shared Documents** library) on the SharePoint site where you will be publishing the form template (also see recipe *7 Publish an Excel workbook to SharePoint*).

3. In InfoPath, create a new browser-compatible form template or use an existing one.

4. Select **Data ➤ Get External Data ➤From Web Service ➤ From REST Web Service**.

5. On the **Data Connection Wizard**, enter the URL of the Excel Services REST web service and the Excel workbook, for example:

```
http://servername/sitename/_vti_bin/ExcelREST.aspx/Shared%20Documents/Leave
Balances.xlsx/model/Ranges('DateDiffCalculation!A3')?$format=atom
```

and click **Next**. Here, **servername** is the name of the SharePoint server and **sitename** is the name of the site where the **LeaveBalances.xlsx** workbook has been stored in the **Shared Documents** document library. **A3** is the cell on the **DateDiffCalculation** worksheet in the Excel workbook that contains the formula to calculate the amount of work days.

6. On the **Data Connection Wizard**, name the data connection **GetWorkdaysDifference**, deselect the **Automatically retrieve data when form is opened** check box, and click **Finish**.

7. Add two **Date Picker** controls to the view of the form template and name them **startDate** and **endDate**, respectively.

8. Add a **Text Box** control to the view of the form template and name it **workdaysDiff**. Make the text box control read-only or change it into a calculated value control, since the user should not be able to change the value of this field.

9. Add an **Action** rule to the **startDate** date picker with a **Condition** that says:

```
startDate is not blank
and
endDate is not blank
```

and that has a first action that says:

```
Change REST URL: GetWorkdaysDifference
```

that changes the **REST Web Service URL** to the following formula:

```
concat("http://servername/sitename/_vti_bin/ExcelREST.aspx/Shared%20Documen
ts/LeaveBalances.xlsx/model/Ranges('DateDiffCalculation!A3')?Ranges('DateDi
ffCalculation!A1')=", ., "&Ranges('DateDiffCalculation!A2')=", endDate,
"&$format=atom")
```

Add a second action that says:

```
Query using a data connection: GetWorkdaysDifference
```

The first action sets the values of the parameters for the start date and the end date in the REST web service URL.

```
Ranges('DateDiffCalculation!A1')=.
```

sets the value of cell **A1** on the **DateDiffCalculation** worksheet in the Excel workbook to be equal to the value of the **startDate** date picker control and

```
Ranges('DateDiffCalculation!A2')=endDate
```

sets the value of cell **A2** on the **DateDiffCalculation** worksheet in the Excel workbook to be equal to the value of the **endDate** date picker control. The second action queries the data connection and returns the result from cell **A3**, which is specified through

```
Ranges('DateDiffCalculation!A3')
```

in the REST web service URL.

10. Add an **Action** rule to the **endDate** date picker with a **Condition** that says:

```
startDate is not blank
and
endDate is not blank
```

and that has a first action that says:

```
Change REST URL: GetWorkdaysDifference
```

that changes the **REST Web Service URL** to the following formula:

```
concat("http://servername/sitename/_vti_bin/ExcelREST.aspx/Shared%20Documen
ts/LeaveBalances.xlsx/model/Ranges('DateDiffCalculation!A3')?Ranges('DateDi
ffCalculation!A1')=", startDate, "&Ranges('DateDiffCalculation!A2')=", .,
"&$format=atom")
```

Add a second action that says:

```
Query using a data connection: GetWorkdaysDifference
```

The first action sets the values of the parameters for the start date and the end date in the REST web service URL.

```
Ranges('DateDiffCalculation!A1')=startDate
```

sets the value of cell **A1** on the **DateDiffCalculation** worksheet in the Excel workbook to be equal to the value of the **startDate** date picker control and

```
Ranges('DateDiffCalculation!A2')=.
```

sets the value of cell **A2** on the **DateDiffCalculation** worksheet in the Excel workbook to be equal to the value of the **endDate** date picker control. The second action queries the data connection and returns the result from cell **A3**, which is specified through

```
Ranges('DateDiffCalculation!A3')
```

in the REST web service URL.

11. Set the **Default Value** of the **workdaysDiff** field to be equal to:

<u>v</u>

where **v** is located under the **c** group node under the **row** group node under the **range** group node under the **content** group node under the **entry** group node in the **GetWorkdaysDifference** secondary data source. Leave the **Refresh value when formula is recalculated** check box selected on the **Field or Group Properties** dialog box.

12. Publish the form template to a SharePoint form library.

In SharePoint, navigate to the form library where you published the form template and add a new form. When the form opens, select a start date and an end date and verify that the calculated amount of work days is correct.

Discussion

The **NETWORKDAYS** function in Excel returns the number of whole work days between a start date and an end date. Work days exclude weekends and any dates identified as holidays. You can use the **NETWORKDAYS** function to take holidays into account by specifying a range of cells that contains dates for holidays in the Excel workbook as the third argument of the **NETWORKDAYS** function.

In the solution described above, you used the **NETWORKDAYS** function together with the Excel Services REST web service to set values in an Excel workbook, calculate the difference between two dates, and return the result to an InfoPath form.

To make the formula that makes use of the **NETWORKDAYS** function a little bit more user-friendly, you may want to define meaningful names for the cells. For example, you could define **workdaysDifference** as the name for cell **A3** in the Excel workbook (also see *How to create a named range in Excel* in the Appendix) and then use this name in the REST web service URL as follows:

```
http://servername/sitename/_vti_bin/ExcelREST.aspx/Shared%20Documents/WorkDaysCa
lculator.xlsx/model/Ranges('workdaysDifference')?Ranges('A1')=2013-07-
01&Ranges('A2')=2013-07-10&$format=atom
```

Refer to the beginning of the *Use the Excel Services REST Web Service* section in this chapter for general information about using the Excel Services REST web service in InfoPath and for an explanation of the different parts of the REST URL.

If you do not want to use or are unable to make Excel Services REST web service calls on your SharePoint server, you can still make use of Excel Services calculations by going through its SOAP web service.

33 Calculate remaining leave in InfoPath using Excel

Problem

You have two date picker controls on an InfoPath form and want to calculate the difference in business days between two dates excluding holidays and weekends. In addition, you want to retrieve the amount of leave the currently logged on user has from an Excel workbook, subtract the calculated amount of business days from the amount of leave, and then submit the new leave balance to the Excel workbook for storage.

Solution

You can create an Excel workbook that contains the calculations for the amount of work days between two dates with a list of dates for holidays and that performs calculations using the **VLOOKUP** and **MATCH** functions, publish this Excel workbook to a trusted file location for Excel Services, and then call the Excel Services REST and SOAP web services from within an InfoPath form to perform calculations and then update the data in the Excel workbook.

To calculate remaining leave in an InfoPath form using Excel:

1. In Excel, modify the **LeaveBalances.xlsx** Excel workbook of recipe *10 Get the value of an Excel cell in InfoPath* (or download the **LeaveBalances.xlsx** sample file from www.bizsupportonline.com) and add the following formula to cell **A3** on the **Calculations** worksheet:

    ```
    =MATCH(A1,Sheet1!A1:A3,0)
    ```

    where cell **A1** contains a user name for which an exact match should be found in cells **A1** through **A3** on **Sheet1** in the Excel workbook. The Excel formula uses the **MATCH** function to perform the lookup. This function should return a row number, which can then be used to change the value of the leave balance in a particular row for a particular user.

2. Click **File ➤ Save & Send ➤ Save to SharePoint ➤ Save As** and save the entire workbook (including all of its sheets) to a document library (for example the **Shared**

Documents library) on the SharePoint site where you will be publishing the form template (also see recipe *7 Publish an Excel workbook to SharePoint*).

3. In InfoPath, use the same form template from recipe *32 Calculate work days between two dates in InfoPath using Excel*.

4. Select **Data ➤ Get External Data ➤From Web Service ➤ From REST Web Service**.

5. On the **Data Connection Wizard**, enter the URL of the Excel Services REST web service and the Excel workbook, for example:

```
http://servername/sitename/_vti_bin/ExcelREST.aspx/Shared%20Documents/Leave
Balances.xlsx/model/Ranges('Calculations!A2')?Ranges('Calculations!A1')=&$f
ormat=atom
```

and click **Next**. Here, **servername** is the name of the SharePoint server and **sitename** is the name of the site where the **LeaveBalances.xlsx** Excel workbook has been stored in the **Shared Documents** document library. **A2** is the cell on the **Calculations** worksheet in the Excel workbook that looks up the amount of leave for the user passed to cell **A1**.

6. On the **Data Connection Wizard**, name the data connection **GetLeaveBalance**, deselect the **Automatically retrieve data when form is opened** check box, and click **Finish**.

7. Select **Data ➤ Get External Data ➤From Web Service ➤ From REST Web Service**.

8. On the **Data Connection Wizard**, enter the URL of the Excel Services REST web service and the Excel workbook, for example:

```
http://servername/sitename/_vti_bin/ExcelREST.aspx/Shared%20Documents/Leave
Balances.xlsx/model/Ranges('Calculations!A3')?Ranges('Calculations!A1')&$fo
rmat=atom
```

and click **Next**. Here, **servername** is the name of the SharePoint server and **sitename** is the name of the site where the **LeaveBalances.xlsx** Excel workbook has been stored in the **Shared Documents** document library. **A3** is the cell on the **Calculations** worksheet in the Excel workbook that looks up a row number for the user passed to cell **A1**.

9. On the **Data Connection Wizard**, name the data connection **GetRowNumber**, deselect the **Automatically retrieve data when form is opened** check box, and click **Finish**.

10. Click **Data ➤ Rules ➤ Form Load**, and then on the **Rules** task pane, add an **Action** rule with an action that says:

```
Change REST URL: GetLeaveBalance
```

that changes the **REST Web Service URL** to the following formula:

177

```
concat("http://servername/sitename/_vti_bin/ExcelREST.aspx/Shared%20Documen
ts/LeaveBalances.xlsx/model/Ranges('Calculations!A2')?Ranges('Calculations!
A1')=", userName(), "&$format=atom")
```

This REST web service URL sets the value of cell **A1** on the **Calculations** worksheet in the Excel workbook to be equal to the **userName()** function. Making this call should return the amount of leave for the currently logged on user in cell **A2** of the **Calculations** worksheet in the Excel workbook.

Add a second action that says:

```
Query using a data connection: GetLeaveBalance
```

11. On the **Rules** task pane, add another **Action** rule with an action that says:

```
Change REST URL: GetRowNumber
```

that changes the **REST Web Service URL** to the following formula:

```
concat("http://servername/sitename/_vti_bin/ExcelREST.aspx/Shared%20Documen
ts/LeaveBalances.xlsx/model/Ranges('Calculations!A3')?Ranges('Calculations!
A1')=", userName(), "&$format=atom")
```

This REST web service URL sets the value of cell **A1** on the **Calculations** worksheet in the Excel workbook to be equal to the **userName()** function. Making this call should return a row number for the currently logged on user from cell **A3** of the **Calculations** worksheet in the Excel workbook.

Add a second action that says:

```
Query using a data connection: GetRowNumber
```

12. Add a **Text Box** control to the view of the form template and name it **remainingLeave**. Make the text box control read-only or change it into a calculated value control, since the user should not be able to change the value of this field.

13. Set the **Default Value** of the **remainingLeave** text box to be equal to the following formula:

```
v - workdaysDiff
```

where **v** is a field located under the **c** group node under the **row** group node under the **range** group node under the **content** group node under the **entry** group node in the **GetLeaveBalance** secondary data source and **workdaysDiff** is located in the Main data source. Leave the **Refresh value when formula is recalculated** check box selected on the **Field or Group Properties** dialog box.

14. Select **Data ➤ Get External Data ➤ From Web Service ➤ From SOAP Web Service** to add a **Receive** data connection for the **OpenWorkbookForEditing** operation of the Excel Services web service (also see recipe *18 Get the value of an Excel cell in InfoPath* for detailed instructions on how to connect to the Excel Services

SOAP web service) and configure its parameters as follows:

Parameter	Value
tns:workbookPath	`http://servername/sitename/libraryname/LeaveBalances.xlsx` where **servername** is the name of the SharePoint server, **sitename** is the name of the site, and **libraryname** is the name of the document library and Excel Services trusted file location where the **LeaveBalances.xlsx** Excel workbook is located.
tns:uiCultureName	
tns:dataCultureName	

Leave the **Store a copy of the data in the form template** check box deselected, name the data connection **OpenWorkbookForEditing**, and deselect the **Automatically retrieve data when form is opened** check box. You will use this data connection to open the Excel workbook and get a session ID that you can use for all subsequent calls you make to Excel Services.

15. Select **Data ➤ Get External Data ➤ From Web Service ➤ From SOAP Web Service** to add a **Receive** data connection for the **SetCell** operation of the Excel Services web service (also see recipe *19 Set the value of an Excel cell in InfoPath*). Leave all parameters as is, leave the **Store a copy of the data in the form template** check box deselected, name the data connection **SetCell**, and deselect the **Automatically retrieve data when form is opened** check box. You will use this data connection to change the leave balance for the currently logged on user in the Excel workbook. At this point, the fields in the **SetCell** secondary data source are still blank; you will use a rule later to set their values before making the web service call.

16. Select **Data ➤ Get External Data ➤ From Web Service ➤ From SOAP Web Service** to add a **Receive** data connection for the **CloseWorkbook** operation of the Excel Services web service. Leave the **sessionId** parameter as is, leave the **Store a copy of the data in the form template** check box deselected, name the data connection **CloseWorkbook**, and deselect the **Automatically retrieve data when form is opened** check box. You will use this data connection to close the Excel workbook and Excel Services session.

17. Add a **Button** control to the view of the form template and label it **Update Leave Balance**.

18. Add an **Action** rule to the **Update Leave Balance** button with the following 9 actions:

```
Query using a data connection: OpenWorkbookForEditing
```

This action calls the **OpenWorkbookForEditing** web service operation to retrieve a session ID.

```
Set a field's value: sessionId = OpenWorkbookForEditingResult
```

where **sessionId** is located under the **SetCell** group node under the **queryFields** group node in the **SetCell** secondary data source and **OpenWorkbookForEditingResult** is located under the **OpenWorkbookForEditingResponse** group node under the **dataFields** group node in the **OpenWorkbookForEditing** secondary data source.

```
Set a field's value: sheetName = "Sheet1"
```

where **sheetName** is located under the **SetCell** group node under the **queryFields** group node in the **SetCell** secondary data source and **Sheet1** is a static piece of text representing the name of the worksheet in the Excel workbook where the leave balances are located.

```
Set a field's value: column = 1
```

where **column** is located under the **SetCell** group node under the **queryFields** group node in the **SetCell** secondary data source and **1** is a number representing column **B** in the Excel workbook that contains the amount of leave that should be changed.

```
Set a field's value: row = v - 1
```

where **row** is located under the **SetCell** group node under the **queryFields** group node in the **SetCell** secondary data source and **v** is located under the **c** group node under the **row** group node under the **range** group node under the **content** group node under the **entry** group node in the **GetRowNumber** secondary data source. Because row and column numbers that are passed to the Excel Services SOAP web service **SetCell** operation should be zero-based, but row and column numbers used in Excel start at 1, you must subtract a 1 from the value of the **v** field before passing it to Excel Services.

```
Set a field's value: cellValue = remainingLeave
```

where **cellValue** is located under the **SetCell** group node under the **queryFields** group node in the **SetCell** secondary data source and **remainingLeave** is located in the Main data source.

```
Query using a data connection: SetCell
```

This action calls the **SetCell** web service operation to update the value of a cell in the Excel workbook.

```
Set a field's value: sessionId = OpenWorkbookForEditingResult
```

where **sessionId** is located under the **CloseWorkbook** group node under the **queryFields** group node in the **CloseWorkbook** secondary data source and **OpenWorkbookForEditingResult** is located under the **OpenWorkbookForEditingResponse** group node under the **dataFields** group node in the **OpenWorkbookForEditing** secondary data source.

```
Query using a data connection: CloseWorkbook
```

This action closes the workbook and the Excel Services session.

19. Publish the form template to a SharePoint form library.

In SharePoint, navigate to the form library where you published the form template and add a new form. When the form opens, the remaining leave for the currently logged on user should appear on the form. Select a start date and an end date that represent a new leave period. The new leave balance should appear in the **remainingLeave** text box. Click the **Update Leave Balance** button and close the form. Navigate to the SharePoint document library where the **LeaveBalances.xlsx** Excel workbook is located, open the workbook, and verify that the new leave balance appears behind the name of the user who requested leave.

Discussion

In the solution described above, you saw how to combine the Excel Services REST and SOAP web services to be able to look up the amount of leave that is available for a particular user, calculate a new leave balance based on a leave period, and then update the leave balance in an Excel workbook with the newly calculated amount of leave.

While you could have also used Excel Services SOAP web service operations instead of making REST web service calls, the Excel Services REST web service is easier to use and you generally only need to perform one request instead of at least two when you use the Excel Services SOAP web service.

The Excel workbook used a **VLOOKUP** formula to look up the amount of leave for a particular user and a **MATCH** formula to find the vertical position (row number) of the cell in which a particular user name was located. The **MATCH** function searches for a specified item in a range of cells, and then returns the relative position of that item in the range. You can read more about the **MATCH** function and get examples of its usage in the Excel documentation.

In the solution described above, the **MATCH** function was used to first look up the name of the logged on user in cells **A1** through **A3** on **Sheet1** of the Excel workbook, and if a match was found, the corresponding relative position in the range of cells was returned. The relative position in the range of cells was in this case equivalent to the row number of the cell in which the user name was found, since the range of cells started at cell **A1**. This means that if you use a range that does not start on the first row of a worksheet, you should apply a correction, so that the correct row number is used together with the **SetCell** web service operation to update the value of a cell in the Excel workbook.

The sequence of Excel Services SOAP web service operation calls to store the new leave balance in the Excel table was as follows:

1. Call **OpenWorkbookForEditing** to get an Excel Services session ID, which allowed you to edit the Excel workbook.

2. Call **SetCell** using the row number that was retrieved from a previous Excel Services request that made use of the **MATCH** function in the Excel workbook. While you could have also used the **SetCellA1** web service operation, it is much easier to use the **SetCell** web service operation in this case, because you are working with row numbers instead of cell names.

3. Call **CloseWorkbook** to save the changes, close the workbook, and end the Excel Services session.

Note:

When you use the **OpenWorkbookForEditing** web service operation to open an Excel workbook for editing, you generally do not need to explicitly call the **SaveWorkbook** operation to save the changes made to the workbook before calling the **CloseWorkbook** operation to close the workbook, since any changes made to the workbook should automatically and permanently be stored in the workbook when you close it. But if the changes you made are not being persisted in your workbook, you may want to try adding the **SaveWorkbook** operation (see for example recipe *20 Update an Excel chart on an InfoPath form*) just before calling the **CloseWorkbook** operation to see whether the additional operation solves the issue.

34 Get the amount of records in an Excel table from within InfoPath

Problem

You have an Excel workbook that contains a table. You want to know how many rows are present in the table from within an InfoPath form.

Solution

You can use the Excel Services REST web service to retrieve the result of an Excel calculation (in this case a **ROWS** calculation), and return the result to an InfoPath form.

To get the amount of records in an Excel table from within an InfoPath form:

1. In Excel, create an Excel workbook that has a list of items, for example foods and then select **Home ➤ Styles ➤ Format as Table** to convert the list into a table. Ensure that you select the **My table has headers** check box on the **Format As**

Table dialog box if your table contains a header row and name the table **Foods**. Add a new worksheet named **RowCount** to the Excel workbook and add the following formula to cell **A1** of the **RowCount** worksheet:

```
=ROWS(Foods)
```

This formula returns the amount of rows in the **Foods** Excel table. Name the Excel workbook **Foods.xlsx**. You can also download a file named **Foods.xlsx** from www.bizsupportonline.com for use with this recipe.

2. Click **File ➤ Save & Send ➤ Save to SharePoint ➤ Save As** and save the entire workbook (including all of its sheets) to a document library (for example the **Shared Documents** library) on the SharePoint site to which the InfoPath form will be connecting (also see recipe *7 Publish an Excel workbook to SharePoint*).

3. In InfoPath, create a new browser-compatible form template or use an existing one.

4. Select **Data ➤ Get External Data ➤From Web Service ➤ From REST Web Service**.

5. On the **Data Connection Wizard**, enter the URL of the Excel Services REST web service and the Excel workbook, for example:

```
http://servername/sitename/_vti_bin/ExcelREST.aspx/Shared%20Documents/Foods
.xlsx/model/Ranges('RowCount!A1')?$format=atom
```

and click **Next**. Here, **servername** is the name of the SharePoint server and **sitename** is the name of the site where the **Foods.xlsx** workbook has been stored in the **Shared Documents** document library. **A1** is the name of the cell on the **RowCount** worksheet in the Excel workbook that uses the **ROWS** function to retrieve the amount of rows in the **Foods** Excel table.

6. On the **Data Connection Wizard**, name the data connection **GetRowCount**, leave the **Automatically retrieve data when form is opened** check box selected, and click **Finish**.

7. On the **Fields** task pane, select **GetRowCount (Secondary)** from the **Fields** drop-down list box, expand all of the nodes under the **content** group node, and then drag-and-drop the **v** field onto the view of the form template. It should automatically get bound to a text box control.

8. Publish the form template to a SharePoint form library.

In SharePoint, navigate to the form library where you published the form template and add a new form. When the form opens, you should see the amount of rows that are present in the Excel table appear in the text box.

Discussion

In the solution described above, you used the Excel Services REST web service and the **ROWS** function in an Excel workbook to retrieve the amount of rows contained in a table in the Excel workbook. The **ROWS** function in Excel returns the number of rows in a reference or array.

You could have also used Excel Services SOAP web service operations to retrieve the amount of rows contained in a table in an Excel workbook using the technique discussed in recipe *18 Get the value of an Excel cell in InfoPath*. For this, you would have had to call the **OpenWorkbook**, **GetCellA1** or **GetCell**, and **CloseWorkbook** web service operations to achieve the same result as described in the solution in this recipe.

Once you have retrieved the amount of rows that are present in an Excel table, you can use this amount to sequentially navigate through the records of the Excel table as described in recipe *35 Sequentially navigate through rows of an Excel table – method 1* and *36 Sequentially navigate through rows of an Excel table – method 2*, or you can use it to append a new row to the Excel table as described in recipe *37 Add a new row to an Excel table from within InfoPath*.

35 Sequentially navigate through rows of an Excel table – method 1

Problem

You have an Excel workbook that contains a table. You want to sequentially navigate through the rows that are present in the table from within an InfoPath form.

Solution

You can use Excel Services SOAP web service operations to retrieve data from a specific row and column in an Excel table and return this data to an InfoPath form for display while using a counter to navigate forward and backward through the table records.

To sequentially navigate through rows of an Excel table from within an InfoPath form:

1. Use the same InfoPath form template and Excel workbook you created in recipe *34 Get the amount of records in an Excel table from within InfoPath*.

2. In InfoPath, select **Data ➤ Get External Data ➤ From Web Service ➤ From SOAP Web Service** to add a **Receive** data connection for the **OpenWorkbook** operation of the Excel Services web service (also see recipe *18 Get the value of an Excel cell in InfoPath* for detailed instructions on how to connect to the Excel Services SOAP web service) and configure its parameters as follows:

Parameter	Value
tns:workbookPath	`http://servername/sitename/libraryname/Foods.xlsx` where **servername** is the name of the SharePoint server, **sitename** is the name of the site, and **libraryname** is the name of the document library and Excel Services trusted file location where the **Foods.xlsx** Excel workbook is located.
tns:uiCultureName	
tns:dataCultureName	

Leave the **Store a copy of the data in the form template** check box deselected, name the data connection **OpenWorkbook**, and deselect the **Automatically retrieve data when form is opened** check box. You will use this data connection to open the Excel workbook and get a session ID that you can use for all subsequent calls you make to Excel Services.

3. Select **Data ➤ Get External Data ➤ From Web Service ➤ From SOAP Web Service** to add a **Receive** data connection for the **GetCell** operation of the Excel Services web service and configure its parameters as follows:

Parameter	Value
tns:sessionId	
tns:sheetName	Foods where **Foods** is a static piece of text representing the name of the worksheet in the Excel workbook where a table containing food items is located.
tns:row	1 where **1** is a number representing the second row of a worksheet in the Excel workbook. The data in the table starts on the second row of the **Foods** worksheet.
tns:column	0 where **0** is a number representing the first column of a worksheet in the Excel workbook.

tns:formatted*	false

Note that the **sessionId** parameter is left blank since its value will be set later through a rule. Leave the **Store a copy of the data in the form template** check box deselected, name the data connection **GetCell**, and deselect the **Automatically retrieve data when form is opened** check box. You will use this data connection to retrieve the value of the **Name** field (first column) of a particular row in the Excel table.

4. Select **Data ➤ Get External Data ➤ From Web Service ➤ From SOAP Web Service** to add a **Receive** data connection for the **CloseWorkbook** operation of the Excel Services web service. Leave the **sessionId** parameter as is, leave the **Store a copy of the data in the form template** check box deselected, name the data connection **CloseWorkbook**, and deselect the **Automatically retrieve data when form is opened** check box. You will use this data connection to close the Excel workbook and Excel Services session.

5. On the **Fields** task pane, select **GetCell (Secondary)** from the **Fields** drop-down list box, expand the **dataFields** group node, expand the **GetCellResponse** group node, and then drag-and-drop the **GetCellResult** field onto the view of the form template. It should automatically get bound to a text box control.

6. On the **Fields** task pane, select **Main** from the **Fields** drop-down list box, and then add a **Field (element)** with the name **pos**, the data type **Whole Number (integer)**, and a default value equal to **1** to the Main data source.

7. Add two **Button** controls to the view of the form template and label them **Previous** and **Next**, respectively.

8. Add a **Formatting** rule to the **Previous** button with a **Condition** that says:

```
pos = 1
```

and a formatting of **Disable this control**. This formatting rule disables the **Previous** button if the value of the **pos** field is pointing to the first record in the Excel table.

9. Add a **Formatting** rule to the **Next** button with a **Condition** that says:

```
pos ≥ v
```

and a formatting of **Disable this control**. Here **v** is located under the **c** group node under the **row** group node under the **range** group node under the **content** group node under the **entry** group node in the **GetRowCount** secondary data source. This formatting rule disables the **Next** button if the value of the **pos** field is greater than or equal to the number of the last record in the Excel table.

10. Add an **Action** rule to the **Next** button with the following 7 actions:

```
Set a field's value: pos = pos + 1
```

This action increases the value of the **pos** field in the Main data source by **1**.

```
Query using a data connection: OpenWorkbook
```

This action calls the **OpenWorkbook** web service operation to retrieve a session ID.

```
Set a field's value: sessionId = OpenWorkbookResult
```

where **sessionId** is located under the **GetCell** group node under the **queryFields** group node in the **GetCell** secondary data source and **OpenWorkbookResult** is located under the **OpenWorkbookResponse** group node under the **dataFields** group node in the **OpenWorkbook** secondary data source.

```
Set a field's value: row = pos
```

where **row** is located under the **GetCell** group node under the **queryFields** group node in the **GetCell** secondary data source and **pos** is located in the Main data source.

```
Query using a data connection: GetCell
```

This action calls the **GetCell** web service operation to retrieve the value of the **Name** field (first column) in the Excel table on the row specified by the value of the **pos** field in the Main data source.

```
Set a field's value: sessionId = OpenWorkbookResult
```

where **sessionId** is located under the **CloseWorkbook** group node under the **queryFields** group node in the **CloseWorkbook** secondary data source and **OpenWorkbookResult** is located under the **OpenWorkbookResponse** group node under the **dataFields** group node in the **OpenWorkbook** secondary data source.

```
Query using a data connection: CloseWorkbook
```

This action closes the workbook and the Excel Services session.

11. On the **Rules** task pane, copy the **Action** rule from the **Next** button, paste it onto the **Previous** button, and then change the first action of the newly pasted rule on the **Previous** button to say:

```
Set a field's value: pos = pos - 1
```

This action decreases the value of the **pos** field in the Main data source by **1**.

12. Select the **Next** button and then on the **Rules** task pane, copy the **Action** rule from the **Next** button, click **Data ➤ Rules ➤ Form Load** to switch to the **Rules** task pane for the **Form Load** event, and then click **Paste Rule** to paste the rule. Change the first action of the newly pasted rule to say:

```
pos = 1
```

This action sets the value of the **pos** field in the Main data source to be equal to **1**.

13. Publish the form template to a SharePoint form library.

In SharePoint, navigate to the form library where you published the form template and add a new form. When the form opens, the first record should appear. Click the **Next** and **Previous** buttons to navigate through the records. When you reach the last record, the **Next** button should be disabled, and when you navigate back to the first record, the **Previous** button should be disabled.

Discussion

In the solution described above, you saw how to use Excel Services SOAP web service operations to sequentially navigate through data that is stored in a table in an Excel workbook.

You could also use the Excel Services REST web service to achieve the same result, but would have to construct the range name every time before you make a call. For example, you could use the **concat()** function to append the value of the **pos** field to an **A** to return **A1**, **A2**, **A3**, **A4**, etc. to be able to navigate through the rows in the first column (also see recipe *36 Sequentially navigate through rows of an Excel table – method 2*).

And while you could have also used the **GetCellA1** operation instead of the **GetCell** operation as in the solution described above, the **GetCell** operation makes it easier to pass and retrieve data from the Excel workbook using a counter (the value of the **pos** field in this case) that represents a specific number for a row. Had you used the **GetCellA1** operation, you would have had to construct the name of the cell that should be retrieved, in much the same way as you would have had to do if you used the Excel REST web service.

Warning:

Because the amount of requests a user is allowed to make via an InfoPath browser form is capped by default, too many clicks while navigating back and forth through Excel data may cause InfoPath Forms Services to eventually raise an error. Therefore, it is recommended that you find a way to reduce the amount of requests made by not continuously opening and closing the workbook with each click of a button, using REST instead of SOAP as described in recipe *36 Sequentially navigate through rows of an Excel table – method 2*, or provide the user with a way to search the data (see for example recipe *38 Perform exact and wildcard searches in an Excel table from within InfoPath*) instead of sequentially navigating through it.

36 Sequentially navigate through rows of an Excel table – method 2

Problem

You have an Excel workbook that contains a table. You want to sequentially navigate through the rows that are present in the table from within an InfoPath form and retrieve the values in specific fields of each row.

Solution

You can use the Excel Services REST web service to retrieve data from a specific range of cells in a row of an Excel table and return this data to an InfoPath form for display while using a counter to navigate forward and backward through the table records.

To sequentially navigate through rows of an Excel table from within an InfoPath form:

1. Use the same InfoPath form template and Excel workbook you created in recipe *34 Get the amount of records in an Excel table from within InfoPath*.

2. In InfoPath, on the **Fields** task pane, add a **Field (element)** with the name **pos**, the data type **Whole Number (integer)**, and a default value equal to **2** to the Main data source.

3. Select **Data ➤ Get External Data ➤ From Web Service ➤ From REST Web Service**.

4. On the **Data Connection Wizard**, enter the URL of the Excel Services REST web service and the Excel workbook, for example:

    ```
    http://servername/sitename/_vti_bin/ExcelREST.aspx/Shared%20Documents/Foods
    .xlsx/model/Ranges('Foods!A2%7CF2')?$format=atom
    ```

    and click **Next**. Here, **servername** is the name of the SharePoint server and **sitename** is the name of the site where the **Foods.xlsx** Excel workbook has been stored in the **Shared Documents** document library. A2%7CF2 (cells **A2** through **F2** where %7C represents a pipe symbol) is the range of cells on the **Foods** worksheet in the Excel workbook that contains data for the first row in the **Foods** Excel table.

5. On the **Data Connection Wizard**, name the data connection **GetRow**, leave the **Automatically retrieve data when form is opened** check box selected, and click **Finish**.

6. On the **Fields** task pane, select **GetRow (Secondary)** from the **Fields** drop-down list box, expand all of the group nodes under the **content** group node, right-click the **c** repeating group node, drag it to the view of the form template, drop it, and select **Repeating Section with Controls** from the context menu that appears.

189

7. Delete the **v** field with its corresponding label, and then change the label for the **fv** field to **Name**, which is the name of the first column in the Excel table.

8. Add a **Formatting** rule to the **c** repeating section with a **The Expression** condition that says:

```
count(preceding-sibling::*) != 0
```

and a formatting of **Hide this control**. This formatting rule hides a **c** group node if it has sibling nodes preceding it. So what this rule effectively does is hide all of the **fv** fields except for the **fv** field that corresponds to the first column in the Excel table.

9. Repeat the previous 3 steps 5 times, but change the labels to **Weight (g)**, **Calories**, **Protein (g)**, **Fat (g)**, and **Carbs (g)**, respectively, and change the expression for the condition of the **Formatting** rules to:

```
count(preceding-sibling::*) != 1
```

for the **Weight (g)** repeating section,

```
count(preceding-sibling::*) != 2
```

for the **Calories** repeating section,

```
count(preceding-sibling::*) != 3
```

for the **Protein (g)** repeating section,

```
count(preceding-sibling::*) != 4
```

for the **Fat (g)** repeating section, and

```
count(preceding-sibling::*) != 5
```

for the **Carbs (g)** repeating section.

10. Add two **Button** controls to the view of the form template and label them **Previous** and **Next**, respectively.

11. Add a **Formatting** rule to the **Previous** button with a condition that says:

```
pos = 2
```

and a formatting of **Disable this control**. This formatting rule disables the **Previous** button if the value of the **pos** field is pointing to the first record in the Excel table.

12. Add a **Formatting** rule to the **Next** button with a condition that says:

```
pos ≥ v + 1
```

and a formatting of **Disable this control**. Here **v** is located under the **c** group node under the **row** group node under the **range** group node under the **content** group node under the **entry** group node in the **GetRowCount** secondary data source. This formatting rule disables the **Next** button if the value of the **pos** field is greater than or equal to the number of the last record in the Excel table.

13. Add an **Action** rule to the **Next** button with the following 3 actions:

```
Set a field's value: pos = pos + 1
```

This action increases the value of the **pos** field in the Main data source by **1**.

```
Change REST URL: GetRow
```

where you must change the formula that sets the value of the **REST Web Service URL** to be the following:

```
concat("http://servername/sitename/_vti_bin/ExcelREST.aspx/Shared%20Documen
ts/Foods.xlsx/model/Ranges('Foods!A", pos, "%7CF", pos, "')?$format=atom")
```

where **pos** is the field in the Main data source that is used to keep track of the row number in the Excel table. With this you have made the REST URL dynamic by using the **concat()** function to construct the REST URL based on a static base URL and the value of a field on the InfoPath form.

```
Query using a data connection: GetRow
```

This action refreshes the data in the **GetRow** secondary data source by retrieving values from the Excel table on the row indicated by the value of the **pos** field in the Main data source.

14. On the **Rules** task pane, copy the **Action** rule from the **Next** button, paste it onto the **Previous** button, and then change the first action of the newly pasted rule on the **Previous** button to say:

```
pos = pos - 1
```

This action decreases the value of the **pos** field in the Main data source by **1**.

15. Publish the form template to a SharePoint form library.

In SharePoint, navigate to the form library where you published the form template and add a new form. When the form opens, the values for the first record should appear. Click the **Next** and **Previous** buttons to navigate through the records. When you reach the last record, the **Next** button should be disabled, and when you navigate back to the first record, the **Previous** button should be disabled.

Discussion

In the solution described above, you saw how to use the Excel Services REST web service to sequentially navigate through data that is stored in a table in an Excel workbook. If you want to use Excel Services SOAP web service operations to achieve the same result, see recipe *35 Sequentially navigate through rows of an Excel table – method 1*.

Note that the value of the **pos** field is used in the **concat()** function to repeatedly change the REST URL whenever a user clicks on either the **Previous** or the **Next** button.

```
concat("http://servername/sitename/_vti_bin/ExcelREST.aspx/Shared%20Documents/Fo
ods.xlsx/model/Ranges('Foods!A", pos, "%7CF", pos, "')?$format=atom")
```

37   Add a new row to an Excel table from within InfoPath

Problem

You have a table in an Excel workbook to which you would like to add a new row from within an InfoPath form.

Solution

You can use the Excel Services REST web service to retrieve the total amount of rows that are present in a table in an Excel workbook, calculate a new row number to use, and then use this row number together with Excel Services SOAP web service operations to add a new row to the Excel table from within an InfoPath form.

To add a new row to an Excel table from within an InfoPath form:

1.   Use the same InfoPath form template and Excel workbook you created in recipe *34 Get the amount of records in an Excel table from within InfoPath*.

2.   In InfoPath, add a **Text Box** control to the view of the form template and name it **field1**. You will use this text box to set the value of the food item's name in the new row of the Excel table.

3.   Add a **Button** control to the view of the form template and label it **Add New Row**.

4.   Select **Data ➤ Get External Data ➤ From Web Service ➤ From SOAP Web Service** to add a **Receive** data connection for the **OpenWorkbookForEditing** operation of the Excel Services web service (also see recipe *18 Get the value of an Excel cell in InfoPath* for detailed instructions on how to connect to the Excel Services SOAP web service) and configure its parameters as follows:

Parameter	Value
tns:workbookPath	`http://servername/sitename/libraryname/Foods.xlsx`
	where **servername** is the name of the SharePoint server, **sitename** is the name of the site, and **libraryname** is the name of the document library and Excel Services trusted file location where the **Foods.xlsx** Excel workbook is located.

tns:uiCultureName

tns:dataCultureName

Leave the **Store a copy of the data in the form template** check box deselected, name the data connection **OpenWorkbookForEditing**, and deselect the **Automatically retrieve data when form is opened** check box. You will use this data connection to open the Excel workbook and get a session ID that you can use for all subsequent calls you make to Excel Services.

5. Select **Data ➤ Get External Data ➤ From Web Service ➤ From SOAP Web Service** to add a **Receive** data connection for the **SetCell** operation of the Excel Services web service (also see recipe *19 Set the value of an Excel cell in InfoPath*). Leave all parameters as is, leave the **Store a copy of the data in the form template** check box deselected, name the data connection **SetCell**, and deselect the **Automatically retrieve data when form is opened** check box. You will use this data connection to set a value in the new Excel table row. At this point, the fields in the **SetCell** secondary data source are still blank; you will use a rule later to set their values before making the web service call.

6. Select **Data ➤ Get External Data ➤ From Web Service ➤ From SOAP Web Service** to add a **Receive** data connection for the **CloseWorkbook** operation of the Excel Services web service. Leave the **sessionId** parameter as is, leave the **Store a copy of the data in the form template** check box deselected, name the data connection **CloseWorkbook**, and deselect the **Automatically retrieve data when form is opened** check box. You will use this data connection to close the Excel workbook and Excel Services session.

7. Add an **Action** rule to the **Add New Row** button with the following 10 actions:

```
Query using a data connection: GetRowCount
```

This action requeries the **GetRowCount** secondary data connection to retrieve the latest total amount of rows in the Excel table.

```
Query using a data connection: OpenWorkbookForEditing
```

This action calls the **OpenWorkbookForEditing** web service operation to retrieve a session ID.

```
Set a field's value: sessionId = OpenWorkbookForEditingResult
```

where **sessionId** is located under the **SetCell** group node under the **queryFields** group node in the **SetCell** secondary data source and **OpenWorkbookForEditingResult** is located under the **OpenWorkbookForEditingResponse** group node under the **dataFields** group node in the **OpenWorkbookForEditing** secondary data source.

```
Set a field's value: sheetName = "Foods"
```

where **sheetName** is located under the **SetCell** group node under the **queryFields** group node in the **SetCell** secondary data source and **Foods** is a static piece of text representing the name of the worksheet in the Excel workbook where the table is located. Note that you could also provide an extra field on the form so that the value of the name of the worksheet can be dynamically changed by users at runtime.

```
Set a field's value: row = v + 2 - 1
```

where **row** is located under the **SetCell** group node under the **queryFields** group node in the **SetCell** secondary data source and **v** is located under the **c** group node under the **row** group node under the **range** group node under the **content** group node under the **entry** group node in the **GetRowCount** secondary data source. A **2** is added to the value of **v**, because the table rows start on row number **2** on the **Foods** worksheet. And a **1** is subtracted to apply a correction to get the correct row number to use when calling the **SetCell** operation (also see the discussion section for more information). Note that you can also use a formula such as **v + 1** instead of **v + 2 − 1**. The **2 − 1** is kept here to make it clear which row number the table starts at (row number **2**), since you can also replace the **2** by a field in a secondary data source for a second REST web service call that is used to dynamically retrieve the number of the first row of a table using the **ROW** function (see the discussion section for more information).

```
Set a field's value: column = 0
```

where **column** is located under the **SetCell** group node under the **queryFields** group node in the **SetCell** secondary data source and **0** is a number representing the first column on the worksheet, so the first field in the Excel table row.

```
Set a field's value: cellValue = field1
```

where **cellValue** is located under the **SetCell** group node under the **queryFields** group node in the **SetCell** secondary data source and **field1** is located in the Main data source of the form.

```
Query using a data connection: SetCell
```

This action calls the **SetCell** web service operation to set the value of the first field in a new row in the table in the Excel workbook.

```
Set a field's value: sessionId = OpenWorkbookForEditingResult
```

where **sessionId** is located under the **CloseWorkbook** group node under the **queryFields** group node in the **CloseWorkbook** secondary data source and **OpenWorkbookForEditingResult** is located under the **OpenWorkbookForEditingResponse** group node under the **dataFields** group node in the **OpenWorkbookForEditing** secondary data source.

```
Query using a data connection: CloseWorkbook
```

This action closes the workbook and the Excel Services session.

8. Publish the form template to a SharePoint form library.

In SharePoint, navigate to the form library where you published the form template and add a new form. When the form opens, the amount of rows that are currently present in the Excel table should appear in the **v** text box. Enter a piece of text in the **field1** text box, and then click the **Add New Row** button. Enter another piece of text in the **field1** text box, and then click the **Add New Row** button again. Close the form and navigate to the SharePoint document library where the Excel workbook that contains the table is located. Open the Excel workbook and verify that the table contains two new records.

Discussion

In the solution described above, you combined the Excel Services REST web service with the Excel Services SOAP web service to be able to first determine the row number that should be used to add a new row to a table in an Excel workbook, and then submit data to the table. Note that you could have implemented the functionality using only the Excel Services SOAP web service, but because the REST web service requires less steps, it was used in the solution described above.

You also made an assumption that the records in the Excel table started on row number **2**. If you want to dynamically determine which row number an Excel table starts at, you can use the **ROW** function to do so. For example **ROW(Foods)** would return **2** as its value. You can add this formula to a cell on the **RowCount** worksheet in the Excel workbook and retrieve the calculated value dynamically through Excel Services just like you retrieved the total amount of rows (**ROWS(Foods)**) in the Excel table. You would then have to change the **Set a field's value** action in step 7 from

```
Set a field's value: row = v + 2 - 1
```

to

```
Set a field's value: row = v + v - 1
```

where the first **v** refers to the total amount of rows from the **GetRowCount** secondary data source and the second **v** refers to the starting row number from the second secondary data source you would have to add to dynamically retrieve the starting row number of the Excel table using the **ROW** function.

And if you wanted to do the same for the columns, you could use **COLUMN(Foods)** to determine the column number the Excel table starts at and **COLUMNS(Foods)** to determine how many columns the Excel table spans.

The **ROW** function returns the row number of a reference, the **ROWS** function returns the number of rows in a reference or array, the **COLUMN** function returns the column number of a reference, and the **COLUMNS** function returns the number of columns in a reference or array.

Because it is much easier to work with row and column numbers instead of cell names such as **A1**, **B2**, etc. when adding rows to an Excel table, the solution described above used the **SetCell** operation instead of the **SetCellA1** operation to set the value of a cell in the Excel table. The only thing you have to remember is that **SetCell** starts its row and column numbers at **0** (so the row and column numbers for cell **A1** would be equal to **0** and **0**, respectively), while an Excel worksheet starts counting at **1** (so the row and column numbers for cell **A1** are equal to **1** and **1**, respectively). This means that you must apply a correction of **-1** when using the **SetCell** operation.

For example, if the row numbers for an Excel table on a worksheet start at **2** and there are **20** rows in the table, the new row number would be **22** (2 + 20), but because row numbers start at **0** when using the **SetCell** operation, the new row number to use with the **SetCell** operation would be **21** (22 - 1).

In the solution described above, the value of only one field in a new row was set. If you wanted to set the values of more fields in the new row, you would have to use actions to repeatedly call the **SetCell** operation with the appropriate row and column numbers for each field you want to set before calling the **CloseWorkbook** operation to save all of the changes for the new table row. For example, the sequence of calls to set the first and second fields in a new row (on the 21st position) in the Excel table would be as follows:

1. Call **OpenWorkbookForEditing** to get an Excel Services session ID, which allows you to edit the Excel workbook.

2. Call **SetCell** with row number equal to **21**, column number equal to **0**, and **cellValue** equal to whatever value you want to set the first field to.

3. Call **SetCell** with row number equal to **21**, column number equal to **1**, and **cellValue** equal to whatever value you want to set the second field to.

4. Call **CloseWorkbook** to save the changes, close the workbook, and end the Excel Services session.

Note:

When you use the **OpenWorkbookForEditing** web service operation to open an Excel workbook for editing, you generally do not need to explicitly call the **SaveWorkbook** operation to save the changes made to the workbook before calling the **CloseWorkbook** operation to close the workbook, since any changes made to the workbook should automatically and permanently be stored in the workbook when you close it. But if the changes you made are not being persisted in your workbook, you may want to try adding the **SaveWorkbook** operation (see for example recipe *20 Update an Excel chart on an InfoPath form*) just before calling the **CloseWorkbook** operation to see whether the additional operation solves the issue.

38 Perform exact and wildcard searches in an Excel table from within InfoPath

Problem

You have an Excel workbook that contains a range of cells that serves as a database. You want to enter part of or an entire word in a text box on an InfoPath form and then click a button to search for the word and retrieve a value from the Excel workbook.

Solution

You can use the **DGET** function in Excel together with the Excel Services REST web service to search for a value in a range of cells that defines a database in an Excel workbook.

To perform exact and wildcard searches in an Excel table from within an InfoPath form:

1. In Excel, use the same workbook you created in recipe *34 Get the amount of records in an Excel table from within InfoPath*, but add a new worksheet named **FindRecord** with the text **Name** in cell **A1**, and the following formula in cell **A3**:

    ```
    =DGET(Foods!A1:AE21, "Calories", A1:A2)
    ```

    This formula retrieves the amount of **Calories** per 100 grams of the food item specified through its **Name** (the label in cell **A1**) in cell **A2**. The database is defined by the range of cells (**A1** through **AE21**) on the **Foods** worksheet. The InfoPath form is going to pass the search criteria to cell **A2** and retrieve the amount of calories from cell **A3** on the **FindRecord** worksheet. You can also download a file named **Foods.xlsx** from www.bizsupportonline.com for use with this recipe.

2. Click **File ➤ Save & Send ➤ Save to SharePoint ➤ Save As** and save the entire workbook (including all of its sheets) to a document library (for example the **Shared Documents** library) on the SharePoint site to which the InfoPath form will be connecting (also see recipe *7 Publish an Excel workbook to SharePoint*).

3. In InfoPath, create a new browser-compatible form template or use an existing one.

4. Select **Data ➤ Get External Data ➤From Web Service ➤ From REST Web Service**.

5. On the **Data Connection Wizard**, enter the URL of the Excel Services REST web service and the Excel workbook, for example:

    ```
    http://servername/sitename/_vti_bin/ExcelREST.aspx/Shared%20Documents/Foods
    .xlsx/model/Ranges('FindRecord!A3')?Ranges('FindRecord!A2')=App&$format=ato
    m
    ```

    and click **Next**. Here, **servername** is the name of the SharePoint server and **sitename** is the name of the site where the **Foods.xlsx** Excel workbook has been stored in the **Shared Documents** document library. Cell **A2** on the **FindRecord**

197

worksheet receives the search term from the InfoPath form, while cell **A3** on the **FindRecord** worksheet returns the amount of calories if the food item is found.

6. On the **Data Connection Wizard**, name the data connection **GetCalories**, deselect the **Automatically retrieve data when form is opened** check box, and click **Finish**.

7. Add a **Text Box** control to the view of the form template and name it **searchTerm**. Users will use this text box to search for a particular food item. For example, entering **App** should return the amount of calories for apples and entering ***rrots*** should return the amount of calories for carrots.

8. On the **Fields** task pane, select **GetCalories (Secondary)** from the **Fields** drop-down list box, expand all of the group nodes under the **content** group node, and then drag-and-drop the **fv** field onto the view of the form template. It should automatically get bound to a text box control.

9. Add a **Button** control to the view of the form template and label it **Get Calories**.

10. Add an **Action** rule to the **Get Calories** button with the following 2 actions:

```
Change REST URL: GetCalories
```

where you must change the formula that sets the value of the **REST Web Service URL** to be the following:

```
concat("http://servername/sitename/_vti_bin/ExcelREST.aspx/Shared%20Documen
ts/Foods.xlsx/model/Ranges('FindRecord!A3')?Ranges('FindRecord!A2')=",
searchTerm, "&$format=atom")
```

where **searchTerm** is the field in the Main data source that is used to enter the name of the food item to search for in the Excel table. With this you have made the REST URL dynamic by using the **concat()** function to construct the REST URL based on a static base URL and the value of a field on the InfoPath form.

```
Query using a data connection: GetCalories
```

This action refreshes the data in the **GetCalories** secondary data source by running the **DGET** formula on the Excel table and returning the data to the InfoPath form.

11. Publish the form template to a SharePoint form library.

In SharePoint, navigate to the form library where you published the form template and add a new form. When the form opens, enter part of the name of a food item (for example **App**) in the **searchTerm** text box and then click the **Get Calories** button. The amount of calories for apples should appear in the **fv** text box. Repeat the search but this time do a wildcard search (for example ***rrots***). Repeat the search with a food item that does not exist (for example **?Bee**). You should see **#VALUE!** appear in the **fv** text box. Repeat the search but this time enter just one character, for example **C**. Because there are multiple records starting with a **C**, you should see **#NUM!** appear in the **fv** text box.

Discussion

The **DGET** function extracts a single value from a column of a list or database that matches conditions you specify. The **DGET** function returns the **#VALUE!** error value when no record matches the criteria and it returns the **#NUM!** error value when more than one record matches the criteria. You can use a question mark (**?**) in the search criteria to find any single character and an asterisk (*****) to find any number of characters. For more information about the **DGET** function, consult the Excel documentation.

In the solution described above, you used the **DGET** function in an Excel workbook along with the Excel Services REST web service to search in a database defined by cells **A1** through **AE21** on a worksheet named **Foods** in an Excel workbook.

```
=DGET(Foods!A1:AE21, "Calories", A1:A2)
```

Cell **A1** on another worksheet named **FindRecord** contained the name of the field to search on (**Name** in this case) and cell **A2** contained the search criteria (for example ***rrots***). These two cells together defined the search criteria that was passed as the third argument to the **DGET** function (**A1:A2**). And finally, the amount of calories, defined by the **Calories** field in the database, was returned. Note that **Calories** is the label of one of the columns in the table that spans cells **A1** through **AE21** on the **Foods** worksheet.

The value of cell **A3** on the **FindRecord** worksheet was retrieved through the following Excel Services REST URL

```
http://servername/sitename/_vti_bin/ExcelREST.aspx/Shared%20Documents/Foods.xlsx
/model/Ranges('FindRecord!A3')
```

after passing the value of the **searchTerm** text box on the InfoPath form to set the value of cell **A2** on the **FindRecord** worksheet to serve as an input parameter for the **DGET** function.

```
?Ranges('FindRecord!A2')= searchTerm
```

Also see recipe *11 Set the value of an Excel cell in InfoPath* for an explanation of how to use the Excel Services REST web service to retrieve the result of an Excel calculation and refer to the beginning of the *Use the Excel Services REST Web Service* section in this chapter for general information about using the Excel Services REST web service in InfoPath and for an explanation of the different parts of the REST URL.

Chapter 3: InfoPath with Excel Programming

Programming for InfoPath with Excel can take place either in Excel or in InfoPath. The most common scenarios in both cases include:

1. **Creating documents**
   Create an Excel workbook from within InfoPath or create an InfoPath form from within Excel.

2. **Getting data**
   Retrieve data from an Excel workbook to populate an InfoPath form or retrieve data from an InfoPath form to populate cells in an Excel workbook.

3. **Sending data**
   Send data from an Excel workbook to an InfoPath form for storage or send data from an InfoPath form to an Excel workbook for storage.

Both InfoPath forms and Excel workbooks can be stored locally on disk or in SharePoint. When stored locally, you can use Visual Basic for Applications (VBA) code in Excel to create or get/set data in InfoPath forms, and you can use the Excel Object Model or the Open XML SDK in InfoPath to create or get/set data in Excel workbooks. When stored in SharePoint, you can use User-Defined Functions (UDFs) to pull data from InfoPath forms into Excel workbooks, and you can use the Open XML SDK in InfoPath to create or get/set data in Excel workbooks.

While you can also use the Excel Object Model with Visual Studio Tools for Office (VSTO) to do Excel programming, this book only covers writing VBA code and creating UDFs for Excel. Note that you will need to have Visual Studio 2010 installed to be able to create UDFs for Excel.

While writing code may often help you implement functionality that you may otherwise not be able to implement without writing code, you are not always required to write code if you want to create or get/set data in Excel workbooks. Refer to Chapter 2 for codeless solutions that create or get/set data in Excel workbooks before you consider writing code.

Use VBA in Excel

39 Generate an InfoPath form from Excel data

Problem

You have an Excel workbook, which you want to use to programmatically create a new InfoPath form that is based on a particular form template and which contains data from the Excel workbook.

Solution

You can use `Microsoft.XMLDOM` and `Scripting.FileSystemObject` objects to programmatically contruct an InfoPath form using VBA code in Excel and then save the form locally on disk.

To generate an InfoPath form from Excel data:

1. In InfoPath, create a new form template or use an existing one. If you are creating your own form template, continue with step 2. If you want to use a sample form template, you can download a file named **GenerateFromExcel.xsn** from www.bizsupportonline.com, follow the instructions below, and then continue with step 5.

    To use the downloaded form template:

    a. In Windows Explorer, navigate to the location where you saved the form template (.xsn).

    b. Right-click the form template (.xsn), and select **Design** from the context menu that appears. This should open the form template in InfoPath Designer 2010.

    c. In InfoPath, click **Save** and save the form template to a location on disk.

2. Add a **Text Box** control to the view of the form template and name it **field1**.

3. Add a **Repeating Table** control with 3 columns to the view of the form template, and ensure that the fields within the repeating table are named **field2**, **field3**, and **field4**, respectively.

4. Save the form template locally on disk.

5. In Windows Explorer, navigate to the location where you saved the form template, double-click it, and then when it opens in InfoPath Filler, save the InfoPath form as a file named **BlankForm.xml**.

6. In Excel, create a new workbook or open an existing one.

7. Click **File ➤ Save As**.

8. On the **Save As** dialog box, browse to a location on disk where you want to save the workbook, enter a suitable file name (for example **GenerateIPForm**) in the **File name** text box, select **Excel Macro-Enabled Workbook (*.xlsm)** from the **Save as type** drop-down list box, and then click **Save**.

9. In Excel, add data to **Sheet1** in the workbook. For example, you could fill column **A** with the names of fruits and column **B** with the colors of fruits.

10. If the **Developer** tab is not present on the Ribbon, click **File ➤ Options**. On the **Excel Options** dialog box, click **Customize Ribbon**, and then on the right-hand side of the dialog box, select **Main Tabs** from the **Customize the Ribbon** drop-down list box, ensure that the **Developer** check box is selected, and then click **OK**.

11. Click **Developer ➤ Controls ➤ Insert**, and then under **ActiveX Controls**, click the icon that represents a **Button** control. The cursor should change into a cross. Click in an empty cell on **Sheet1**, hold the mouse button pressed down, move the mouse pointer to the bottom-right corner of the empty cell, and then release the mouse button. A button should appear with the text **CommandButton1** displayed on it.

12. With the button still selected, click **Developer ➤ Controls ➤ Properties** to open the **Properties** pane.

13. On the **Properties** pane, change the **(Name)** of the button from **CommandButton1** to **GenerateIPFormButton**, and change the **Caption** from **CommandButton1** to **Generate InfoPath Form**. Close the **Properties** pane and then resize the button on **Sheet1** if necessary so that you can see its entire caption.

14. Double-click the **GenerateIPFormButton** button to add a `GenerateIPFormButton_Click()` event handler in code. Microsoft Visual Basic for Applications should automatically open and add a **Sub** procedure to **Sheet1**.

    ```
    Private Sub GenerateIPFormButton_Click()

    End Sub
    ```

15. In Microsoft Visual Basic for Applications, click **Insert ➤ Module** to add a new module to the VBA project. The code window for **Module1** should automatically open. If it does not, double-click **Module1** in the **Project – VBAProject** pane to open its code window.

16. Add the following code to **Module1** (*code #: 21E427DD-C26C-4AAA-BF92-911430473153*):

    ```
    Function CreateFieldOrGroup( _
      ByRef xmlDoc, ByVal nodeName, ByVal namespaceURI, ByVal nodeValue) _
      As Object

      Dim xmlNode
      Set xmlNode = xmlDoc.CreateNode(1, nodeName, namespaceURI)
      xmlNode.Text = nodeValue
      Set CreateFieldOrGroup = xmlNode
    ```

```
End Function

Sub CreateFileWithContents(ByVal contents, ByVal fullFilePath)

  Dim fso, tf
  Set fso = CreateObject("Scripting.FileSystemObject")
  Set tf = fso.CreateTextFile(fullFilePath, True)
  tf.Write (contents)
  tf.Close

End Sub
```

The `CreateFieldOrGroup()` procedure is a helper function that can be used to add a node (a field or a group in an InfoPath form) to an XML document, while the `CreateFileWithContents()` procedure can be used to create a new file on disk.

17. Double-click **Sheet1 (Sheet1)** in the **Project – VBAProject** pane to open its code window.

18. Add the following code to the `GenerateIPFormButton_Click()` event handler (*code #: 8CDB5F00-50FF-437B-B97E-A97F60371EF9*):

```
Dim xmlDoc, ns, root
Dim field1, field2, field3, field4, group1, group2

Set xmlDoc = CreateObject("Microsoft.XMLDOM")
xmlDoc.async = False
Call xmlDoc.LoadXML("<?xml version=""1.0"" encoding=""UTF-8""?>" & _
  "<?mso-infoPathSolution solutionVersion=""1.0.0.2"" " & _
  "productVersion=""14.0.0"" PIVersion=""1.0.0.0"" " & _
  "href=""file:///E:\GenerateFromExcel.xsn"" " & _
  "name=""urn:schemas-microsoft-com:office:infopath:GenerateFromExcel:" & _
  "-myXSD-2012-07-27T03-59-09"" ?>" & _
  "<?mso-application progid=""InfoPath.Document"" " & _
  "versionProgid=""InfoPath.Document.3""?>" & _
  "<my:myFields " & _
  "xmlns:my=""http://schemas.microsoft.com/office/infopath/2003/myXSD/"" & _
  "2012-07-27T03:59:09"" xml:lang=""en-us""></my:myFields>")

ns = "http://schemas.microsoft.com/office/infopath/2003/myXSD/" & _
  "2012-07-27T03:59:09"

Set root = xmlDoc.DocumentElement

Set field1 = CreateFieldOrGroup(xmlDoc, "field1", ns, "Generated by Excel")
Call root.appendChild(field1)

Set group1 = CreateFieldOrGroup(xmlDoc, "group1", ns, "")
Call root.appendChild(group1)

If Selection.Areas.Count > 0 Then

  For Each area In Selection.Areas

    Set group2 = CreateFieldOrGroup(xmlDoc, "group2", ns, "")

    For Each cell In area

      If cell.column = 1 Then
        Set field2 = CreateFieldOrGroup(xmlDoc, "field2", ns, cell.Value)
```

```
        Call group2.appendChild(field2)
      End If

      If cell.column = 2 Then
        Set field3 = CreateFieldOrGroup(xmlDoc, "field3", ns, cell.Value)
        Call group2.appendChild(field3)

        Set field4 = CreateFieldOrGroup(xmlDoc, "field4", ns, "")
        Call group2.appendChild(field4)

        Call group1.appendChild(group2)
        Set group2 = CreateFieldOrGroup(xmlDoc, "group2", ns, "")
      End If

    Next cell

  Next area

End If

Call CreateFileWithContents(xmlDoc.XML, "E:\GeneratedForm.xml")
```

where you must replace **E:\GeneratedForm.xml** with the correct location on disk and file name where you want to save the generated InfoPath form. You must also change the value of the ns variable to be equal to the correct namespace URI for the **my** namespace prefix for your own InfoPath form template. You can find the namespace URI by opening the InfoPath form in Notepad and then searching for **xmlns:my=**. In addition, you must replace the initial XML fragment that is passed to the LoadXML() method by the XML contained in the **BlankForm.xml** file you saved earlier as follows:

a. In Windows Explorer, navigate to the location on disk where the **BlankForm.xml** file is located.

b. Right-click the **BlankForm.xml** file and select **Open with ➤ Notepad** from the context menu that appears.

c. In Notepad, delete all of the nodes that are located between the <my:myFields> and </my:myFields> nodes.

d. Select all of the text and press **Ctrl+C** to copy the text to the clipboard.

e. Close Notepad without saving the file.

f. In Microsoft Visual Basic for Applications, select all of the text contained in the LoadXML() method, and then press **Ctrl+V** to paste the text from the clipboard and replace the existing text.

g. Replace all double quotes (") in the newly pasted text by two double quotes (""). Remember to leave the first and last double-quotes as single double quotes, since these are used to enclose the text as a string.

19. Click **File ➤ Save GenerateIPForm.xlsm** to save the code.

In Excel, click **Developer ➤ Controls ➤ Design Mode** to toggle design mode off. Select a range of cells you want to use to create a new InfoPath form, and then click the

Generate InfoPath Form button. In Windows Explorer, navigate to the location on disk where the new InfoPath form should have been created, double-click it to open it in InfoPath Filler 2010, and verify that it contains the data from the cells you selected in the Excel workbook.

Discussion

In the solution described above, you saw how to write VBA code that creates a new InfoPath form and uses data from an Excel workbook to populate the newly created form. Because an InfoPath form is an XML file, you can use objects that are typically used in solutions that contain script code to create an XML file that can be opened as an InfoPath form.

In the solution described above, you first created an InfoPath form template and then used it to create a blank InfoPath form, which provided you with the basic XML content of the InfoPath form you wanted to create. Note that the InfoPath form template was saved to disk and not published. In a real-world scenario, you should first publish the form template (to a network location or to SharePoint) and then create a blank form using the published form template.

The code in the solution described above uses the `Microsoft.XMLDOM` class to load the basic XML content of a blank InfoPath form into an `XMLDOM` object.

```
Set xmlDoc = CreateObject("Microsoft.XMLDOM")
xmlDoc.async = False
Call xmlDoc.LoadXML("<?xml version=""1.0"" encoding=""UTF-8""?>" & _
  "<?mso-infoPathSolution solutionVersion=""1.0.0.2"" " & _
  "productVersion=""14.0.0"" PIVersion=""1.0.0.0"" " & _
  "href=""file:///E:\GenerateFromExcel.xsn"" " & _
  "name=""urn:schemas-microsoft-com:office:infopath:GenerateFromExcel:" & _
  "-myXSD-2012-07-27T03-59-09"" ?>" & _
  "<?mso-application progid=""InfoPath.Document"" " & _
  "versionProgid=""InfoPath.Document.3""?>" & _
  "<my:myFields " & _
  "xmlns:my=""http://schemas.microsoft.com/office/infopath/2003/myXSD/" & _
  "2012-07-27T03:59:09"" xml:lang=""en-us""></my:myFields>")
```

Note that the XML that is loaded into the `XMLDOM` object only contains the root element (**myFields** in this case) and no child elements, since the child elements are created afterwards through code using a procedure named `CreateFieldOrGroup()` which is defined in **Module1**.

The first field of the InfoPath form (**field1**) is added to the XML document using the `CreateFieldOrGroup()` procedure and the `appendChild()` method of the root element as follows:

```
Set field1 = CreateFieldOrGroup(xmlDoc, "field1", ns, "Generated by Excel")
Call root.appendChild(field1)
```

where `root` refers to the root element of the XML document.

```
Set root = xmlDoc.DocumentElement
```

and ns refers to the namespace URI of the **my** namespace prefix in the InfoPath form.

```
ns = "http://schemas.microsoft.com/office/infopath/2003/myXSD/" & _
    "2012-07-27T03:59:09"
```

Once the first field has been added, it is time to add the main group node (**group1**) for the repeating table on the InfoPath form in much the same way you added the first field, but then without assigning a value to it.

```
Set group1 = CreateFieldOrGroup(xmlDoc, "group1", ns, "")
Call root.appendChild(group1)
```

The code then creates the first repeating group node (**group2**) for the repeating table on the InfoPath form

```
Set group2 = CreateFieldOrGroup(xmlDoc, "group2", ns, "")
```

when it starts to loop through the selected areas and cells in each selected area on the Excel worksheet.

```
If Selection.Areas.Count > 0 Then

  For Each area In Selection.Areas

    Set group2 = CreateFieldOrGroup(xmlDoc, "group2", ns, "")

    For Each cell In area

      ...

    Next cell

  Next area

End If
```

Note that because the code loops through all of the selected areas, the areas a user selects need not be adjacent. For example, a user could select cells **A1** through **B2** and also cells **A5** through **B6** (so two separate non-adjacent areas) and all of data from the selected cells would be placed in the repeating table on the InfoPath form.

The code that loops through all of the cells in a particular area checks the column number, and based on this number adds either a **field2** or a **field3** to the **group2** element. Note that **field4** is left blank in the repeating table, since the assumption is made that data from only two columns on the worksheet are added to the repeating table in **field2** and **field3**. So even if the user selects areas that have 3 columns the code would ignore the last column.

```
For Each cell In area

  If cell.column = 1 Then
    Set field2 = CreateFieldOrGroup(xmlDoc, "field2", ns, cell.Value)
    Call group2.appendChild(field2)
  End If

  If cell.column = 2 Then
    Set field3 = CreateFieldOrGroup(xmlDoc, "field3", ns, cell.Value)
    Call group2.appendChild(field3)

    Set field4 = CreateFieldOrGroup(xmlDoc, "field4", ns, "")
    Call group2.appendChild(field4)

    Call group1.appendChild(group2)
    Set group2 = CreateFieldOrGroup(xmlDoc, "group2", ns, "")
  End If

Next cell
```

If you want a user to be able to select areas that have 3 columns and place the values in the 3 fields in the repeating table on the InfoPath form, you must modify the code to check for a third column as follows:

```
For Each cell In area

  If cell.Column = 1 Then
    Set field2 = CreateFieldOrGroup(xmlDoc, "field2", ns, cell.Value)
    Call group2.appendChild(field2)
  End If

  If cell.Column = 2 Then
    Set field3 = CreateFieldOrGroup(xmlDoc, "field3", ns, cell.Value)
    Call group2.appendChild(field3)
  End If

  If cell.Column = 3 Then
    Set field4 = CreateFieldOrGroup(xmlDoc, "field4", ns, cell.Value)
    Call group2.appendChild(field4)

    Call group1.appendChild(group2)
    Set group2 = CreateFieldOrGroup(xmlDoc, "group2", ns, "")
  End If

Next cell
```

Note that if a user selects an area that spans only 2 columns, the code shown above would ignore the data in that area and not add it to the repeating table on the InfoPath form. So users are forced to select areas that span at least 3 columns for the code to add rows to the repeating table on the InfoPath form.

Once the entire XML document has been constructed using data from Excel, a procedure named CreateFileWithContents() that uses a Scripting.FileSystemObject object is called to save the XML document to disk.

```
Call CreateFileWithContents(xmlDoc.XML, "E:\GeneratedForm.xml")
```

And because the XML document contains InfoPath processing instructions, its icon should automatically be the icon of an InfoPath form, so you can also double-click the file to open it in InfoPath Filler 2010.

The solution described above is dynamic in that it allows users to select a range of cells to create an InfoPath form, but you could have also used a static range of cells instead. For example, if you wanted to write data from cell **B2** to **field1** on the InfoPath form, you could use the following code:

```
Set field1 = CreateFieldOrGroup(xmlDoc, "field1", ns, Sheet1.Cells(2, 2))
Call root.appendChild(field1)
```

or

```
Set field1 = CreateFieldOrGroup(xmlDoc, "field1", ns, Sheet1.Range("B2"))
Call root.appendChild(field1)
```

Consult the *Excel 2010 Developer Reference* in the Excel Help file for more information about writing VBA code for Excel. To access the help file, click the blue **Help** icon or press **F1** in Microsoft Visual Basic for Applications.

40 Populate an InfoPath repeating table with Excel data

Problem

You have an InfoPath form that has a repeating table on it which you want to populate with data from an Excel workbook.

Solution

You can use a `Microsoft.XMLDOM` object to programmatically populate a repeating table on an existing InfoPath form and then save the form.

To populate a repeating table on an InfoPath form with Excel data:

1. In InfoPath, create a new form template, use an existing one, or use the **GenerateFromExcel.xsn** form template from step 1 of recipe *39 Generate an InfoPath form from Excel data*. Create a form using the form template of your choice, save the InfoPath form somewhere locally on disk, and name the file **BlankForm.xml**.

2. In Excel, create a new workbook or open an existing one.

3. Click **File ➤ Save As**.

4. On the **Save As** dialog box, browse to a location on disk where you want to save the workbook, enter a suitable file name (for example **PopulateRepeatingTableFromExcel**) in the **File name** text box, select **Excel**

Macro-Enabled Workbook (*.xlsm) from the **Save as type** drop-down list box, and then click **Save**.

5. In Excel, add data to **Sheet1** in the workbook. For example, you could fill column **A** with the names of fruits and column **B** with the colors of fruits.

6. If the **Developer** tab is not present on the Ribbon, click **File ➤ Options**. On the **Excel Options** dialog box, click **Customize Ribbon**, and then on the right-hand side of the dialog box, select **Main Tabs** from the **Customize the Ribbon** drop-down list box, ensure that the **Developer** check box is selected, and then click **OK**.

7. Click **Developer ➤ Controls ➤ Insert**, and then under **ActiveX Controls**, click the icon that represents a **Button** control. The cursor should change into a cross. Click in an empty cell on **Sheet1**, hold the mouse button pressed down, move the mouse pointer to the bottom-right corner of the empty cell, and then release the mouse button. A button should appear with the text **CommandButton1** displayed on it.

8. With the button still selected, click **Developer ➤ Controls ➤ Properties** to open the **Properties** pane.

9. On the **Properties** pane, change the **(Name)** of the button from **CommandButton1** to **PopulateRepTblButton**, and change the **Caption** from **CommandButton1** to **Populate Repeating Table**. Close the **Properties** pane and then resize the button on **Sheet1** if necessary so that you can see its entire caption.

10. Double-click the **PopulateRepTblButton** button to add a `PopulateRepTblButton_Click()` event handler in code. Microsoft Visual Basic for Applications should automatically open and add a **Sub** procedure to **Sheet1**.

```
Private Sub PopulateRepTblButton_Click()

End Sub
```

11. In Microsoft Visual Basic for Applications, click **Insert ➤ Module** to add a new module to the VBA project. The code window for **Module1** should automatically open. If it does not, double-click **Module1** in the **Project – VBAProject** pane to open its code window.

12. Add the following code to **Module1** (*code #: 8E353467-77D7-4E2F-BBBD-E0A789C612CB*):

```
Function CreateFieldOrGroup( _
  ByRef xmlDoc, ByVal nodeName, ByVal namespaceURI, ByVal nodeValue) _
  As Object

  Dim xmlNode
  Set xmlNode = xmlDoc.CreateNode(1, nodeName, namespaceURI)
  xmlNode.Text = nodeValue
  Set CreateFieldOrGroup = xmlNode

End Function
```

The `CreateFieldOrGroup()` procedure is a helper function that can be used to add a node (a field or a group in an InfoPath form) to an XML document.

13. Double-click **Sheet1 (Sheet1)** in the **Project – VBAProject** pane to open its code window.

14. Add the following code to the `PopulateRepTblButton_Click()` event handler (*code #: 56436984-4D22-4D45-9ED7-5D9A059A9E3B*):

```
Dim xmlDoc As Object
Dim group1 As Object
Dim group2 As Object
Dim field2 As Object
Dim field3 As Object
Dim field4 As Object
Dim formFilePath As String
Dim namespaceURI As String

formFilePath = "E:\BlankForm.xml"
namespaceURI = "http://schemas.microsoft.com/office/infopath/2003/" & _
  "myXSD/2012-07-27T03:59:09"

Set xmlDoc = CreateObject("Microsoft.XMLDOM")
xmlDoc.async = False
Call xmlDoc.Load(formFilePath)
Call xmlDoc.setProperty("SelectionNamespaces", "xmlns:my='" & _
  namespaceURI & "'")
Call xmlDoc.setProperty("SelectionLanguage", "XPath")

Set group1 = xmlDoc.SelectSingleNode("//my:group1")

If Selection.Areas.Count > 0 Then

  For Each area In Selection.Areas

    For Each cell In area

      If cell.Column = 1 Then
        Set group2 = CreateFieldOrGroup( _
          xmlDoc, "my:group2", namespaceURI, "")
        Set field2 = CreateFieldOrGroup( _
          xmlDoc, "my:field2", namespaceURI, cell.Value)
        Call group2.appendChild(field2)
      End If

      If cell.Column = 2 Then
        Set field3 = CreateFieldOrGroup( _
          xmlDoc, "my:field3", namespaceURI, cell.Value)
        Call group2.appendChild(field3)
      End If

      If cell.Column = 3 Then
        Set field4 = CreateFieldOrGroup( _
          xmlDoc, "my:field4", namespaceURI, cell.Value)
        Call group2.appendChild(field4)
        Call group1.appendChild(group2)
      End If

    Next cell
```

```
        Set group2 = Nothing
        Set field2 = Nothing
        Set field3 = Nothing
        Set field4 = Nothing

    Next area

End If

Call xmlDoc.Save(formFilePath)
```

where you must replace **E:\BlankForm.xml** with the correct location and file name where the InfoPath form you want to modify is located on disk. In addition, you must replace the namespace URI for the **my** namespace prefix with the correct namespace URI for your own InfoPath form template. You can find the namespace URI by opening the InfoPath form in Notepad and then searching for **xmlns:my=**. Note that if you are using an InfoPath form template that contains other namespaces, you must declare them in code using the `setProperty()` method of the XMLDOM object similar to how the **my** namespace prefix has been defined in the code, so that you can use the namespaces in XPath expressions.

15. Click **File ➤ Save PopulateRepeatingTableFromExcel.xlsm** to save the code.

In Excel, click **Developer ➤ Controls ➤ Design Mode** to toggle design mode off. Select a range of cells (that has 3 columns) you want to use to populate the repeating table on the InfoPath form, and then click the **Populate Repeating Table** button. In Windows Explorer, navigate to the location on disk where the InfoPath form is located, double-click it to open it in InfoPath Filler 2010, and verify that it contains the data from the cells you selected in Excel.

Note that while selected areas must contain 3 columns for this solution to work, you do not have to select adjacent rows. For example you could select the data from rows 1 and 3 by holding the **Ctrl** key pressed down while you select the data in Excel and then send only those 2 rows to the repeating table on the InfoPath form.

Discussion

In the solution described above, you saw how to write VBA code that adds one or more rows to a repeating table control on an existing InfoPath form. Unlike the code in recipe *39 Generate an InfoPath form from Excel data*, the code in this solution uses the `Load()` method of a `Microsoft.XMLDOM` object to open an existing InfoPath form that is located on disk.

```
Set xmlDoc = CreateObject("Microsoft.XMLDOM")
xmlDoc.async = False
Call xmlDoc.Load(formFilePath)
```

It then uses the `setproperty()` method to prepare the XMLDOM object for node retrieval using XPath expressions and namespace prefixes.

```
Call xmlDoc.setProperty("SelectionNamespaces", "xmlns:my='" & _
  namespaceURI & "'")
Call xmlDoc.setProperty("SelectionLanguage", "XPath")
```

The code retrieves the main group node (**group1**) of the repeating table on the InfoPath form

```
Set group1 = xmlDoc.SelectSingleNode("//my:group1")
```

before it starts to loop through all of the cells in all of the areas that a user may have selected.

```
If Selection.Areas.Count > 0 Then

  For Each area In Selection.Areas

    For Each cell In area

      ...

    Next cell

    Set group2 = Nothing
    Set field2 = Nothing
    Set field3 = Nothing
    Set field4 = Nothing

  Next area

End If
```

For each row in a selected area, the code creates a **group2** node, and then walks through each column in a row to add a field (**field2**, **field3**, and **field4**) to the **group2** node. If a third column is present in a row, the **group2** node is added to the main group node of the repeating table (**group1**). This effectively means that a user is forced to select areas that have at least 3 columns for the code to work (also see the discussion section of recipe *39 Generate an InfoPath form from Excel data*).

```
For Each cell In area

  If cell.Column = 1 Then
    Set group2 = CreateFieldOrGroup( _
      xmlDoc, "my:group2", namespaceURI, "")
    Set field2 = CreateFieldOrGroup( _
      xmlDoc, "my:field2", namespaceURI, cell.Value)
    Call group2.appendChild(field2)
  End If

  If cell.Column = 2 Then
    Set field3 = CreateFieldOrGroup( _
      xmlDoc, "my:field3", namespaceURI, cell.Value)
    Call group2.appendChild(field3)
  End If

  If cell.Column = 3 Then
```

```
   Set field4 = CreateFieldOrGroup( _
     xmlDoc, "my:field4", namespaceURI, cell.Value)
   Call group2.appendChild(field4)
   Call group1.appendChild(group2)
 End If

Next cell
```

And finally, the `Save()` method of the `XMLDOM` object is called to save the changes in the InfoPath form.

```
Call xmlDoc.Save(formFilePath)
```

Note that the code in this solution does not overwrite the contents of a repeating table on an InfoPath form, but rather adds to it. So a user can select any row(s) on the worksheet, click the button, and continue to add rows to the repeating table on the InfoPath form this way.

You could extend this solution by providing users with the ability to dynamically select an InfoPath form through for example a drop-down list box or by entering data in a particular cell on a worksheet in the Excel workbook.

Consult the *Excel 2010 Developer Reference* in the Excel Help file for more information about writing VBA code for Excel. To access the help file, click the blue **Help** icon or press **F1** in Microsoft Visual Basic for Applications.

41   Populate Excel with InfoPath repeating table data

Problem

You have an InfoPath form that has a repeating table from which you would like to import data into an Excel workbook.

Solution

You can write VBA code in a macro in Excel to import data from a repeating table on an existing InfoPath form, and copy that data to cells on a worksheet in the Excel workbook.

To populate an Excel worksheet with data from a repeating table on an InfoPath form:

1.   In InfoPath, create a new form template that has a repeating table control with the name **group1** for its container group node and the name **group2** for its repeating group node. You can add as many or as little columns as you like to the repeating table.

2.   Fill out a new form based on the form template you created in step 1 and name the filled out form **PopulateExcelFromRepeatingTable.xml**. You can also download a sample file named **PopulateExcelFromRepeatingTable.xml** from www.bizsupportonline.com for use with this recipe.

3. In Excel, create a new Excel workbook and save it as an **Excel Macro-Enabled Workbook (.xlsm)** file.

4. Click **Developer ➤ Code ➤ Macros**. If the **Developer** tab is not present on the Ribbon, click **File ➤ Options**. On the **Excel Options** dialog box, click **Customize Ribbon**, and then on the right-hand side of the dialog box, select **Main Tabs** from the **Customize the Ribbon** drop-down list box, ensure that the **Developer** check box is selected, and then click **OK**.

5. On the **Macro** dialog box, enter **ImportRepeatingTableData** in the **Macro name** text box, select **This Workbook** from the **Macros in** drop-down list box, and then click **Create**. This should open Microsoft Visual Basic for Applications.

6. In Microsoft Visual Basic for Applications, add the following procedure to **Module1** (*code #: 31708B4D-59FF-4112-89EF-90A62E45D064*):

```
Function IsGroupNode(ByVal Node As Object) As Boolean

  If Not Node Is Nothing Then

    Dim objChildNodeList As Object
    Set objChildNodeList = Node.SelectNodes("*")

    If objChildNodeList.Length > 0 Then
      IsGroupNode = True
    End If

  End If

End Function
```

This procedure determines whether the node passed to it is a group node and returns True if it is.

7. Add the following code to the ImportRepeatingTableData() procedure in **Module1** (*code #: C7434D24-A3B0-4429-A4ED-E84131A40F9F*):

```
Dim xmlDoc As Object
Dim objNodeList As Object
Dim parentNode As Object
Dim startingRowIndex As Integer
Dim startingColIndex As Integer
Dim rIndex As Integer
Dim cIndex As Integer
Dim newRow As Boolean

Set xmlDoc = CreateObject("Microsoft.XMLDOM")
xmlDoc.async = False
Call xmlDoc.Load("C:\PopulateExcelFromRepeatingTable.xml")
Call xmlDoc.setProperty("SelectionLanguage", "XPath")
Set objNodeList = xmlDoc.DocumentElement.SelectNodes( _
  "//*[local-name() = 'group1']//*")

rIndex = 0
cIndex = 0
startingRowIndex = 0
```

```
startingColIndex = 0
newRow = False

If Selection.Areas.Count > 0 Then
  startingRowIndex = Selection.Areas(1).Cells(1, 1).Row
  startingColIndex = Selection.Areas(1).Cells(1, 1).Column
End If

For Each Node In objNodeList

  If IsGroupNode(Node) Then
    Set parentNode = Node
    cIndex = 0
    newRow = True
  Else
    cIndex = cIndex + 1
    If newRow = True Then
      rIndex = rIndex + 1
      newRow = False
    End If

    Cells(startingRowIndex + rIndex - 1, _
      startingColIndex + cIndex - 1) _
     .Value = Node.Text
  End If

Next Node
```

where you must replace `C:\PopulateExcelFromRepeatingTable.xml` with the correct location of the InfoPath form you saved in step 2.

8. Save the VBA project.

In Excel, select a cell (for example **C4**) and then click **Developer ➤ Code ➤ Macros**. On the **Macro** dialog box, select **ImportRepeatingTableData**, and then click **Run**. The data from the repeating table on the InfoPath form that was specified in the `Load()` method of the `XMLDOM` object should have been loaded into cells starting from cell **C4** and the amount of columns in the repeating table should have been automatically detected to fill the correct amount of columns on the worksheet in the Excel workbook.

Discussion

In the solution described above, you saw how to use a macro to import data from a repeating table on an existing InfoPath form into a range of cells on a worksheet in an Excel workbook.

The code first loads an existing InfoPath form into a `Microsoft.XMLDOM` object

```
Set xmlDoc = CreateObject("Microsoft.XMLDOM")
xmlDoc.async = False
Call xmlDoc.Load("C:\PopulateExcelFromRepeatingTable.xml")
```

and then uses an XPath expression to retrieve all of the nodes under the main group node of the repeating table on the InfoPath form.

```
Call xmlDoc.setProperty("SelectionLanguage", "XPath")
Set objNodeList = xmlDoc.DocumentElement.SelectNodes( _
  "//*[local-name() = 'group1']//*")
```

The code then retrieves the numbers for the row and column of the cell the user selected on the Excel worksheet

```
If Selection.Areas.Count > 0 Then
  startingRowIndex = Selection.Areas(1).Cells(1, 1).Row
  startingColIndex = Selection.Areas(1).Cells(1, 1).Column
End If
```

before it starts to loop through all of the nodes (group nodes and fields) from the repeating table and fill the cells on the Excel worksheet.

```
For Each Node In objNodeList

  If IsGroupNode(Node) Then
    Set parentNode = Node
    cIndex = 0
    newRow = True
  Else
    cIndex = cIndex + 1
    If newRow = True Then
      rIndex = rIndex + 1
      newRow = False
    End If

    Cells(startingRowIndex + rIndex - 1, _
      startingColIndex + cIndex - 1) _
      .Value = Node.Text
  End If

Next Node
```

The code is written in a way that it can recognize and skip group nodes using a procedure named IsGroupNode() and thereby also keep track of row numbers and rewind column numbers when populating cells on the Excel worksheet.

If you want to import all of the data from an InfoPath form that not only contains a repeating table, you can replace the line of code where the nodes are selected

```
Set objNodeList = xmlDoc.DocumentElement.SelectNodes( _
  "//*[local-name() = 'group1']//*")
```

with the following line of code

```
Set objNodeList = xmlDoc.DocumentElement.SelectNodes("//*")
```

This should import all of the data from the InfoPath form instead of only data from the repeating table.

Consult the *Excel 2010 Developer Reference* in the Excel Help file for more information about writing VBA code for Excel. To access the help file, click the blue **Help** icon or press **F1** in Microsoft Visual Basic for Applications.

42 Link Excel cells to document library columns

Problem

You have a couple of cells in an Excel workbook, which you want to fill out. These cells correspond to columns in a SharePoint document library where items represent records. So whenever a cell is filled out in the Excel workbook, the corresponding column in the SharePoint document library for the item corresponding to the Excel workbook should be updated with the same value of the cell in the Excel workbook.

Solution

You can use VBA code to synchronize cells in an Excel workbook with columns in a SharePoint document library.

To link Excel cells to SharePoint document library columns:

1. In SharePoint, click **Site Actions ➤ More Options**.

2. On the **Create** page, select **Library** under the **Filter By** catergory, select **Document Library**, and then click **More Options**.

3. On the **Create** page, enter a **Name** for the document library (for example **ExcelDIPLib**), select **Microsoft Excel spreadsheet** as the **Document Template**, and click **Create**.

4. Once the document library has been created, click **Library Tools ➤ Library ➤ Manage Views ➤ Create Column**, follow the instructions to create a **Single line of text** column named **Col1**, and then repeat the process to create a second **Single line of text** column named **Col2**. These columns are automatically copied onto the default content type for the document library, which you should then be able to access from within Excel.

5. In Excel, create a new workbook or open an existing one.

6. Click **File ➤ Save As**.

7. On the **Save As** dialog box, browse to a location on disk where you want to save the workbook, enter a suitable file name (for example **ExcelDIP**) in the **Filename** text box, select **Excel Macro-Enabled Workbook (*.xlsm)** from the **Save as type** drop-down list box, and then click **Save**.

8. In Excel, click **File ➤ Save & Send ➤ Save to SharePoint ➤ Save As** and follow the instructions to save the Excel workbook to the **ExcelDIPLib** document library you created earlier (also see recipe *7 Publish an Excel workbook to SharePoint*). This

should allow the properties of the default content type of the SharePoint document library to be exposed to the Excel workbook.

9. Let us assume that you want to use cell **B3** on **Sheet1** to fill out **Col1** in the SharePoint document library, and cell **C4** on **Sheet2** to fill out **Col2** in the SharePoint document library. Click **Developer ➤ Code ➤ Visual Basic**. If the **Developer** tab is not present on the Ribbon, click **File ➤ Options**. On the **Excel Options** dialog box, click **Customize Ribbon**, and then on the right-hand side of the dialog box, select **Main Tabs** from the **Customize the Ribbon** drop-down list box, ensure that the **Developer** check box is selected, and then click **OK**.

10. In Microsoft Visual Basic for Applications, on the **Project – VBAProject** pane, double-click **Sheet1 (Sheet1)**.

11. In the code window for **Sheet1**, select **Worksheet** in the first drop-down list box, and then select **Change** in the second drop-down list box to add a `Worksheet_Change()` event handler.

```
Private Sub Worksheet_Change(ByVal Target As Range)

End Sub
```

12. Add the following code to the `Worksheet_Change()` event handler (*code #: 8B0ED553-C173-43E2-BBDC-AE95CDBA7BB2*):

```
Dim CellRef As String

CellRef = Replace(Target.AddressLocal, "$", "")

If CellRef = "B3" Then
  ThisWorkbook.ContentTypeProperties("Col1").Value = Range("B3").Value
End If
```

This code first retrieves a user-friendly name for the cell being changed on **Sheet1** and if that cell is cell **B3**, the value of the **Col1** property of the content type is set to be equal to the value of cell **B3**.

13. Repeat steps 10 through 12 for **Sheet2** and cell **C4**, but add the following code to the `Worksheet_Change()` event handler (*code #: 8457EC66-BCE6-4806-ADE6-608E2258D4B3*):

```
Dim CellRef As String

CellRef = Replace(Target.AddressLocal, "$", "")

If CellRef = "C4" Then
  ThisWorkbook.ContentTypeProperties("Col2").Value = Range("C4").Value
End If
```

This code first retrieves a user-friendly name for the cell being changed on **Sheet2** and if that cell is cell **C4**, the value of the **Col2** property of the content type is set to be equal to the value of cell **C4**.

14. The code in steps 10 through 13 writes data from the Excel workbook to SharePoint document library columns. If you only require one-way updating from Excel to SharePoint, you can skip this and the next two steps. To retrieve data from SharePoint document library columns and display it in the Excel workbook as soon as the workbook opens in Excel, in Microsoft Visual Basic for Applications, on the **Project – VBAProject** pane, double-click **ThisWorkbook**.

15. In the code window for **ThisWorkbook**, select **Workbook** in the first drop-down list box. **Open** should automatically be selected in the second drop-down list box and a `Workbook_Open()` event handler added to the code window.

```
Private Sub Workbook_Open()

End Sub
```

16. Add the following code to the `Workbook_Open()` event handler (*code #: 0F20299D-ECDF-4A60-A8D6-8D42AA522083*):

```
Sheet1.Range("B3").Value = ThisWorkbook.ContentTypeProperties("Col1").Value
Sheet2.Range("C4").Value = ThisWorkbook.ContentTypeProperties("Col2").Value
```

This code sets the values of cell **B3** on **Sheet1** and cell **C4** on **Sheet2** to be equal to the values of the **Col1** and **Col2** properties of the content type when the workbook opens in the Excel client application.

17. Click **File ➤ Save ExcelDIP.xlsm** to save the code.

In Excel, enter a piece of text in cell **B3** of **Sheet1** and then click **Save**. In SharePoint, navigate to the document library where the Excel workbook is stored, and verify that the **Col1** column for the item representing the Excel workbook in the SharePoint document library contains the value you entered in Excel. Repeat the process for cell **C4** on **Sheet2**.

Discussion

In the solution described above, you saw how to use VBA code to write data from an Excel workbook to columns in a SharePoint document library.

In this case, the values of properties (**Col1** and **Col2**) that were defined on the default content type of a SharePoint document library were set using the following code in the `Change()` event handler of a worksheet:

```
Dim CellRef As String

CellRef = Replace(Target.AddressLocal, "$", "")

If CellRef = "B3" Then
  ThisWorkbook.ContentTypeProperties("Col1").Value = Range("B3").Value
End If
```

If you do not know which properties are available on a content type, you can sequentially display all of the content type properties that are available by adding the following code to a macro or a procedure:

```
For Each Prop In ThisWorkbook.ContentTypeProperties
  MsgBox Prop.Name
Next Prop
```

Consult the *Excel 2010 Developer Reference* in the Excel Help file for more information about the `Workbook.ContentTypeProperties` property and about writing VBA code for Excel. To access the help file, click the blue **Help** icon or press **F1** in Microsoft Visual Basic for Applications.

In the solution described above, you changed the values directly in cells on two worksheets. However, you could also use an InfoPath form in Excel, called a Document Information Panel, to modify the metadata stored in the SharePoint document library. To see the values from the SharePoint document library displayed in the Document Information Panel in Excel, you must open the Document Information Panel by selecting **File ➤ Info ➤ Properties ➤ Show Document Panel**.

Figure 55. The Show Document Panel command in Excel 2010.

43 Create a new Excel workbook through a SharePoint Designer workflow

Problem

You want to use a SharePoint Designer 2010 workflow to create a new Excel workbook that contains cells that should be populated with data from fields in an InfoPath form.

Solution

You can set a macro-enabled Excel workbook to be the document template of a SharePoint document library, ensure that the workbook can read/write values of content type properties, and then create a SharePoint Designer workflow that can be started when an InfoPath form is submitted to a form library, so that it can extract data from the InfoPath form and set the values of properties of the content type on the document library, so that cells in the workbook can automatically be populated when the workbook is opened in the Excel client application.

There are three parts to this solution:

1. Create a macro-enabled Excel workbook and set it to be the document template of the default content type of a SharePoint document library.

2. Create and publish an InfoPath form template that can be used to extract data and start a workflow.

3. Create a SharePoint Designer workflow that can create a new macro-enabled Excel workbook based on data from an InfoPath form.

To change the document template of the default content type of a SharePoint document library from a macro-free workbook to a macro-enabled workbook:

1. Follow the instructions of recipe *42 Link Excel cells to document library columns* to create a macro-enabled workbook that is linked to SharePoint document library columns.

2. In SharePoint, navigate to the SharePoint document library where the Excel workbook is stored (**ExcelDIPLib** in this example), and click **Library Tools ➤ Library ➤ Settings ➤ Library Settings**.

3. On the **Document Library Settings** page, under **General Settings**, click **Advanced settings**.

4. On the **Advanced Settings** page, under **Content Types**, select the **Yes** option to allow management of content types, and then click **OK**.

5. On the **Document Library Settings** page, under **Content Types**, click **Document**.

6. On the **Document** page, under **Settings**, click **Advanced settings**.

7. On the **Advanced Settings** page, under **Document Template**, leave the **Enter the URL of an existing document template** option selected, enter the URL to the macro-enabled workbook you created in step 1, and click **OK**. The URL should resemble the following:

```
/sitename/ExcelDIPLib/ExcelDIP.xlsm
```

where **sitename** is the SharePoint site where the **ExcelDIPLib** document library is located where the **ExcelDIP.xlsm** macro-enabled workbook is stored.

You should now be able to manually create a macro-enabled Excel workbook by selecting **Library Tools ➤ Documents ➤ New ➤ New Document ➤ Document**, and then when the document opens in Excel, fill it out, and save it back to the SharePoint document library as a macro-enabled workbook.

To create an InfoPath form on which a SharePoint Designer workflow can run:

1. In InfoPath, create a new browser-compatible form template or use an existing one.

2. Add two **Text Box** controls to the view of the form template and name them **field1** and **field2**, respectively.

3. Click **File ➤ Info ➤ Form Options**.

4. On the **Form Options** dialog box, select **Property Promotion** in the **Category** list, and click the **Add** button that is located in the top half section of the dialog box.

5. On the **Select a Field or Group** dialog box, select **field1**, leave the **Column name** as **Field 1**, and click **OK**.

6. Repeat steps 4 and 5 for **field2** and leave the column name as **Field 2**.

7. On the **Form Options** dialog box, click **OK**.

8. Publish the form template to a SharePoint form library (named for example **CreateExcelWBFormLib**) on the same site where the document library that contains the Excel workbook is located.

You will use this form template to create InfoPath forms that can start the SharePoint Designer workflow and use the data entered in **field1** and **field2** to fill out the columns of the SharePoint document library where the Excel workbook should be created and also fill out the cells in the Excel workbook when the Excel workbook is opened in Excel.

To create a SharePoint Designer 2010 workflow that creates an Excel workbook:

1. In SharePoint Designer 2010, open the SharePoint site where the **ExcelDIPLib** document library and the **CreateExcelWBFormLib** form library are located.

2. Select **Site ➤ New ➤ List Workflow ➤ CreateExcelWBFormLib** to create a new list workflow that runs on the **CreateExcelWBFormLib** form library.

3. On the **Create List Workflow** dialog box, name the workflow **CreateExcelWBWF**, and click **OK**.

4. On the workflow editor, click to place the cursor inside of **Step 1**, and then select **Workflow ➤ Insert ➤ Action ➤ List Actions ➤ Create List Item** to add a **Create List Item** workflow action to **Step 1**.

5. Click **this list** in the sentence for the workflow action.

6. On the **Create New List Item** dialog box, select the **ExcelDIPLib** document library from the **List** drop-down list box. The **Content Type ID** in the fields list should automatically be set to **Document**, which is the default content type of the document library.

7. On the **Create New List Item** dialog box, select **Path and Name (*)** in the fields list, and click **Modify**.

8. On the **Value Assignment** dialog box, click the ellipsis button (first button) behind the **To this value** text box.

9. On the **String Builder** dialog box, click **Add or Change Lookup**.

10. On the **Lookup for String** dialog box, leave **Current Item** selected in the **Data source** drop-down list box (this is the InfoPath form the workflow is running on), select **ID** from the **Field from source** drop-down list box, and click **OK**.

11. On the **String Builder** dialog box, append **.xlsm** to the text that was already added. The final text should say:

    ```
    [%CurrentItem:ID%].xlsm
    ```

    Click **OK** when you are done. This string constructs a file name for the new Excel workbook based on the ID of the InfoPath form.

12. On the **Value Assignment** dialog box, click **OK**.

13. On the **Create New List Item** dialog box, click **Add**.

14. On the **Value Assignment** dialog box, select **Col1** from the **Set this field** drop-down list box, and then click the formula button (second button) behind the **To this value** text box.

15. On the **Lookup for Single line of text** dialog box, leave **Current Item** selected in the **Data source** drop-down list box (this is the InfoPath form the workflow is running on), select **Field 1** from the **Field from source** drop-down list box, and click **OK**.

16. On the **Value Assignment** dialog box, click **OK**. With this you have set the value of the **Col1** property of the content type to be equal to the value of the **Field 1** field in the InfoPath form.

17. Repeat steps 13 through 16 to set the value of **Col2** to be equal to the value of **Field 2** in the InfoPath form.

18. On the **Create New List Item** dialog box, click **OK**.

19. Click **Workflow ➤ Manage ➤ Workflow Settings**.

20. On the workflow settings page under the **Start Options** section, select the **Start workflow automatically when an item is created** check box.

21. Click **Workflow Settings ➤ Save ➤ Publish** to publish the workflow.

In SharePoint, navigate to the **CreateExcelWBFormLib** form library and add a new form. Fill out the form and then save it back to the form library. The workflow should automatically start. After the workflow has run and completed, navigate to the **ExcelDIPLib** document library and verify that a new Excel workbook was created. Open the workbook in Excel (the client application; not Excel Web Access) and verify that the cells contain the values that were entered in the InfoPath form.

Discussion

In the solution described above, you saw how to create and fill out a macro-enabled Excel workbook through a SharePoint Designer workflow. If you do not want to create a macro-enabled Excel workbook and are not required to use a workflow, but still want the functionality of being able to create and fill out an Excel workbook, refer to the techniques discussed in recipes *23 Create a new Excel workbook in SharePoint from within an InfoPath form*, *24 Update an Excel workbook when submitting an InfoPath form to SharePoint*, and *25 Submit SharePoint List form values to a new Excel workbook*.

Because VBA projects are not supported when you open an Excel workbook in the browser (Excel Web Access), you must open macro-enabled workbooks in the Excel client application, so that you can see the values that were written by the workflow to columns of the document library displayed in cells in the Excel workbook.

Note that if you only want to create a new Excel workbook through a workflow without writing any data to its cells, you can use a macro-free workbook instead of a macro-enabled workbook. The latter is only required if you want to read/write data between Excel and SharePoint as discussed in recipe *42 Link Excel cells to document library columns*.

To learn more about the use of SharePoint Designer workflows with InfoPath forms, refer to Chapter 5 of *InfoPath 2010 Cookbook 2*.

Use the Excel Object Model in VSTA

44   Create a new Excel workbook from within InfoPath

Problem

You have an InfoPath Filler form and want to create a new Excel workbook from within the InfoPath form.

Solution

You can use the Excel Object Model in VSTA to create a new Excel workbook from within an InfoPath form.

To create a new Excel workbook from within InfoPath:

1. In InfoPath, create a new InfoPath Filler Form template or use an existing one.

2. Add a **Text Box** control to the view of the form template and name it **field1**.

3. Add a **Button** control to the view of the form template and label it **Create Excel File**.

4. With the button still selected, click **Control Tools ➤ Properties ➤ Button ➤ Custom Code** to add an event handler for the **Clicked** event of the **Create Excel File** button.

5. In VSTA, add a reference to the **Microsoft Excel 14.0 Object Library** (**Microsoft.Office.Interop.Excel**) COM component.

6. Add the following **using** statement to the **FormCode.cs** file:

```
using ExcelLib = Microsoft.Office.Interop.Excel;
```

Or add the following **Imports** statement to the **FormCode.vb** file:

```
Imports ExcelLib = Microsoft.Office.Interop.Excel
```

7. Add the following C# or Visual Basic code to the `Clicked()` event handler for the **Create Excel File** button (*code #: 61F05104-8B12-4853-96F0-48EBA14D9F39*):

C#

```
XPathNavigator mainDS = MainDataSource.CreateNavigator();
string fileName = mainDS.SelectSingleNode(
  "//my:field1", NamespaceManager).Value;

ExcelLib.Application app =
  new Microsoft.Office.Interop.Excel.Application();

ExcelLib.Workbook wb = app.Workbooks.Add(System.Type.Missing);

try
{
  wb.SaveAs(@"C:\" + fileName, System.Type.Missing,
    System.Type.Missing, System.Type.Missing, System.Type.Missing,
    System.Type.Missing, ExcelLib.XlSaveAsAccessMode.xlNoChange,
    System.Type.Missing, System.Type.Missing, System.Type.Missing,
    System.Type.Missing, System.Type.Missing);
}
finally
{
  wb.Close(false, System.Type.Missing, System.Type.Missing);
}
```

Visual Basic

```
Dim mainDS As XPathNavigator = MainDataSource.CreateNavigator()
Dim fileName As String = mainDS.SelectSingleNode( _
  "//my:field1", NamespaceManager).Value

Dim app As New Microsoft.Office.Interop.Excel.Application()

Dim wb As ExcelLib.Workbook = _
  app.Workbooks.Add(System.Type.Missing)

Try

  wb.SaveAs("C:\" & fileName, System.Type.Missing, _
    System.Type.Missing, System.Type.Missing, System.Type.Missing, _
    System.Type.Missing, ExcelLib.XlSaveAsAccessMode.xlNoChange, _
    System.Type.Missing, System.Type.Missing, System.Type.Missing, _
    System.Type.Missing, System.Type.Missing)

Finally

  wb.Close(False, System.Type.Missing, System.Type.Missing)

End Try
```

8. Save and build the project.

9. In InfoPath, click **File ➤ Info ➤ Form Options**.

10. On the **Form Options** dialog box, select **Security and Trust** in the **Category** list, deselect the **Automatically determine security level (recommended)** check box, select the **Full Trust** option, and then click **OK**.

11. Preview the form.

When the form opens, enter a new file name (with or without the **.xlsx** extension) into the text box control and then click the button. Open Windows Explorer, navigate to the C-drive and verify that the Excel workbook was created.

Discussion

In the solution described above, you saw how to write code that makes use of the Excel Object Model to create a new Excel workbook on disk from within an InfoPath form. The code first retrieves the value of the text box control on the InfoPath form.

C#

```
XPathNavigator mainDS = MainDataSource.CreateNavigator();
string fileName = mainDS.SelectSingleNode(
  "//my:field1", NamespaceManager).Value;
```

Visual Basic

```
Dim mainDS As XPathNavigator = MainDataSource.CreateNavigator()
Dim fileName As String = mainDS.SelectSingleNode( _
  "//my:field1", NamespaceManager).Value
```

It then creates an `Application` object

C#

```
ExcelLib.Application app = new Microsoft.Office.Interop.Excel.Application();
```

Visual Basic

```
Dim app As New Microsoft.Office.Interop.Excel.Application()
```

so that a `Workbook` object can be added

C#

```
ExcelLib.Workbook wb = app.Workbooks.Add(System.Type.Missing);
```

Visual Basic

```
Dim wb As ExcelLib.Workbook = app.Workbooks.Add(System.Type.Missing)
```

and the `Workbook` object then used to create a new Excel workbook on disk thereby using the `SaveAs()` method of the `Workbook` object and the value from the text box control on the InfoPath form.

<u>**C#**</u>

```
wb.SaveAs(@"C:\" + fileName, System.Type.Missing,
  System.Type.Missing, System.Type.Missing, System.Type.Missing,
  System.Type.Missing, ExcelLib.XlSaveAsAccessMode.xlNoChange,
  System.Type.Missing, System.Type.Missing, System.Type.Missing,
  System.Type.Missing, System.Type.Missing);
```

<u>**Visual Basic**</u>

```
wb.SaveAs("C:\" & fileName, System.Type.Missing, _
  System.Type.Missing, System.Type.Missing, System.Type.Missing, _
  System.Type.Missing, ExcelLib.XlSaveAsAccessMode.xlNoChange, _
  System.Type.Missing, System.Type.Missing, System.Type.Missing, _
  System.Type.Missing, System.Type.Missing)
```

And finally, the `Workbook` object is closed.

<u>**C#**</u>

```
wb.Close(false, System.Type.Missing, System.Type.Missing);
```

<u>**Visual Basic**</u>

```
wb.Close(False, System.Type.Missing, System.Type.Missing)
```

To learn more about writing code that calls into the Excel Object Model, consult the documentation on the MSDN web site.

Warning:

> If you do not make use of error-handling and an error takes place after opening an Excel workbook and performing an action, the code for closing the workbook will not run. Therefore, you may not be able to open Excel afterwards, since a process for Excel is still/already active. To correct this issue, you would have to manually end the EXCEL.EXE process via the **Processes** tab on the **Windows Task Manager** dialog box. To avoid having to manually end processes, ensure that you always close an Excel workbook through code by adding a `Try-Catch-Finally` block around your code and placing the code that closes the workbook in the `Finally` block.

45 Get the value of an Excel cell in InfoPath

Problem

You have an InfoPath Filler form, which you want to use to retrieve and display the value of a cell in an Excel workbook that is located locally on disk.

Solution

You can use the Excel Object Model in VSTA to retrieve the value of a cell in an Excel workbook from within an InfoPath form.

To get the value of an Excel cell from within an InfoPath form:

1. In InfoPath, create a new InfoPath Filler Form template or use an existing one.

2. Add two **Text Box** controls to the view of the form template and name them **field1** and **field2**, respectively.

3. Add a **Button** control to the view of the form template and label it **Get Excel Value**.

4. With the button still selected, click **Control Tools ▶ Properties ▶ Button ▶ Custom Code** to add an event handler for the **Clicked** event of the **Get Excel Value** button.

5. In VSTA, add a reference to the **Microsoft Excel 14.0 Object Library** (**Microsoft.Office.Interop.Excel**) COM component.

6. Add the following **using** statement to the **FormCode.cs** file:

```
using ExcelLib = Microsoft.Office.Interop.Excel;
```

Or add the following **Imports** statement to the **FormCode.vb** file:

```
Imports ExcelLib = Microsoft.Office.Interop.Excel
```

7. Add the following C# or Visual Basic code to the `Clicked()` event handler for the **Get Excel Value** button (*code #: B992C7D8-2BB0-47E7-9CD8-53627410BED1*):

C#

```
XPathNavigator mainDS = MainDataSource.CreateNavigator();

XPathNavigator field1 = mainDS.SelectSingleNode(
  "//my:field1", NamespaceManager);

XPathNavigator field2 = mainDS.SelectSingleNode(
  "//my:field2", NamespaceManager);

ExcelLib.Application app =
  new Microsoft.Office.Interop.Excel.Application();

ExcelLib.Workbook wb = app.Workbooks.Open(
```

```
   @"C:\ExistingWorkbook.xlsx",
   System.Type.Missing, System.Type.Missing, System.Type.Missing,
   System.Type.Missing, System.Type.Missing, System.Type.Missing,
   System.Type.Missing, System.Type.Missing, System.Type.Missing,
   System.Type.Missing, System.Type.Missing, System.Type.Missing,
   System.Type.Missing, System.Type.Missing);

try
{
   ExcelLib.Worksheet sheet = (ExcelLib.Worksheet)wb.Worksheets["Sheet1"];
   ExcelLib.Range cell = sheet.get_Range(field1.Value, System.Type.Missing);
   field2.SetValue(cell.Value2.ToString());
}
finally
{
   wb.Close(false, System.Type.Missing, System.Type.Missing);
}
```

Visual Basic

```
Dim mainDS As XPathNavigator = MainDataSource.CreateNavigator()

Dim field1 As XPathNavigator = mainDS.SelectSingleNode( _
   "//my:field1", NamespaceManager)

Dim field2 As XPathNavigator = mainDS.SelectSingleNode( _
   "//my:field2", NamespaceManager)

Dim app As New Microsoft.Office.Interop.Excel.Application()

Dim wb As ExcelLib.Workbook = app.Workbooks.Open( _
   "C:\ExistingWorkbook.xlsx", _
   System.Type.Missing, System.Type.Missing, System.Type.Missing, _
   System.Type.Missing, System.Type.Missing, System.Type.Missing, _
   System.Type.Missing, System.Type.Missing, System.Type.Missing, _
   System.Type.Missing, System.Type.Missing, System.Type.Missing, _
   System.Type.Missing, System.Type.Missing)

Try

   Dim sheet As ExcelLib.Worksheet = wb.Worksheets("Sheet1")
   Dim cell As ExcelLib.Range = sheet.Range( _
     field1.Value, System.Type.Missing)
   field2.SetValue(cell.Value.ToString())

Finally

   wb.Close(False, System.Type.Missing, System.Type.Missing)

End Try
```

where you must replace `C:\ExistingWorkbook.xlsx` with the path to the Excel workbook from which you want to get the value of a cell.

8. Save and build the project.

9. In InfoPath, click **File ➤ Info ➤ Form Options**.

10. On the **Form Options** dialog box, select **Security and Trust** in the **Category** list, deselect the **Automatically determine security level (recommended)** check box, select the **Full Trust** option, and then click **OK**.

11. Preview the form.

When the form opens, enter the name of the cell from which you want to retrieve a value (for example **C4**) in the first text box and then click the button. The value corresponding to the cell you entered in the first text box should appear in the second text box.

Discussion

In the solution described above, you saw how to write code that makes use of the Excel Object Model to retrieve the value of a cell from an Excel workbook that is located on disk. The code first retrieves XPathNavigator objects pointing to the text boxes on the InfoPath form.

C#

```
XPathNavigator mainDS = MainDataSource.CreateNavigator();

XPathNavigator field1 = mainDS.SelectSingleNode(
  "//my:field1", NamespaceManager);

XPathNavigator field2 = mainDS.SelectSingleNode(
  "//my:field2", NamespaceManager);
```

Visual Basic

```
Dim mainDS As XPathNavigator = MainDataSource.CreateNavigator()

Dim field1 As XPathNavigator = mainDS.SelectSingleNode( _
  "//my:field1", NamespaceManager)

Dim field2 As XPathNavigator = mainDS.SelectSingleNode( _
  "//my:field2", NamespaceManager)
```

It then creates an Application object

C#

```
ExcelLib.Application app = new Microsoft.Office.Interop.Excel.Application();
```

Visual Basic

```
Dim app As New Microsoft.Office.Interop.Excel.Application()
```

and uses the Open() method of the Workbooks property of the Application object to open an existing Excel workbook.

C#

```
ExcelLib.Workbook wb = app.Workbooks.Open(
```

```
@"C:\ExistingWorkbook.xlsx",
System.Type.Missing, System.Type.Missing, System.Type.Missing,
System.Type.Missing, System.Type.Missing, System.Type.Missing,
System.Type.Missing, System.Type.Missing, System.Type.Missing,
System.Type.Missing, System.Type.Missing, System.Type.Missing,
System.Type.Missing, System.Type.Missing);
```

Visual Basic

```
Dim wb As ExcelLib.Workbook = app.Workbooks.Open( _
  "C:\ExistingWorkbook.xlsx", _
  System.Type.Missing, System.Type.Missing, System.Type.Missing, _
  System.Type.Missing, System.Type.Missing, System.Type.Missing, _
  System.Type.Missing, System.Type.Missing, System.Type.Missing, _
  System.Type.Missing, System.Type.Missing, System.Type.Missing, _
  System.Type.Missing, System.Type.Missing)
```

The code then retrieves a `Worksheet` object pointing to **Sheet1** in the workbook and uses the `get_Range()` method (C#) or the `Range` property (Visual Basic) of the `Worksheet` object to retrieve a `Range` object that has the cell reference specified in the first text box (**field1**), and then uses the `Value2` property (C#) or the `Value` property (Visual Basic) of the `Range` object to set the value of the second text box (**field2**).

C#

```
ExcelLib.Worksheet sheet = (ExcelLib.Worksheet)wb.Worksheets["Sheet1"];
ExcelLib.Range cell = sheet.get_Range(field1.Value, System.Type.Missing);
field2.SetValue(cell.Value2.ToString());
```

Visual Basic

```
Dim sheet As ExcelLib.Worksheet = wb.Worksheets("Sheet1")
Dim cell As ExcelLib.Range = sheet.Range(field1.Value, System.Type.Missing)
field2.SetValue(cell.Value.ToString())
```

If you want to retrieve the value of a cell on a different worksheet, you must change the static text "Sheet1" into the name or the index number of the worksheet that has the cell for which you want to retrieve its value, or you can place an extra field on the InfoPath form which users can use to specify the name of the worksheet to use.

And finally, the `Workbook` object is closed.

C#

```
wb.Close(false, System.Type.Missing, System.Type.Missing);
```

Visual Basic

```
wb.Close(False, System.Type.Missing, System.Type.Missing)
```

Note that you can also use the `get_Range()` method (C#) or `Range` property (Visual Basic) of the `Application` object to retrieve the value of a cell. And since you would not be specifying a particular worksheet to use, the first worksheet in the Excel workbook (**Sheet1** in this case) would automatically be used unless the name of the cell you specified is a named range (also see *How to create a named range in Excel* in the Appendix) that has been defined on a specific cell on a worksheet in the Excel workbook. If you are not working with cells on specific worksheets in an Excel workbook, but instead are working with named ranges, you can use the `Application` object instead of a `Worksheet` object to retrieve a `Range` object to retrieve the value of a cell.

<u>**C#**</u>

```
ExcelLib.Range cell = app.get_Range(field1.Value, System.Type.Missing);
field2.SetValue(cell.Value2.ToString());
```

<u>**Visual Basic**</u>

```
Dim cell As ExcelLib.Range = app.Range(field1.Value, System.Type.Missing)
field2.SetValue(cell.Value.ToString())
```

To learn more about writing code that calls into the Excel Object Model, consult the documentation on the MSDN web site.

Warning:

If you do not make use of error-handling and an error takes place after opening an Excel workbook and performing an action, the code for closing the workbook will not run. Therefore, you may not be able to open Excel afterwards, since a process for Excel is still/already active. To correct this issue, you would have to manually end the EXCEL.EXE process via the **Processes** tab on the **Windows Task Manager** dialog box. To avoid having to manually end processes, ensure that you always close an Excel workbook through code by adding a `Try-Catch-Finally` block around your code and placing the code that closes the workbook in the `Finally` block.

46 Set the value of an Excel cell from within InfoPath

Problem

You have an InfoPath Filler form, which you want to use to enter a value and an Excel cell reference, and then save the data to an Excel workbook that is located locally on disk.

Solution

You can use the Excel Object Model in VSTA to update the value of a cell in an Excel workbook from within an InfoPath form.

InfoPath 2010 Cookbook 5

To set the value of an Excel cell from within an InfoPath form:

1. In InfoPath, create a new InfoPath Filler Form template or use an existing one.

2. Add two **Text Box** controls to the view of the form template and name them **field1** and **field2**, respectively.

3. Add a **Button** control to the view of the form template and label it **Update Excel File**.

4. With the button still selected, click **Control Tools ➤ Properties ➤ Button ➤ Custom Code** to add an event handler for the **Clicked** event of the **Update Excel File** button.

5. In VSTA, add a reference to the **Microsoft Excel 14.0 Object Library** (**Microsoft.Office.Interop.Excel**) COM component.

6. Add the following **using** statement to the **FormCode.cs** file:

    ```
    using ExcelLib = Microsoft.Office.Interop.Excel;
    ```

    Or add the following **Imports** statement to the **FormCode.vb** file:

    ```
    Imports ExcelLib = Microsoft.Office.Interop.Excel
    ```

7. Add the following C# or Visual Basic code to the `Clicked()` event handler for the **Update Excel File** button (*code #: 8BB2C13B-E052-4EFF-8B8D-EEA79D0EF38C*):

    C#

    ```
    XPathNavigator mainDS = MainDataSource.CreateNavigator();

    string newCellValue = mainDS.SelectSingleNode(
      "//my:field1", NamespaceManager).Value;

    string cellRef = mainDS.SelectSingleNode(
      "//my:field2", NamespaceManager).Value;

    ExcelLib.Application app =
      new Microsoft.Office.Interop.Excel.Application();

    ExcelLib.Workbook wb = app.Workbooks.Open(
      @"C:\ExistingWorkbook.xlsx",
      System.Type.Missing, System.Type.Missing, System.Type.Missing,
      System.Type.Missing, System.Type.Missing, System.Type.Missing,
      System.Type.Missing, System.Type.Missing, System.Type.Missing,
      System.Type.Missing, System.Type.Missing, System.Type.Missing,
      System.Type.Missing, System.Type.Missing);

    try
    {
      ExcelLib.Worksheet sheet = (ExcelLib.Worksheet)wb.Worksheets["Sheet1"];
      ExcelLib.Range cell = sheet.get_Range(cellRef, System.Type.Missing);
      cell.Value2 = newCellValue;

      wb.Save();
    }
    finally
    ```

234

```
{
  wb.Close(false, System.Type.Missing, System.Type.Missing);
}
```

<u>Visual Basic</u>

```
Dim mainDS As XPathNavigator = MainDataSource.CreateNavigator()

Dim newCellValue As String = mainDS.SelectSingleNode( _
  "//my:field1", NamespaceManager).Value

Dim cellRef As String = mainDS.SelectSingleNode( _
  "//my:field2", NamespaceManager).Value

Dim app As New Microsoft.Office.Interop.Excel.Application()

Dim wb As ExcelLib.Workbook = app.Workbooks.Open( _
  "C:\ExistingWorkbook.xlsx", _
  System.Type.Missing, System.Type.Missing, System.Type.Missing, _
  System.Type.Missing, System.Type.Missing, System.Type.Missing, _
  System.Type.Missing, System.Type.Missing, System.Type.Missing, _
  System.Type.Missing, System.Type.Missing, System.Type.Missing, _
  System.Type.Missing, System.Type.Missing)

Try

  Dim sheet As ExcelLib.Worksheet = wb.Worksheets("Sheet1")
  Dim cell As ExcelLib.Range = sheet.Range(cellRef, System.Type.Missing)
  cell.Value = newCellValue

  wb.Save()

Finally

  wb.Close(False, System.Type.Missing, System.Type.Missing)

End Try
```

where you must replace `C:\ExistingWorkbook.xlsx` with the path to the Excel workbook in which you want to set the value of a cell.

8. Save and build the project.

9. In InfoPath, click **File ➤ Info ➤ Form Options**.

10. On the **Form Options** dialog box, select **Security and Trust** in the **Category** list, deselect the **Automatically determine security level (recommended)** check box, select the **Full Trust** option, and then click **OK**.

11. Preview the form.

When the form opens, enter a value into the first text box, enter the name of the cell you want to update (for example **C4**) into the second text box, and then click the button. Navigate to the location on disk where the **ExitingWorkbook.xlsx** Excel workbook is located, open the file, and verify that the value you entered into the InfoPath form was written to the cell you specified from within the InfoPath form.

Discussion

In the solution described above, you saw how to write code that makes use of the Excel Object Model to set the value of a cell on a particular worksheet in an Excel workbook that is located on disk. The code first uses XPathNavigator objects to retrieve the values of the text boxes on the InfoPath form.

C#

```
XPathNavigator mainDS = MainDataSource.CreateNavigator();

string newCellValue = mainDS.SelectSingleNode(
  "//my:field1", NamespaceManager).Value;

string cellRef = mainDS.SelectSingleNode(
  "//my:field2", NamespaceManager).Value;
```

Visual Basic

```
Dim mainDS As XPathNavigator = MainDataSource.CreateNavigator()

Dim newCellValue As String = mainDS.SelectSingleNode( _
  "//my:field1", NamespaceManager).Value

Dim cellRef As String = mainDS.SelectSingleNode( _
  "//my:field2", NamespaceManager).Value
```

It then creates an Application object

C#

```
ExcelLib.Application app = new Microsoft.Office.Interop.Excel.Application();
```

Visual Basic

```
Dim app As New Microsoft.Office.Interop.Excel.Application()
```

and uses the Open() method of the Workbooks property of the Application object to open an existing Excel workbook.

C#

```
ExcelLib.Workbook wb = app.Workbooks.Open(
  @"C:\ExistingWorkbook.xlsx",
  System.Type.Missing, System.Type.Missing, System.Type.Missing,
  System.Type.Missing, System.Type.Missing, System.Type.Missing,
  System.Type.Missing, System.Type.Missing, System.Type.Missing,
  System.Type.Missing, System.Type.Missing, System.Type.Missing,
  System.Type.Missing, System.Type.Missing);
```

Visual Basic

```
Dim wb As ExcelLib.Workbook = app.Workbooks.Open( _
  "C:\ExistingWorkbook.xlsx", _
  System.Type.Missing, System.Type.Missing, System.Type.Missing, _
```

```
System.Type.Missing, System.Type.Missing, System.Type.Missing, _
System.Type.Missing, System.Type.Missing, System.Type.Missing, _
System.Type.Missing, System.Type.Missing, System.Type.Missing, _
System.Type.Missing, System.Type.Missing)
```

The code then retrieves a `Worksheet` object pointing to **Sheet1** in the workbook and uses the `get_Range()` method (C#) or the `Range` property (Visual Basic) of the `Worksheet` object to retrieve a `Range` object that has the cell reference specified in the second text box (**field2**), and then uses the `Value2` property (C#) or the `Value` property (Visual Basic) of the `Range` object to set the value of the cell to be equal to the value of the first text box (**field1**).

C#

```
ExcelLib.Worksheet sheet = (ExcelLib.Worksheet)wb.Worksheets["Sheet1"];
ExcelLib.Range cell = sheet.get_Range(cellRef, System.Type.Missing);
cell.Value2 = newCellValue;
```

Visual Basic

```
Dim sheet As ExcelLib.Worksheet = wb.Worksheets("Sheet1")
Dim cell As ExcelLib.Range = sheet.Range(cellRef, System.Type.Missing)
cell.Value = newCellValue
```

If you want to update the value of a cell on a different worksheet, you must change the static text "Sheet1" into the name or the index number of the worksheet that has the cell you want to update, or you can place an extra field on the InfoPath form which users can use to specify the name of the worksheet to use.

And finally, the `Workbook` object is saved and closed.

C#

```
try
{
  ...
  wb.Save();
}
finally
{
  wb.Close(false, System.Type.Missing, System.Type.Missing);
}
```

Visual Basic

```
Try

  ...
  wb.Save()

Finally

  wb.Close(False, System.Type.Missing, System.Type.Missing)

End Try
```

Note that you can also use the `get_Range()` method (C#) or `Range` property (Visual Basic) of the `Application` object to update the value of a cell. And since you would not be specifying a particular worksheet to use, the first worksheet in the Excel workbook (**Sheet1** in this case) would automatically be used unless the name of the cell you specified is a named range (also see *How to create a named range in Excel* in the Appendix) that has been defined on a specific cell on a worksheet in the Excel workbook. If you are not working with cells on specific worksheets in an Excel workbook, but instead are working with named ranges, you can use the `Application` object instead of a `Worksheet` object to retrieve a `Range` object to update the value of a cell.

C#

```
ExcelLib.Range cell = app.get_Range(cellRef, System.Type.Missing);
cell.Value2 = newCellValue;
```

Visual Basic

```
Dim cell As ExcelLib.Range = app.Range(cellRef, System.Type.Missing)
cell.Value = newCellValue
```

To learn more about writing code that calls into the Excel Object Model, consult the documentation on the MSDN web site.

Warning:

> If you do not make use of error-handling and an error takes place after opening an Excel workbook and performing an action, the code for closing the workbook will not run. Therefore, you may not be able to open Excel afterwards, since a process for Excel is still/already active. To correct this issue, you would have to manually end the EXCEL.EXE process via the **Processes** tab on the **Windows Task Manager** dialog box. To avoid having to manually end processes, ensure that you always close an Excel workbook through code by adding a `Try-Catch-Finally` block around your code and placing the code that closes the workbook in the `Finally` block.

47   Populate a repeating table with Excel data

Problem

You have a repeating table on an InfoPath form, which you want to use to retrieve and display values from a range of cells in an Excel workbook that is stored locally on disk.

Solution

You can use the Excel Object Model in VSTA to open an existing Excel workbook, read data from a range of cells, and then write the data to a repeating table on an InfoPath form.

To populate a repeating table on an InfoPath form with data from an Excel workbook:

1. In Excel, create a new Excel workbook named **Fruits.xlsx** that contains a named range called **Fruits** that spans cells **A2** through **B6** on **Sheet1**. You can also download the **Fruits.xlsx** Excel workbook from www.bizsupportonline.com for use with this recipe.

2. In InfoPath, create a new InfoPath Filler Form template or use an existing one.

3. Add a **Repeating Table** control with 2 columns to the view of the form template, and name the fields within the repeating table **field1** and **field2**, respectively.

4. Click **Data ➤ Form Data ➤ Default Values**.

5. On the **Edit Default Values** dialog box, expand the **group1** node, clear the check box in front of the **group2** node, and then click **OK**. This will ensure that the repeating table does not start up with a row that contains empty fields.

6. Add a **Button** control to the view of the form template and label it **Retrieve From Excel**.

7. With the button still selected, click **Control Tools ➤ Properties ➤ Button ➤ Custom Code** to add an event handler for the **Clicked** event of the **Retrieve From Excel** button.

8. In VSTA, add a reference to the **Microsoft Excel 14.0 Object Library** (**Microsoft.Office.Interop.Excel**) COM component.

9. Add the following **using** statement to the **FormCode.cs** file:

```
using ExcelLib = Microsoft.Office.Interop.Excel;
```

Or add the following **Imports** statement to the **FormCode.vb** file:

```
Imports ExcelLib = Microsoft.Office.Interop.Excel
```

10. Add the following C# or Visual Basic code to the `Clicked()` event handler for the **Retrieve From Excel** button (*code #: 38DB8784-29BC-41EB-9B08-C1300D590FFA*):

<u>C#</u>

```
ExcelLib.Application app =
  new Microsoft.Office.Interop.Excel.Application();

ExcelLib.Workbook wb = app.Workbooks.Open(
  @"C:\Fruits.xlsx",
  System.Type.Missing, System.Type.Missing, System.Type.Missing,
  System.Type.Missing, System.Type.Missing, System.Type.Missing,
  System.Type.Missing, System.Type.Missing, System.Type.Missing,
```

```
      System.Type.Missing, System.Type.Missing, System.Type.Missing,
      System.Type.Missing, System.Type.Missing);

  try
  {
    ExcelLib.Range range = app.get_Range("Fruits", System.Type.Missing);

    XPathNavigator mainDS = MainDataSource.CreateNavigator();
    XPathNavigator group1 = mainDS.SelectSingleNode(
      "/my:myFields/my:group1", NamespaceManager);

    for (int i = 1; i <= range.Rows.Count; i++)
    {
      group1.AppendChildElement("my", "group2",
        NamespaceManager.LookupNamespace("my"), "");

      XPathNavigator lastGroup2 = mainDS.SelectSingleNode(
        "/my:myFields/my:group1/my:group2[last()]", NamespaceManager);

      if (lastGroup2 != null)
      {
        lastGroup2.AppendChildElement("my", "field1",
          NamespaceManager.LookupNamespace("my"), "");
        lastGroup2.AppendChildElement("my", "field2",
          NamespaceManager.LookupNamespace("my"), "");

        for (int j = 1; j <= range.Columns.Count; j++)
        {
          ExcelLib.Range cell = (ExcelLib.Range)range[i, j];
          string val = cell.Value2.ToString();

          switch (j)
          {
            case 1:
              lastGroup2.SelectSingleNode(
                "my:field1", NamespaceManager).SetValue(val);
                break;
            case 2:
              lastGroup2.SelectSingleNode(
                "my:field2", NamespaceManager).SetValue(val);
              break;
            default:
              break;
          }
        }
      }
    }
  }
  finally
  {
    wb.Close(false, System.Type.Missing, System.Type.Missing);
  }
```

Visual Basic

```
Dim app As New Microsoft.Office.Interop.Excel.Application()

Dim wb As ExcelLib.Workbook = app.Workbooks.Open( _
  "C:\Fruits.xlsx", _
  System.Type.Missing, System.Type.Missing, System.Type.Missing, _
  System.Type.Missing, System.Type.Missing, System.Type.Missing, _
  System.Type.Missing, System.Type.Missing, System.Type.Missing, _
```

```
    System.Type.Missing, System.Type.Missing, System.Type.Missing, _
    System.Type.Missing, System.Type.Missing)

Try

  Dim range As ExcelLib.Range = app.Range("Fruits", System.Type.Missing)

  Dim mainDS As XPathNavigator = MainDataSource.CreateNavigator()
  Dim group1 As XPathNavigator = mainDS.SelectSingleNode( _
    "/my:myFields/my:group1", NamespaceManager)

  For i As Integer = 1 To range.Rows.Count

    group1.AppendChildElement("my", "group2", _
      NamespaceManager.LookupNamespace("my"), "")

    Dim lastGroup2 As XPathNavigator = mainDS.SelectSingleNode( _
      "/my:myFields/my:group1/my:group2[last()]", NamespaceManager)

    If lastGroup2 IsNot Nothing Then

      lastGroup2.AppendChildElement("my", "field1", _
        NamespaceManager.LookupNamespace("my"), "")
      lastGroup2.AppendChildElement("my", "field2", _
        NamespaceManager.LookupNamespace("my"), "")

      For j As Integer = 1 To range.Columns.Count

        Dim cell As ExcelLib.Range = range(i, j)
        Dim val As String = cell.Value.ToString()

        Select Case j
          Case 1
            lastGroup2.SelectSingleNode( _
              "my:field1", NamespaceManager).SetValue(val)
          Case 2
            lastGroup2.SelectSingleNode( _
              "my:field2", NamespaceManager).SetValue(val)
          Case Else
            ' Do nothing
        End Select

      Next j

    End If

  Next i

Finally

  wb.Close(False, System.Type.Missing, System.Type.Missing)

End Try
```

where you must replace C:\Fruits.xlsx with the path to the Excel workbook from which you want to retrieve the data for the repeating table.

11. Save and build the project.

12. In InfoPath, click **File ➤ Info ➤ Form Options**.

13. On the **Form Options** dialog box, select **Security and Trust** in the **Category** list, deselect the **Automatically determine security level (recommended)** check box, select the **Full Trust** option, and then click **OK**.

14. Preview the form.

When the form opens, click the **Retrieve From Excel** button. The data from the Excel workbook should appear in the repeating table on the InfoPath form.

Discussion

In the solution described above, you saw how to write code that makes use of the Excel Object Model to populate rows of a repeating table control on an InfoPath form with data from a range of cells on a particular worksheet in an Excel workbook that is located on disk. The code first creates an `Application` object

C#

```
ExcelLib.Application app = new Microsoft.Office.Interop.Excel.Application();
```

Visual Basic

```
Dim app As New Microsoft.Office.Interop.Excel.Application()
```

and uses the `Open()` method of the `Workbooks` property of the `Application` object to open the **Fruits.xlsx** Excel workbook.

C#

```
ExcelLib.Workbook wb = app.Workbooks.Open(
  @"C:\Fruits.xlsx",
  System.Type.Missing, System.Type.Missing, System.Type.Missing,
  System.Type.Missing, System.Type.Missing, System.Type.Missing,
  System.Type.Missing, System.Type.Missing, System.Type.Missing,
  System.Type.Missing, System.Type.Missing, System.Type.Missing,
  System.Type.Missing, System.Type.Missing);
```

Visual Basic

```
Dim wb As ExcelLib.Workbook = app.Workbooks.Open( _
  "C:\Fruits.xlsx", _
  System.Type.Missing, System.Type.Missing, System.Type.Missing, _
  System.Type.Missing, System.Type.Missing, System.Type.Missing, _
  System.Type.Missing, System.Type.Missing, System.Type.Missing, _
  System.Type.Missing, System.Type.Missing, System.Type.Missing, _
  System.Type.Missing, System.Type.Missing)
```

The code then uses the `get_Range()` method (C#) or `Range` property (Visual Basic) of the `Application` object to get a reference to the **Fruits** named range in the Excel workbook.

C#

```
ExcelLib.Range range = app.get_Range("Fruits", System.Type.Missing);
```

Visual Basic

```
Dim range As ExcelLib.Range = app.Range("Fruits", System.Type.Missing)
```

Because the **Fruits** named range has a scope of **Workbook**, it should automatically be found by the code. However, you could have also used a specific worksheet (**Sheet1** in this case) and range of cells (cells **A2** through **B6** in this case) to retrieve a reference to a Range object as follows:

C#

```
ExcelLib.Worksheet sheet = (ExcelLib.Worksheet)wb.Worksheets["Sheet1"];
ExcelLib.Range range = sheet.get_Range("A2", "B6");
```

Visual Basic

```
Dim sheet As ExcelLib.Worksheet = wb.Worksheets("Sheet1")
Dim range As ExcelLib.Range = sheet.Range("A2", "B6")
```

The code goes on to loop through the rows and columns contained in the Range object and add rows containing data to the repeating table control on the InfoPath form.

C#

```
XPathNavigator mainDS = MainDataSource.CreateNavigator();
XPathNavigator group1 = mainDS.SelectSingleNode(
  "/my:myFields/my:group1", NamespaceManager);

for (int i = 1; i <= range.Rows.Count; i++)
{
  group1.AppendChildElement("my", "group2",
    NamespaceManager.LookupNamespace("my"), "");

  XPathNavigator lastGroup2 = mainDS.SelectSingleNode(
    "/my:myFields/my:group1/my:group2[last()]", NamespaceManager);

  if (lastGroup2 != null)
  {
    lastGroup2.AppendChildElement("my", "field1",
      NamespaceManager.LookupNamespace("my"), "");
    lastGroup2.AppendChildElement("my", "field2",
      NamespaceManager.LookupNamespace("my"), "");

    for (int j = 1; j <= range.Columns.Count; j++)
    {
      ExcelLib.Range cell = (ExcelLib.Range)range[i, j];
      string val = cell.Value2.ToString();

      switch (j)
      {
        case 1:
          lastGroup2.SelectSingleNode(
            "my:field1", NamespaceManager).SetValue(val);
```

```
              break;
         case 2:
           lastGroup2.SelectSingleNode(
             "my:field2", NamespaceManager).SetValue(val);
           break;
         default:
           break;
     }
    }
  }
}
```

Visual Basic

```
Dim mainDS As XPathNavigator = MainDataSource.CreateNavigator()
Dim group1 As XPathNavigator = mainDS.SelectSingleNode( _
  "/my:myFields/my:group1", NamespaceManager)

For i As Integer = 1 To range.Rows.Count

  group1.AppendChildElement("my", "group2", _
    NamespaceManager.LookupNamespace("my"), "")

  Dim lastGroup2 As XPathNavigator = mainDS.SelectSingleNode( _
    "/my:myFields/my:group1/my:group2[last()]", NamespaceManager)

  If lastGroup2 IsNot Nothing Then

    lastGroup2.AppendChildElement("my", "field1", _
      NamespaceManager.LookupNamespace("my"), "")
    lastGroup2.AppendChildElement("my", "field2", _
      NamespaceManager.LookupNamespace("my"), "")

    For j As Integer = 1 To range.Columns.Count

      Dim cell As ExcelLib.Range = range(i, j)
      Dim val As String = cell.Value.ToString()

      Select Case j
       Case 1
         lastGroup2.SelectSingleNode( _
           "my:field1", NamespaceManager).SetValue(val)
       Case 2
         lastGroup2.SelectSingleNode( _
           "my:field2", NamespaceManager).SetValue(val)
       Case Else
         ' Do nothing
         End Select

    Next j

  End If

Next i
```

And finally, the `Workbook` object is closed.

C#

```
wb.Close(false, System.Type.Missing, System.Type.Missing);
```

<u>Visual Basic</u>

```
wb.Close(False, System.Type.Missing, System.Type.Missing)
```

To learn more about writing code that calls into the Excel Object Model, consult the documentation on the MSDN web site.

Warning:

> If you do not make use of error-handling and an error takes place after opening an Excel workbook and performing an action, the code for closing the workbook will not run. Therefore, you may not be able to open Excel afterwards, since a process for Excel is still/already active. To correct this issue, you would have to manually end the EXCEL.EXE process via the **Processes** tab on the **Windows Task Manager** dialog box. To avoid having to manually end processes, ensure that you always close an Excel workbook through code by adding a `Try-Catch-Finally` block around your code and placing the code that closes the workbook in the `Finally` block.

48 Populate an Excel workbook with InfoPath repeating table data

Problem

You have a repeating table on an InfoPath form and want to send the data that is contained in the fields of the repeating table to an Excel workbook that is stored locally on disk.

Solution

You can use the Excel Object Model in VSTA to open an existing Excel workbook and write data from a repeating table to it.

To populate an Excel workbook with data from a repeating table on an InfoPath form:

1. In Excel, create a new Excel workbook or use an existing one. In this recipe, you will use a new Excel workbook named **ExistingWorkbook.xlsx**.

2. In InfoPath, create a new InfoPath Filler Form template or use an existing one.

3. Add a **Repeating Table** control with 3 columns to the view of the form template, and name the fields within the repeating table **field1**, **field2**, and **field3**, respectively.

4. Add two **Text Box** controls with data type **Whole Number (integer)** to the view of the form template and name them **rowIndex** and **colIndex**, respectively. Set the **Default Value** of both text boxes to be equal to **1**.

5. Add a **Button** control to the view of the form template and label it **Send To Excel**.

6. With the button still selected, click **Control Tools ➤ Properties ➤ Button ➤ Custom Code** to add an event handler for the **Clicked** event of the **Send To Excel** button.

7. In VSTA, add a reference to the **Microsoft Excel 14.0 Object Library** (**Microsoft.Office.Interop.Excel**) COM component.

8. Add the following **using** statement to the **FormCode.cs** file:

```
using ExcelLib = Microsoft.Office.Interop.Excel;
```

Or add the following **Imports** statement to the **FormCode.vb** file:

```
Imports ExcelLib = Microsoft.Office.Interop.Excel
```

9. Add the following C# or Visual Basic code to the `Clicked()` event handler for the **Send To Excel** button (*code #: 1D6DF472-8357-4295-A721-A976045455E2*):

<u>C#</u>

```
ExcelLib.Application app =
  new Microsoft.Office.Interop.Excel.Application();

ExcelLib.Workbook wb = app.Workbooks.Open(
  @"C:\ExistingWorkbook.xlsx",
  System.Type.Missing, System.Type.Missing, System.Type.Missing,
  System.Type.Missing, System.Type.Missing, System.Type.Missing,
  System.Type.Missing, System.Type.Missing, System.Type.Missing,
  System.Type.Missing, System.Type.Missing, System.Type.Missing,
  System.Type.Missing, System.Type.Missing);

if (wb.Worksheets.Count >= 2)
{
  try
  {
    ExcelLib.Worksheet ws = (ExcelLib.Worksheet)wb.Worksheets["Sheet2"];

    XPathNavigator mainDS = MainDataSource.CreateNavigator();
    XPathNavigator row = mainDS.SelectSingleNode(
      "//my:rowIndex", NamespaceManager);
    XPathNavigator col = mainDS.SelectSingleNode(
      "//my:colIndex", NamespaceManager);
    XPathNodeIterator iter = mainDS.Select(
      "//my:group2", NamespaceManager);

    int rowIndex = Int32.Parse(row.Value);
    int colIndex = Int32.Parse(col.Value);

    while (iter.MoveNext())
    {
      ((ExcelLib.Range)ws.Cells[rowIndex, colIndex]).Value2 =
        iter.Current.SelectSingleNode(
```

```
      "my:field1", NamespaceManager).Value;

   ((ExcelLib.Range)ws.Cells[rowIndex, colIndex + 1]).Value2 =
      iter.Current.SelectSingleNode(
      "my:field2", NamespaceManager).Value;

   ((ExcelLib.Range)ws.Cells[rowIndex, colIndex + 2]).Value2 =
      iter.Current.SelectSingleNode(
      "my:field3", NamespaceManager).Value;

   rowIndex++;
   }

   wb.Save();

   }
   finally
   {
      wb.Close(true, System.Type.Missing, System.Type.Missing);
   }
}
```

Visual Basic

```
Dim app As New Microsoft.Office.Interop.Excel.Application()

Dim wb As ExcelLib.Workbook = app.Workbooks.Open( _
   "C:\ExistingWorkbook.xlsx", _
   System.Type.Missing, System.Type.Missing, System.Type.Missing, _
   System.Type.Missing, System.Type.Missing, System.Type.Missing, _
   System.Type.Missing, System.Type.Missing, System.Type.Missing, _
   System.Type.Missing, System.Type.Missing, System.Type.Missing, _
   System.Type.Missing, System.Type.Missing)

If wb.Worksheets.Count >= 2 Then

   Try

      Dim ws As ExcelLib.Worksheet = wb.Worksheets("Sheet2")

      Dim mainDS As XPathNavigator = MainDataSource.CreateNavigator()
      Dim row As XPathNavigator = mainDS.SelectSingleNode( _
         "//my:rowIndex", NamespaceManager)
      Dim col As XPathNavigator = mainDS.SelectSingleNode( _
         "//my:colIndex", NamespaceManager)
      Dim iter As XPathNodeIterator = mainDS.Select( _
         "//my:group2", NamespaceManager)

      Dim rowIndex As Integer = Int32.Parse(row.Value)
      Dim colIndex As Integer = Int32.Parse(col.Value)

      While iter.MoveNext()

        ws.Cells(rowIndex, colIndex).Value = _
           iter.Current.SelectSingleNode( _
           "my:field1", NamespaceManager).Value

        ws.Cells(rowIndex, colIndex + 1).Value = _
           iter.Current.SelectSingleNode( _
           "my:field2", NamespaceManager).Value

        ws.Cells(rowIndex, colIndex + 2).Value = _
```

247

```
        iter.Current.SelectSingleNode( _
        "my:field3", NamespaceManager).Value

    rowIndex = rowIndex + 1

  End While

  wb.Save()

Finally

  wb.Close(True, System.Type.Missing, System.Type.Missing)

End Try

End If
```

where you must replace `C:\ExistingWorkbook.xlsx` with the path to the Excel workbook to which you want to write the data from the repeating table.

10. Save and build the project.

11. In InfoPath, click **File ➤ Info ➤ Form Options**.

12. On the **Form Options** dialog box, select **Security and Trust** in the **Category** list, deselect the **Automatically determine security level (recommended)** check box, select the **Full Trust** option, and then click **OK**.

13. Preview the form.

When the form opens, add a couple of rows to the repeating table, fill the fields in the repeating table with data, change the row and column index numbers if you wish (these numbers represent the row and column numbers of the cell in the upper-left corner of the range of cells that will be populated in the Excel workbook), and then click the **Send To Excel** button. Open Windows Explorer, navigate to the location on disk where the **ExitingWorkbook.xlsx** Excel workbook is located, open the file, and verify that the data from the repeating table on the InfoPath form was written to it.

Discussion

In the solution described above, you saw how to write code that makes use of the Excel Object Model to populate a range of cells on a particular worksheet in an Excel workbook that is located on disk with data from a repeating table control on an InfoPath form. The code first creates an `Application` object

C#

```
ExcelLib.Application app = new Microsoft.Office.Interop.Excel.Application();
```

Visual Basic

```
Dim app As New Microsoft.Office.Interop.Excel.Application()
```

and uses the Open() method of the Workbooks property of the Application object to open an existing Excel workbook.

C#

```
ExcelLib.Workbook wb = app.Workbooks.Open(
  @"C:\ExistingWorkbook.xlsx",
  System.Type.Missing, System.Type.Missing, System.Type.Missing,
  System.Type.Missing, System.Type.Missing, System.Type.Missing,
  System.Type.Missing, System.Type.Missing, System.Type.Missing,
  System.Type.Missing, System.Type.Missing, System.Type.Missing,
  System.Type.Missing, System.Type.Missing);
```

Visual Basic

```
Dim wb As ExcelLib.Workbook = app.Workbooks.Open( _
  "C:\ExistingWorkbook.xlsx", _
  System.Type.Missing, System.Type.Missing, System.Type.Missing, _
  System.Type.Missing, System.Type.Missing, System.Type.Missing, _
  System.Type.Missing, System.Type.Missing, System.Type.Missing, _
  System.Type.Missing, System.Type.Missing, System.Type.Missing, _
  System.Type.Missing, System.Type.Missing)
```

The code then checks whether there are two or more worksheets in the workbook, and if there are, it retrieves a reference to the **Sheet2** worksheet.

C#

```
if (wb.Worksheets.Count >= 2)
{
  try
  {
    ExcelLib.Worksheet ws = (ExcelLib.Worksheet)wb.Worksheets["Sheet2"];
    ...
  }
}
```

Visual Basic

```
If wb.Worksheets.Count >= 2 Then

  Try

    Dim ws As ExcelLib.Worksheet = wb.Worksheets("Sheet2")
    ...

  End Try

End If
```

Note that you can also use a number (for example **2** in this case) to get a reference to the second worksheet in the Excel workbook (**Sheet2**) as follows:

C#

```
ExcelLib.Worksheet ws = (ExcelLib.Worksheet)wb.Worksheets[2];
```

Visual Basic

```
Dim ws As ExcelLib.Worksheet = wb.Worksheets(2)
```

You could also provide users with an extra field on the form in which the worksheet name or number can be specified and then use that value in code.

The code goes on to retrieve XPathNavigator objects pointing to the two text boxes and an XPathNodeIterator object for the repeating group nodes (**group2**) of the repeating table.

C#

```
XPathNavigator mainDS = MainDataSource.CreateNavigator();
XPathNavigator row = mainDS.SelectSingleNode(
  "//my:rowIndex", NamespaceManager);
XPathNavigator col = mainDS.SelectSingleNode(
  "//my:colIndex", NamespaceManager);
XPathNodeIterator iter = mainDS.Select(
  "//my:group2", NamespaceManager);
```

Visual Basic

```
Dim mainDS As XPathNavigator = MainDataSource.CreateNavigator()
Dim row As XPathNavigator = mainDS.SelectSingleNode( _
  "//my:rowIndex", NamespaceManager)
Dim col As XPathNavigator = mainDS.SelectSingleNode( _
  "//my:colIndex", NamespaceManager)
Dim iter As XPathNodeIterator = mainDS.Select( _
  "//my:group2", NamespaceManager)
```

After retrieving the values of the **rowIndex** and **colIndex** text boxes

C#

```
int rowIndex = Int32.Parse(row.Value);
int colIndex = Int32.Parse(col.Value);
```

Visual Basic

```
Dim rowIndex As Integer = Int32.Parse(row.Value)
Dim colIndex As Integer = Int32.Parse(col.Value)
```

the code loops through all of the rows in the repeating table and uses the Cells property of the Worksheet object to populate cells in a range of cells where the upper-left corner has the row and column numbers that were specified in the **rowIndex** and **colIndex** text boxes on the InfoPath form.

C#

```
while (iter.MoveNext())
{
  ((ExcelLib.Range)ws.Cells[rowIndex, colIndex]).Value2 =
    iter.Current.SelectSingleNode(
```

```
          "my:field1", NamespaceManager).Value;

      ((ExcelLib.Range)ws.Cells[rowIndex, colIndex + 1]).Value2 =
        iter.Current.SelectSingleNode(
        "my:field2", NamespaceManager).Value;

      ((ExcelLib.Range)ws.Cells[rowIndex, colIndex + 2]).Value2 =
        iter.Current.SelectSingleNode(
        "my:field3", NamespaceManager).Value;

      rowIndex++;
}
```

Visual Basic

```
While iter.MoveNext()

    ws.Cells(rowIndex, colIndex).Value = _
      iter.Current.SelectSingleNode( _
      "my:field1", NamespaceManager).Value

    ws.Cells(rowIndex, colIndex + 1).Value = _
      iter.Current.SelectSingleNode( _
      "my:field2", NamespaceManager).Value

    ws.Cells(rowIndex, colIndex + 2).Value = _
      iter.Current.SelectSingleNode( _
      "my:field3", NamespaceManager).Value

    rowIndex = rowIndex + 1

End While
```

Note that the rowIndex variable starts at the row number specified in the **rowIndex** text box on the InfoPath form and is incremented by 1 for each row in the repeating table while looping through the rows. The colIndex variable starts at the column number specified in the **colIndex** text box on the InfoPath form and is then incremented by 1 for the second field and by 2 for the third field in each row. And unlike the rowIndex variable, the colIndex variable restarts every time at the column number specified in the **colIndex** text box on the InfoPath form while looping through the rows. Note that row and column numbers start at 1 when using the Excel Object Model. So cell **A1** has row and column number 1.

And finally, the Workbook object is saved and then closed.

C#

```
try
{
  ...
  wb.Save();
}
finally
{
  wb.Close(true, System.Type.Missing, System.Type.Missing);
}
```

Visual Basic

```
Try

  ...
  wb.Save()

Finally

  wb.Close(True, System.Type.Missing, System.Type.Missing)

End Try
```

To learn more about writing code that calls into the Excel Object Model, consult the documentation on the MSDN web site.

Warning:

> If you do not make use of error-handling and an error takes place after opening an Excel workbook and performing an action, the code for closing the workbook will not run. Therefore, you may not be able to open Excel afterwards, since a process for Excel is still/already active. To correct this issue, you would have to manually end the EXCEL.EXE process via the **Processes** tab on the **Windows Task Manager** dialog box. To avoid having to manually end processes, ensure that you always close an Excel workbook through code by adding a `Try-Catch-Finally` block around your code and placing the code that closes the workbook in the `Finally` block.

Use Open XML for Excel in SharePoint

All of the solutions in this section require you to have the Open XML SDK 2.0 installed on your system. You can download it from Microsoft's web site.

49 Create a new Excel workbook in SharePoint from within InfoPath

Problem

You have an InfoPath form and want to use it to create a new Excel workbook in a SharePoint document library.

Solution

You can use the Open XML SDK to create a new Excel workbook and then use the **Copy** web service to store the workbook in a SharePoint document library.

To create a new Excel workbook in SharePoint from within an InfoPath form:

1. In SharePoint, enter the URL of the **CopyIntoItems** operation of the **Copy** web service in the browser's address bar. For example:

    ```
    http://servername/sitename/_vti_bin/Copy.asmx?op=CopyIntoItems
    ```

2. Copy the XML fragment that is located in the **soap:Body** element of the SOAP request. For example:

    ```
    <CopyIntoItems xmlns="http://schemas.microsoft.com/sharepoint/soap/">
      <SourceUrl>string</SourceUrl>
      <DestinationUrls>
        <string>string</string>
        <string>string</string>
      </DestinationUrls>
      <Fields>
        <FieldInformation Type="Invalid or Integer or Text or Note or DateTime
    or Counter or Choice or Lookup or Boolean or Number or Currency or URL or
    Computed or Threading or Guid or MultiChoice or GridChoice or Calculated or
    File or Attachments or User or Recurrence or CrossProjectLink or ModStat or
    AllDayEvent or Error" DisplayName="string" InternalName="string" Id="guid"
    Value="string" />
        <FieldInformation Type="Invalid or Integer or Text or Note or DateTime
    or Counter or Choice or Lookup or Boolean or Number or Currency or URL or
    Computed or Threading or Guid or MultiChoice or GridChoice or Calculated or
    File or Attachments or User or Recurrence or CrossProjectLink or ModStat or
    AllDayEvent or Error" DisplayName="string" InternalName="string" Id="guid"
    Value="string" />
      </Fields>
      <Stream>base64Binary</Stream>
    </CopyIntoItems>
    ```

    Open Notepad and paste the XML fragment you just copied, remove all line-breaks and whitespaces between the elements, and then save the file as **CopyIntoItemsRequest.xml**. You can also download this file from www.bizsupportonline.com for use with this recipe.

3. Copy the XML fragment that is located in the **soap:Body** element of the SOAP response. For example:

    ```
    <CopyIntoItemsResponse
    xmlns="http://schemas.microsoft.com/sharepoint/soap/">
      <CopyIntoItemsResult>unsignedInt</CopyIntoItemsResult>
      <Results>
        <CopyResult ErrorCode="Success or DestinationInvalid or DestinationMWS
    or SourceInvalid or DestinationCheckedOut or InvalidUrl or Unknown"
    ErrorMessage="string" DestinationUrl="string" />
        <CopyResult ErrorCode="Success or DestinationInvalid or DestinationMWS
    or SourceInvalid or DestinationCheckedOut or InvalidUrl or Unknown"
    ErrorMessage="string" DestinationUrl="string" />
      </Results>
    </CopyIntoItemsResponse>
    ```

Open Notepad and paste the XML fragment you just copied, remove all line-breaks and whitespaces between the elements, and then save the file as **CopyIntoItemsResponse.xml**. You can also download this file from www.bizsupportonline.com for use with this recipe.

4. In InfoPath, create a new browser-compatible form template or use an existing one.

5. Select **Data ➤ Get External Data ➤ From Other Sources ➤ From XML File** and follow the instructions to add an XML data connection for the **CopyIntoItemsRequest.xml** file. Leave the **Automatically retrieve data when form is opened** check box selected and name the data connection **CopyIntoItemsRequest**.

6. Select **Data ➤ Get External Data ➤ From Other Sources ➤ From XML File** and follow the instructions to add an XML data connection for the **CopyIntoItemsResponse.xml** file. Leave the **Automatically retrieve data when form is opened** check box selected and name the data connection **CopyIntoItemsResponse**.

7. Select **Data ➤ Submit Form ➤ To Other Locations ➤ To Web Service**.

8. On the **Data Connection Wizard**, enter the URL of the **Copy** web service, for example:

    ```
    http://servername/sitename/_vti_bin/Copy.asmx
    ```

    and click **Next**. Here **servername** is the name of the SharePoint server where a site named **sitename** on which the **Copy** web service is located.

9. On the **Data Connection Wizard**, select the **CopyIntoItems** operation from the list of operations, and click **Next**.

10. On the **Data Connection Wizard**, configure the parameters as follows:

Parameter	Element
ns1:SourceUrl	/ns1:CopyIntoItems/ns1:SourceUrl
	where **SourceUrl** is a field located in the **CopyIntoItemsRequest** secondary data source.
ns1:DestinationUrls	/ns1:CopyIntoItems/ns1:DestinationUrls
	where **DestinationsUrls** is a group node located in the **CopyIntoItemsRequest** secondary data source.
ns1:Fields	/ns1:CopyIntoItems/ns1:Fields
	where **Fields** is a group node located in the **CopyIntoItemsRequest** secondary data source.
ns1:Stream	/ns1:CopyIntoItems/ns1:Stream
	where **Stream** is a field located in the **CopyIntoItemsRequest** secondary data source.

Select **Text and child elements only** from the **Include** drop-down list box and leave the **Submit data as a string** check box deselected for all of the parameters. Accept the default data connection name of **Web Service Submit** and deselect the **Set as the default submit connection** check box. You will use this data connection to upload the new Excel workbook to a SharePoint document library.

11. Add a **Text Box** control to the view of the form template and name it **excelFileName**.

12. Add a **Button** control to the view of the form template and label it **Create Excel File**.

13. With the button still selected, click **Control Tools ➤ Properties ➤ Button ➤ Custom Code** to add an event handler for the **Clicked** event of the button.

14. In VSTA, add references to the **DocumentFormat.OpenXml** and **WindowsBase** assemblies.

15. Add the following **using** statements to the **FormCode.cs** file:

```
using System.IO;
using DocumentFormat.OpenXml;
using DocumentFormat.OpenXml.Packaging;
using DocumentFormat.OpenXml.Spreadsheet;
```

Or add the following **Imports** statements to the **FormCode.vb** file:

```
Imports System.IO
Imports DocumentFormat.OpenXml
Imports DocumentFormat.OpenXml.Packaging
Imports DocumentFormat.OpenXml.Spreadsheet
```

16. Add the following C# or Visual Basic code to the `Clicked()` event handler for the **Create Excel File** button (*code #: 89B0503E-CD8E-4465-85FC-B7CAAD6AA719*):

C#

```csharp
XPathNavigator mainDS = MainDataSource.CreateNavigator();
string excelFileName = mainDS.SelectSingleNode(
  "//my:excelFileName", NamespaceManager).Value;

byte[] bytes = null;

using (MemoryStream sr = new MemoryStream())
{
  using (SpreadsheetDocument spreadSheet =
    SpreadsheetDocument.Create(sr, SpreadsheetDocumentType.Workbook))
  {
    spreadSheet.AddWorkbookPart();
    spreadSheet.WorkbookPart.Workbook = new Workbook();
    WorksheetPart wsPart =
      spreadSheet.WorkbookPart.AddNewPart<WorksheetPart>();

    wsPart.Worksheet = new Worksheet();
    SheetData sheetData = wsPart.Worksheet.AppendChild(new SheetData());
    wsPart.Worksheet.Save();

    spreadSheet.WorkbookPart.Workbook.AppendChild(new Sheets());
    Sheet sheet1 = new Sheet();
    sheet1.Id = spreadSheet.WorkbookPart.GetIdOfPart(wsPart);
    sheet1.SheetId = 1;
    sheet1.Name = "Sheet1";
    spreadSheet.WorkbookPart.Workbook.GetFirstChild<Sheets>().AppendChild(
      sheet1);

    spreadSheet.WorkbookPart.Workbook.Save();
  }

  bytes = sr.ToArray();
  sr.Close();
}

string siteUrl = "http://servername/sitename/";

XPathNavigator secDS =
  DataSources["CopyIntoItemsRequest"].CreateNavigator();

XPathNavigator sourceUrl = secDS.SelectSingleNode(
  "/ns1:CopyIntoItems/ns1:SourceUrl", NamespaceManager);
XPathNavigator destUrl = secDS.SelectSingleNode(
  "/ns1:CopyIntoItems/ns1:DestinationUrls/ns1:string[1]",
NamespaceManager);

XPathNavigator secondDestUrl = secDS.SelectSingleNode(
  "/ns1:CopyIntoItems/ns1:DestinationUrls/ns1:string[2]",
```

```
      NamespaceManager);
  if (secondDestUrl != null)
    secondDestUrl.DeleteSelf();

  XPathNodeIterator fields = secDS.Select(
    "/ns1:CopyIntoItems/ns1:Fields/ns1:FieldInformation", NamespaceManager);
  if (fields != null && fields.Count > 0)
  {
    int count = fields.Count;
    XPathNavigator firstChild = secDS.SelectSingleNode(
      "/ns1:CopyIntoItems/ns1:Fields/ns1:FieldInformation[1]",
      NamespaceManager);
    XPathNavigator lastChild = secDS.SelectSingleNode(
      "/ns1:CopyIntoItems/ns1:Fields/ns1:FieldInformation["
      + count.ToString() + "]",
      NamespaceManager);
    firstChild.DeleteRange(lastChild);
  }

  XPathNavigator stream2 = secDS.SelectSingleNode(
    "/ns1:CopyIntoItems/ns1:Stream", NamespaceManager);

  string libName = "DocLib";

  destUrl.SetValue(siteUrl + libName + "/" + excelFileName);
  sourceUrl.SetValue(destUrl.Value);
  stream2.SetValue(Convert.ToBase64String(bytes));

  XPathNavigator response =
    DataSources["CopyIntoItemsResponse"].CreateNavigator()
    .SelectSingleNode("/ns1:CopyIntoItemsResponse", NamespaceManager);

  ((WebServiceConnection)DataConnections["Web Service Submit"])
    .Execute(secDS, response, null);
```

Visual Basic

```
Dim mainDS As XPathNavigator = MainDataSource.CreateNavigator()
Dim excelFileName As String = mainDS.SelectSingleNode( _
  "//my:excelFileName", NamespaceManager).Value

Dim bytes As Byte() = Nothing

Using sr As New MemoryStream()

  Using spreadSheet As SpreadsheetDocument = _
    SpreadsheetDocument.Create(sr, SpreadsheetDocumentType.Workbook)

    spreadSheet.AddWorkbookPart()
    spreadSheet.WorkbookPart.Workbook = New Workbook()
    Dim wsPart As WorksheetPart = _
      spreadSheet.WorkbookPart.AddNewPart(Of WorksheetPart)()

    wsPart.Worksheet = New Worksheet()
    Dim sheetData As SheetData = wsPart.Worksheet.AppendChild( _
      New SheetData())
    wsPart.Worksheet.Save()

    spreadSheet.WorkbookPart.Workbook.AppendChild(New Sheets())
    Dim sheet1 As Sheet = New Sheet()
    sheet1.Id = spreadSheet.WorkbookPart.GetIdOfPart(wsPart)
    sheet1.SheetId = 1
```

```
      sheet1.Name = "Sheet1"
      spreadSheet.WorkbookPart.Workbook.GetFirstChild(Of Sheets)() _
        .AppendChild(sheet1)

      spreadSheet.WorkbookPart.Workbook.Save()

    End Using

    bytes = sr.ToArray()
    sr.Close()

End Using

Dim siteUrl As String = "http://servername/sitename/"

Dim secDS As XPathNavigator = _
  DataSources("CopyIntoItemsRequest").CreateNavigator()

Dim sourceUrl As XPathNavigator = secDS.SelectSingleNode( _
  "/ns1:CopyIntoItems/ns1:SourceUrl", NamespaceManager)
Dim destUrl As XPathNavigator = secDS.SelectSingleNode( _
  "/ns1:CopyIntoItems/ns1:DestinationUrls/ns1:string[1]", NamespaceManager)

Dim secondDestUrl As XPathNavigator = secDS.SelectSingleNode( _
  "/ns1:CopyIntoItems/ns1:DestinationUrls/ns1:string[2]", NamespaceManager)

If secondDestUrl IsNot Nothing Then
  secondDestUrl.DeleteSelf()
End If

Dim fields As XPathNodeIterator = secDS.Select( _
  "/ns1:CopyIntoItems/ns1:Fields/ns1:FieldInformation", NamespaceManager)

If fields IsNot Nothing Then
  If fields.Count > 0 Then
    Dim count As UInt16Value = fields.Count
    Dim firstChild As XPathNavigator = secDS.SelectSingleNode( _
      "/ns1:CopyIntoItems/ns1:Fields/ns1:FieldInformation[1]", _
      NamespaceManager)
    Dim lastChild As XPathNavigator = secDS.SelectSingleNode( _
      "/ns1:CopyIntoItems/ns1:Fields/ns1:FieldInformation[" & _
      count.ToString() & "]", NamespaceManager)
    firstChild.DeleteRange(lastChild)
  End If
End If

Dim stream2 As XPathNavigator = secDS.SelectSingleNode( _
  "/ns1:CopyIntoItems/ns1:Stream", NamespaceManager)

Dim libName As String = "DocLib"

destUrl.SetValue(siteUrl & libName & "/" & excelFileName)
sourceUrl.SetValue(destUrl.Value)
stream2.SetValue(Convert.ToBase64String(bytes))

Dim response As XPathNavigator = _
DataSources("CopyIntoItemsResponse").CreateNavigator() _
  .SelectSingleNode("/ns1:CopyIntoItemsResponse", NamespaceManager)

CType(DataConnections("Web Service Submit"), WebServiceConnection) _
  .Execute(secDS, response, Nothing)
```

where you must replace **DocLib** with the name of the SharePoint document library where the Excel workbook should be saved and replace `http://servername/sitename/` with the correct URL of the site where the document library is located.

17. Save and build the project.

18. Preview the form.

When the form opens, enter a file name (including a file extension of **.xlsx**) for the new Excel workbook into the **excelFileName** text box and then click the **Create Excel File** button. Close the form and navigate to the SharePoint document library where the Excel workbook should have been created. Verify that the Excel workbook is present and then open it to verify that it contains one worksheet named **Sheet1**.

Discussion

In the solution described above, you saw how to create a new Excel workbook and store it in SharePoint from within an InfoPath form using the Open XML SDK and the **Copy** web service. The solution consists of two parts:

1. Create a new Excel workbook using the Open XML SDK.

2. Use the **CopyIntoItems** operation of the **Copy** web service to upload the newly created Excel workbook to a SharePoint document library.

The code first retrieves the value of the text box control on the InfoPath form.

C#

```
XPathNavigator mainDS = MainDataSource.CreateNavigator();
string excelFileName = mainDS.SelectSingleNode(
  "//my:excelFileName", NamespaceManager).Value;
```

Visual Basic

```
Dim mainDS As XPathNavigator = MainDataSource.CreateNavigator()
Dim excelFileName As String = mainDS.SelectSingleNode( _
  "//my:excelFileName", NamespaceManager).Value
```

To create the Excel workbook, the code:

1. Adds a `WorkbookPart` object to a `SpreadsheetDocument` object.

   C#

   ```
   spreadSheet.AddWorkbookPart();
   ```

   Visual Basic

   ```
   spreadSheet.AddWorkbookPart()
   ```

2. Creates a new `Workbook` object for the `WorkbookPart` object.

   C#

```
spreadSheet.WorkbookPart.Workbook = new Workbook();
```

Visual Basic

```
spreadSheet.WorkbookPart.Workbook = New Workbook()
```

3. Adds a new `WorksheetPart` object to the `WorkbookPart` object.

   C#

   ```
   WorksheetPart wsPart =
     spreadSheet.WorkbookPart.AddNewPart<WorksheetPart>();
   ```

   Visual Basic

   ```
   Dim wsPart As WorksheetPart = _
     spreadSheet.WorkbookPart.AddNewPart(Of WorksheetPart)()
   ```

4. Creates a new `Worksheet` object for the `WorksheetPart` object.

   C#

   ```
   wsPart.Worksheet = new Worksheet();
   ```

   Visual Basic

   ```
   wsPart.Worksheet = New Worksheet()
   ```

5. Adds a new `SheetData` object to the `Worksheet` object.

   C#

   ```
   SheetData sheetData = wsPart.Worksheet.AppendChild(new SheetData());
   ```

   Visual Basic

   ```
   Dim sheetData As SheetData = _
     wsPart.Worksheet.AppendChild(New SheetData())
   ```

6. Saves the `Worksheet` object.

   C#

   ```
   wsPart.Worksheet.Save();
   ```

   Visual Basic

   ```
   wsPart.Worksheet.Save()
   ```

7. Adds a new `Sheets` object to the `Workbook` object.

   C#

   ```
   spreadSheet.WorkbookPart.Workbook.AppendChild(new Sheets());
   ```

   Visual Basic

   ```
   spreadSheet.WorkbookPart.Workbook.AppendChild(New Sheets())
   ```

8. Adds a new `Sheet` object to the `Sheets` object.

C#

```
Sheet sheet1 = new Sheet();
sheet1.Id = spreadSheet.WorkbookPart.GetIdOfPart(wsPart);
sheet1.SheetId = 1;
sheet1.Name = "Sheet1";
spreadSheet.WorkbookPart.Workbook.GetFirstChild<Sheets>().AppendChild(
    sheet1);
```

Visual Basic

```
Dim sheet1 As Sheet = New Sheet()
sheet1.Id = spreadSheet.WorkbookPart.GetIdOfPart(wsPart)
sheet1.SheetId = 1
sheet1.Name = "Sheet1"
spreadSheet.WorkbookPart.Workbook.GetFirstChild(Of Sheets)() _
    .AppendChild(sheet1)
```

9. Saves the `Workbook` object.

C#

```
spreadSheet.WorkbookPart.Workbook.Save();
```

Visual Basic

```
spreadSheet.WorkbookPart.Workbook.Save()
```

Once the spreadsheet document has been created, the code converts the `MemoryStream` object that contains the spreadsheet document into a `Byte` array and closes the stream.

C#

```
bytes = sr.ToArray();
sr.Close();
```

Visual Basic

```
bytes = sr.ToArray()
sr.Close()
```

Refer to the Open XML SDK documentation and the article entitled *Generating Excel 2010 Workbooks by using the Open XML SDK 2.0* on the MSDN web site to learn more about using the Open XML SDK to work with data in Excel workbooks.

In the second part of the solution, the code uses the **Copy** web service of SharePoint to upload the newly created Excel workbook to a SharePoint document library. The code for using the **Copy** web service to upload a document to SharePoint was extensively explained in recipe *98 Use an InfoPath form to upload a file to a SharePoint document library* of *InfoPath 2010 Cookbook 3* and *InfoPath 2010 Cookbook 4*, but the essence of it is that it first populates the parameters with values for the source and destination URLs in addition to setting the value of the **Stream** parameter to be equal to the base64-encoded string for the `Byte` array

C#

```
destUrl.SetValue(siteUrl + libName + "/" + excelFileName);
sourceUrl.SetValue(destUrl.Value);
stream2.SetValue(Convert.ToBase64String(bytes));
```

Visual Basic

```
destUrl.SetValue(siteUrl & libName & "/" & excelFileName)
sourceUrl.SetValue(destUrl.Value)
stream2.SetValue(Convert.ToBase64String(bytes))
```

before calling the `Execute()` method of the data connection for the **CopyIntoItems** operation of the **Copy** web service to upload the Excel workbook to SharePoint.

C#

```
((WebServiceConnection)DataConnections["Web Service Submit"])
  .Execute(secDS, response, null);
```

Visual Basic

```
CType(DataConnections("Web Service Submit"), WebServiceConnection) _
  .Execute(secDS, response, Nothing)
```

50   Get the value of a cell in an Excel workbook

Problem

You have an Excel workbook stored in a SharePoint document library and would like to retrieve the value of a cell in the Excel workbook for display on an InfoPath form.

Solution

You can download an existing Excel workbook from a SharePoint document library into an InfoPath form, use the Open XML SDK to open the workbook, read data from it, and then display that data on the InfoPath form.

To get the value of a cell in an Excel workbook:

1.   In InfoPath, create a new browser-compatible form template or use an existing one.

2.   Select **Data ➤ Get External Data ➤ From Web Service ➤ From SOAP Web Service**.

3.   On the **Data Connection Wizard**, enter the URL of the **Copy** web service, for example:

```
http://servername/sitename/_vti_bin/Copy.asmx
```

and click **Next**. Here **servername** is the name of the SharePoint server where a site named **sitename** on which the **Copy** web service is located.

4. On the **Data Connection Wizard**, select the **GetItem** operation, and click **Next**.

5. On the **Data Connection Wizard**, leave the parameter as is, and click **Next**.

6. On the **Data Connection Wizard**, leave the **Store a copy of the data in the form template** check box deselected, and click **Next**.

7. On the **Data Connection Wizard**, name the data connection **GetItem**, deselect the **Automatically retrieve data when form is opened** check box, and click **Finish**.

8. Add two **Text Box** controls to the view of the form template and name them **field1** and **field2**, respectively.

9. Add a **Button** control to the view of the form template and label it **Get From Excel**.

10. With the button still selected, click **Control Tools ➤ Properties ➤ Button ➤ Custom Code** to add an event handler for the **Clicked** event of the button.

11. In VSTA, add references to the **DocumentFormat.OpenXml** and **WindowsBase** assemblies.

12. If you are writing C# code, add a new class file named **InfoPathExcel.cs** to the project, open the file and replace the code in the **InfoPathExcel.cs** file with the code displayed in *InfoPathExcel.cs* in the Appendix (*code #: C6EE40D6-96BC-485A-A1FD-12511A8E91D2*); or if you are writing Visual Basic code, add a new module file named **InfoPathExcel.vb** to the project, open the file and replace the code in the **InfoPathExcel.vb** file with the code displayed in *InfoPathExcel.vb* in the Appendix (*code #: 9DFDBC84-9A61-43E3-92FD-E819BEB95D21*).

13. Add the following **using** statements to the **FormCode.cs** file:

```
using System.IO;
using DocumentFormat.OpenXml;
using DocumentFormat.OpenXml.Packaging;
using DocumentFormat.OpenXml.Spreadsheet;
```

Or add the following **Imports** statements to the **FormCode.vb** file:

```
Imports System.IO
Imports DocumentFormat.OpenXml
Imports DocumentFormat.OpenXml.Packaging
Imports DocumentFormat.OpenXml.Spreadsheet
```

14. Add the following C# or Visual Basic code to the `Clicked()` event handler for the **Get From Excel** button (*code #: A78172C4-E187-4A09-8A2D-F6B44A82284D*):

<u>C#</u>

```
string workbookPath = "http://servername/sitename/libname/MyWorkbook.xlsx";

XPathNavigator mainDS = MainDataSource.CreateNavigator();
XPathNavigator field1 = mainDS.SelectSingleNode(
  "//my:field1", NamespaceManager);
XPathNavigator field2 = mainDS.SelectSingleNode(
  "//my:field2", NamespaceManager);

XPathNavigator getItemDS = DataSources["GetItem"].CreateNavigator();
getItemDS.SelectSingleNode(
  "/dfs:myFields/dfs:queryFields/tns:GetItem/tns:Url",
  NamespaceManager).SetValue(workbookPath);

DataSources["GetItem"].QueryConnection.Execute();

XPathNavigator stream = getItemDS.SelectSingleNode(
  "/dfs:myFields/dfs:dataFields/tns:GetItemResponse/tns:Stream",
  NamespaceManager);

if (stream != null)
{
  string base64 = stream.Value;
  byte[] bytes = Convert.FromBase64String(base64);

  using (MemoryStream ms = new MemoryStream(bytes))
  {
    using (SpreadsheetDocument document =
      SpreadsheetDocument.Open(ms, false))
    {
      WorkbookPart wbPart = document.WorkbookPart;
      field2.SetValue(
        BizSupportOnline.InfoPathExcel.GetCellData(
        "Sheet1", field1.Value, wbPart)
      );
      document.Close();
    }

    ms.Close();
  }

}
```

Visual Basic

```
Dim workbookPath As String = _
  "http://servername/sitename/libname/MyWorkbook.xlsx"

Dim mainDS As XPathNavigator = MainDataSource.CreateNavigator()
Dim field1 As XPathNavigator = mainDS.SelectSingleNode( _
  "//my:field1", NamespaceManager)
Dim field2 As XPathNavigator = mainDS.SelectSingleNode( _
  "//my:field2", NamespaceManager)

Dim getItemDS As XPathNavigator = DataSources("GetItem").CreateNavigator()
getItemDS.SelectSingleNode( _
  "/dfs:myFields/dfs:queryFields/tns:GetItem/tns:Url", _
  NamespaceManager).SetValue(workbookPath)

DataSources("GetItem").QueryConnection.Execute()

Dim stream As XPathNavigator = getItemDS.SelectSingleNode( _
  "/dfs:myFields/dfs:dataFields/tns:GetItemResponse/tns:Stream", _
```

```
        NamespaceManager)

If stream IsNot Nothing Then

    Dim base64 As String = stream.Value
    Dim bytes As Byte() = Convert.FromBase64String(base64)

    Using ms As New MemoryStream(bytes)

        Using document As SpreadsheetDocument = _
          SpreadsheetDocument.Open(ms, False)

            Dim wbPart As WorkbookPart = document.WorkbookPart
            field2.SetValue( _
              BizSupportOnline.InfoPathExcel.GetCellData( _
              "Sheet1", field1.Value, wbPart))
            document.Close()

        End Using

        ms.Close()

    End Using

End If
```

where you must replace the value of the `workbookPath` variable with the correct URL for the Excel workbook that is located in a SharePoint document library and from which you want to retrieve a value.

15. Save and build the project.

16. Preview the form.

When the form opens, enter a cell reference (for example **C4**) in the first text box and then click the **Get From Excel** button. The value from the cell in the Excel workbook should appear in the second text box.

Discussion

In the solution described above, you saw how to use the Open XML SDK together with the **Copy** web service to retrieve a value from a particular cell in an Excel workbook and display this value on an InfoPath form. The solution consists of two parts:

1. Use the **GetItem** operation of the **Copy** web service to download an existing Excel workbook from a SharePoint document library. Note that you could have also used the **GetWorkbook** operation of the Excel Services web service to download the Excel workbook from SharePoint as described in recipe *51 Set the value of a cell in an Excel workbook*.

2. Open the Excel workbook and read data from it using the Open XML SDK.

The code first declares a variable containing the URL of an existing Excel workbook in SharePoint and creates `XPathNavigator` objects pointing to the fields that are bound to the two text box controls on the InfoPath form.

InfoPath 2010 Cookbook 5

C#

```
string workbookPath = "http://servername/sitename/libname/MyWorkbook.xlsx";

XPathNavigator mainDS = MainDataSource.CreateNavigator();
XPathNavigator field1 = mainDS.SelectSingleNode(
  "//my:field1", NamespaceManager);
XPathNavigator field2 = mainDS.SelectSingleNode(
  "//my:field2", NamespaceManager);
```

Visual Basic

```
Dim workbookPath As String = _
  "http://servername/sitename/libname/MyWorkbook.xlsx"

Dim mainDS As XPathNavigator = MainDataSource.CreateNavigator()
Dim field1 As XPathNavigator = mainDS.SelectSingleNode( _
  "//my:field1", NamespaceManager)
Dim field2 As XPathNavigator = mainDS.SelectSingleNode( _
  "//my:field2", NamespaceManager)
```

The code then retrieves the base64-encoded string representation of the Excel workbook by using the **GetItem** operation of the **Copy** web service.

C#

```
XPathNavigator getItemDS = DataSources["GetItem"].CreateNavigator();
getItemDS.SelectSingleNode(
  "/dfs:myFields/dfs:queryFields/tns:GetItem/tns:Url",
  NamespaceManager).SetValue(workbookPath);

DataSources["GetItem"].QueryConnection.Execute();

XPathNavigator stream = getItemDS.SelectSingleNode(
  "/dfs:myFields/dfs:dataFields/tns:GetItemResponse/tns:Stream",
  NamespaceManager);
```

Visual Basic

```
Dim getItemDS As XPathNavigator = DataSources("GetItem").CreateNavigator()
getItemDS.SelectSingleNode( _
  "/dfs:myFields/dfs:queryFields/tns:GetItem/tns:Url", _
  NamespaceManager).SetValue(workbookPath)

DataSources("GetItem").QueryConnection.Execute()

Dim stream As XPathNavigator = getItemDS.SelectSingleNode( _
  "/dfs:myFields/dfs:dataFields/tns:GetItemResponse/tns:Stream", _
  NamespaceManager)
```

The code then converts the base64-encoded string into a `Byte` array

C#

```
string base64 = stream.Value;
byte[] bytes = Convert.FromBase64String(base64);
```

Visual Basic

```
Dim base64 As String = stream.Value
Dim bytes As Byte() = Convert.FromBase64String(base64)
```

so that it can be used with classes from the Open XML SDK to open and retrieve data from the Excel workbook.

C#

```
using (MemoryStream ms = new MemoryStream(bytes))
{
  using (SpreadsheetDocument document =
    SpreadsheetDocument.Open(ms, false))
  {
    WorkbookPart wbPart = document.WorkbookPart;
    field2.SetValue(
      BizSupportOnline.InfoPathExcel.GetCellData(
      "Sheet1", field1.Value, wbPart)
    );
    document.Close();
  }

  ms.Close();
}
```

Visual Basic

```
Using ms As New MemoryStream(bytes)

  Using document As SpreadsheetDocument = _
    SpreadsheetDocument.Open(ms, False)

    Dim wbPart As WorkbookPart = document.WorkbookPart
    field2.SetValue( _
      BizSupportOnline.InfoPathExcel.GetCellData( _
      "Sheet1", field1.Value, wbPart))
    document.Close()

  End Using

  ms.Close()

End Using
```

Note that the code that retrieves data from the Excel workbook makes use of a procedure named GetCellData(), which has been defined in the InfoPathExcel C# class or Visual Basic module. The GetCellData() procedure makes use of classes from the Open XML SDK to retrieve data from a particular cell on a worksheet in an Excel workbook. Refer to the Open XML SDK documentation and the article entitled *Generating Excel 2010 Workbooks by using the Open XML SDK 2.0* on the MSDN web site to learn more about using the Open XML SDK to work with data in Excel workbooks.

Also note that the code retrieves data from **Sheet1** in the Excel workbook. You could make the solution dynamic by for example providing an extra field on the InfoPath form in which users can enter the name of the worksheet from which to retrieve data.

51 Set the value of a cell in an Excel workbook

Problem

You have an Excel workbook stored in a SharePoint document library and would like to write the value of a field on an InfoPath form to a cell in the Excel workbook.

Solution

You can download an existing Excel workbook from a SharePoint document library into an InfoPath form, use the Open XML SDK to open the workbook, modify it, and then upload it back to the SharePoint document library.

To set the value of a cell in an Excel workbook:

1. Follow steps 1 through 10 of recipe *49 Create a new Excel workbook in SharePoint from within InfoPath*, but name the data connection **UploadFile** instead of **Web Service Submit**.

2. Select **Data ➤ Get External Data ➤ From Web Service ➤ From SOAP Web Service** to add a **Receive** data connection for the **OpenWorkbook** operation of the Excel Services web service. Leave all of the parameters as is, leave the **Store a copy of the data in the form template** check box deselected, name the data connection **OpenWorkbook**, and deselect the **Automatically retrieve data when form is opened** check box. You will use this data connection to open the Excel workbook and retrieve a session ID you can use for all subsequent calls to Excel Services.

3. Select **Data ➤ Get External Data ➤ From Web Service ➤ From SOAP Web Service** to add a **Receive** data connection for the **GetWorkbook** operation of the Excel Services web service. Leave all of the parameters as is, leave the **Store a copy of the data in the form template** check box deselected, name the data connection **GetWorkbook**, and deselect the **Automatically retrieve data when form is opened** check box. You will use this data connection to download an entire Excel workbook from SharePoint.

4. Select **Data ➤ Get External Data ➤ From Web Service ➤ From SOAP Web Service** to add a **Receive** data connection for the **CloseWorkbook** operation of the Excel Services web service. Leave the **sessionId** parameter as is, leave the **Store a copy of the data in the form template** check box deselected, name the data connection **CloseWorkbook**, and deselect the **Automatically retrieve data when form is opened** check box. You will use this data connection to close the Excel workbook and Excel Services session.

5. Add two **Text Box** controls to the view of the form template and name them **field1** and **field2**, respectively.

6. Add a **Button** control to the view of the form template and label it **Save To Excel**.

7. With the button still selected, click **Control Tools ➤ Properties ➤ Button ➤ Custom Code** to add an event handler for the **Clicked** event of the button.

8. In VSTA, add references to the **DocumentFormat.OpenXml** and **WindowsBase** assemblies.

9. If you are writing C# code, add a new class file named **InfoPathExcel.cs** to the project, open the file and replace the code in the **InfoPathExcel.cs** file with the code displayed in *InfoPathExcel.cs* in the Appendix (*code #: C6EE40D6-96BC-485A-A1FD-12511A8E91D2*); or if you are writing Visual Basic code, add a new module file named **InfoPathExcel.vb** to the project, open the file and replace the code in the **InfoPathExcel.vb** file with the code displayed in *InfoPathExcel.vb* in the Appendix (*code #: 9DFDBC84-9A61-43E3-92FD-E819BEB95D21*).

10. Add the following **using** statements to the **FormCode.cs** file:

```
using System.IO;
using DocumentFormat.OpenXml;
using DocumentFormat.OpenXml.Packaging;
using DocumentFormat.OpenXml.Spreadsheet;
```

Or add the following **Imports** statements to the **FormCode.vb** file:

```
Imports System.IO
Imports DocumentFormat.OpenXml
Imports DocumentFormat.OpenXml.Packaging
Imports DocumentFormat.OpenXml.Spreadsheet
```

11. Add the following C# or Visual Basic code to the Clicked() event handler for the **Save To Excel** button (*code #: CB58D768-9F02-4604-8451-BC8C8C2F631C*):

C#

```
string workbookPath = "http://servername/sitename/libname/MyWorkbook.xlsx";

XPathNavigator mainDS = MainDataSource.CreateNavigator();
XPathNavigator field1 = mainDS.SelectSingleNode(
    "//my:field1", NamespaceManager);
XPathNavigator field2 = mainDS.SelectSingleNode(
    "//my:field2", NamespaceManager);

XPathNavigator openWBDS = DataSources["OpenWorkbook"].CreateNavigator();
XPathNavigator getWBDS = DataSources["GetWorkbook"].CreateNavigator();
XPathNavigator closeWBDS = DataSources["CloseWorkbook"].CreateNavigator();

openWBDS.SelectSingleNode(
    "/dfs:myFields/dfs:queryFields/ns2:OpenWorkbook/ns2:workbookPath",
    NamespaceManager).SetValue(workbookPath);
DataSources["OpenWorkbook"].QueryConnection.Execute();

string sessionId = openWBDS.SelectSingleNode(
    "/dfs:myFields/dfs:dataFields/ns2:OpenWorkbookResponse" +
    "/ns2:OpenWorkbookResult", NamespaceManager).Value;

getWBDS.SelectSingleNode(
    "/dfs:myFields/dfs:queryFields/ns2:GetWorkbook/ns2:sessionId",
```

```
    NamespaceManager).SetValue(sessionId);
  getWBDS.SelectSingleNode(
    "/dfs:myFields/dfs:queryFields/ns2:GetWorkbook/ns2:workbookType",
    NamespaceManager).SetValue("FullWorkbook");
  DataSources["GetWorkbook"].QueryConnection.Execute();

  closeWBDS.SelectSingleNode(
    "/dfs:myFields/dfs:queryFields/ns2:CloseWorkbook/ns2:sessionId",
    NamespaceManager).SetValue(sessionId);
  DataSources["CloseWorkbook"].QueryConnection.Execute();

  string stream = getWBDS.SelectSingleNode(
    "/dfs:myFields/dfs:dataFields/ns2:GetWorkbookResponse" +
    "/ns2:GetWorkbookResult", NamespaceManager).Value;

  if (!String.IsNullOrEmpty(stream))
  {
    byte[] bytes = Convert.FromBase64String(stream);

    using (MemoryStream ms = new MemoryStream())
    {
      ms.Position = 0;
      ms.Write(bytes, 0, (int)bytes.Length);

      using (SpreadsheetDocument document =
        SpreadsheetDocument.Open(ms, true))
      {
        WorkbookPart wbPart = document.WorkbookPart;
        BizSupportOnline.InfoPathExcel.SetCellData(
          "Sheet1", field1.Value, CellValues.String, field2.Value, wbPart);
        wbPart.Workbook.Save();
        document.Close();
      }

      XPathNavigator secDS =
        DataSources["CopyIntoItemsRequest"].CreateNavigator();

      XPathNavigator sourceUrl = secDS.SelectSingleNode(
        "/ns1:CopyIntoItems/ns1:SourceUrl", NamespaceManager);
      XPathNavigator destUrl = secDS.SelectSingleNode(
        "/ns1:CopyIntoItems/ns1:DestinationUrls/ns1:string[1]",
        NamespaceManager);

      XPathNavigator secondDestUrl = secDS.SelectSingleNode(
        "/ns1:CopyIntoItems/ns1:DestinationUrls/ns1:string[2]",
        NamespaceManager);
      if (secondDestUrl != null)
        secondDestUrl.DeleteSelf();

      XPathNodeIterator fields = secDS.Select(
        "/ns1:CopyIntoItems/ns1:Fields/ns1:FieldInformation",
        NamespaceManager);
      if (fields != null && fields.Count > 0)
      {
        int count = fields.Count;
        XPathNavigator firstChild = secDS.SelectSingleNode(
          "/ns1:CopyIntoItems/ns1:Fields/ns1:FieldInformation[1]",
          NamespaceManager);
        XPathNavigator lastChild = secDS.SelectSingleNode(
          "/ns1:CopyIntoItems/ns1:Fields/ns1:FieldInformation["
          + count.ToString() + "]", NamespaceManager);
        firstChild.DeleteRange(lastChild);
```

```
      }

      XPathNavigator stream2 = secDS.SelectSingleNode(
        "/ns1:CopyIntoItems/ns1:Stream", NamespaceManager);

      destUrl.SetValue(workbookPath);
      sourceUrl.SetValue(destUrl.Value);
      stream2.SetValue(Convert.ToBase64String(ms.ToArray()));

      XPathNavigator response =
        DataSources["CopyIntoItemsResponse"].CreateNavigator()
        .SelectSingleNode("/ns1:CopyIntoItemsResponse", NamespaceManager);

      ((WebServiceConnection)DataConnections["UploadFile"])
        .Execute(secDS, response, null);

      ms.Close();
    }

}
```

Visual Basic

```
Dim workbookPath As String = _
  "http://servername/sitename/libname/MyWorkbook.xlsx"

Dim mainDS As XPathNavigator = MainDataSource.CreateNavigator()
Dim field1 As XPathNavigator = mainDS.SelectSingleNode( _
  "//my:field1", NamespaceManager)
Dim field2 As XPathNavigator = mainDS.SelectSingleNode( _
  "//my:field2", NamespaceManager)

Dim openWBDS As XPathNavigator = _
  DataSources("OpenWorkbook").CreateNavigator()
Dim getWBDS As XPathNavigator = _
  DataSources("GetWorkbook").CreateNavigator()
Dim closeWBDS As XPathNavigator = _
  DataSources("CloseWorkbook").CreateNavigator()

openWBDS.SelectSingleNode( _
  "/dfs:myFields/dfs:queryFields/ns2:OpenWorkbook/ns2:workbookPath", _
  NamespaceManager).SetValue(workbookPath)
DataSources("OpenWorkbook").QueryConnection.Execute()

Dim sessionId As String = openWBDS.SelectSingleNode( _
  "/dfs:myFields/dfs:dataFields/ns2:OpenWorkbookResponse" & _
  "/ns2:OpenWorkbookResult", NamespaceManager).Value

getWBDS.SelectSingleNode( _
  "/dfs:myFields/dfs:queryFields/ns2:GetWorkbook/ns2:sessionId", _
  NamespaceManager).SetValue(sessionId)
getWBDS.SelectSingleNode( _
  "/dfs:myFields/dfs:queryFields/ns2:GetWorkbook/ns2:workbookType", _
  NamespaceManager).SetValue("FullWorkbook")
DataSources("GetWorkbook").QueryConnection.Execute()

closeWBDS.SelectSingleNode( _
  "/dfs:myFields/dfs:queryFields/ns2:CloseWorkbook/ns2:sessionId", _
  NamespaceManager).SetValue(sessionId)
DataSources("CloseWorkbook").QueryConnection.Execute()

Dim stream As String = getWBDS.SelectSingleNode( _
```

```vbnet
    "/dfs:myFields/dfs:dataFields/ns2:GetWorkbookResponse" & _
    "/ns2:GetWorkbookResult", NamespaceManager).Value

If Not String.IsNullOrEmpty(stream) Then

  Dim bytes As Byte() = Convert.FromBase64String(stream)

  Using ms As New MemoryStream()

    ms.Position = 0
    ms.Write(bytes, 0, CInt(bytes.Length))

    Using document As SpreadsheetDocument = _
      SpreadsheetDocument.Open(ms, True)

      Dim wbPart As WorkbookPart = document.WorkbookPart
      BizSupportOnline.InfoPathExcel.SetCellData( _
        "Sheet1", field1.Value, CellValues.String, field2.Value, wbPart)
      wbPart.Workbook.Save()
      document.Close()

    End Using

    Dim secDS As XPathNavigator = _
      DataSources("CopyIntoItemsRequest").CreateNavigator()

    Dim sourceUrl As XPathNavigator = secDS.SelectSingleNode( _
      "/ns1:CopyIntoItems/ns1:SourceUrl", NamespaceManager)
    Dim destUrl As XPathNavigator = secDS.SelectSingleNode( _
      "/ns1:CopyIntoItems/ns1:DestinationUrls/ns1:string[1]", _
      NamespaceManager)

    Dim secondDestUrl As XPathNavigator = secDS.SelectSingleNode( _
      "/ns1:CopyIntoItems/ns1:DestinationUrls/ns1:string[2]", _
      NamespaceManager)

    If secondDestUrl IsNot Nothing Then
      secondDestUrl.DeleteSelf()
    End If

    Dim fields As XPathNodeIterator = secDS.Select( _
      "/ns1:CopyIntoItems/ns1:Fields/ns1:FieldInformation", _
      NamespaceManager)

    If fields IsNot Nothing Then
      If fields.Count > 0 Then

        Dim count As Integer = fields.Count
        Dim firstChild As XPathNavigator = secDS.SelectSingleNode( _
          "/ns1:CopyIntoItems/ns1:Fields/ns1:FieldInformation[1]", _
          NamespaceManager)
        Dim lastChild As XPathNavigator = secDS.SelectSingleNode( _
          "/ns1:CopyIntoItems/ns1:Fields/ns1:FieldInformation[" _
          & count.ToString() & "]", NamespaceManager)
        firstChild.DeleteRange(lastChild)

      End If
    End If

    Dim stream2 As XPathNavigator = secDS.SelectSingleNode( _
      "/ns1:CopyIntoItems/ns1:Stream", NamespaceManager)
```

```
        destUrl.SetValue(workbookPath)
        sourceUrl.SetValue(destUrl.Value)
        stream2.SetValue(Convert.ToBase64String(ms.ToArray()))

        Dim response As XPathNavigator = _
          DataSources("CopyIntoItemsResponse").CreateNavigator() _
          .SelectSingleNode("/ns1:CopyIntoItemsResponse", NamespaceManager)

        CType(DataConnections("UploadFile"), WebServiceConnection) _
          .Execute(secDS, response, Nothing)

        ms.Close()

    End Using

End If
```

where you must replace the value of the `workbookPath` variable with the correct URL for the Excel workbook that is located in a SharePoint document library and which you want to modify.

12. Save and build the project.

13. Preview the form.

When the form opens, enter a cell reference (for example **C4**) in the first text box, enter a piece of text in the second text box, and then click the **Save To Excel** button. In SharePoint, navigate to the document library where the Excel workbook is located, open the workbook, and verify that the value of the cell you specified in the InfoPath form was saved in the Excel workbook.

Discussion

In the solution described above, you saw how to use the Open XML SDK together with Excel Services web service operations and the **Copy** web service to download an entire Excel workbook from SharePoint, modify it, and then upload it back to SharePoint. The solution consists of three parts:

1. Use the **OpenWorkbook**, **GetWorkbook**, and **CloseWorkbook** Excel Services web service operations to download an existing Excel workbook from a SharePoint document library. Note that you could have also used the **GetItem** operation of the **Copy** web service to download the Excel workbook as described in recipe *50 Get the value of a cell in an Excel workbook*.

2. Open the Excel workbook and modify data in it using the Open XML SDK.

3. Use the **CopyIntoItems** operation of the **Copy** web service to upload the Excel workbook back to the SharePoint document library.

The download code first retrieves three `XPathNavigator` objects pointing to the **OpenWorkbook**, **GetWorkbook**, and **CloseWorkbook** secondary data sources.

<u>C#</u>

```
XPathNavigator openWBDS = DataSources["OpenWorkbook"].CreateNavigator();
XPathNavigator getWBDS = DataSources["GetWorkbook"].CreateNavigator();
XPathNavigator closeWBDS = DataSources["CloseWorkbook"].CreateNavigator();
```

Visual Basic

```
Dim openWBDS As XPathNavigator = DataSources("OpenWorkbook").CreateNavigator()
Dim getWBDS As XPathNavigator = DataSources("GetWorkbook").CreateNavigator()
Dim closeWBDS As XPathNavigator = DataSources("CloseWorkbook").CreateNavigator()
```

The code then sets the value of the **workbookPath** parameter of the **OpenWorkbook** secondary data source before querying the data source and retrieving the value returned for the session ID.

<u>C#</u>

```
openWBDS.SelectSingleNode(
  "/dfs:myFields/dfs:queryFields/ns2:OpenWorkbook/ns2:workbookPath",
  NamespaceManager).SetValue(workbookPath);
DataSources["OpenWorkbook"].QueryConnection.Execute();

string sessionId = openWBDS.SelectSingleNode(
  "/dfs:myFields/dfs:dataFields/ns2:OpenWorkbookResponse" +
  "/ns2:OpenWorkbookResult", NamespaceManager).Value;
```

Visual Basic

```
openWBDS.SelectSingleNode( _
  "/dfs:myFields/dfs:queryFields/ns2:OpenWorkbook/ns2:workbookPath", _
  NamespaceManager).SetValue(workbookPath)
DataSources("OpenWorkbook").QueryConnection.Execute()

Dim sessionId As String = openWBDS.SelectSingleNode( _
  "/dfs:myFields/dfs:dataFields/ns2:OpenWorkbookResponse" & _
  "/ns2:OpenWorkbookResult", NamespaceManager).Value
```

The code then uses the session ID to set the **sessionId** parameter of the **GetWorkbook** secondary data source before querying it. In addition, the second parameter (**workbookType**) is set to be equal to the static piece of text "FullWorkbook".

<u>C#</u>

```
getWBDS.SelectSingleNode(
  "/dfs:myFields/dfs:queryFields/ns2:GetWorkbook/ns2:sessionId",
  NamespaceManager).SetValue(sessionId);
getWBDS.SelectSingleNode(
  "/dfs:myFields/dfs:queryFields/ns2:GetWorkbook/ns2:workbookType",
  NamespaceManager).SetValue("FullWorkbook");
DataSources["GetWorkbook"].QueryConnection.Execute();
```

Visual Basic

```
getWBDS.SelectSingleNode( _
  "/dfs:myFields/dfs:queryFields/ns2:GetWorkbook/ns2:sessionId", _
  NamespaceManager).SetValue(sessionId)
```

```
getWBDS.SelectSingleNode( _
  "/dfs:myFields/dfs:queryFields/ns2:GetWorkbook/ns2:workbookType", _
  NamespaceManager).SetValue("FullWorkbook")
DataSources("GetWorkbook").QueryConnection.Execute()
```

The code also uses the session ID to set the **sessionId** parameter of the **CloseWorkbook** secondary data source before querying it to close the workbook and the Excel Services session.

C#

```
closeWBDS.SelectSingleNode(
  "/dfs:myFields/dfs:queryFields/ns2:CloseWorkbook/ns2:sessionId",
  NamespaceManager).SetValue(sessionId);
DataSources["CloseWorkbook"].QueryConnection.Execute();
```

Visual Basic

```
closeWBDS.SelectSingleNode( _
  "/dfs:myFields/dfs:queryFields/ns2:CloseWorkbook/ns2:sessionId", _
  NamespaceManager).SetValue(sessionId)
DataSources("CloseWorkbook").QueryConnection.Execute()
```

The last part of the download code retrieves a base64-encoded string representing the Excel workbook that was downloaded using the **GetWorkbook** secondary data source.

C#

```
string stream = getWBDS.SelectSingleNode(
  "/dfs:myFields/dfs:dataFields/ns2:GetWorkbookResponse" +
  "/ns2:GetWorkbookResult", NamespaceManager).Value;
```

Visual Basic

```
Dim stream As String = getWBDS.SelectSingleNode( _
  "/dfs:myFields/dfs:dataFields/ns2:GetWorkbookResponse" & _
  "/ns2:GetWorkbookResult", NamespaceManager).Value
```

To modify the value of a cell in the Excel workbook, the code makes use of a procedure named `SetCellData()`, which has been defined in the `InfoPathExcel` C# class or Visual Basic module. The `SetCellData()` procedure makes use of classes from the Open XML SDK to write data to a particular cell on a worksheet in an Excel workbook. Refer to the Open XML SDK documentation and the article entitled *Generating Excel 2010 Workbooks by using the Open XML SDK 2.0* on the MSDN web site to learn more about using Open XML to work with data in Excel workbooks.

C#

```
using (SpreadsheetDocument document = SpreadsheetDocument.Open(ms, true))
{
  WorkbookPart wbPart = document.WorkbookPart;
  BizSupportOnline.InfoPathExcel.SetCellData(
    "Sheet1", field1.Value, CellValues.String, field2.Value, wbPart);
  wbPart.Workbook.Save();
```

```
    document.Close();
}
```

```
Using document As SpreadsheetDocument = SpreadsheetDocument.Open(ms, True)

    Dim wbPart As WorkbookPart = document.WorkbookPart
    BizSupportOnline.InfoPathExcel.SetCellData( _
        "Sheet1", field1.Value, CellValues.String, field2.Value, wbPart)
    wbPart.Workbook.Save()
    document.Close()

End Using
```

Refer to the discussion section of recipe *49 Create a new Excel workbook in SharePoint from within InfoPath* for an explanation of the upload code that uploads the modified Excel workbook back to the SharePoint document library.

Warning:

Writing code that makes use of the Open XML SDK to modify data in Excel workbooks has the potential to corrupt documents. So be very careful when using the Open XML SDK to modify data in Excel workbooks. In the event that an Excel workbook is corrupted, open it in the Excel client application, so that Excel can try to fix the problem. If Excel manages to fix the problem it will display a dialog box with information about what it fixed. You can then use this information to debug your code and investigate what caused the corruption.

52 Populate a repeating table with Excel data

Problem

You have an Excel workbook stored in a SharePoint document library and would like to retrieve the values of a range of cells from the Excel workbook for display in a repeating table on an InfoPath form.

Solution

You can download an existing Excel workbook from a SharePoint document library into an InfoPath form, use the Open XML SDK to open the workbook, read data from it, and then display this data on the InfoPath form.

Suppose you have an Excel workbook named **Fruits.xlsx** that is stored in a SharePoint document library and that contains a named range called **Fruits** that spans cells **A2** through **B6** on **Sheet1**. You can also download the **Fruits.xlsx** Excel workbook from www.bizsupportonline.com for use with this recipe.

To populate a repeating table with data from a range of cells in an Excel workbook:

1. In InfoPath, create a new browser-compatible form template or use an existing one.

2. Select **Data ➤ Get External Data ➤ From Web Service ➤ From SOAP Web Service**.

3. On the **Data Connection Wizard**, enter the URL of the **Copy** web service, for example:

    ```
    http://servername/sitename/_vti_bin/Copy.asmx
    ```

    and click **Next**. Here **servername** is the name of the SharePoint server where a site named **sitename** on which the **Copy** web service is located.

4. On the **Data Connection Wizard**, select the **GetItem** operation, and click **Next**.

5. On the **Data Connection Wizard**, leave the parameter as is, and click **Next**.

6. On the **Data Connection Wizard**, leave the **Store a copy of the data in the form template** check box deselected, and click **Next**.

7. On the **Data Connection Wizard**, name the data connection **GetItem**, deselect the **Automatically retrieve data when form is opened** check box, and click **Finish**.

8. Add a **Repeating Table** control with 2 columns to the view of the form template and name the fields in the repeating table **field1** and **field2**, respectively.

9. Click **Data ➤ Form Data ➤ Default Values**.

10. On the **Edit Default Values** dialog box, expand the **group1** node, deselect the check box in front of the **group2** node so that the repeating table does not start up with a row that contains empty fields, and then click **OK**.

11. Add a **Button** control to the view of the form template and label it **Get From Excel**.

12. With the button still selected, click **Control Tools ➤ Properties ➤ Button ➤ Custom Code** to add an event handler for the **Clicked** event of the button.

13. In VSTA, add references to the **DocumentFormat.OpenXml** and **WindowsBase** assemblies.

14. If you are writing C# code, add a new class file named **InfoPathExcel.cs** to the project, open the file and replace the code in the **InfoPathExcel.cs** file with the code displayed in *InfoPathExcel.cs* in the Appendix (*code #: C6EE40D6-96BC-485A-A1FD-12511A8E91D2*); or if you are writing Visual Basic code, add a new module file named **InfoPathExcel.vb** to the project, open the file and replace the code in the **InfoPathExcel.vb** file with the code displayed in *InfoPathExcel.vb* in the Appendix (*code #: 9DFDBC84-9A61-43E3-92FD-E819BEB95D21*).

15. Add the following **using** statements to the **FormCode.cs** file:

```
using System.Collections.Generic;
using System.IO;
using System.Text;
using System.Text.RegularExpressions;
using DocumentFormat.OpenXml;
using DocumentFormat.OpenXml.Packaging;
using DocumentFormat.OpenXml.Spreadsheet;
```

Or add the following **Imports** statements to the **FormCode.vb** file:

```
Imports System.Collections.Generic
Imports System.IO
Imports System.Text
Imports System.Text.RegularExpressions
Imports DocumentFormat.OpenXml
Imports DocumentFormat.OpenXml.Packaging
Imports DocumentFormat.OpenXml.Spreadsheet
```

16. Add the following C# or Visual Basic code to the `Clicked()` event handler for the **Get From Excel** button (*code #: 38C0BA5B-FBA6-46AE-B73B-8DBC8575C6E4*):

<u>C#</u>

```
string workbookPath = "http://servername/sitename/libname/Fruits.xlsx";

XPathNavigator mainDS = MainDataSource.CreateNavigator();
string my = NamespaceManager.LookupNamespace("my");

XPathNavigator getItemDS = DataSources["GetItem"].CreateNavigator();
getItemDS.SelectSingleNode(
  "/dfs:myFields/dfs:queryFields/tns:GetItem/tns:Url",
  NamespaceManager).SetValue(workbookPath);

DataSources["GetItem"].QueryConnection.Execute();

XPathNavigator stream = getItemDS.SelectSingleNode(
  "/dfs:myFields/dfs:dataFields/tns:GetItemResponse/tns:Stream",
  NamespaceManager);

if (stream != null)
{
  string base64 = stream.Value;
  byte[] bytes = Convert.FromBase64String(base64);

  using (MemoryStream ms = new MemoryStream(bytes))
  {
    using (SpreadsheetDocument document =
      SpreadsheetDocument.Open(ms, false))
    {
      WorkbookPart wbPart = document.WorkbookPart;
      string namedRangeRef =
        BizSupportOnline.InfoPathExcel.GetNamedRange("Fruits", wbPart);

      string sheetName = namedRangeRef.Substring(
        0, namedRangeRef.IndexOf("!"));
      string cellRange = namedRangeRef.Substring(
        namedRangeRef.IndexOf("!") + 1);
      string[] cells = cellRange.Split(':');
```

```csharp
string startCell = string.Empty;
string endCell = string.Empty;
Regex regEx = new Regex(@"\d");
int rStart = 0;
int rEnd = 0;
string cStart = string.Empty;
string cEnd = string.Empty;

if (cells.Length == 2)
{
  startCell = cells[0].Replace("$", "");
  endCell = cells[1].Replace("$", "");

  Match match = regEx.Match(startCell);
  if (match.Index > 0)
  {
    if (int.TryParse(
      startCell.Substring(match.Index), out rStart) == true)
    {
      cStart = startCell.Substring(0, match.Index);
    }
  }

  match = regEx.Match(endCell);
  if (match.Index > 0)
  {
    if (int.TryParse(
      endCell.Substring(match.Index), out rEnd) == true)
    {
      cEnd = endCell.Substring(0, match.Index);
    }
  }

}

List<string> colRefs = new List<string>();
colRefs.AddRange(new string[] { "A", "B", "C", "D", "E" });
// Add as many column names to the collection
// as is required by your Excel workbook

string cellValue1 = string.Empty;
string cellValue2 = string.Empty;
StringBuilder sb = null;

for (int i = rStart; i <= rEnd; i++)
{
  cellValue1 = BizSupportOnline.InfoPathExcel.GetCellData(
    sheetName, cStart + i.ToString(), wbPart);

  string cNext = colRefs[colRefs.IndexOf(cStart) + 1];
  if (colRefs.IndexOf(cNext) <= colRefs.IndexOf(cEnd))
  {
    cellValue2 = BizSupportOnline.InfoPathExcel.GetCellData(
      sheetName, cNext + i.ToString(), wbPart);
  }

  sb = new StringBuilder();
  sb.AppendFormat("<my:group2 xmlns:my=\"{0}\">", my);
  sb.AppendFormat("<my:field1 xmlns:my=\"{0}\">", my);
  sb.AppendFormat("{0}</my:field1>", cellValue1);
  sb.AppendFormat("<my:field2 xmlns:my=\"{0}\">", my);
  sb.AppendFormat("{0}</my:field2>", cellValue2);
```

```
            sb.Append("</my:group2>");
            MainDataSource.CreateNavigator().SelectSingleNode(
              "/my:myFields/my:group1",
              NamespaceManager).AppendChild(sb.ToString());
          }

          document.Close();
        }

      ms.Close();
    }
  }
```

Visual Basic

```
Dim workbookPath As String = _
  "http://servername/sitename/libname/Fruits.xlsx"

Dim mainDS As XPathNavigator = MainDataSource.CreateNavigator()
Dim myNs As String = NamespaceManager.LookupNamespace("my")

Dim getItemDS As XPathNavigator = DataSources("GetItem").CreateNavigator()
getItemDS.SelectSingleNode( _
  "/dfs:myFields/dfs:queryFields/tns:GetItem/tns:Url", _
  NamespaceManager).SetValue(workbookPath)

DataSources("GetItem").QueryConnection.Execute()

Dim stream As XPathNavigator = getItemDS.SelectSingleNode( _
  "/dfs:myFields/dfs:dataFields/tns:GetItemResponse/tns:Stream", _
  NamespaceManager)

If stream IsNot Nothing Then

  Dim base64 As String = stream.Value
  Dim bytes As Byte() = Convert.FromBase64String(base64)

  Using ms As New MemoryStream(bytes)

    Using document As SpreadsheetDocument = _
      SpreadsheetDocument.Open(ms, False)

      Dim wbPart As WorkbookPart = document.WorkbookPart
      Dim namedRangeRef As String = _
        BizSupportOnline.InfoPathExcel.GetNamedRange("Fruits", wbPart)

      Dim sheetName As String = namedRangeRef.Substring( _
        0, namedRangeRef.IndexOf("!"))
      Dim cellRange As String = namedRangeRef.Substring( _
        namedRangeRef.IndexOf("!") + 1)
      Dim cells As String() = cellRange.Split(":")
      Dim startCell As String = String.Empty
      Dim endCell As String = String.Empty
      Dim regEx As Regex = New Regex("\d")
      Dim rStart As Integer = 0
      Dim rEnd As Integer = 0
      Dim cStart As String = String.Empty
      Dim cEnd As String = String.Empty

      If cells.Length = 2 Then

        startCell = cells(0).Replace("$", "")
```

```vb
    endCell = cells(1).Replace("$", "")

  Dim match As Match = regEx.Match(startCell)
  If match.Index > 0 Then
    If Integer.TryParse( _
      startCell.Substring(match.Index), rStart) = True Then
        cStart = startCell.Substring(0, match.Index)
    End If
  End If

  match = regEx.Match(endCell)

  If match.Index > 0 Then
    If Integer.TryParse( _
      endCell.Substring(match.Index), rEnd) = True Then
        cEnd = endCell.Substring(0, match.Index)
    End If
  End If

End If

Dim colRefs As List(Of String) = New List(Of String)()
colRefs.AddRange(New String() {"A", "B", "C", "D", "E"})
' Add as many column names to the collection
' as is required by your Excel workbook

Dim cellValue1 As String = String.Empty
Dim cellValue2 As String = String.Empty
Dim sb As StringBuilder = Nothing

For i As Integer = rStart To rEnd

  cellValue1 = BizSupportOnline.InfoPathExcel.GetCellData( _
    sheetName, cStart & i.ToString(), wbPart)

  Dim cNext As String = colRefs(colRefs.IndexOf(cStart) + 1)

  If colRefs.IndexOf(cNext) <= colRefs.IndexOf(cEnd) Then
    cellValue2 = BizSupportOnline.InfoPathExcel.GetCellData( _
      sheetName, cNext & i.ToString(), wbPart)
  End If

  sb = New StringBuilder()
  sb.AppendFormat("<my:group2 xmlns:my=""{0}"">", myNs)
  sb.AppendFormat("<my:field1 xmlns:my=""{0}"">", myNs)
  sb.AppendFormat("{0}</my:field1>", cellValue1)
  sb.AppendFormat("<my:field2 xmlns:my=""{0}"">", myNs)
  sb.AppendFormat("{0}</my:field2>", cellValue2)
  sb.Append("</my:group2>")
  MainDataSource.CreateNavigator().SelectSingleNode( _
    "/my:myFields/my:group1", _
    NamespaceManager).AppendChild(sb.ToString())

Next

document.Close()

End Using

ms.Close()

End Using
```

```
End If
```

where you must replace the value of the `workbookPath` variable with the correct URL for the Excel workbook that is located in a SharePoint document library and from which you want to retrieve data.

17. Save and build the project.

18. Preview the form.

When the form opens, click the **Get From Excel** button. The values from the range of cells in the Excel workbook should appear in the repeating table.

Discussion

In the solution described above, you saw how to use the Open XML SDK together with the **Copy** web service to download an entire Excel workbook from SharePoint, open it, read data from a range of cells, and then populate a repeating table with this data. The solution consists of two main parts:

1. Use the **GetItem** operation of the **Copy** web service to download an existing Excel workbook from a SharePoint document library. Note that you could have also used the **GetWorkbook** operation of the Excel Services web service to download the Excel workbook from SharePoint as described in recipe *51 Set the value of a cell in an Excel workbook*.

2. Open the Excel workbook, read data from it using the Open XML SDK, and use this data to populate a repeating table on an InfoPath form.

The code first declares a variable containing the URL of an existing Excel workbook in SharePoint and looks up the URI of the **my** namespace prefix, so that it can be used later to add rows to the repeating table on the InfoPath form.

<u>**C#**</u>

```
string workbookPath = "http://servername/sitename/libname/Fruits.xlsx";

XPathNavigator mainDS = MainDataSource.CreateNavigator();
string my = NamespaceManager.LookupNamespace("my");
```

<u>**Visual Basic**</u>

```
Dim workbookPath As String = "http://servername/sitename/libname/Fruits.xlsx"

Dim mainDS As XPathNavigator = MainDataSource.CreateNavigator()
Dim myNs As String = NamespaceManager.LookupNamespace("my")
```

The code then retrieves the base64-encoded string representation of the Excel workbook by using the **GetItem** operation of the **Copy** web service.

C#

```csharp
XPathNavigator getItemDS = DataSources["GetItem"].CreateNavigator();
getItemDS.SelectSingleNode(
  "/dfs:myFields/dfs:queryFields/tns:GetItem/tns:Url",
  NamespaceManager).SetValue(workbookPath);

DataSources["GetItem"].QueryConnection.Execute();

XPathNavigator stream = getItemDS.SelectSingleNode(
  "/dfs:myFields/dfs:dataFields/tns:GetItemResponse/tns:Stream",
  NamespaceManager);
```

Visual Basic

```vbnet
Dim getItemDS As XPathNavigator = DataSources("GetItem").CreateNavigator()
getItemDS.SelectSingleNode( _
  "/dfs:myFields/dfs:queryFields/tns:GetItem/tns:Url", _
  NamespaceManager).SetValue(workbookPath)

DataSources("GetItem").QueryConnection.Execute()

Dim stream As XPathNavigator = getItemDS.SelectSingleNode( _
  "/dfs:myFields/dfs:dataFields/tns:GetItemResponse/tns:Stream", _
  NamespaceManager)
```

The code then converts the base64-encoded string into a `Byte` array

C#

```csharp
string base64 = stream.Value;
byte[] bytes = Convert.FromBase64String(base64);
```

Visual Basic

```vbnet
Dim base64 As String = stream.Value
Dim bytes As Byte() = Convert.FromBase64String(base64)
```

so that it can be used with classes from the Open XML SDK to open and retrieve data from the Excel workbook.

C#

```csharp
using (MemoryStream ms = new MemoryStream(bytes))
{
  using (SpreadsheetDocument document = SpreadsheetDocument.Open(ms, false))
  {
    ...
  }

  ms.Close();
}
```

Visual Basic

```vbnet
Using ms As New MemoryStream(bytes)

  Using document As SpreadsheetDocument = SpreadsheetDocument.Open(ms, False)
```

```
    ...

  End Using

  ms.Close()

End Using
```

The code that retrieves data from the Excel workbook makes use of a procedure named `GetNamedRange()` to return the full reference for a named range. For example, the full reference for the **Fruits** named range would be **Sheet1!$A$2:$B$6**. The code parses this full reference to extract the worksheet name and the characters and numbers for the starting and ending cells that the range spans.

<u>C#</u>

```
WorkbookPart wbPart = document.WorkbookPart;
string namedRangeRef =
  BizSupportOnline.InfoPathExcel.GetNamedRange("Fruits", wbPart);

string sheetName = namedRangeRef.Substring(0, namedRangeRef.IndexOf("!"));
string cellRange = namedRangeRef.Substring(namedRangeRef.IndexOf("!") + 1);
string[] cells = cellRange.Split(':');
string startCell = string.Empty;
string endCell = string.Empty;
Regex regEx = new Regex(@"\d");
int rStart = 0;
int rEnd = 0;
string cStart = string.Empty;
string cEnd = string.Empty;

if (cells.Length == 2)
{
  startCell = cells[0].Replace("$", "");
  endCell = cells[1].Replace("$", "");

  Match match = regEx.Match(startCell);
  if (match.Index > 0)
  {
    if (int.TryParse(
      startCell.Substring(match.Index), out rStart) == true)
    {
      cStart = startCell.Substring(0, match.Index);
    }
  }

  match = regEx.Match(endCell);
  if (match.Index > 0)
  {
    if (int.TryParse(
      endCell.Substring(match.Index), out rEnd) == true)
    {
      cEnd = endCell.Substring(0, match.Index);
    }
  }

}
```

Visual Basic

```vb
Dim wbPart As WorkbookPart = document.WorkbookPart
Dim namedRangeRef As String = _
  BizSupportOnline.InfoPathExcel.GetNamedRange("Fruits", wbPart)

Dim sheetName As String = namedRangeRef.Substring( _
  0, namedRangeRef.IndexOf("!"))
Dim cellRange As String = namedRangeRef.Substring( _
  namedRangeRef.IndexOf("!") + 1)
Dim cells As String() = cellRange.Split(":")
Dim startCell As String = String.Empty
Dim endCell As String = String.Empty
Dim regEx As Regex = New Regex("\d")
Dim rStart As Integer = 0
Dim rEnd As Integer = 0
Dim cStart As String = String.Empty
Dim cEnd As String = String.Empty

If cells.Length = 2 Then

  startCell = cells(0).Replace("$", "")
  endCell = cells(1).Replace("$", "")

  Dim match As Match = regEx.Match(startCell)
  If match.Index > 0 Then
    If Integer.TryParse( _
      startCell.Substring(match.Index), rStart) = True Then
        cStart = startCell.Substring(0, match.Index)
    End If
  End If

  match = regEx.Match(endCell)

  If match.Index > 0 Then
    If Integer.TryParse( _
      endCell.Substring(match.Index), rEnd) = True Then
        cEnd = endCell.Substring(0, match.Index)
    End If
  End If

End If
```

Once the starting and ending numbers and characters of the cells of the named range are known, they are then used together with the GetCellData() procedure, which has been defined in the InfoPathExcel C# class or Visual Basic module to retrieve the data from the named range in the Excel workbook and use this data to add rows to the repeating table on the InfoPath form.

C#

```csharp
List<string> colRefs = new List<string>();
colRefs.AddRange(new string[] { "A", "B", "C", "D", "E" });
// Add as many column names to the collection
// as is required by your Excel workbook

string cellValue1 = string.Empty;
string cellValue2 = string.Empty;
StringBuilder sb = null;
```

```
for (int i = rStart; i <= rEnd; i++)
{
  cellValue1 = BizSupportOnline.InfoPathExcel.GetCellData(
    sheetName, cStart + i.ToString(), wbPart);

  string cNext = colRefs[colRefs.IndexOf(cStart) + 1];
  if (colRefs.IndexOf(cNext) <= colRefs.IndexOf(cEnd))
  {
    cellValue2 = BizSupportOnline.InfoPathExcel.GetCellData(
      sheetName, cNext + i.ToString(), wbPart);
  }

  sb = new StringBuilder();
  sb.AppendFormat("<my:group2 xmlns:my=\"{0}\">", my);
  sb.AppendFormat("<my:field1 xmlns:my=\"{0}\">", my);
  sb.AppendFormat("{0}</my:field1>", cellValue1);
  sb.AppendFormat("<my:field2 xmlns:my=\"{0}\">", my);
  sb.AppendFormat("{0}</my:field2>", cellValue2);
  sb.Append("</my:group2>");
  MainDataSource.CreateNavigator().SelectSingleNode(
    "/my:myFields/my:group1",
    NamespaceManager).AppendChild(sb.ToString());
}
```

Visual Basic

```
Dim colRefs As List(Of String) = New List(Of String)()
colRefs.AddRange(New String() {"A", "B", "C", "D", "E"})
' Add as many column names to the collection
' as is required by your Excel workbook

Dim cellValue1 As String = String.Empty
Dim cellValue2 As String = String.Empty
Dim sb As StringBuilder = Nothing

For i As Integer = rStart To rEnd

  cellValue1 = BizSupportOnline.InfoPathExcel.GetCellData( _
    sheetName, cStart & i.ToString(), wbPart)

  Dim cNext As String = colRefs(colRefs.IndexOf(cStart) + 1)

  If colRefs.IndexOf(cNext) <= colRefs.IndexOf(cEnd) Then
    cellValue2 = BizSupportOnline.InfoPathExcel.GetCellData( _
      sheetName, cNext & i.ToString(), wbPart)
  End If

  sb = New StringBuilder()
  sb.AppendFormat("<my:group2 xmlns:my=""{0}"">", myNs)
  sb.AppendFormat("<my:field1 xmlns:my=""{0}"">", myNs)
  sb.AppendFormat("{0}</my:field1>", cellValue1)
  sb.AppendFormat("<my:field2 xmlns:my=""{0}"">", myNs)
  sb.AppendFormat("{0}</my:field2>", cellValue2)
  sb.Append("</my:group2>")
  MainDataSource.CreateNavigator().SelectSingleNode( _
    "/my:myFields/my:group1", _
    NamespaceManager).AppendChild(sb.ToString())

Next
```

Note that this solution only works for ranges that consist of adjacent cells, since the code sequentially goes through all of the rows and columns in a named range using the cell in the upper-left corner and the cell in the lower-right corner of the named range as references. If your Excel workbook contains non-adjacent cells in a named range, you may have to find another way to import the data into the repeating table on the InfoPath form. Refer to the Open XML SDK documentation and the article entitled *Generating Excel 2010 Workbooks by using the Open XML SDK 2.0* on the MSDN web site to learn more about using the Open XML SDK to work with data in Excel workbooks.

53 Populate an Excel workbook with InfoPath repeating table data

Problem

You have an Excel workbook stored in a SharePoint document library and would like to write data from a repeating table on an InfoPath form to cells in the Excel workbook.

Solution

You can download an existing Excel workbook from a SharePoint document library into an InfoPath form, use the Open XML SDK to open the workbook, modify it, and then upload it back to the SharePoint document library.

To populate an Excel workbook with data from a repeating table on an InfoPath form:

1. Follow steps 1 through 4 of recipe *51 Set the value of a cell in an Excel workbook*.

2. Add a **Repeating Table** control with 3 columns to the view of the form template and name the fields in the repeating table **field1**, **field2**, and **field3**, respectively.

3. Add a **Button** control to the view of the form template and label it **Save To Excel**.

4. With the button still selected, click **Control Tools ➤ Properties ➤ Button ➤ Custom Code** to add an event handler for the **Clicked** event of the button.

5. In VSTA, add references to the **DocumentFormat.OpenXml** and **WindowsBase** assemblies.

6. If you are writing C# code, add a new class file named **InfoPathExcel.cs** to the project, open the file and replace the code in the **InfoPathExcel.cs** file with the code displayed in *InfoPathExcel.cs* in the Appendix (*code #: C6EE40D6-96BC-485A-A1FD-12511A8E91D2*); or if you are writing Visual Basic code, add a new module file named **InfoPathExcel.vb** to the project, open the file and replace the code in the **InfoPathExcel.vb** file with the code displayed in *InfoPathExcel.vb* in the Appendix (*code #: 9DFDBC84-9A61-43E3-92FD-E819BEB95D21*).

7. Add the following **using** statements to the **FormCode.cs** file:

```
using System.IO;
```

```
using System.Collections.Generic;
using DocumentFormat.OpenXml;
using DocumentFormat.OpenXml.Packaging;
using DocumentFormat.OpenXml.Spreadsheet;
```

Or add the following **Imports** statements to the **FormCode.vb** file:

```
Imports System.IO
Imports System.Collections.Generic
Imports DocumentFormat.OpenXml
Imports DocumentFormat.OpenXml.Packaging
Imports DocumentFormat.OpenXml.Spreadsheet
```

8. Add the following C# or Visual Basic code to the `Clicked()` event handler for the **Save To Excel** button (*code #: 10C9944D-4E54-48B9-A31D-C9B0FFB62ED0*):

C#

```
string workbookPath = "http://servername/sitename/libname/MyWorkbook.xlsx";

XPathNavigator mainDS = MainDataSource.CreateNavigator();
XPathNavigator field1 = mainDS.SelectSingleNode(
  "//my:field1", NamespaceManager);
XPathNavigator field2 = mainDS.SelectSingleNode(
  "//my:field2", NamespaceManager);

XPathNodeIterator iter = mainDS.Select(
  "//my:group2", NamespaceManager);
Dictionary<string, string> repTblValues = new Dictionary<string, string>();
uint counter = 1;

while (iter.MoveNext())
{
  repTblValues.Add(
    "A" + counter.ToString(),
    iter.Current.SelectSingleNode(
    "my:field1", NamespaceManager).Value);

  repTblValues.Add(
    "B" + counter.ToString(),
    iter.Current.SelectSingleNode(
    "my:field2", NamespaceManager).Value);

  repTblValues.Add(
    "C" + counter.ToString(),
    iter.Current.SelectSingleNode(
    "my:field3", NamespaceManager).Value);

  counter++;
}

XPathNavigator openWBDS = DataSources["OpenWorkbook"].CreateNavigator();
XPathNavigator getWBDS = DataSources["GetWorkbook"].CreateNavigator();
XPathNavigator closeWBDS = DataSources["CloseWorkbook"].CreateNavigator();

openWBDS.SelectSingleNode(
  "/dfs:myFields/dfs:queryFields/ns2:OpenWorkbook/ns2:workbookPath",
  NamespaceManager).SetValue(workbookPath);
DataSources["OpenWorkbook"].QueryConnection.Execute();

string sessionId = openWBDS.SelectSingleNode(
```

```
  "/dfs:myFields/dfs:dataFields/ns2:OpenWorkbookResponse" +
  "/ns2:OpenWorkbookResult", NamespaceManager).Value;

getWBDS.SelectSingleNode(
  "/dfs:myFields/dfs:queryFields/ns2:GetWorkbook/ns2:sessionId",
  NamespaceManager).SetValue(sessionId);
getWBDS.SelectSingleNode(
  "/dfs:myFields/dfs:queryFields/ns2:GetWorkbook/ns2:workbookType",
  NamespaceManager).SetValue("FullWorkbook");
DataSources["GetWorkbook"].QueryConnection.Execute();

closeWBDS.SelectSingleNode(
  "/dfs:myFields/dfs:queryFields/ns2:CloseWorkbook/ns2:sessionId",
  NamespaceManager).SetValue(sessionId);
DataSources["CloseWorkbook"].QueryConnection.Execute();

string stream = getWBDS.SelectSingleNode(
  "/dfs:myFields/dfs:dataFields/ns2:GetWorkbookResponse" +
  "/ns2:GetWorkbookResult", NamespaceManager).Value;

if (!String.IsNullOrEmpty(stream))
{
  byte[] bytes = Convert.FromBase64String(stream);

  using (MemoryStream ms = new MemoryStream())
  {
    ms.Position = 0;
    ms.Write(bytes, 0, (int)bytes.Length);

    using (SpreadsheetDocument document =
      SpreadsheetDocument.Open(ms, true))
    {
      WorkbookPart wbPart = document.WorkbookPart;
      BizSupportOnline.InfoPathExcel.SetRangeData(
        repTblValues, "Sheet1", wbPart);
      wbPart.Workbook.Save();
      document.Close();
    }

    XPathNavigator secDS =
      DataSources["CopyIntoItemsRequest"].CreateNavigator();

    XPathNavigator sourceUrl = secDS.SelectSingleNode(
      "/ns1:CopyIntoItems/ns1:SourceUrl", NamespaceManager);
    XPathNavigator destUrl = secDS.SelectSingleNode(
      "/ns1:CopyIntoItems/ns1:DestinationUrls/ns1:string[1]",
      NamespaceManager);

    XPathNavigator secondDestUrl = secDS.SelectSingleNode(
      "/ns1:CopyIntoItems/ns1:DestinationUrls/ns1:string[2]",
      NamespaceManager);
    if (secondDestUrl != null)
      secondDestUrl.DeleteSelf();

    XPathNodeIterator fields = secDS.Select(
      "/ns1:CopyIntoItems/ns1:Fields/ns1:FieldInformation",
      NamespaceManager);
    if (fields != null && fields.Count > 0)
    {
      int count = fields.Count;
      XPathNavigator firstChild = secDS.SelectSingleNode(
        "/ns1:CopyIntoItems/ns1:Fields/ns1:FieldInformation[1]",
```

```
        NamespaceManager);
      XPathNavigator lastChild = secDS.SelectSingleNode(
        "/ns1:CopyIntoItems/ns1:Fields/ns1:FieldInformation["
        + count.ToString() + "]", NamespaceManager);
      firstChild.DeleteRange(lastChild);
    }

    XPathNavigator stream2 = secDS.SelectSingleNode(
      "/ns1:CopyIntoItems/ns1:Stream", NamespaceManager);

    destUrl.SetValue(workbookPath);
    sourceUrl.SetValue(destUrl.Value);
    stream2.SetValue(Convert.ToBase64String(ms.ToArray()));

    XPathNavigator response =
      DataSources["CopyIntoItemsResponse"].CreateNavigator()
      .SelectSingleNode("/ns1:CopyIntoItemsResponse", NamespaceManager);

    ((WebServiceConnection)DataConnections["UploadFile"])
      .Execute(secDS, response, null);

    ms.Close();
  }

}
```

Visual Basic

```
Dim workbookPath As String = _
  "http://servername/sitename/libname/MyWorkbook.xlsx"

Dim mainDS As XPathNavigator = MainDataSource.CreateNavigator()
Dim field1 As XPathNavigator = mainDS.SelectSingleNode( _
  "//my:field1", NamespaceManager)
Dim field2 As XPathNavigator = mainDS.SelectSingleNode( _
  "//my:field2", NamespaceManager)

Dim iter As XPathNodeIterator = mainDS.Select( _
  "//my:group2", NamespaceManager)
Dim repTblValues As Dictionary(Of String, String) = _
  New Dictionary(Of String, String)()
Dim counter As UInteger = 1

While iter.MoveNext()

  repTblValues.Add( _
    "A" & counter.ToString(), _
    iter.Current.SelectSingleNode( _
    "my:field1", NamespaceManager).Value)

  repTblValues.Add( _
    "B" & counter.ToString(), _
    iter.Current.SelectSingleNode( _
    "my:field2", NamespaceManager).Value)

  repTblValues.Add( _
    "C" & counter.ToString(), _
    iter.Current.SelectSingleNode( _
    "my:field3", NamespaceManager).Value)

  counter = counter + 1
```

```vb
End While

Dim openWBDS As XPathNavigator = _
  DataSources("OpenWorkbook").CreateNavigator()
Dim getWBDS As XPathNavigator = _
  DataSources("GetWorkbook").CreateNavigator()
Dim closeWBDS As XPathNavigator = _
  DataSources("CloseWorkbook").CreateNavigator()

openWBDS.SelectSingleNode( _
  "/dfs:myFields/dfs:queryFields/ns2:OpenWorkbook/ns2:workbookPath", _
  NamespaceManager).SetValue(workbookPath)
DataSources("OpenWorkbook").QueryConnection.Execute()

Dim sessionId As String = openWBDS.SelectSingleNode( _
  "/dfs:myFields/dfs:dataFields/ns2:OpenWorkbookResponse" & _
  "/ns2:OpenWorkbookResult", NamespaceManager).Value

getWBDS.SelectSingleNode( _
  "/dfs:myFields/dfs:queryFields/ns2:GetWorkbook/ns2:sessionId", _
  NamespaceManager).SetValue(sessionId)
getWBDS.SelectSingleNode( _
  "/dfs:myFields/dfs:queryFields/ns2:GetWorkbook/ns2:workbookType", _
  NamespaceManager).SetValue("FullWorkbook")
DataSources("GetWorkbook").QueryConnection.Execute()

closeWBDS.SelectSingleNode( _
  "/dfs:myFields/dfs:queryFields/ns2:CloseWorkbook/ns2:sessionId", _
  NamespaceManager).SetValue(sessionId)
DataSources("CloseWorkbook").QueryConnection.Execute()

Dim stream As String = getWBDS.SelectSingleNode( _
  "/dfs:myFields/dfs:dataFields/ns2:GetWorkbookResponse" & _
  "/ns2:GetWorkbookResult", NamespaceManager).Value

If Not String.IsNullOrEmpty(stream) Then

  Dim bytes As Byte() = Convert.FromBase64String(stream)

  Using ms As New MemoryStream()

    ms.Position = 0
    ms.Write(bytes, 0, CInt(bytes.Length))

    Using document As SpreadsheetDocument = _
      SpreadsheetDocument.Open(ms, True)

      Dim wbPart As WorkbookPart = document.WorkbookPart
      BizSupportOnline.InfoPathExcel.SetRangeData( _
        repTblValues, "Sheet1", wbPart)
      wbPart.Workbook.Save()
      document.Close()

    End Using

    Dim secDS As XPathNavigator = _
      DataSources("CopyIntoItemsRequest").CreateNavigator()

    Dim sourceUrl As XPathNavigator = secDS.SelectSingleNode( _
      "/ns1:CopyIntoItems/ns1:SourceUrl", NamespaceManager)
    Dim destUrl As XPathNavigator = secDS.SelectSingleNode( _
      "/ns1:CopyIntoItems/ns1:DestinationUrls/ns1:string[1]", _
```

```
        NamespaceManager)

    Dim secondDestUrl As XPathNavigator = secDS.SelectSingleNode( _
        "/ns1:CopyIntoItems/ns1:DestinationUrls/ns1:string[2]", _
        NamespaceManager)

    If secondDestUrl IsNot Nothing Then
        secondDestUrl.DeleteSelf()
    End If

    Dim fields As XPathNodeIterator = secDS.Select( _
        "/ns1:CopyIntoItems/ns1:Fields/ns1:FieldInformation", _
        NamespaceManager)

    If fields IsNot Nothing Then
        If fields.Count > 0 Then

            Dim count As Integer = fields.Count
            Dim firstChild As XPathNavigator = secDS.SelectSingleNode( _
                "/ns1:CopyIntoItems/ns1:Fields/ns1:FieldInformation[1]", _
                NamespaceManager)
            Dim lastChild As XPathNavigator = secDS.SelectSingleNode( _
                "/ns1:CopyIntoItems/ns1:Fields/ns1:FieldInformation[" _
                & count.ToString() & "]", NamespaceManager)
            firstChild.DeleteRange(lastChild)

        End If
    End If

    Dim stream2 As XPathNavigator = secDS.SelectSingleNode( _
        "/ns1:CopyIntoItems/ns1:Stream", NamespaceManager)

    destUrl.SetValue(workbookPath)
    sourceUrl.SetValue(destUrl.Value)
    stream2.SetValue(Convert.ToBase64String(ms.ToArray()))

    Dim response As XPathNavigator = _
        DataSources("CopyIntoItemsResponse").CreateNavigator() _
        .SelectSingleNode("/ns1:CopyIntoItemsResponse", NamespaceManager)

    CType(DataConnections("UploadFile"), WebServiceConnection) _
        .Execute(secDS, response, Nothing)

    ms.Close()

  End Using

End If
```

where you must replace the value of the `workbookPath` variable with the correct URL for the Excel workbook that is located in a SharePoint document library and which you want to modify.

9. Save and build the project.

10. Preview the form.

When the form opens, add a couple of rows with data to the repeating table and then click the **Save To Excel** button. In SharePoint, navigate to the document library where the Excel workbook is located, open the workbook, and verify that the repeating table data you specified on the InfoPath form was written to the Excel workbook.

Discussion

In the solution described above, you saw how to use the Open XML SDK together with Excel Services web service operations and the **Copy** web service to download an entire Excel workbook from SharePoint, modify it, and then upload it back to SharePoint. The solution consists of three parts:

1. Use the **OpenWorkbook**, **GetWorkbook**, and **CloseWorkbook** Excel Services web service operations to download an existing Excel workbook from a SharePoint document library. Note that you could have also used the **GetItem** operation of the **Copy** web service to download the Excel workbook as described in recipe *50 Get the value of a cell in an Excel workbook*.

2. Open the Excel workbook and modify data in it using the Open XML SDK.

3. Use the **CopyIntoItems** operation of the **Copy** web service to upload the Excel workbook back to the SharePoint document library.

Refer to the discussion section of recipe *51 Set the value of a cell in an Excel workbook* for an explanation of the download and upload code.

To modify the Excel workbook by setting the values of a range of cells to be equal to values from rows in the repeating table on the InfoPath form, the code makes use of a procedure named SetRangeData(), which has been defined in the InfoPathExcel C# class or Visual Basic module. The SetRangeData() procedure makes use of classes from the Open XML SDK to write data to a range of cells on a worksheet in an Excel workbook. Refer to the Open XML SDK documentation and the article entitled *Generating Excel 2010 Workbooks by using the Open XML SDK 2.0* on the MSDN web site to learn more about using the Open XML SDK to work with data in Excel workbooks.

C#

```
using (SpreadsheetDocument document = SpreadsheetDocument.Open(ms, true))
{
  WorkbookPart wbPart = document.WorkbookPart;
  BizSupportOnline.InfoPathExcel.SetRangeData(
    repTblValues, "Sheet1", wbPart);
  wbPart.Workbook.Save();
  document.Close();
}
```

Visual Basic

```
Using document As SpreadsheetDocument = SpreadsheetDocument.Open(ms, True)

  Dim wbPart As WorkbookPart = document.WorkbookPart
  BizSupportOnline.InfoPathExcel.SetRangeData( _
    repTblValues, "Sheet1", wbPart)
  wbPart.Workbook.Save()
  document.Close()
```

```
End Using
```

Note that the `SetRangeData()` procedure has a `Dictionary` object as its first argument. This `Dictionary` object should contain cell names (references) and cell values as key/value pairs. The `Dictionary` object is filled in code by looping through the rows of the repeating table on the InfoPath form before it is passed to the `SetRangeData()` procedure.

C#

```csharp
XPathNodeIterator iter = mainDS.Select("//my:group2", NamespaceManager);
Dictionary<string, string> repTblValues = new Dictionary<string, string>();
uint counter = 1;

while (iter.MoveNext())
{
  repTblValues.Add(
    "A" + counter.ToString(),
    iter.Current.SelectSingleNode(
    "my:field1", NamespaceManager).Value);

  repTblValues.Add(
    "B" + counter.ToString(),
    iter.Current.SelectSingleNode(
    "my:field2", NamespaceManager).Value);

  repTblValues.Add(
    "C" + counter.ToString(),
    iter.Current.SelectSingleNode(
    "my:field3", NamespaceManager).Value);

  counter++;
}
```

Visual Basic

```vb
Dim iter As XPathNodeIterator = mainDS.Select("//my:group2", NamespaceManager)
Dim repTblValues As Dictionary(Of String, String) = _
  New Dictionary(Of String, String)()
Dim counter As UInteger = 1

While iter.MoveNext()

  repTblValues.Add( _
    "A" & counter.ToString(), _
    iter.Current.SelectSingleNode( _
    "my:field1", NamespaceManager).Value)

  repTblValues.Add( _
    "B" & counter.ToString(), _
    iter.Current.SelectSingleNode( _
    "my:field2", NamespaceManager).Value)

  repTblValues.Add( _
    "C" & counter.ToString(), _
    iter.Current.SelectSingleNode( _
    "my:field3", NamespaceManager).Value)
```

```
counter = counter + 1

End While
```

Warning:

> Writing code that makes use of the Open XML SDK to modify data in Excel
> workbooks has the potential to corrupt documents. So be very careful when using
> the Open XML SDK to modify data in Excel workbooks. In the event that an
> Excel workbook is corrupted, open it in the Excel client application, so that Excel
> can try to fix the problem. If Excel manages to fix the problem it will display a
> dialog box with information about what it fixed. You can then use this information
> to debug your code and investigate what caused the corruption.

54 Create and attach a new Excel workbook to an InfoPath form

Problem

You have an InfoPath form and want to use it to create a new Excel workbook and store
this workbook in a file attachment control on the InfoPath form itself.

Solution

You can use the Open XML SDK to create a new Excel workbook and then encode the
file so that it can be stored in a file attachment control on an InfoPath form.

To create and attach a new Excel workbook to an InfoPath form:

1. In InfoPath, create a new browser-compatible form template or use an existing one.

2. Add a **Text Box** control to the view of the form template, name it **field1**, and select
   its **Cannot Be Blank** property to make it a required field.

3. Add a **File Attachment** control to the view of the form template and name it **field2**.

4. Add a **Button** control to the view of the form template and label it **Create Excel
   File**.

5. With the button still selected, click **Control Tools ➤ Properties ➤ Button ➤
   Custom Code** to add an event handler for the **Clicked** event of the button.

6. In VSTA, add a new class with the name **InfoPathAttachmentEncoder** to the
   project and add the code from *InfoPathAttachmentEncoder.cs* or
   InfoPathAttachmentEncoder.vb listed in the Appendix to the new class file. You can
   also download the **InfoPathAttachmentEncoder.cs** or

InfoPathAttachmentEncoder.vb file from www.bizsupportonline.com and then add it to your VSTA project.

7. Add references to the **DocumentFormat.OpenXml** and **WindowsBase** assemblies.

8. Add the following **using** statements to the **FormCode.cs** file:

```
using System.IO;
using DocumentFormat.OpenXml;
using DocumentFormat.OpenXml.Packaging;
using DocumentFormat.OpenXml.Spreadsheet;
```

Or add the following **Imports** statements to the **FormCode.vb** file:

```
Imports System.IO
Imports DocumentFormat.OpenXml
Imports DocumentFormat.OpenXml.Packaging
Imports DocumentFormat.OpenXml.Spreadsheet
```

9. Add the following C# or Visual Basic code to the `Clicked()` event handler for the **Create Excel File** button (*code #: 5BF9773D-F411-462B-A892-A2CF92E92F47*):

<u>C#</u>

```
XPathNavigator mainDS = MainDataSource.CreateNavigator();
string excelFileName = mainDS.SelectSingleNode(
  "//my:field1", NamespaceManager).Value;
XPathNavigator field2 = mainDS.SelectSingleNode(
  "//my:field2", NamespaceManager);

using (MemoryStream sr = new MemoryStream())
{
  using (SpreadsheetDocument spreadSheet =
    SpreadsheetDocument.Create(sr, SpreadsheetDocumentType.Workbook))
  {
    spreadSheet.AddWorkbookPart();
    spreadSheet.WorkbookPart.Workbook = new Workbook();
    WorksheetPart wsPart =
      spreadSheet.WorkbookPart.AddNewPart<WorksheetPart>();

    wsPart.Worksheet = new Worksheet();
    SheetData sheetData = wsPart.Worksheet.AppendChild(new SheetData());
    wsPart.Worksheet.Save();

    spreadSheet.WorkbookPart.Workbook.AppendChild(new Sheets());
    Sheet sheet1 = new Sheet();
    sheet1.Id = spreadSheet.WorkbookPart.GetIdOfPart(wsPart);
    sheet1.SheetId = 1;
    sheet1.Name = "Sheet1";
    spreadSheet.WorkbookPart.Workbook.GetFirstChild<Sheets>().AppendChild(
      sheet1);

    spreadSheet.WorkbookPart.Workbook.Save();
  }

  byte[] bytes = sr.ToArray();
  sr.Close();
```

```
  if (field2.MoveToAttribute("nil", field2.LookupNamespace("xsi")))
  {
    field2.DeleteSelf();
  }

  BizSupportOnline.InfoPathAttachmentEncoder encoder =
    new BizSupportOnline.InfoPathAttachmentEncoder(excelFileName, bytes);

  field2.SetValue(encoder.ToBase64String());
}
```

Visual Basic

```
Dim mainDS As XPathNavigator = MainDataSource.CreateNavigator()
Dim excelFileName As String = mainDS.SelectSingleNode( _
  "//my:field1", NamespaceManager).Value
Dim field2 As XPathNavigator = mainDS.SelectSingleNode( _
  "//my:field2", NamespaceManager)

Using sr As New MemoryStream()

  Using spreadSheet As SpreadsheetDocument = SpreadsheetDocument.Create( _
    sr, SpreadsheetDocumentType.Workbook)

    spreadSheet.AddWorkbookPart()
    spreadSheet.WorkbookPart.Workbook = New Workbook()
    Dim wsPart As WorksheetPart = _
      spreadSheet.WorkbookPart.AddNewPart(Of WorksheetPart)()

    wsPart.Worksheet = New Worksheet()
    Dim sheetData As SheetData = wsPart.Worksheet.AppendChild( _
      New SheetData())
    wsPart.Worksheet.Save()

    spreadSheet.WorkbookPart.Workbook.AppendChild(New Sheets())
    Dim sheet1 As Sheet = New Sheet()
    sheet1.Id = spreadSheet.WorkbookPart.GetIdOfPart(wsPart)
    sheet1.SheetId = 1
    sheet1.Name = "Sheet1"
    spreadSheet.WorkbookPart.Workbook _
      .GetFirstChild(Of Sheets)().AppendChild(sheet1)

    spreadSheet.WorkbookPart.Workbook.Save()

  End Using

  Dim bytes As Byte() = sr.ToArray()
  sr.Close()

  If field2.MoveToAttribute("nil", field2.LookupNamespace("xsi")) Then
    field2.DeleteSelf()
  End If

  Dim encoder As New BizSupportOnline.InfoPathAttachmentEncoder( _
    excelFileName, bytes)

  field2.SetValue(encoder.ToBase64String())

End Using
```

10. Save and build the project.

11. Preview the form.

When the form opens, enter a file name for the new Excel workbook (including its file extension) into the **field1** text box and then click the **Create Excel File** button. The newly created Excel workbook should appear in the file attachment control.

Discussion

In the solution described above, you saw how to use the Open XML SDK to create a new Excel workbook and store it in a file attachment control on an InfoPath form. This solution consists of two main parts:

1. Use the Open XML SDK to create a new Excel workbook.

2. Convert the `MemoryStream` object for the Excel workbook created using the Open XML SDK into a `Byte` array, and then convert the `Byte` array into a base64-encoded string by encoding it so that it can be stored in a file attachment control on an InfoPath form.

The code first retrieves the value of **field1**, which should contain the file name to use for the new Excel workbook, and an `XPathNavigator` object pointing to **field2**, which is bound to the file attachment control.

C#

```
XPathNavigator mainDS = MainDataSource.CreateNavigator();
string excelFileName = mainDS.SelectSingleNode(
  "//my:field1", NamespaceManager).Value;
XPathNavigator field2 = mainDS.SelectSingleNode(
  "//my:field2", NamespaceManager);
```

Visual Basic

```
Dim mainDS As XPathNavigator = MainDataSource.CreateNavigator()
Dim excelFileName As String = mainDS.SelectSingleNode( _
  "//my:field1", NamespaceManager).Value
Dim field2 As XPathNavigator = mainDS.SelectSingleNode( _
  "//my:field2", NamespaceManager)
```

The code then creates a new `MemoryStream` object that can be used with classes from the Open XML SDK to create a new Excel workbook.

C#

```
using (MemoryStream sr = new MemoryStream())
{
  using (SpreadsheetDocument spreadSheet =
    SpreadsheetDocument.Create(sr, SpreadsheetDocumentType.Workbook))
  {
    ...
  }
}
```

Visual Basic

```
Using sr As New MemoryStream()

  Using spreadSheet As SpreadsheetDocument = SpreadsheetDocument.Create( _
    sr, SpreadsheetDocumentType.Workbook)

    ...

  End Using

End Using
```

See the discussion section of recipe *49 Create a new Excel workbook in SharePoint from within InfoPath* for an explanation of the sequence of code that is required to create a new spreadsheet document using classes from the Open XML SDK. Once the spreadsheet document has been created, the code then converts the MemoryStream object that contains the spreadsheet document into a Byte array and closes the stream.

C#

```
byte[] bytes = sr.ToArray();
sr.Close();
```

Visual Basic

```
Dim bytes As Byte() = sr.ToArray()
sr.Close()
```

If the field that is bound to the file attachment control has a **nil** attribute set on it, the attribute is removed.

C#

```
if (field2.MoveToAttribute("nil", field2.LookupNamespace("xsi")))
{
  field2.DeleteSelf();
}
```

Visual Basic

```
If field2.MoveToAttribute("nil", field2.LookupNamespace("xsi")) Then
  field2.DeleteSelf()
End If
```

The Byte array is encoded using the InfoPathAttachmentEncoder class and the file name specified in the **field1** text box on the InfoPath form.

C#

```
BizSupportOnline.InfoPathAttachmentEncoder encoder =
  new BizSupportOnline.InfoPathAttachmentEncoder(excelFileName, bytes);
```

Visual Basic

299

```
Dim encoder As New BizSupportOnline.InfoPathAttachmentEncoder( _
  excelFileName, bytes)
```

And finally, the base64-encoded string for the `Byte` array is stored in the file attachment control.

C#

```
field2.SetValue(encoder.ToBase64String());
```

Visual Basic

```
field2.SetValue(encoder.ToBase64String())
```

If you want to access data that is stored in an Excel workbook that is attached to an InfoPath form, see recipe *55 Get data from an Excel workbook attached to an InfoPath form*.

Refer to the Open XML SDK documentation and the article entitled *Generating Excel 2010 Workbooks by using the Open XML SDK 2.0* on the MSDN web site to learn more about using the Open XML SDK to work with data in Excel workbooks.

55   Get data from an Excel workbook attached to an InfoPath form

Problem

You have a file attachment control on an InfoPath form that contains an Excel workbook and would like to be able to retrieve the value of a cell in the Excel workbook so that you can display it on the InfoPath form.

Solution

You can decode the file representing an Excel workbook that is stored in a file attachment control on an InfoPath form, store the file in a `MemoryStream` object, and then use the Open XML SDK to open the Excel workbook, read data from it, and then display this data on the InfoPath form.

To get data from an Excel workbook attached to an InfoPath form:

1.   In InfoPath, create a new browser-compatible form template or use an existing one.

2.   Add a **File Attachment** control to the view of the form template and name it **field1**.

3.   Add two **Text Box** controls to the view of the form template and name them **field2** and **field3**, respectively.

4.   Add a **Button** control to the view of the form template and label it **Get From Excel**.

5. With the button still selected, click **Control Tools ➤ Properties ➤ Button ➤ Custom Code** to add an event handler for the **Clicked** event of the button.

6. In VSTA, add references to the **DocumentFormat.OpenXml** and **WindowsBase** assemblies.

7. Add a new class with the name **InfoPathAttachmentDecoder** to the project and add the code from *InfoPathAttachmentDecoder.cs* or *InfoPathAttachmentDecoder.vb* listed in the Appendix to the new class file. You can also download the **InfoPathAttachmentDecoder.cs** or **InfoPathAttachmentDecoder.vb** file from www.bizsupportonline.com and then add it to your VSTA project.

8. If you are writing C# code, add a new class file named **InfoPathExcel.cs** to the project, open the file and replace the code in the **InfoPathExcel.cs** file with the code displayed in *InfoPathExcel.cs* in the Appendix (*code #: C6EE40D6-96BC-485A-A1FD-12511A8E91D2*); or if you are writing Visual Basic code, add a new module file named **InfoPathExcel.vb** to the project, open the file and replace the code in the **InfoPathExcel.vb** file with the code displayed in *InfoPathExcel.vb* in the Appendix (*code #: 9DFDBC84-9A61-43E3-92FD-E819BEB95D21*).

9. Add the following **using** statements to the **FormCode.cs** file:

```
using System.IO;
using DocumentFormat.OpenXml;
using DocumentFormat.OpenXml.Packaging;
using DocumentFormat.OpenXml.Spreadsheet;
```

Or add the following **Imports** statements to the **FormCode.vb** file:

```
Imports System.IO
Imports DocumentFormat.OpenXml
Imports DocumentFormat.OpenXml.Packaging
Imports DocumentFormat.OpenXml.Spreadsheet
```

10. Add the following C# or Visual Basic code to the Clicked() event handler for the **Get From Excel** button (*code #: 25DDC7DA-D09C-4FD3-8D55-4B5143EA3666*):

__C#__

```
XPathNavigator mainDS = MainDataSource.CreateNavigator();

XPathNavigator field1 = mainDS.SelectSingleNode(
  "/my:myFields/my:field1", NamespaceManager);
XPathNavigator field2 = mainDS.SelectSingleNode(
  "/my:myFields/my:field2", NamespaceManager);
XPathNavigator field3 = mainDS.SelectSingleNode(
  "/my:myFields/my:field3", NamespaceManager);

BizSupportOnline.InfoPathAttachmentDecoder dec =
  new BizSupportOnline.InfoPathAttachmentDecoder(field1.Value);
byte[] bytes = dec.DecodedAttachment;

using (MemoryStream ms = new MemoryStream(bytes))
{
  using (SpreadsheetDocument document =
```

```
      SpreadsheetDocument.Open(ms, false))
  {
    WorkbookPart wbPart = document.WorkbookPart;
    field3.SetValue(
      BizSupportOnline.InfoPathExcel.GetCellData(
      "Sheet1", field2.Value, wbPart)
    );
    document.Close();
  }

  ms.Close();
}
```

<u>Visual Basic</u>

```
Dim mainDS As XPathNavigator = MainDataSource.CreateNavigator()

Dim field1 As XPathNavigator = mainDS.SelectSingleNode( _
  "/my:myFields/my:field1", NamespaceManager)
Dim field2 As XPathNavigator = mainDS.SelectSingleNode( _
  "/my:myFields/my:field2", NamespaceManager)
Dim field3 As XPathNavigator = mainDS.SelectSingleNode( _
  "/my:myFields/my:field3", NamespaceManager)

Dim dec As New BizSupportOnline.InfoPathAttachmentDecoder(field1.Value)
Dim bytes As Byte() = dec.DecodedAttachment

Using ms As New MemoryStream(bytes)

  Using document As SpreadsheetDocument = _
    SpreadsheetDocument.Open(ms, False)

    Dim wbPart As WorkbookPart = document.WorkbookPart

    field3.SetValue( _
      BizSupportOnline.InfoPathExcel.GetCellData( _
      "Sheet1", field2.Value, wbPart))

    document.Close()

  End Using

  ms.Close()

End Using
```

11. Save and build the project.

12. Preview the form.

When the form opens, attach an Excel workbook that contains data on a worksheet named **Sheet1** to the InfoPath form, enter a cell reference (for example **C4**) in the first text box, and then click the **Get From Excel** button. The value of the cell in the Excel workbook should appear in the second text box.

Discussion

In the solution described above, you saw how to use the Open XML SDK to read data from an Excel workbook that is stored in a file attachment control on an InfoPath form. This solution consists of two main parts:

1. Decode the file representing an Excel workbook that is stored in a file attachment control on an InfoPath form and store it in a `MemoryStream` object.

2. Use the `MemoryStream` object and the Open XML SDK to read data from the Excel workbook similar to the technique described in recipe *50 Get the value of a cell in an Excel workbook*.

The code first retrieves `XPathNavigator` objects pointing to the file attachment control and the two text box controls on the InfoPath form.

C#

```
XPathNavigator mainDS = MainDataSource.CreateNavigator();

XPathNavigator field1 = mainDS.SelectSingleNode(
  "/my:myFields/my:field1", NamespaceManager);
XPathNavigator field2 = mainDS.SelectSingleNode(
  "/my:myFields/my:field2", NamespaceManager);
XPathNavigator field3 = mainDS.SelectSingleNode(
  "/my:myFields/my:field3", NamespaceManager);
```

Visual Basic

```
Dim mainDS As XPathNavigator = MainDataSource.CreateNavigator()

Dim field1 As XPathNavigator = mainDS.SelectSingleNode( _
  "/my:myFields/my:field1", NamespaceManager)
Dim field2 As XPathNavigator = mainDS.SelectSingleNode( _
  "/my:myFields/my:field2", NamespaceManager)
Dim field3 As XPathNavigator = mainDS.SelectSingleNode( _
  "/my:myFields/my:field3", NamespaceManager)
```

It then uses the `InfoPathAttachmentDecoder` class to decode the base64-encoded string stored in the file attachment control and retrieve the `Byte` array for the file.

C#

```
BizSupportOnline.InfoPathAttachmentDecoder dec =
  new BizSupportOnline.InfoPathAttachmentDecoder(field1.Value);
byte[] bytes = dec.DecodedAttachment;
```

Visual Basic

```
Dim dec As New BizSupportOnline.InfoPathAttachmentDecoder(field1.Value)
Dim bytes As Byte() = dec.DecodedAttachment
```

The `Byte` array is then used to create a `MemoryStream` object that can be used with objects from the Open XML SDK to extract the value of a cell on **Sheet1** in the Excel workbook that is specified through the value of **field2** on the InfoPath form and then store this value in the second text box control (**field3**) on the InfoPath form.

C#

```
using (MemoryStream ms = new MemoryStream(bytes))
{
  using (SpreadsheetDocument document = SpreadsheetDocument.Open(ms, false))
  {
    WorkbookPart wbPart = document.WorkbookPart;
    field3.SetValue(BizSupportOnline.InfoPathExcel.GetCellData(
      "Sheet1", field2.Value, wbPart)
    );
    document.Close();
  }

  ms.Close();
}
```

Visual Basic

```
Using ms As New MemoryStream(bytes)

  Using document As SpreadsheetDocument = SpreadsheetDocument.Open(ms, False)

    Dim wbPart As WorkbookPart = document.WorkbookPart

    field3.SetValue(BizSupportOnline.InfoPathExcel.GetCellData( _
      "Sheet1", field2.Value, wbPart))

    document.Close()

  End Using

  ms.Close()

End Using
```

The same way you can read data from an Excel workbook that is stored in a file attachment control on an InfoPath form, you can also save data from fields on an InfoPath form to an Excel workbook that is stored in a file attachment control on the InfoPath form. To implement such functionality you must:

1. Decode the file representing an Excel workbook that is stored in a file attachment control on an InfoPath form and store it in a `MemoryStream` object.

2. Use the `MemoryStream` object and the Open XML SDK to open the Excel workbook for editing, write the data to the Excel workbook, and then save the changes back to the `MemoryStream` object similar to the technique used in recipe *51 Set the value of a cell in an Excel workbook*.

3. Encode the bytes of the `MemoryStream` object, so that the data can be stored back in the file attachment control on the InfoPath form similar to the technique used in recipe *54 Create and attach a new Excel workbook to an InfoPath form*.

Refer to the Open XML SDK documentation and the article entitled *Generating Excel 2010 Workbooks by using the Open XML SDK 2.0* on the MSDN web site to learn more about using the Open XML SDK to work with data in Excel workbooks.

Use User-Defined Functions

56 Populate an Excel cell with InfoPath form field data using a UDF

Problem

You have a text box control on an InfoPath form and want to retrieve the data that is contained in this text box from within a cell in an Excel workbook that is stored in SharePoint.

Solution

You can use a User-Defined Function (UDF) in Excel to retrieve a particular InfoPath form that is stored in a SharePoint form library, extract data from a text box on the form, and then display this data in a cell on a worksheet in the Excel workbook.

To populate a cell in an Excel workbook with data from a field on an InfoPath form using a UDF:

1. In InfoPath, create a new browser-compatible form template or use an existing one.

2. Add a **Text Box** control to the view of the form template and name it **field1**.

3. Publish the form template to a SharePoint form library.

4. In Excel, create a new Excel workbook or use an existing one.

5. Select cell **C4** on a worksheet, and then enter the following formula into the formula text box:

    ```
    =GetFormFieldValue("fieldname", "servername", "sitename", "libraryname",
    "formname")
    ```

    where **fieldname** is the name of the field bound to the text box control on the InfoPath form, **servername** is the name of the SharePoint server (without `http://` prepended) where a site named **sitename** where a form library named **libraryname** is located. The form library should be the same form library as the form library where you published the InfoPath form template in step 3. **formname** is the name of an InfoPath form including its file extension, so for example **form01.xml**. A concrete example would be:

```
=GetFormFieldValue("field1", "win-ji2o5062vat", "infopath2010cookbook5",
"SimpleFormLib", "form01.xml")
```

6. Click **File ➤ Save & Send ➤ Save to SharePoint ➤ Save As** and save the entire workbook (including all of its sheets) to a SharePoint document library (for example the **Shared Documents** library). Name the workbook **UDFWorkbook.xlsx** (also see recipe *7 Publish an Excel workbook to SharePoint*).

7. In Visual Studio 2010, select **File ➤ New ➤ Project**.

8. On the **New Project** dialog box, select **Windows** under **Visual C#** or **Visual Basic** from the list of **Installed Templates**, select **.NET Framework 3.5** from the drop-down list box, select **Class Library**, enter a name for the project (for example **UDFLib**), select a location where to save the solution, enter a name for the solution, and click **OK**.

9. On the **Solution Explorer** pane, add references to the **Microsoft.SharePoint** and **Microsoft.Office.Excel.Server.Udf** (Excel Services Application UDF Framework) assemblies.

10. Add the following **using** or **Imports** statements to the **Class1** file:

    C#

    ```
    using System.Xml;
    using System.Xml.XPath;
    using System.IO;
    using Microsoft.Office.Excel.Server.Udf;
    using Microsoft.SharePoint;
    ```

    Visual Basic

    ```
    Imports System.Xml
    Imports System.Xml.XPath
    Imports System.IO
    Imports Microsoft.Office.Excel.Server.Udf
    Imports Microsoft.SharePoint
    ```

11. Add a **UdfClass** attribute to **Class1** as follows:

    C#

    ```
    [UdfClass]
    public class Class1
    {
      ...
    }
    ```

    Visual Basic

    ```
    <UdfClass()>
    Public Class Class1
      ...
    End Class
    ```

12. Add the following UDF method to **Class1** (*code #: 8D689482-8444-4AFE-816F-21FB190678CF*):

C#

```csharp
[UdfMethod(IsVolatile = true)]
public string GetFormFieldValue(string fieldname, string servername, string
sitename, string libname, string formname)
{
  try
  {
    string formUrl = "http://" + servername + "/" + sitename
      + "/" + libname + "/" + formname;

    using (SPSite site = new SPSite("http://" + servername))
    {
      using (SPWeb web = site.AllWebs[sitename])
      {
        SPDocumentLibrary docLib = (SPDocumentLibrary)web.Lists[libname];
        SPFile file = docLib.RootFolder.Files[formname];

        byte[] formData = file.OpenBinary();

        XPathDocument doc = null;
        using (MemoryStream ms = new MemoryStream(formData))
        {
          doc = new XPathDocument(ms);
          ms.Close();
        }

        if (doc != null)
        {
          XPathNavigator root = doc.CreateNavigator();
          XPathNavigator formField = root.SelectSingleNode(
            "//*[local-name() = '" + fieldname + "']");

          if (formField != null)
          {
            return formField.Value;
          }
        }
      }
    }

    return null;

  }
  catch (Exception ex)
  {
    return ex.Message;
  }

}
```

Visual Basic

```vb
<UdfMethod(IsVolatile:=True)> _
Public Function GetFormFieldValue( _
  ByVal fieldname As String, ByVal servername As String, _
  ByVal sitename As String, ByVal libname As String, _
  ByVal formname As String) As String
```

```
Try

    Dim formUrl As String = "http://" & servername & "/" & sitename _
      & "/" & libname & "/" & formname

    Using site As SPSite = New SPSite("http://" & servername)

      Using web As SPWeb = site.AllWebs(sitename)

        Dim docLib As SPDocumentLibrary = _
          CType(web.Lists(libname), SPDocumentLibrary)
        Dim file As SPFile = docLib.RootFolder.Files(formname)

        Dim formData As Byte() = file.OpenBinary()

        Dim doc As XPathDocument = Nothing
        Using ms As New MemoryStream(formData)
          doc = New XPathDocument(ms)
          ms.Close()
        End Using

        If doc IsNot Nothing Then

          Dim root As XPathNavigator = doc.CreateNavigator()
          Dim formField As XPathNavigator = root.SelectSingleNode( _
            "//*[local-name() = '" & fieldname & "']")

          If formField IsNot Nothing Then
            Return formField.Value
          End If

        End If

      End Using

    End Using

    Return Nothing

  Catch ex As Exception

      Return ex.Message

  End Try

End Function
```

13. Save and build the project.

14. In Windows Explorer, create a new folder named **Udfs** on the C-drive, and copy the DLL from the **bin** folder of the project to `C:\Udfs`.

15. In SharePoint Central Administration, click **Manage service applications** under **Application Management**.

16. On the **Service Applications** page, click **Excel Services Application**.

17. On the **Manage Excel Services Application** page, click **User Defined Function Assemblies**.

18. On the **User-Defined Functions** page, click **Add User-Defined Function Assembly**.

19. On the **Add User-Defined Function Assembly** page, enter the path to the UDF (for example `C:\Udfs\UDFLib.dll`) in the text box under **Assembly**, select the **File path** option under **Assembly Location**, and click **OK**.

20. Navigate back to the **Excel Services Application** page, and click **Trusted File Locations**.

21. On the **Trusted File Locations** page, click **Add Trusted File Location**.

22. On the **Add Trusted File Location** page, enter the URL of the SharePoint document library where the **UDFWorkbook.xlsx** file is located into the text box under **Address** under the **Location** section, select the **User-defined functions allowed** check box under the **User-Defined Functions** section, and click **OK**.

23. Reset IIS.

In SharePoint, navigate to the form library where you published the InfoPath form template and add a new form. Fill out the form and then save the form as **form01.xml** or whatever form name you used in the formula in the **UDFWorkbook.xlsx** Excel workbook. Navigate to the document library where the **UDFWorkbook.xlsx** Excel workbook is located, and click the file to open it in the browser (Excel Web Access). When the file opens in the browser, the value you entered into the text box on the InfoPath form should appear in cell **C4** of the Excel workbook.

Discussion

In the solution described above, you saw how to use a User-Defined Function (UDF) in an Excel workbook to pull data in from an InfoPath form that is stored in a SharePoint form library. Note that the UDF runs within the context of SharePoint, so you must open the Excel workbook in the browser (through Excel Web Access) for it to work.

The main steps for getting the value of a field on an InfoPath form and then displaying this value in a cell of an Excel workbook using a User-Defined Function are:

1. Retrieve the InfoPath form from the SharePoint form library in which it is stored.

   C#

   ```
   SPDocumentLibrary docLib = (SPDocumentLibrary)web.Lists[libname];
   SPFile file = docLib.RootFolder.Files[formname];
   ```

   Visual Basic

   ```
   Dim docLib As SPDocumentLibrary = _
     CType(web.Lists(libname), SPDocumentLibrary)
   Dim file As SPFile = docLib.RootFolder.Files(formname)
   ```

2. Open the InfoPath form and retrieve the value of a form field.

C#

```
byte[] formData = file.OpenBinary();

XPathDocument doc = null;
using (MemoryStream ms = new MemoryStream(formData))
{
  doc = new XPathDocument(ms);
  ms.Close();
}

if (doc != null)
{
  XPathNavigator root = doc.CreateNavigator();
  XPathNavigator formField = root.SelectSingleNode(
    "//*[local-name() = '" + fieldname + "']");
  ...
}
```

Visual Basic

```
Dim formData As Byte() = file.OpenBinary()

Dim doc As XPathDocument = Nothing
Using ms As New MemoryStream(formData)
  doc = New XPathDocument(ms)
  ms.Close()
End Using

If doc IsNot Nothing Then

  Dim root As XPathNavigator = doc.CreateNavigator()
  Dim formField As XPathNavigator = root.SelectSingleNode( _
    "//*[local-name() = '" & fieldname & "']")
  ...

End If
```

3. Return the value of the InfoPath form field to the Excel workbook so that it can be used in a formula to populate a cell.

    C#

```
if (formField != null)
{
  return formField.Value;
}
```

    Visual Basic

```
If formField IsNot Nothing Then
  Return formField.Value
End If
```

Note that if an error occurs in code, the error message will be returned to the Excel workbook instead of the form field value.

<u>C#</u>

```csharp
try
{
  ...
}
catch (Exception ex)
{
  return ex.Message;
}
```

Visual Basic

```vbnet
Try

  ...

Catch ex As Exception

  Return ex.Message

End Try
```

The solution described above *pulls* data from an InfoPath form into an Excel workbook using a User-Defined Function in a formula. If you want to push data from an InfoPath form into an Excel workbook, see recipe *19 Set the value of an Excel cell in InfoPath*, recipe *46 Set the value of an Excel cell from within InfoPath*, or recipe *51 Set the value of a cell in an Excel workbook*.

To learn more about User-Defined Functions, consult the SharePoint documentation on the MSDN web site.

Tip:

> If you get an error that says *FileNotFoundException was unhandled. The web application at ... could not be found.*, ensure that the compile platform for the Visual Studio project has been set to **AnyCPU**. If you are writing C# code, you can set this value by opening the project's **Properties** window and then on the **Build** tab, select **AnyCPU** from the **Platform target** drop-down list box. If you are writing Visual Basic code, open the project's **Properties** window, and then on **Compile** tab, click **Advanced Compile Options**, and then on the **Advanced Compile Options** dialog box, select **AnyCPU** from the **Target CPU** drop-down list box.

57   Populate an Excel workbook with InfoPath repeating table data using a UDF

Problem

You have a repeating table on an InfoPath form and want to retrieve the data that it contains from within cells in an Excel workbook that is stored in a SharePoint document library.

Solution

You can use a User-Defined Function (UDF) in Excel to retrieve a particular InfoPath form that is stored in a SharePoint form library, extract the data from a repeating table on the form, and display this data in cells on a worksheet in an Excel workbook.

To populate an Excel workbook with data from an InfoPath repeating table using a UDF:

1.   In InfoPath, create a new browser-compatible form template or use an existing one.

2.   Add a **Repeating Table** control with 3 columns to the view of the form template, and name the fields within the repeating table **field1**, **field2**, and **field3**, respectively.

3.   Publish the form template to a SharePoint form library.

4.   In Excel, create a new Excel workbook or use an existing one.

5.   Select an area covering cells **A1** through **C5** on a worksheet, and then enter the following formula into the formula text box:

```
=GetRowsOfRepeatingTable("servername", "sitename", "libraryname",
"formname")
```

where **servername** is the name of the SharePoint server (without `http://` prepended) where a site named **sitename** where a form library named **libraryname** is located. The form library should be the same form library as the form library where you published the InfoPath form template in step 3. **formname** is the name of an InfoPath form including its file extension, so for example **form01.xml**. A concrete example would be:

```
=GetRowsOfRepeatingTable("win-ji2o5062vat", "infopath2010cookbook5",
"SimpleFormLib", "form01.xml")
```

6.   With the cursor still in the formula text box, press **Ctrl+Shift+Enter**. The formula should then change into the following array formula:

```
{=GetRowsOfRepeatingTable("servername", "sitename", "libraryname",
"formname")}
```

7.   Click **File ➤ Save & Send ➤ Save to SharePoint ➤ Save As** and save the entire workbook (including all of its sheets) to a SharePoint document library (for example

the **Shared Documents** library). Name the workbook **UDFWorkbook.xlsx** (also see recipe *7 Publish an Excel workbook to SharePoint*).

8. In Visual Studio 2010, select **File ➤ New ➤ Project**.

9. On the **New Project** dialog box, select **Windows** under **Visual C#** or **Visual Basic** from the list of **Installed Templates**, select **.NET Framework 3.5** from the drop-down list box, select **Class Library**, enter a name for the project (for example **UDFLib**), select a location where to save the solution, enter a name for the solution, and click **OK**.

10. On the **Solution Explorer** pane, add references to the **Microsoft.SharePoint** and **Microsoft.Office.Excel.Server.Udf** (Excel Services Application UDF Framework) assemblies.

11. Add the following **using** or **Imports** statements to the **Class1** file:

C#

```
using System.Xml;
using System.Xml.XPath;
using System.IO;
using Microsoft.Office.Excel.Server.Udf;
using Microsoft.SharePoint;
```

Visual Basic

```
Imports System.Xml
Imports System.Xml.XPath
Imports System.IO
Imports Microsoft.Office.Excel.Server.Udf
Imports Microsoft.SharePoint
```

12. Add a **UdfClass** attribute to **Class1** as follows:

C#

```
[UdfClass]
public class Class1
{
  . . .
}
```

Visual Basic

```
<UdfClass()>
Public Class Class1
 . . .
End Class
```

13. Add the following UDF method to **Class1** (*code #: BCB82DB8-963D-4EE6-BD32-15E0DEA91221*):

C#

```
[UdfMethod(IsVolatile = true)]
public object[,] GetRowsOfRepeatingTable(string servername, string
```

```
sitename, string libname, string formname)
{
  try
  {
    string formUrl = "http://" + servername + "/" + sitename
      + "/" + libname + "/" + formname;

    using (SPSite site = new SPSite("http://" + servername))
    {
      using (SPWeb web = site.AllWebs[sitename])
      {
        SPDocumentLibrary docLib = (SPDocumentLibrary)web.Lists[libname];
        SPFile file = docLib.RootFolder.Files[formname];

        byte[] formData = file.OpenBinary();

        XPathDocument doc = null;
        using (MemoryStream ms = new MemoryStream(formData))
        {
          doc = new XPathDocument(ms);
          ms.Close();
        }

        if (doc != null)
        {
          XPathNavigator root = doc.CreateNavigator();
          XPathNodeIterator iter = root.Select(
            "//*[local-name() = 'group2']");

          int counter = 1;

          if (iter != null)
          {
            object[,] toExcelGrid = new object[iter.Count, 3];

            while (iter.MoveNext())
            {
              toExcelGrid[counter - 1, 0] = iter.Current.SelectSingleNode(
                "*[local-name() = 'field1']").Value;
              toExcelGrid[counter - 1, 1] = iter.Current.SelectSingleNode(
                "*[local-name() = 'field2']").Value;
              toExcelGrid[counter - 1, 2] = iter.Current.SelectSingleNode(
                "*[local-name() = 'field3']").Value;

              counter++;
            }

            return toExcelGrid;
          }
        }
      }
    }

    return null;

  }
  catch (Exception ex)
  {
    object[,] error = new object[1, 1];
    error[0, 0] = ex.Message;
    return error;
```

```
    }

}
```

Visual Basic

```vb
<UdfMethod(IsVolatile:=True)> _
Public Function GetRowsOfRepeatingTable( _
  ByVal servername As String, ByVal sitename As String, _
  ByVal libname As String, ByVal formname As String) As Object(,)

  Try

    Dim formUrl As String = "http://" & servername & "/" & sitename _
      & "/" & libname & "/" & formname

    Using site As SPSite = New SPSite("http://" & servername)

      Using web As SPWeb = site.AllWebs(sitename)

        Dim docLib As SPDocumentLibrary = _
          CType(web.Lists(libname), SPDocumentLibrary)
        Dim file As SPFile = docLib.RootFolder.Files(formname)

        Dim formData As Byte() = file.OpenBinary()

        Dim doc As XPathDocument = Nothing

        Using ms As New MemoryStream(formData)
          doc = New XPathDocument(ms)
          ms.Close()
        End Using

        If doc IsNot Nothing Then

          Dim root As XPathNavigator = doc.CreateNavigator()
          Dim iter As XPathNodeIterator = root.Select( _
            "//*[local-name() = 'group2']")

          Dim counter As Integer = 1

          If iter IsNot Nothing Then

            Dim toExcelGrid(,) As Object = New Object(iter.Count - 1, 3) {}

            While (iter.MoveNext())
              toExcelGrid(counter - 1, 0) = _
                iter.Current.SelectSingleNode( _
                "*[local-name() = 'field1']").Value
              toExcelGrid(counter - 1, 1) = _
                iter.Current.SelectSingleNode( _
                "*[local-name() = 'field2']").Value
              toExcelGrid(counter - 1, 2) = _
                iter.Current.SelectSingleNode( _
                "*[local-name() = 'field3']").Value

              counter = counter + 1
            End While

            Return toExcelGrid

          End If
```

```
          End If

        End Using

      End Using

      Return Nothing

   Catch ex As Exception

      Dim err(,) As Object = New Object(1, 1) {}
      err(0, 0) = ex.Message
      Return err

   End Try

End Function
```

14. Save and build the project.

15. In Windows Explorer, create a new folder named **Udfs** on the C-drive, and copy the DLL from the **bin** folder of the project to `C:\Udfs`.

16. In SharePoint Central Administration, click **Manage service applications** under **Application Management**.

17. On the **Service Applications** page, click **Excel Services Application**.

18. On the **Manage Excel Services Application** page, click **User Defined Function Assemblies**.

19. On the **User-Defined Functions** page, click **Add User-Defined Function Assembly**.

20. On the **Add User-Defined Function Assembly** page, enter the path to the UDF (for example `C:\Udfs\UDFLib.dll`) in the text box under **Assembly**, select the **File path** option under **Assembly Location**, and click **OK**.

21. Navigate back to the **Excel Services Application** page, and click **Trusted File Locations**.

22. On the **Trusted File Locations** page, click **Add Trusted File Location**.

23. On the **Add Trusted File Location** page, enter the URL of the SharePoint document library where the **UDFWorkbook.xlsx** file is located into the text box under **Address** under the **Location** section, select the **User-defined functions allowed** check box under the **User-Defined Functions** section, and click **OK**.

24. Reset IIS.

In SharePoint, navigate to the form library where you published the InfoPath form template and add a new form. Add a couple of rows with data to the repeating table control on the form and then save the form as **form01.xml** or whatever form name you used in the array formula in the **UDFWorkbook.xlsx** Excel workbook. Navigate to the document library where the **UDFWorkbook.xlsx** Excel workbook is located, and click the file to open it in the browser (Excel Web Access). When the file opens, the first 5 rows of the repeating table contained in the InfoPath form should be displayed in cells **A1** through **C5** of the Excel workbook.

Discussion

In the solution described above, you saw how to use a User-Defined Function (UDF) in an Excel workbook to pull data in from an InfoPath form that is stored in a SharePoint form library. Note that the UDF runs within the context of SharePoint, so you must open the Excel workbook in the browser (through Excel Web Access) for it to work.

The main steps for reading data from a repeating table on an InfoPath form and then displaying this data in an Excel workbook using a User-Defined Function are:

1. Retrieve the InfoPath form from the SharePoint form library in which it is stored.

    C#

    ```
    SPDocumentLibrary docLib = (SPDocumentLibrary)web.Lists[libname];
    SPFile file = docLib.RootFolder.Files[formname];
    ```

    Visual Basic

    ```
    Dim docLib As SPDocumentLibrary = _
      CType(web.Lists(libname), SPDocumentLibrary)
    Dim file As SPFile = docLib.RootFolder.Files(formname)
    ```

2. Open the InfoPath form and retrieve data from the repeating table.

    C#

    ```
    byte[] formData = file.OpenBinary();

    XPathDocument doc = null;
    using (MemoryStream ms = new MemoryStream(formData))
    {
      doc = new XPathDocument(ms);
      ms.Close();
    }

    if (doc != null)
    {
      XPathNavigator root = doc.CreateNavigator();
      XPathNodeIterator iter = root.Select(
        "//*[local-name() = 'group2']");
      ...
    }
    ```

    Visual Basic

    ```
    Dim formData As Byte() = file.OpenBinary()

    Dim doc As XPathDocument = Nothing

    Using ms As New MemoryStream(formData)
      doc = New XPathDocument(ms)
      ms.Close()
    ```

```
End Using

If doc IsNot Nothing Then

  Dim root As XPathNavigator = doc.CreateNavigator()
  Dim iter As XPathNodeIterator = root.Select( _
    "//*[local-name() = 'group2']")
  ...

End If
```

3. Fill a two-dimensional array while looping through the rows of the repeating table. The first dimension of the array contains the index number for a table row and the second dimension contains the index number for a column in the row specified by the first dimension.

C#

```csharp
object[,] toExcelGrid = new object[iter.Count, 3];

while (iter.MoveNext())
{
  toExcelGrid[counter - 1, 0] = iter.Current.SelectSingleNode(
    "*[local-name() = 'field1']").Value;
  toExcelGrid[counter - 1, 1] = iter.Current.SelectSingleNode(
    "*[local-name() = 'field2']").Value;
  toExcelGrid[counter - 1, 2] = iter.Current.SelectSingleNode(
    "*[local-name() = 'field3']").Value;

  counter++;
}
```

Visual Basic

```vb
Dim toExcelGrid(,) As Object = New Object(iter.Count - 1, 3) {}

While (iter.MoveNext())
  toExcelGrid(counter - 1, 0) = iter.Current.SelectSingleNode( _
    "*[local-name() = 'field1']").Value
  toExcelGrid(counter - 1, 1) = iter.Current.SelectSingleNode( _
    "*[local-name() = 'field2']").Value
  toExcelGrid(counter - 1, 2) = iter.Current.SelectSingleNode( _
    "*[local-name() = 'field3']").Value

  counter = counter + 1
End While
```

4. Return the two-dimensional array to the Excel workbook so that it can be used in an array formula to populate a range of cells.

C#

```csharp
return toExcelGrid;
```

Visual Basic

```vb
Return toExcelGrid
```

The solution described above is quite rigid in that you must know in advance how many Excel rows will be populated with data from a repeating table on an InfoPath form. And all of the cells that have the array formula defined on them in the Excel workbook, but which are not populated with data from the repeating table on the InfoPath form will display the **#N/A** value. To prevent this value from being displayed, you could change the UDF method to accept an extra parameter named **maxrows** of type `Integer`.

<u>**C#**</u>

```csharp
[UdfMethod(IsVolatile = true)]
public object[,] GetRowsOfRepeatingTable(string servername, string sitename,
string libname, string formname, int maxrows)
{
   ...
}
```

<u>**Visual Basic**</u>

```vb
<UdfMethod(IsVolatile:=True)> _
Public Function GetRowsOfRepeatingTable( _
  ByVal servername As String, ByVal sitename As String, _
  ByVal libname As String, ByVal formname As String, _
  ByVal maxrows As Integer) As Object(,)

   ...

End Function
```

Note that you must also update the array formula in the Excel workbook to accept this parameter. For example:

```
=GetRowsOfRepeatingTable("servername", "sitename", "libraryname", "formname", 5)
```

where **5** indicates that a maximum of 5 rows can be populated in the Excel workbook. And then if the repeating table contains less rows than the maximum allowable rows in the Excel workbook, size the two-dimentional array to have the maximum amount of rows just before the `While`-loop as follows (*code #: 2A3076A0-4711-4372-BA8D-03841DF10113*):

<u>**C#**</u>

```csharp
object[,] toExcelGrid = null;
if (maxrows > iter.Count)
{
   toExcelGrid = new object[maxrows, 3];
}
else
{
   toExcelGrid = new object[iter.Count, 3];
}
```

<u>**Visual Basic**</u>

```vb
Dim toExcelGrid(,) As Object = Nothing
If maxrows > iter.Count Then
   toExcelGrid = New Object(maxrows - 1, 3) {}
```

319

```
Else
  toExcelGrid = New Object(iter.Count - 1, 3) {}
End If
```

The rest of the code would then populate the array with the amount of rows in the repeating table and then any other rows that are superfluous would be left empty and display an empty string in the Excel workbook instead of the **#N/A** value.

If you require a more flexible solution that does not require you to know in advance how many Excel rows are going to be populated, you can use the solution described in recipe *53 Populate an Excel workbook with InfoPath repeating table data*. Note that such a solution *pushes* data from an InfoPath form into an Excel workbook instead of *pulling* data from an InfoPath form into an Excel workbook as described in the solution above.

To learn more about User-Defined Functions, consult the SharePoint documentation on the MSDN web site.

Tip:

> If you get an error that says *FileNotFoundException was unhandled. The web application at ... could not be found.*, ensure that the compile platform for the Visual Studio project has been set to **AnyCPU**. If you are writing C# code, you can set this value by opening the project's **Properties** window and then on the **Build** tab, select **AnyCPU** from the **Platform target** drop-down list box. If you are writing Visual Basic code, open the project's **Properties** window, and then on **Compile** tab, click **Advanced Compile Options**, and then on the **Advanced Compile Options** dialog box, select **AnyCPU** from the **Target CPU** drop-down list box.

Appendix

Troubleshooting InfoPath with Excel Services web services

A few of the most common reasons for getting errors while using the Excel Services SOAP web service have been listed below.

There was a time-out
Excel Services tends to need to "warm-up" the first time a user calls it. You may see an error such as *An error occurred while querying the data source* displayed in a dialog box or on a page.

Solution: Close the InfoPath form, reopen it, and try again. Or open an Excel workbook in the browser for Excel Services to "warm up" before trying to fill out any InfoPath forms that make use of the Excel Services SOAP web service.

Access to an Excel workbook is denied
The Excel workbook you are trying to access has been either opened or locked by another user. To check whether the Excel workbook has been locked by another user, open it in the Excel client application from within SharePoint. If Excel displays a dialog box saying that you can only get a read-only copy, then the file is in use by another user or locked by Excel Services.

Solution: If locked by a user, ask the user to close the Excel workbook. If locked by Excel Services (for example because an error took place while a user was submitting data to the Excel Services SOAP web service), wait between 5 to 15 minutes for Excel Services to release the Excel workbook.

The Excel workbook cannot be found
The URL for the Excel workbook used in the InfoPath form is incorrect or the Excel workbook does not exist at the location specified in the InfoPath form template.

Solution: Double-check that the InfoPath form template is referencing the correct URL for the Excel workbook, and then republish the form template.

A standard browser form error message is being displayed
You created a normal browser-compatible form template that can be published to a SharePoint form library wihout adding the **ArrayOfAnyType** attribute to its main data source.

Solution: See *How to add an ArrayOfAnyType to the Main data source* below and the three ways to create a form template listed in recipe *19 Set the value of an Excel cell in InfoPath*. Also refer to the next issue listed below.

The form template failed to work

The InfoPath form is not working as intended, is not doing what it is supposed to do, or an error is being displayed.

Solution: Open and fill out the InfoPath form in InfoPath Filler 2010 to get a better error message with details or use VSTA to debug any code you may have written for the form template.

Tip:

When an error occurs when you are testing an InfoPath form that calls Excel Services via the browser, try opening the form in InfoPath Filler and perform the same action(s) that caused the error. InfoPath Filler generally provides more sensible and clearer error messages than SharePoint does.

How to add an ArrayOfAnyType to the Main data source

Problem

You are receiving the error "An error occurred querying a data source", "There has been an error processing the form", or "The given key was not present in the dictionary" after you have designed an InfoPath browser-compatible form template that uses one or more Excel Services SOAP web service operations, have published this form template to SharePoint, and are trying to fill out a form.

Solution

You can try adding an **arrayOfAnyType** node to the Main data source of the form and see whether it resolves the problem. Note that you need not do anything else with the node but just add it to the Main data source of the form. Also note that you must add it to the Main data source and not as a secondary data source.

To add an **arrayOfAnyType** node to the Main data source:

1. In Notepad, create an XML file that has the following contents:

```
<tns:ArrayOfAnyType xmlns:xsd="http://www.w3.org/2001/XMLSchema"
xmlns:xsi="http://www.w3.org/2001/XMLSchema"
xmlns:tns="http://schemas.microsoft.com/office/excel/server/webservices" >
    <tns:anyType type="xsd:string"></tns:anyType>
    <tns:anyType type="xsd:string"></tns:anyType>
</tns:ArrayOfAnyType>
```

and name the XML file **ArrayOfAnyType.xml** or download the
ArrayOfAnyType.xml file from www.bizsupportonline.com.

2. In InfoPath, on the **Fields** task pane, right-click the **myFields** group node, and
select **Add** from the drop-down menu that appears.

3. On the **Add Field or Group** dialog box, select **Complete XML Schema or XML
document** from the **Type** drop-down list box.

4. On the **Data Source Wizard**, click **Browse**, and browse to, select, and open the
ArrayOfAnyType.xml file.

5. On the **Data Source Wizard**, click **Next**.

6. On the **Data Source Wizard**, leave the **No** option selected, and click **Finish**.

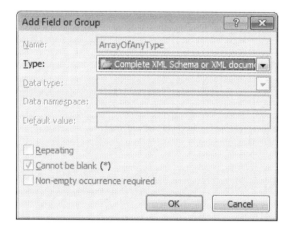

Figure 56. The dialog box after adding the ArrayOfAnyType XML file.

7. On the **Add Field or Group** dialog box, click **OK**.

8. Republish the form template to SharePoint and test it.

Discussion

Excel web service operations that return or use **anyType** elements may require you to
perform the steps described in the solution above if you are designing a normal browser-
compatible form template (**Blank Form** or **SharePoint Form Library**) and have not
bound the Main data source directly to an Excel web service operation by creating a **Web
Service** form template (also see recipe *19 Set the value of an Excel cell in InfoPath*). And
even if an Excel web service operation does not return **anyType** elements, but you still
get one of the errors mentioned in the problem description of this recipe, you can try
adding the **ArrayOfAnyType** XML structure to the Main data source to see whether it
helps.

Web service calls from within InfoPath are very error-prone and can be difficult to debug. So if you get any errors while trying to design a form template that makes use of web service data connections, for example

An error occurred querying a data source

or

There has been an error while processing the form.

with a detailed error message of

There was a form postback error. …, Type: KeyNotFoundException, Exception Message: The given key was not present in the dictionary.)

the first step would be to check the SharePoint log files, which in a default SharePoint installation are located under

```
C:\Program Files\Common Files\Microsoft Shared\Web Server Extensions\14\LOGS
```

to see what the exact error message is. If you are not an administrator, so cannot access the log files, the next step would be to disable all of the action rules in InfoPath, enable them one-by-one, check the values that are returned, and try to narrow down which rule (or action) is causing the error.

Another solution to avoid getting browser form errors when you are using Excel Services SOAP web service operations is to design a **Web Service** InfoPath form template that is based on an Excel Services SOAP web service operation, so is defined as its Main data connection. If you use a **Web Service** InfoPath form template, you do not have to add the **ArrayOfAnyType** node to the Main data source of the form (also see recipe *19 Set the value of an Excel cell in InfoPath*).

How to create a named range in Excel

Problem

You want to give one or more cells on a worksheet in an Excel workbook a friendly name, so that you can easily refer to the cell(s) in formulas.

Solution

You can use the **Define Name** command in Excel to create a named range.

To create a named range in Excel:

1. In Excel, create a new workbook or use an existing one.

2. Select the cells for which you want to create a named range. Note that these cells need not be adjacent. For example, you can create a named range using cells **A1** and **C1** (non-adjacent cells) instead of cells **A1** and **B1** (adjacent cells). To select non-adjacent cells, hold the **Ctrl** key pressed down while clicking on cells.

3.   Click **Formulas ➤ Defined Names ➤ Define Name**.

Figure 57. The Define Name commnad in Excel 2010.

4.   On the **New Name** dialog box, enter a **Name** for the range of cells, select a scope for the named range from the **Scope** drop-down list box, and click **OK**. Note that you can also click the button behind the **Refers to** text box and then select the cells that you want to include in the named range.

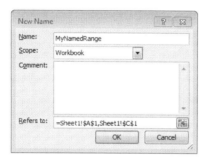

Figure 58. The New Name dialog box to define a named range in Excel 2010.

To edit an existing named range in Excel:

1.   Click **Formulas ➤ Defined Names ➤ Name Manager**.

Figure 59. The Name Manager command in Excel 2010.

2.   On the **Name Manager** dialog box, select the named range you want to edit, and click **Edit**.

3. On the **Edit Name** dialog box, modify the data you want to modify, and click **OK**.

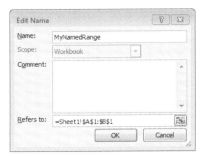

Figure 60. The Edit Name dialog box to modify the settings for a named range in Excel 2010.

4. On the **Name Manager** dialog box, click **Close**.

To delete an existing named range in Excel:

1. Click **Formulas** ➤ **Defined Names** ➤ **Name Manager**.

2. On the **Name Manager** dialog box, select the named range you want to delete, and click **Delete**.

3. On the **Microsoft Excel** dialog box, click **OK**.

4. On the **Name Manager** dialog box, click **Close**.

InfoPathAttachmentEncoder.cs

```
using System;
using System.Text;
using System.IO;
using System.Security.Cryptography;

namespace BizSupportOnline
{
  public class InfoPathAttachmentEncoder
  {
    private string base64EncodedFile = string.Empty;
    private string fileName;
    private byte[] fileData;

    public InfoPathAttachmentEncoder(string fileName, byte[] fileData)
    {
      if (fileName == string.Empty)
        throw new ArgumentException("Must specify file name", "fileName");

      if (fileData.Length == 0)
        throw new ArgumentNullException("fileData", "File is empty");
```

```csharp
      this.fileName = fileName;
      this.fileData = fileData;
    }

    public string ToBase64String()
    {
      if (base64EncodedFile != string.Empty)
        return base64EncodedFile;

      using (MemoryStream ms = new MemoryStream())
      {
        using (MemoryStream msOld = new MemoryStream(fileData))
        {
          using (BinaryReader br = new BinaryReader(msOld))
          {
            string fileName = this.fileName;

            uint fileNameLength = (uint)fileName.Length + 1;

            byte[] fileNameBytes = Encoding.Unicode.GetBytes(fileName);

            using (BinaryWriter bw = new BinaryWriter(ms))
            {
              bw.Write(new byte[] { 0xC7, 0x49, 0x46, 0x41 });

              bw.Write((uint)0x14);
              bw.Write((uint)0x01);
              bw.Write((uint)0x00);

              bw.Write((uint)br.BaseStream.Length);
              bw.Write((uint)fileNameLength);
              bw.Write(fileNameBytes);
              bw.Write(new byte[] { 0, 0 });

              byte[] data = new byte[64 * 1024];
              int bytesRead = 1;

              while (bytesRead > 0)
              {
                bytesRead = br.Read(data, 0, data.Length);
                bw.Write(data, 0, bytesRead);
              }
            }

            br.Close();
          }

          using (MemoryStream msOut = new MemoryStream())
          {
            using (BinaryReader br =
              new BinaryReader(new MemoryStream(ms.ToArray())))
            {
              ToBase64Transform tf = new ToBase64Transform();

              byte[] data = new byte[tf.InputBlockSize];
              byte[] outData = new byte[tf.OutputBlockSize];

              int bytesRead = 1;

              while (bytesRead > 0)
              {
                bytesRead = br.Read(data, 0, data.Length);
```

```
                    if (bytesRead == data.Length)
                      tf.TransformBlock(data, 0, bytesRead, outData, 0);
                    else
                      outData = tf.TransformFinalBlock(data, 0, bytesRead);

                    msOut.Write(outData, 0, outData.Length);
                  }

                  br.Close();
                }

              msOut.Close();

              base64EncodedFile = Encoding.ASCII.GetString(msOut.ToArray());
            }

            msOld.Close();
          }

        ms.Close();
      }

    return base64EncodedFile;
    }
  }
}
```

InfoPathAttachmentEncoder.vb

```
Imports System
Imports System.IO
Imports System.Text
Imports System.Security.Cryptography

Namespace BizSupportOnline

  Public Class InfoPathAttachmentEncoder

    Private base64EncodedFile As String = String.Empty
    Private fileName As String
    Private fileData As Byte()

    Public Sub New(ByVal fileName As String, ByVal fileData As Byte())

      If fileName = String.Empty Then
        Throw New ArgumentException("Must specify file name", "fileName")
      End If

      If fileData.Length = 0 Then
        Throw New ArgumentNullException("fileData", "File is empty")
      End If

      Me.fileName = fileName
      Me.fileData = fileData

    End Sub

    Public Function ToBase64String() As String
```

```
If base64EncodedFile <> String.Empty Then
  Return base64EncodedFile
End If

Using ms As New MemoryStream()

  Using msOld As MemoryStream = New MemoryStream(fileData)

    Using br As BinaryReader = New BinaryReader(msOld)

      Dim fileName As String = Me.fileName
      Dim fileNameLength As UInteger = CUInt(fileName.Length) + 1
      Dim fileNameBytes As Byte() = Encoding.Unicode.GetBytes(fileName)

      Using bw As New BinaryWriter(ms)

        bw.Write(New Byte() {&HC7, &H49, &H46, &H41})

        bw.Write(CUInt(&H14))
        bw.Write(CUInt(&H1))
        bw.Write(CUInt(&H0))

        bw.Write(CUInt((br.BaseStream.Length)))
        bw.Write(CUInt(fileNameLength))
        bw.Write(fileNameBytes)
        bw.Write(New Byte() {0, 0})

        Dim data As Byte() = New Byte(64 * 1024 - 1) {}
        Dim bytesRead As Integer = 1

        While bytesRead > 0
          bytesRead = br.Read(data, 0, data.Length)
          bw.Write(data, 0, bytesRead)
        End While

      End Using

      br.Close()

    End Using


    Using msOut As New MemoryStream()

      Using br As BinaryReader = New BinaryReader( _
      New MemoryStream(ms.ToArray()))

        Dim tf As New ToBase64Transform()

        Dim data As Byte() = New Byte(tf.InputBlockSize - 1) {}
        Dim outData As Byte() = New Byte(tf.OutputBlockSize - 1) {}

        Dim bytesRead As Integer = 1

        While bytesRead > 0
          bytesRead = br.Read(data, 0, data.Length)

          If bytesRead = data.Length Then
            tf.TransformBlock(data, 0, bytesRead, outData, 0)
          Else
            outData = tf.TransformFinalBlock(data, 0, bytesRead)
```

```
                End If

                msOut.Write(outData, 0, outData.Length)

            End While

            br.Close()

          End Using

          base64EncodedFile = Encoding.ASCII.GetString(msOut.ToArray())

          msOut.Close()

        End Using

        msOld.Close()

      End Using

      ms.Close()

    End Using

    Return base64EncodedFile

  End Function

  End Class

End Namespace
```

InfoPathAttachmentDecoder.cs

```csharp
using System;
using System.IO;
using System.Text;

namespace BizSupportOnline
{
  public class InfoPathAttachmentDecoder
  {
    private const int SP1Header_Size = 20;
    private const int FIXED_HEADER = 16;

    private int fileSize;
    private int attachmentNameLength;
    private string attachmentName;
    private byte[] decodedAttachment;

    public InfoPathAttachmentDecoder(string base64EncodedString)
    {
      byte[] data = Convert.FromBase64String(base64EncodedString);
      using (MemoryStream ms = new MemoryStream(data))
      {
        BinaryReader reader = new BinaryReader(ms);
        DecodeAttachment(reader);
        reader.Close();
        ms.Close();
```

```
        }
    }

    private void DecodeAttachment(BinaryReader reader)
    {
      byte[] headerData = new byte[FIXED_HEADER];
      headerData = reader.ReadBytes(headerData.Length);

      fileSize = (int)reader.ReadUInt32();
      attachmentNameLength = (int)reader.ReadUInt32() * 2;

      byte[] fileNameBytes = reader.ReadBytes(attachmentNameLength);

      Encoding enc = Encoding.Unicode;
      attachmentName =
        enc.GetString(fileNameBytes, 0, attachmentNameLength - 2);
      decodedAttachment = reader.ReadBytes(fileSize);
    }

    public void SaveAttachment(string saveLocation)
    {
      string fullFileName = saveLocation;

      if (!fullFileName.EndsWith(Path.DirectorySeparatorChar.ToString()))
        fullFileName += Path.DirectorySeparatorChar;

      fullFileName += attachmentName;

      if (File.Exists(fullFileName))
        File.Delete(fullFileName);

      using (FileStream fs = new FileStream(fullFileName, FileMode.CreateNew))
      {
        BinaryWriter bw = new BinaryWriter(fs);
        bw.Write(decodedAttachment);
        bw.Close();
        fs.Close();
      }
    }

    public string Filename
    {
      get { return attachmentName; }
    }

    public byte[] DecodedAttachment
    {
      get { return decodedAttachment; }
    }
  }
}
```

InfoPathAttachmentDecoder.vb

```
Imports System
Imports System.IO
Imports System.Text

Namespace BizSupportOnline
```

```vb
Public Class InfoPathAttachmentDecoder

  Private Const SP1Header_Size As Integer = 20
  Private Const FIXED_HEADER As Integer = 16

  Private fileSize As Integer
  Private attachmentNameLength As Integer
  Private attachmentName As String
  Private _decodedAttachment As Byte()

  Public Sub New(ByVal base64EncodedString As String)

    Dim data As Byte() = Convert.FromBase64String(base64EncodedString)

    Using ms As New MemoryStream(data)
      Dim reader As BinaryReader = New BinaryReader(ms)
      DecodeAttachment(reader)
      reader.Close()
      ms.Close()
    End Using

  End Sub

  Private Sub DecodeAttachment(ByVal reader As BinaryReader)

    Dim headerData As Byte() = New Byte(FIXED_HEADER - 1) {}
    headerData = reader.ReadBytes(headerData.Length)

    fileSize = CInt(reader.ReadUInt32())
    attachmentNameLength = CInt(reader.ReadUInt32()) * 2

    Dim fileNameBytes As Byte() = reader.ReadBytes(attachmentNameLength)

    Dim enc As Encoding = Encoding.Unicode
    attachmentName = _
      enc.GetString(fileNameBytes, 0, attachmentNameLength - 2)
    Me._decodedAttachment = reader.ReadBytes(fileSize)

  End Sub

  Public Sub SaveAttachment(ByVal saveLocation As String)

    Dim fullFileName As String = saveLocation

    If Not fullFileName.EndsWith( _
    Path.DirectorySeparatorChar.ToString()) Then
      fullFileName += Path.DirectorySeparatorChar
    End If

    fullFileName += attachmentName

    If File.Exists(fullFileName) Then
      File.Delete(fullFileName)
    End If

    Using fs As New FileStream(fullFileName, FileMode.CreateNew)
      Dim bw As BinaryWriter = New BinaryWriter(fs)
      bw.Write(DecodedAttachment)
      bw.Close()
      fs.Close()
    End Using
```

```
      End Sub

    Public ReadOnly Property Filename() As String
      Get
        Return attachmentName
      End Get
    End Property

    Public ReadOnly Property DecodedAttachment() As Byte()
      Get
        Return Me._decodedAttachment
      End Get
    End Property

  End Class

End Namespace
```

InfoPathExcel.cs

```csharp
using System;
using System.Collections.Generic;
using System.Text;
using System.Text.RegularExpressions;
using DocumentFormat.OpenXml;
using DocumentFormat.OpenXml.Packaging;
using DocumentFormat.OpenXml.Spreadsheet;

namespace BizSupportOnline
{
  public static class InfoPathExcel
  {
    public static string GetCellData(
      string sheetName, string cellRef, WorkbookPart wbPart)
    {
      string cellValue = String.Empty;

      if (wbPart != null)
      {
        WorksheetPart worksheetPart = GetWorkSheetPart(sheetName, wbPart);
        SheetData sheetData =
          worksheetPart.Worksheet.GetFirstChild<SheetData>();

        Cell cell = null;
        IEnumerable<Cell> ieCells = sheetData.Descendants<Cell>();
        foreach (Cell ieCell in ieCells)
        {
          if (ieCell.CellReference.Value == cellRef)
          {
            cell = ieCell;
            break;
          }
        }

        if (cell != null)
        {
          if (cell.DataType != null)
          {
```

```
        switch (cell.DataType.Value)
        {
          case CellValues.String:
            cellValue = cell.CellValue.Text;
            break;
          case CellValues.SharedString:
            cellValue = GetSharedStringValue(cell.CellValue.Text, wbPart);
            break;
          default:
            cellValue = cell.CellValue.Text;
            break;
        }
      }
      else
      {
        cellValue = cell.CellValue.Text;
      }
    }

  }

  return cellValue;
}

public static string GetSharedStringValue(string id, WorkbookPart wbPart)
{
  string val = String.Empty;

  if (wbPart != null)
  {
    SharedStringTablePart sharedStringPart = null;
    IEnumerable<SharedStringTablePart> ieSSTableParts =
      wbPart.GetPartsOfType<SharedStringTablePart>();
    foreach (SharedStringTablePart ieSSTablePart in ieSSTableParts)
    {
      sharedStringPart = ieSSTablePart;
      break;
    }

    List<SharedStringItem> list = new List<SharedStringItem>();
    IEnumerable<SharedStringItem> ieSSStringItems =
      sharedStringPart.SharedStringTable
      .Elements<SharedStringItem>();
    foreach (SharedStringItem ieSSStringItem in ieSSStringItems)
    {
      list.Add(ieSSStringItem);
    }
    SharedStringItem[] items = list.ToArray();

    if (items != null && items.Length > 0)
    {
      val = items[int.Parse(id)].InnerText;
    }
  }

  return val;
}

public static string GetNamedRange(
  string namedRange, WorkbookPart wbPart)
{
  string retVal = string.Empty;
```

```
   if (wbPart != null)
   {
     IEnumerable<DefinedName> ieDefNames =
       wbPart.Workbook.DefinedNames.Descendants<DefinedName>();
     foreach (DefinedName ieDefName in ieDefNames)
     {
       if (ieDefName.Name == namedRange)
       {
         retVal = ieDefName.InnerText;
         break;
       }
     }
   }

   return retVal;
}

public static void SetCellData(
   string sheetName, string cellRef, CellValues dataType,
   string cellValue, WorkbookPart wbPart)
{
  Regex regEx = new Regex(@"\d");
  Match match = regEx.Match(cellRef);

  uint rowIndex = 0;
  if (match.Index > 0)
  {
    if (uint.TryParse(
      cellRef.Substring(match.Index),
      out rowIndex) == false)
    {
      return;
    }
  }

  if (rowIndex <= 0)
    return;

  if (wbPart != null)
  {
    WorksheetPart worksheetPart = GetWorkSheetPart(sheetName, wbPart);
    SheetData sheetData =
      worksheetPart.Worksheet.GetFirstChild<SheetData>();

    Row row = null;
    IEnumerable<Row> ieRows = sheetData.Descendants<Row>();
    foreach (Row ieRow in ieRows)
    {
      if (ieRow.RowIndex.Value == rowIndex)
      {
        row = ieRow;
        break;
      }
    }

    if (row == null)
    {
      row = CreateRow(ref sheetData, new UInt32Value(rowIndex));
    }

    Cell cell = null;
```

```
    IEnumerable<Cell> ieCells = sheetData.Descendants<Cell>();
    foreach (Cell ieCell in ieCells)
    {
      if (ieCell.CellReference.Value == cellRef)
      {
        cell = ieCell;
        break;
      }
    }

    if (cell == null)
    {
      AddCell(ref row, dataType, cellValue, cellRef);
    }
    else
    {
      UpdateCell(ref cell, dataType, cellValue, cellRef);
    }

  }

}

public static void SetRangeData(
  Dictionary<string, string> rangeData, string sheetName,
  WorkbookPart wbPart)
{
  if (rangeData == null)
    return;

  foreach (string key in rangeData.Keys)
  {
    SetCellData(sheetName, key, CellValues.String, rangeData[key], wbPart);
  }
}

private static WorksheetPart GetWorkSheetPart(
  string sheetName, WorkbookPart wbPart)
{
  WorksheetPart worksheetPart = null;
  string sheetId = String.Empty;

  if (wbPart != null)
  {
    Sheets sheets = wbPart.Workbook.Sheets;
    Sheet sheet = null;
    IEnumerable<Sheet> ieSheets = sheets.Descendants<Sheet>();
    foreach (Sheet ieSheet in ieSheets)
    {
      if (ieSheet.Name == sheetName)
      {
        sheet = ieSheet;
        break;
      }
    }

    if (sheet != null)
    {
      sheetId = sheet.Id;
      worksheetPart = (WorksheetPart)wbPart.GetPartById(sheetId);
    }
  }
```

```
      return worksheetPart;
   }

   private static Row CreateRow(ref SheetData sheetData, UInt32Value rowIndex)
   {
      Row row = sheetData.AppendChild(new Row());
      row.RowIndex = rowIndex;
      return row;
   }

   private static void AddCell(
      ref Row row, CellValues dataType, string cellValue, string cellRef)
   {
      Cell cell = new Cell();
      cell.DataType = dataType;
      cell.CellValue = new CellValue(cellValue);
      cell.CellReference = new StringValue(cellRef);
      row.AppendChild<Cell>(cell);
   }

   private static void UpdateCell(
      ref Cell cell, CellValues dataType, string cellValue, string cellRef)
   {
      cell.DataType = dataType;
      cell.CellValue = new CellValue(cellValue);
      cell.CellReference = new StringValue(cellRef);
   }

  }
}
```

InfoPathExcel.vb

```
Imports System
Imports System.Collections.Generic
Imports System.Text
Imports System.Text.RegularExpressions
Imports DocumentFormat.OpenXml
Imports DocumentFormat.OpenXml.Packaging
Imports DocumentFormat.OpenXml.Spreadsheet

Namespace BizSupportOnline

  Module InfoPathExcel

    Public Function GetCellData( _
      ByVal sheetName As String, ByVal cellRef As String, _
      ByVal wbPart As WorkbookPart) As String

      Dim cellValue As String = String.Empty

      If wbPart IsNot Nothing Then

        Dim worksheetPart As WorksheetPart = GetWorkSheetPart(SheetName, wbPart)
        Dim sheetData As SheetData = _
          worksheetPart.Worksheet.GetFirstChild(Of SheetData)()

        Dim cell As Cell = Nothing
```

```
      Dim ieCells As IEnumerable(Of Cell) = sheetData.Descendants(Of Cell)()

      For Each ieCell As Cell In ieCells
        If ieCell.CellReference.Value = cellRef Then
          cell = ieCell
          Exit For
        End If
      Next

      If cell IsNot Nothing Then

        If cell.DataType IsNot Nothing Then

          Select Case cell.DataType.Value
            Case CellValues.String
              cellValue = cell.CellValue.Text
            Case CellValues.SharedString
              cellValue = GetSharedStringValue(cell.CellValue.Text, wbPart)
            Case Else
              cellValue = cell.CellValue.Text
          End Select

        Else

          cellValue = cell.CellValue.Text

        End If

      End If

    End If

    Return cellValue

  End Function

  Public Function GetSharedStringValue( _
    ByVal id As String, ByVal wbPart As WorkbookPart) As String

    Dim val As String = String.Empty

    If wbPart IsNot Nothing Then

      Dim sharedStringPart As SharedStringTablePart = Nothing
      Dim ieSSTableParts As IEnumerable(Of SharedStringTablePart) = _
        wbPart.GetPartsOfType(Of SharedStringTablePart)()

      For Each ieSSTablePart As SharedStringTablePart In ieSSTableParts
        sharedStringPart = ieSSTablePart
        Exit For
      Next

      Dim list As New List(Of SharedStringItem)()
      Dim ieSSStringItems As IEnumerable(Of SharedStringItem) = _
        sharedStringPart.SharedStringTable.Elements(Of SharedStringItem)()

      For Each ieSSStringItem As SharedStringItem In ieSSStringItems
        list.Add(ieSSStringItem)
      Next

      Dim items As SharedStringItem() = list.ToArray()
```

```vbnet
        If (items IsNot Nothing) Then
          If (items.Length > 0) Then
            val = items(Int32.Parse(id)).InnerText
          End If
        End If

      End If

      Return val

  End Function

  Public Function GetNamedRange( _
    ByVal namedRange As String, ByVal wbPart As WorkbookPart) As String

    Dim retVal As String = String.Empty

    If wbPart IsNot Nothing Then

      Dim ieDefNames As IEnumerable(Of DefinedName) = _
        wbPart.Workbook.DefinedNames.Descendants(Of DefinedName)()

      For Each ieDefName As DefinedName In ieDefNames
        If ieDefName.Name = namedRange Then
          retVal = ieDefName.InnerText
          Exit For
        End If
      Next

    End If

    Return retVal

  End Function

  Public Sub SetCellData( _
    ByVal sheetName As String, ByVal cellRef As String, _
    ByVal dataType As CellValues, ByVal cellValue As String, _
    ByVal wbPart As WorkbookPart)

    Dim regEx As New Regex("\d")
    Dim match As Match = regEx.Match(cellRef)

    Dim rowIndex As UInteger = 0

    If match.Index > 0 Then
      If UInteger.TryParse( _
        cellRef.Substring(match.Index), rowIndex) = False Then
        Return
      End If
    End If

    If rowIndex <= 0 Then
      Return
    End If

    If wbPart IsNot Nothing Then
      Dim worksheetPart As WorksheetPart = GetWorkSheetPart(sheetName, wbPart)
      Dim sheetData As SheetData = _
        worksheetPart.Worksheet.GetFirstChild(Of SheetData)()

      Dim row As Row = Nothing
```

```
    Dim ieRows As IEnumerable(Of Row) = sheetData.Descendants(Of Row)()

    For Each ieRow As Row In ieRows
      If ieRow.RowIndex.Value = rowIndex Then
        row = ieRow
        Exit For
      End If
    Next

    If row Is Nothing Then
      row = CreateRow(SheetData, New UInt32Value(rowIndex))
    End If

    Dim cell As Cell = Nothing
    Dim ieCells As IEnumerable(Of Cell) = SheetData.Descendants(Of Cell)()

    For Each ieCell As Cell In ieCells
      If ieCell.CellReference.Value = cellRef Then
        cell = ieCell
        Exit For
      End If
    Next

    If cell Is Nothing Then
      AddCell(row, dataType, CellValue, cellRef)
    Else
      UpdateCell(cell, dataType, CellValue, cellRef)
    End If

  End If

End Sub

Public Sub SetRangeData( _
  ByVal rangeData As Dictionary(Of String, String), _
  ByVal sheetName As String, ByVal wbPart As WorkbookPart)

  If rangeData Is Nothing Then
    Return
  End If

  For Each key As String In rangeData.Keys
    SetCellData(sheetName, key, CellValues.String, rangeData(key), wbPart)
  Next

End Sub

Private Function GetWorkSheetPart( _
  ByVal sheetName As String, ByVal wbPart As WorkbookPart) As WorksheetPart

  Dim worksheetPart As WorksheetPart = Nothing
  Dim sheetId As String = String.Empty

  If wbPart IsNot Nothing Then

    Dim sheets As Sheets = wbPart.Workbook.Sheets
    Dim sheet As Sheet = Nothing
    Dim ieSheets As IEnumerable(Of Sheet) = sheets.Descendants(Of Sheet)()

    For Each ieSheet As Sheet In ieSheets
      If ieSheet.Name = SheetName Then
        sheet = ieSheet
```

```vbnet
          Exit For
        End If
      Next

      If sheet IsNot Nothing Then
        sheetId = sheet.Id
        worksheetPart = CType(wbPart.GetPartById(sheetId), WorksheetPart)
      End If

    End If

    Return worksheetPart

  End Function

  Private Function CreateRow( _
    ByRef sheetData As SheetData, ByVal rowIndex As UInt32Value) As Row

    Dim row As Row = sheetData.AppendChild(New Row())
    row.RowIndex = rowIndex
    Return row

  End Function

  Private Sub AddCell( _
    ByRef row As Row, ByVal dataType As CellValues, _
    ByVal cellValue As String, ByVal cellRef As String)

    Dim cell As New Cell()
    cell.DataType = dataType
    cell.CellValue = New CellValue(cellValue)
    cell.CellReference = New StringValue(cellRef)
    row.AppendChild(Of Cell)(cell)

  End Sub

  Private Sub UpdateCell( _
    ByRef cell As Cell, ByVal dataType As CellValues, _
    ByVal cellValue As String, ByVal cellRef As String)

    cell.DataType = dataType
    cell.CellValue = New CellValue(cellValue)
    cell.CellReference = New StringValue(cellRef)

  End Sub

  End Module

End Namespace
```

Index

A

Access
    export data as XML, 11, 29
    export data to Excel, 22
    export data to SharePoint list, 17
    import data from Excel, 9, 20, 24
    import data from SharePoint list, 18
    Import Spreadsheet Wizard, 9, 24
    linked table, 19
    move data to SharePoint, 23
    transform XML data on export, 30
action
    Change REST URL, 56, 58, 170, 173, 177,
       191, 198
    Send data to Web Part, 40, 44
add
    InfoPath form link to Excel workbook, 164–
       69
    new record to Excel table, 192–96
    web part connection in SharePoint Designer,
       46
Add Trusted File Location, 36, 309, 316
Add User-Defined Function, 309, 316
AddressLocal property, 220
An error occurred querying a data source, 324
appendChild method, 206
Application object, 227, 231, 236, 242, 248
    get_Range method, 233, 238, 242
    Range property, 233, 238, 242
    Workbooks property, 227, 231, 236, 242,
       249
Areas collection, 155, 207, 213, 217
array formula in Excel, 44, 145, 158, 312
arrayOfAnyType, 322–24
async property, 206, 212, 216
attach Excel workbook to InfoPath form, 295–
    300

B

business days
    difference calculation, 172–76
    validate amount of, 169–72

C

calculate
    date difference, 172–76

    leave balance, 176–82
Cells property, 217
Change REST URL action, 56, 58, 170, 173, 177,
    191, 198
chart, 45, 60–62, 106–11
Close method, 228, 232, 237, 244, 251
CloseWorkbook, 84, 90, 96, 104, 108, 113, 121,
    126, 130, 135, 142, 147, 152, 160, 165, 179,
    186, 193, 268
COLUMN Excel function, 145, 195
COLUMNS Excel function, 195
Complete XML Schema or XML document data
    type, 323
concat(), 49, 56, 58, 127, 136, 142, 149, 153,
    166, 171, 191, 198
CONCATENATE Excel function, 169
configure web part connection, 41
ContentTypeProperties property, 221
convert
    Excel cells into repeating table, 4
    Excel data to XML data, 5–13
    Excel workbook to InfoPath form template,
       1–5
Convert Existing Form, 1
Copy web service in SharePoint, 254, 262, 277
count(), 51, 66, 70, 73, 75, 190
create
    Excel workbook through a workflow, 221–25
    Excel workbook using Open XML, 252–62
    Excel workbook using VSTA, 225–28
    Excel workbook without code, 124–28, 134–
       39
    InfoPath form from Excel data using VBA,
       202–9
    InfoPath form from Excel data using XSLT,
       23–32
    InfoPath form template from Excel
       workbook, 1–5
    named range in Excel, 324–26
    table in Excel, 14, 182
Create method, 256, 296
CreateNode method, 203, 210
CreateTextFile method, 203
current(), 73

D

data connection
    From REST Web Service, 51–77
    From SOAP Web Service, 81

E

F

G

2203096R00212

Printed in Germany
by Amazon Distribution
GmbH, Leipzig